College Teaching and the Development of Reasoning

A volume in
Science and Engineering Education Sources

Series Editor:
Calvin Kalman, *Concordia University, Montreal*

Science and Engineering Education Sources

Calvin Kalman, Series Editor

College Teaching and the Development of Reasoning (2009)
edited by Robert G. Fuller, Thomas C. Campbell,
Dewey I. Dykstra, Jr., and Scott M. Stevens

College Teaching and the Development of Reasoning

edited by

Robert G. Fuller
University of Nebraska Lincoln

Thomas C. Campbell
Illinois Central College

Dewey I. Dykstra, Jr.
Boise State University

and

Scott M. Stevens
Carnegie Mellon University

Information Age Publishing, Inc.
Charlotte, North Carolina • www.infoagepub.com

Library of Congress Cataloging-in-Publication Data

College teaching and the development of reasoning / edited by Robert G. Fuller ... [et al.].
    p. cm. -- (Science and engineering education sources)
 Includes bibliographical references and index.
 ISBN 978-1-60752-236-2 (pbk.) -- ISBN 978-1-60752-237-9 (hardcover)
 1. College teaching. 2. Reasoning--Study and teaching. 3. Thought and thinking--Study and teaching. I. Fuller, Robert G.
 LB2331.C58 2010
 378.1'25--dc22

                                               2009030516

Copyright © 2009 IAP–Information Age Publishing, Inc.

All rights reserved. No part of this publication may be reproduced, stored in a retrieval system, or transmitted in any form or by any electronic or mechanical means, or by photocopying, microfilming, recording, or otherwise without written permission from the publisher.

Printed in the United States of America

*Dedicated to
Jean Piaget,
Robert Karplus,
and
Arnold B. Arons*

*Their pioneering efforts on behalf of students
transformed our careers
and
provide guidance for the transformation of college teaching*

EDITOR-IN-CHIEF

Calvin S. Kalman, *Concordia University, Montreal, QC*

EDITORIAL BOARD

Dewey Dykstra , *Professor of Physics at Boise State University*
Igal Galili, *Head of The Science Teaching Department Hebrew University*
Charles Henderson, *Chair Committee on Research in Physics Education, American Association of Physics Teachers*
Teresa Larkin, *Chair Physics Department American University*
Michael Matthews, *Editor Science & Education, President International History and Philosophy of Science Teaching Group*
Craig Nelson, *First President, International Society for the Scholarship of Teaching and Learning, Professor of Biology, Indiana University*
Edward Redish, *Professor of Physics University of Maryland founder and Coprincipal investigator of the Maryland University Project in Physics Education and Technology (M.U.P.P.E.T.) and Comprehensive Unified Physics Learning Environment (CUPLE)*
David W. Rudge, *Associate Professor, Biological Sciences & The Mallinson Institute for Science Education Western Michigan University*
Eric Scerri, *Editor, Foundations of Chemistry*

CONTENTS

Acknowledgments	*xi*
Introduction and Rationale	*xiii*
1. How Students Reason	*1*
2. Concrete and Formal Operational Reasoning	*19*
3. Formal Reasoning Patterns	*35*
4. Interviews of College Students	*51*
5. College Student Research Findings	*63*
6. Analysis of Test Questions	*69*
7. Analysis of Textbooks	*75*
8. Self-Regulation	*107*
9. The Learning Cycle	*115*
10. Teaching Goals and Strategies	*135*
11. Implementation and Suggested Readings	*147*
12. Progress Since 1978	*153*
13. Theoretical Foundations for College Learning—Piaget & Vygotsky: Sorting Fact From Fiction	*183*
14. College Programs	*203*

APPENDIX A

Bibliography *219*

A. B. Arons and R. Karplus. (1976). "Implications of Accumulating Data on Levels of Intellectual Development." *Amer. J. Phys., 44*(4), 396. *221*

R. G. Fuller, R. Karplus, and A. E. Lawson. (1977). "Can Physics Develop Reasoning?" *Physics Today, 2,* 23–28. *222*

A. B. Arons. (1976). "Cultivating the capacity for formal reasoning: Objectives and procedures in an introductory physical science course." *Amer. J. Phys. 44*(9), 834–838 *228*

E. T. Carpenter. (circa 1977). "Self-Regulation in Reading a Story." *233*

L. Copes. (1975). "Can College Students Reason?" *241*

J. Piaget. (1972). "Problems of Equilibration." *Jean Piaget Society,* 216. *253*

APPENDIX B

"Physics Teaching and Development of Reasoning Materials" ©1975 AAPT. Cover page and selected pages. *267*

J. W. McKinnon and J. W. Renner. (1971). "Are Colleges Concerned with Intellectual Development?" *Amer. J. Phys., 39*(9), 1047–1052. *288*

J. W. Renner and A. E. Lawson. (1973). "Piagetian Theory and Instruction in Physics." *The Physics Teacher, 11*(3), 165–169. *294*

J. W. Renner and A. E. Lawson. (1973). "Promoting Intellectual Development Through Science Teaching." *The Physics Teacher, 11*(5), 273–276. *290*

A. E. Lawson and W. T. Wollman. (1975). "Physics Problems and the Process of Self-Regulation." *The Physics Teacher, 13*(11), 470–475. *303*

APPENDIX C

Petals Around A Rose *309*

APPENDIX D

College Cognitive Development Programs and their Acronyms *313*
Quotation Sources and Pages *314*

APPENDIX E

Dr. Martin Q. Peterson. "ADAPT Anthropology." *315*

APPENDIX F

Dr. Daniela Weinberg and Dr. Gerald M. Weinberg. "Learning by Design: Constructing Experimental Learning Programs." *319*
Index *325*

ACKNOWLEDGMENTS

We thank Dr. Calvin S. Kalman, Editor-in-Chief, and Information Age Publishers for their willingness to publish this book as the first title in their new series on Science and Engineering Education Sources. We thank Dr. Kalman for his advice and support during the process of putting this book together.

This book would not have been possible without the work of many of our colleagues who have written materials that have become included in this book. The basis of this book is found in the American Association of Physics Teachers materials, contained in Appendix B and made available in its original form from the Digital Commons Web site of the University of Nebraska Lincoln (UNL): http://digitalcommons.unl.edu/adapt/

The College Teaching and Development of Reasoning workshop materials, originally created by the UNL ADAPT Program in 1976, serve as the basis for the first 11 chapters of this book. Those materials were enhanced by the contributions of Martin Peterson and Dani Weinberg (anthropology), Jerry Petr (economics), Robert Narveson, James McShane, and Robert Bergstrom (English), Leslie Duly (history), Melvin Thornton (mathematics), Elizabeth Carpenter (philosophy) and Vernon Williams and David Moshman (psychology). Dr. Moshman also helped us with the Piagetian theory parts of the workshop materials. There are additional contributions from these people on the ADAPT Program archival Web site and we invite you to visit the Piagetian Programs in Higher Education link at http://digitalcommons.unl.edu/adaptessays

We thank the American Association of Physics Teachers and the Lawrence Hall of Science for giving us permission to include some of their materials in this book.

In addition, we have benefited from numerous discussion with faculty colleagues of the years, too many for us to remember or name, but we are grateful for contributions to our understanding of how students develop reasoning.

RGF, TCC, DID, Jr., SMS

The original drafts of Chapters 12, 13 and 14 were written by Scott M. Stevens, Dewey I. Dykstra, Jr. and Thomas C. Campbell, respectively

INTRODUCTION AND RATIONALE

The challenge to higher education in American colleges began in the 1970s. The start was the question, *Are colleges interested in intellectual development?* It was posed in an article by McKinnon and Renner published in the *American Journal of Physics* in 1971. (See Appendix B for the original article.). They reported, according to their investigations, that colleges were NOT interested in the intellectual development of students as they measured it.

The challenge was picked up by Professors Arnold B. Arons, University of Washington, Seattle, and Robert Karplus, University of California Berkley. These two very well known and respected physicists had directed their professional attention to the problems of science education and they saw the challenge of intellectual development during the college years as essential. They issued a call for institutions of higher education to take this challenge seriously in their joint communique in 1976, "Implications of Accumulating Data on Intellectual Development." (See Appendix A for the original paper.)

Professor Karplus had been invited to share his concerns with the broader physics community by the *Physics Today* journal. This journal is sent to every member of any of the professional physics organizations. The Karplusian ideas were presented in an article titled "Can Physics Develop Reasoning?" by Fuller, Karplus and Lawson, published in 1977. (See Appendix A for the original paper.)

Professor Karplus had been active in the development of a complete elementary school science curriculum and he knew the importance of teacher training. Robert Karplus used his leadership position in the American Association of Physics Teachers (AAPT) in 1973 to secure a National Science Foundation grant to produce a workshop on "Physics Teaching and the Development of Reasoning." The first workshop was offered at a national AAPT meeting in Anaheim, CA, in 1975. A revised version of the workshop materials was published by the AAPT in 1975. A complete PDF copy of those original materials can be downloaded from the Digital Commons Web site of the University of Nebraska Lincoln: http://digitalcommons.unl.edu/adapt/. A copy of some of those original materials developed by Karplus et al. are included as Appendix B of this book. In our view, these materials formed the basis for the growth and development of the physics education research (PER) community within physics departments in the United States. The PER community is now an important part of the AAPT.

The AAPT materials were quickly adapted to other disciplines. The Multidisciplinary Piagetian-Based Program for College Freshmen (called the ADAPT [Accent of Developing Abstract Processes of Thought] Program) funded by the Exxon Education Foundation in 1975 offered a College Teaching and Development of Reasoning workshop in March, 1975 at the University of Nebraska Lincoln. Those workshop materials included content in anthropology, economics, English, history, mathematics in addition to physics. The Lawrence Hall of Science produced separate workshop booklets for biology, chemistry, earth science, and general science as well as physics. The AAAS-NSF Chautauqua Program offered "College Science Teaching and the Development of Reasoning" workshops at 11 regional centers from 1976 to 1979.

The ADAPT Program faculty began offering faculty development workshops with their materials in January, 1976, at Xavier University of Louisiana. Over the next decade, they lead more than 100 workshops at a wide variety of colleges and universities. By the time Piaget died in 1980, there were at least 14 college programs in the United States that emphasized the development of reasoning by college students.[1] Those programs are discussed in more detail in chapter 14 of this book.

The importance of the use of formal operational reasoning by college students has once again received attention in recent years as college faculty sought measures to help them predict the growth in conceptual knowledge by college students (Coletta & Phillips, 2005). The Lawson Classroom Test for Scientific Thinking has become the most common instrument to use (Lawson, 1983). It is based on the series of articles on reasoning beyond elementary school published by Karplus et al. (Fuller, 2002).

Piaget's ideas had a broad impact on human development studies in many areas, too numerous for us to discuss in this chapter. However, we do want to mention two areas that seem particularly relevant to college student learning. The first is the work of Kohlberg and Turiel (1971) and Gilligan (1982) in the area of moral development. The second is the work of William Perry (1970) on the intellectual and ethical development of students during their college years. These works took the model of stages of development as suggested by Piaget into moral development and intellectual and ethical development. The results of these studies are particularly helpful for college faculty.

The core of this book contains the ideas that created a kind of "continental divide" in thinking about college student reasoning. Before Arons and Karplus most curriculum reform projects in higher education were based upon a realist epistemology as discussed in chapter 13. After Arons and Karplus the processes going on in the minds of students had to become an essential aspect of any serious curriculum improvements in higher physics education. The insights of William Perry provided additional support to the Arons and Karplus movement. About teaching Perry said, "Every student in my class has a completely different teacher."

We offer this book to enable you to be on this Arons and Karplus side of the "continental divide" and to share in the epistemology and language of this movement. We hope you enjoy this opportunity to think anew about college teaching and the development of reasoning.

NOTE

1. If you want to capture some of the enthusiasm of the Piagetian practitioners of the 1980s we invite you to read the article that was published in *The Chronicle of Higher Education* upon the death of Dr. Piaget in the summer of 1980, "Theories of Piaget, Who Died this Month, Inspire Growing Band of U.S. Professors" by Robert L. Jacobson, *The Chronicle of Higher Education*, Volume XXI, Number 6 (September 29, 1980), pp. 5–6. A PDF version of this article is available at http://digitalcommons.unl.edu/adaptessays/28/

REFERENCES

Coletta, V. P., & Phillips, J. A. (2005). Interpreting FCI scores: Normalized gain, preinstruction scores, and scientific reasoning ability. *Amer. J. Phys.* 73(12), 1172–1182.

Fuller, R. G. (Ed.). (2002). *A love of discovery science education—The second career of Robert Karplus*. New York: Kluwer Academic/Plenum. This book of works by Karplus includes all of his articles on reasoning beyond elementary school that were originally published in *School Science and Mathematics*.

Gilligan, C. (1982). *In a different voice: Psychological theory and women's development*. Cambridge, MA: Harvard University Press.

Kohlberg, L., & Turiel, E. (1971). Moral development and moral education. In G. Lesser (Ed.), *Psychology and educational practice* (pp. 410–465). Glenview, IL: Scott, Foresman.

Perry, W. G., Jr. (and associates). (1970). *Forms of intellectual and ethical development in the college years.* New York: Holt, Rinehart and Winston.

Lawson, A. E. (1983). *A classroom test of scientific reasoning.* Retrieved from http://www.public.asu.edu/~anton1/LawsonAssessments.htm

ADDITIONAL READINGS

Perry, W. G., Jr. (1978). *Sharing in the costs of growth.* In C. A. Parker (Ed.), *Encouraging development in college students* (pp. 267–273). Minneapolis: University of Minnesota Press. "What do you do about the house you leave when you move to a new place?"

Perry, W. G., Jr. (1981). Cognitive and ethical growth: The making of meaning. In A. W. Chickering and associates, (Eds.), *The modern American college: Responding to the new realities of diverse students and a changing society* (pp. 76–116). San Francisco: Jossey-Bass. "I have remarked elsewhere (Perry, 1978) on the importance we have come to ascribe to the student's 'allowing for grief' in the process of growth, especially in the rapid movement from the limitless potentials of youth to the particular realities of adulthood."

CHAPTER 1

HOW STUDENTS REASON

INTRODUCTION

You have probably been puzzled at various times in your teaching career by the thinking strategies that students appear to use to solve problems. It is difficult for most of us to understand that many students do not use reasoning patterns that seem obvious to us. Many students substitute numbers into a formula they remember even though the formulas may not be applicable to the problem at hand. This situation quite naturally leads us to wonder about the reasoning that students utilize when we would employ mental operations such as separating variables, excluding an irrelevant factor, or applying a mathematical relationship such as ratios.

Objective of This Chapter

To assist you in distinguishing among various patterns of reasoning students use to solve simple problems.

Procedure

The content of this chapter is based on student responses to four different puzzles—the Islands Puzzle, the Mealworm Puzzle, the Mr. Short/Mr. Tall Puzzle and the Treasure Hunt Puzzle. For each of the puzzles *you should solve it first, then read the student responses*. You may complete the four puzzles in any order. We have put the student responses into two different categories which we have labeled A and B. Please reflect on the properties of the two categories as you read the student responses. We will explain our use of these two categories in chapter 2, but first please wade into the murky water of student reasoning!

After you have completed the four puzzles, please complete the self-check at the end of this chapter.

THE ISLANDS PUZZLE

The puzzle is about Islands A, B, C, and D in the ocean. People have been traveling among these islands by boat for many years, but recently an airline started in business. Carefully read the clues about possible plane trips at present. The trips may be direct or include stops and plane changes on an island. When a trip is possible, it can be made in either direction between the islands. You may make notes or marks on the map to help use the clues.

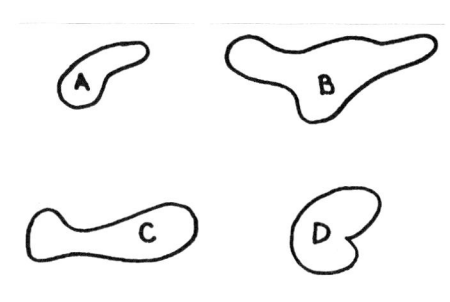

Figure 1.1. The Islands Puzzle. © 1975 American Association of Physics Teachers, edited by ADAPT circa 1980.

First Clue: People can go by plane between Islands C and D.

Second Clue: People cannot go by plane between Island A and B, even indirectly.

Use these two clues to answer Question 1. Do not read the next clue yet.
Question 1: Can people go by plane between Island B and D?
       Yes_____ No_____ Can't tell from the two clues
       Please explain your answer.

Third Clue: (Do not change your answer to Question 1 now) People can go by plane between Island B and D.

Use all three clues to answer Question 2 and 3.
Question 2: Can people go by plane between Island B and C?
       Yes_____ No_____ Can't tell from the three clues_____
       Please explain your answer.
Question 3: Can people go by plane between Island A and C?
       Yes_____ No_____ Can't tell from the three clues_____
       Please explain your answer.

Island Puzzle—Students' Responses

Before reading the student responses, please take a few minutes to reflect on the reasoning patterns you used to solve the Island Puzzle.

What type of thinking did you do while completing the Islands Puzzle? For example, did you need to recall any information beyond that given in the puzzle itself? Did you use combinations of information? Did you separate one piece of information from another? Did you exclude any information because it was irrelevant? Record your observations.

On the following previous pages of this section of the chapter we present written student responses to the Island Puzzle. Please read the student responses, and then compare them with the reasoning you used in solving the Island Puzzle. Record your observations and conclusions about the types of thinking you used as compared with Students A and Students B.

Students' Responses

Student A1 John Blake (16)

1. Answer: Can't tell from the two clues.
   Explanation: You don't know why you *can't go* from island to island.
2. Answer: Yes.
   Explanation: They can't go to Island B from Island C, then on to Island D.
3. Answer: Can't tell from the two clues.
   Explanation: You can't go from Island A to Island B. You don't know if you can go directly to A from C.

Student A2 Deloris Johnson (19)

1. Answer: Can't tell from the two clues.
   Explanation: There was no information given concerning the two.

Student A2 Deloris Johnson (19) continued

2. Answer: Yes.
   Explanation: They can fly from C to D, have a lay over and catch the plane from D to B.
3. Answer: No.
   Explanation: It was said you cannot go from A to B. There is no information about a flight direct from C to A—only C to D.

Student A3 (College Student—Age 17)

1. Answer: Can't tell from the clues given.
   Explanation: The two clues don't relate the upper islands to the lower ones.

2. Answer: Yes.

   Explanation: They can go from B to D and then to C, even if there are no direct flights.

3. Answer: No.

   Explanation: If they could go from C to A, then the people on B could go first to D, then to C, and then on to A. But this contradicts the second clue, that they can't go by plane between B and A.

Student A4 David Kenting (19)

1. Answer: Can't tell from the two clues.

   Explanation: By information given they could if appropriate landing facilities were on Island B.

2. Answer: Yes.

   Explanation: Yes, because planes go from C to D or vice versa & B to D and vice versa. Therefore all have facilities.

3. Answer: No.

   Explanation: No, because Island A has no landing facilities mentioned.

Student A5 Norma Kuhn (20)

1. Answer: Yes.

   Explanation: If the trip from C to D includes a stop on B. The clues only state that one cannot go by plane between A and B. The introduction states that the flights need not be direct.

2. Answer: Yes.

   Explanation: By way of D.

3. Answer: Can't tell from the three clues.

   Explanation: The clues do not give any connections to A except via boat.

Student A6 Barbara Downing (21)

1. Answer: Can't tell from the two clues.

   Explanation: The clues tell nothing of the relation of B and D.

2. Answer: Yes.

   Explanation: If you can go from C to D and D to B, C to B should also be possible.

3. Answer: No.

   Explanation: If you can go from C to B, but not B to A, you should not be able to go from C to A.

Student B1 (High School Student—Age 18)

1. Answer: No.

   Explanation: B and D are not far enough apart.

Student responses continued on next page.

2. Answer: Yes.

    Explanation: They are a long distance apart .

3. Answer: No.

    Explanation: Not far enough apart.

Student B2 (College Student—Age 17)

1. Answer: Yes.

    Explanation: Because the people can go north from Island D because in the clue it could be made in both directions.

2. Answer: No.

    Explanation: I am presuming both directions doesn't include a 45 degree angle from B to C.

3. Answer: Yes.

    Explanation: Because Island C is right below Island A.

Student B3 (College Student, age 30)

1. Answer: Yes.

    Explanation: You can't go from B to A but you can go from D to B, or go from D to C then to Island B.

2. Answer: Yes.

    Explanation: It doesn't say that you can't go. It says you can't go from A to B islands, you can cut across or go through D.

3. Answer: Yes.

    Explanation: You can as long as you don't go on to Island B.

Student B4 (Harold O'Keefe, age 20)

1. Answer: Yes.

    Explanation: Because B is bigger than D and listing is the same sequence.

2. Answer: No.

    Explanation: The sequence is broken.

3. Answer: Yes.

    Explanation: They are listing the same as in Question One.

Before proceeding to another puzzle please compare the student reasoning with the reasoning you used in solving the Island Puzzle. Record your observations and conclusions about the types of reasoning you used as compared with Students A and Students B.

Now proceed to another puzzle or the self-check at the end of this chapter.

THE MEALWORM PUZZLE

Some experimenters wanted to test the response of mealworms to light and moisture. To do this they set up four boxes as shown in the diagram below. They used lamps for light sources and constantly watered pieces of paper in the boxes for moisture. In the center of each box they placed 20 mealworms. One day later they returned to count the number of mealworms that had crawled to the different ends of the boxes.

What can you conclude from these diagrams? The diagrams show that mealworms respond to (response means move toward or away from):

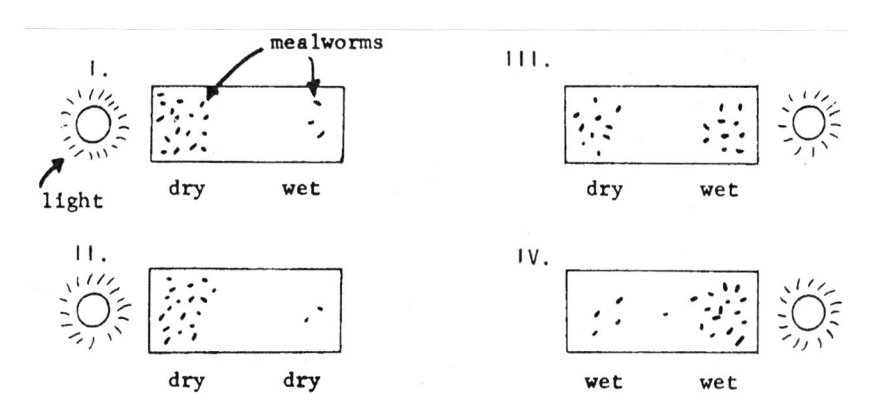

Figure 1.2. Boxes of mealworms. ©1975 The Regents of the University of California, Lawrence Hall of Science.

(a) light but not moisture
(b) moisture but not light
(c) both light and moisture
(d) neither light nor moisture

Please explain your choice.

How did you reason your way through this puzzle? Did you think at once of the way to do it, or did you first think of a way that had to be modified or abandoned? Record your notes here.

Now examine a collection of student responses, beginning on the next page.

The Mealworm Puzzle—Students' Responses

Read these responses and compare them with your own. Look for similarities and differences between type B and type A responses.

Student B1 (College Junior)
D. No definite pattern was followed by the mealworms.

Student B2 (Norma Kuhn—Age 20)
D. Because even though the light was moved in different places the mealworms didn't do the same things.

Student B3 (College Freshman)
A. They usually went to the end of the box with the light.

Student B4 (High School Sophomore)
A. Because there are 17 worms by the light and there are only 3 by the moisture.

Student B6 (Harold O'Keefe—Age 20)
A. Because in all situations, the majority go where there's light. Wetness doesn't seem to make a difference.

Student responses continued on next page.

Student A1 (Barbara Downing—Age 21)
C. Boxes I and II show they prefer dry and light to wet and dark, Box IV eliminates dryness as a factor, so they do respond to light only. Box III shows that wetness cancels the effect of the light, so it seems they prefer dry. (It would be clearer if one of the boxes was wet-dry with no light).

Student A2 (David Kenting—Age 19)
C. When the light was on the dry side they all crowded to the dry side. When it was on the wet side, an equal amount went to each side.

Student A3 (High School Freshman)
C. In experiment 3 the mealworms split 1/2 wet, 1/2 dry. So it's safe to assume that light was not the only factor involved.

Student A4 (Delores Johnson—Age 19)

B. I, II, and IV show that mealworms seem to like the light, but in III they seem to be equally spaced. This leads one to believe that mealworms like the dryness and the reason in pictures III and IV they are by the light is because of the heat that the light produces which gives a dryness effect.

Student A5 (John Blake—Age 16)

C. The mealworms in all cases respond to light. However, in box 3 the division is about 1:1. This shows that they worms are attracted to the light but do not like the situations where the dry area was next to the light. When there is no choice between wet and dry such as in case IV the worms turn to the light. Note: We might also test a box like this wet dry with no light to further verify the effect of moisture.

MEALWORM PUZZLE QUESTIONS

1. What similarities did you find among the type A responses? Please record your analyses here.

2. What similarities did you find among the type B responses? Please record your analyses here.

3. What features do you find that distinguish type A from type B responses?

4. Looking back, did your own solution resemble any of the above? If so, how?

Now proceed to another puzzle or the self-check at the end of this chapter.

THE MR. SHORT / MR. TALL PUZZLE

Figure 1.3 is called Mr. Short. We used large round buttons laid side-by-side to measure Mr. Short's height, starting from the floor between his feet and going to the top of his head. His height was *four* buttons. Then we took a similar figure called Mr. Tall and measured it in the same way with the same buttons. Mr. Tall was *six* buttons high.

Now please do these things:

1. Measure the height of Mr. Short using paper clips in a chain provided below.

   The height is _____

2. Predict the height of Mr. Tall if he were measured with the same paper clips.

   _____

3. Explain how you figured out your predictions. (You may use diagrams, words, or calculations. Please explain your steps carefully.)

   _____
   _____
   _____
   _____
   _____
   _____
   _____
   _____

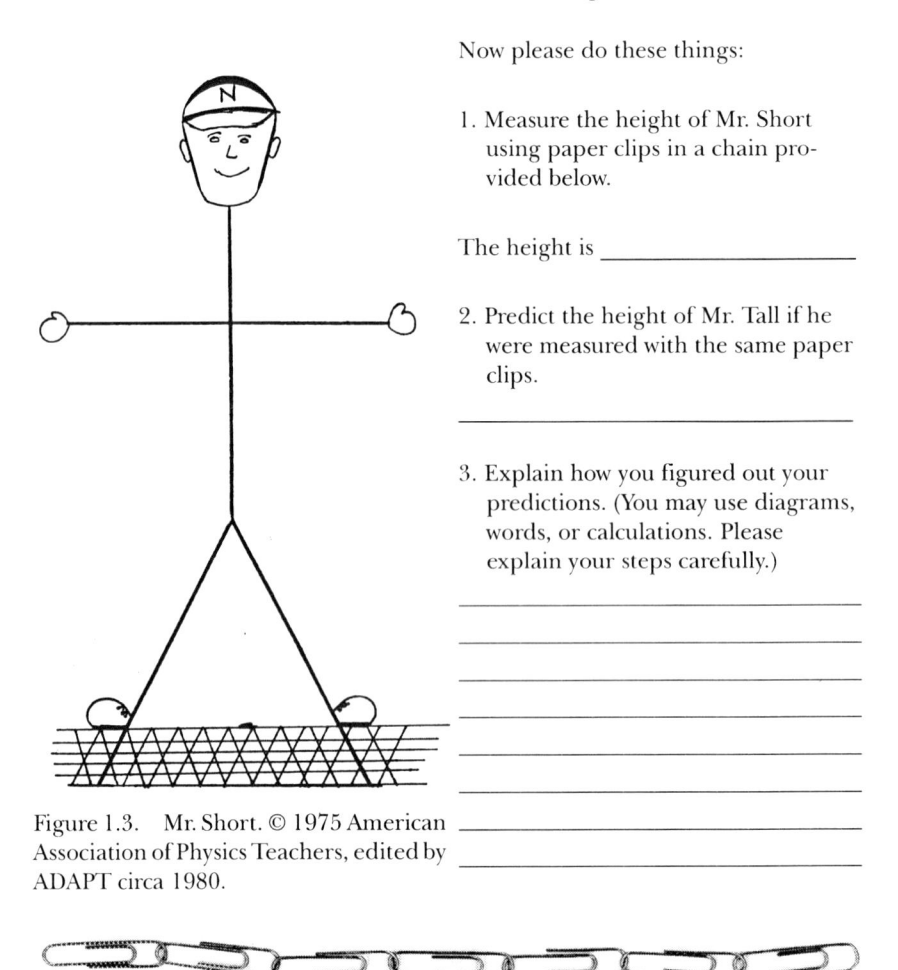

Figure 1.3. Mr. Short. © 1975 American Association of Physics Teachers, edited by ADAPT circa 1980.

Figure 1.4. Chain of paperclips.

When you have completed this puzzle, examine the collection of student responses.

Mr. Short/Mr. Tall—Students' Responses

Student A1 (Age 16)
Prediction for Mr. Tall: 9

Explanation: Figured it out by seeing that Mr. Tall is half again as tall as Mr. Short, so I took half of Mr. Short's height in clips and added it on to his present height in clips and came up with my prediction.

Student A2 (Age 16)
Prediction for Mr. Tall: 9 paper clips

Explanation: I figured that the ratio of paper clips to buttons to be approximately 1–1/2; so two more buttons would make approximately 3 more clips. Since it's 1–1/2:1, he is approximately 9 clips tall.

Student A3 (Age 16)
Prediction for Mr. Tall: 9 clips

Explanation: I took the relationship of the clips to the buttons on Mr. Short and the unknown clips to buttons of Mr. Tall and found the unknown, algebraically.

Student A4 John Blake (Age 16)
Prediction for Mr. Tall: 9 paper clips

Explanation: Mr. Tall is 1.5 times the height of Mr. Short, as measured with buttons, and if the measurement techniques were identical, would be 1.5 times Mr. Short's height with any measurement medium. Assuming that the measurement techniques are identical, Mr. Tall's height in clips is 1.5 x 6, which is 9.

Student A5 Barbara Downing (Age 21)
Prediction for Mr. Tall: 9 paper clips

Explanation: The ratio using buttons of height of Mr. Short and Mr. Tall is 2.3. Figuring out algebraically and solving for x: $2/3 = 6/x$, gives you 9 as the height in paper clips.

Student A6 Delores Johnson (Age 19)
Prediction for Mr. Tall: 9 paper clips tall

Explanation: I figured this out by figuring that Mr. Small is 2/3 as tall as Mr. Tall.

Student B1 (Age 16)
Prediction for Mr. Tall: 8 clips

Explanation: If he is 2 buttons taller, I guess he is 2 clips bigger, which would make it 8.

Student responses continued on next page.

Student B2 (Age 18)
Prediction for Mr. Tall: 8 clips
Explanation: Because he is two times as high as Mr. Short.

Student B3 David Kenting (Age 19)
Prediction for Mr. Tall: 9
Explanation: I figured the buttons the same size as the clips.

Student B4 (Age 16)
Prediction for Mr. Tall: 12 clips
Explanation: Mr. Tall was 12 buttons taller than Mr. Short. The buttons must be larger than the paper clips. So I doubled Mr. Short's height in paper clips for Mr. Tall's height.

Student B5 Norma Kuhn (Age 20)
Prediction for Mr. Tall: 8 clips
Explanation: Mr. Tall is 8 paper clips tall because when using buttons as a unit of measure he is 2 units taller. When Mr. Short is measured with paper clips as a unit of measurement he is 6 paper clips. Therefore, Mr. Tall is 2 units taller in comparison, which totals 8.

Student B6 Harold (Age 20)
Prediction for Mr. Tall: 8 paper clips tall
Explanation: If Mr. Short measures 4 buttons or 6 paper clips (2 pieces more than buttons), then Mr. Tall should be 2 paper clips more than buttons.

Student B7 (Age 25)
Prediction for Mr. Tall: 8 paper clips tall
Explanation: 4 buttons reached top of Mr. Short's head. Mr. Tall is 6 buttons tall. 6 paper clips Mr. Short. Mr. Tall is 8 paper clips tall. Paper clips are approximately 1 inch long and the buttons were probably the same.

Student B8 (Age 15)
Prediction for Mr. Tall: 8 paper clips tall
Explanation: As 4 is to 6, 6 is to 8.

Mr. Short/Mr. Tall—Questions:

1. What comparisons can you make between your response and those of the students? Record those comparisons here.

2. Center your attention on several of those responses which were different from yours. What common elements you can detect among those responses that disagree with yours. Record those common elements here.

3. Center your attention on those responses which agree with yours. What common elements you can detect among those student responses that agree with yours. List those common elements here.

4. Compare Type A responses to Type B responses.

Now proceed to another puzzle or the self-check at the end of this chapter.

Figure 1.5. The Dig.   Figure 1.6. The Hut.

THE TREASURE HUNT PUZZLE

At the beginning of his novel *The Hamlet*, William Faulkner mentions a legend of a treasure buried on an old plantation. Readers expect, naturally, that before the novel ends there will be a search for the treasure, and Faulkner does not disappoint them.

Four major characters are soon introduced: Will, who is chief landowner thereabouts; Jody, Will's son and heir-apparent; Flem, a shrewd fellow working for Will; and Ratliff, an itinerant sewing machine salesman.

Faulkner had to decide who among these four characters would be "in on" the hunt for the buried treasure. Someday you may read the novel and find out what his decision was. For the present though speculation will have to do. See if you can list all of the options that Faulkner has as possible choices among these four to be "in on" the hunt. You may wish to use the letters W, J, F, and R to save space.

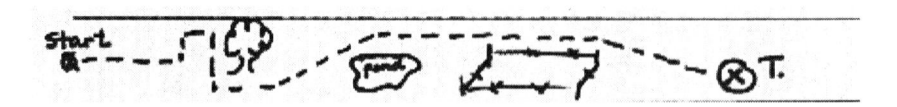

Figure 1.7. The Hunt. © 1980 ADAPT

Looking back, how did you think your way through the problem? Did you think at once of the way to do it, or did you first think of a way that had to be modified or abandoned?

When you are done, examine the collection of student responses, beginning on the next page.

The Treasure Hunt—Students' Responses

The following are typical student responses to the Treasure Hunt. As you look over the responses, compare Student B and Student A responses.

Student B1 (High School senior)
    F, R

Student B2 (Dave Kenting—Age 19)
    WR, WJ, W, RJ, JF, FR

Student B3 (College Junior)
    W, J, F, R

Student B4 (Delores Johnson—Age 19)
    W, J, F, R

Student B5 (Barbatra Downing—Age 21)
    W, J, F, R, WR, WF, RJ, RF, JF, WJ

Student B6 (High School Junior)

WRJF	WRJF	JRWF	RWFJ
WR,	RW	WRJ	JRW
WJ,	JW	WRF	FRW
WF,	FW	WJF	FJW
RJ,	JR	WFR	RFW
RF,	FR		
JF,	FJ		
FJR,	RJF		
FJW,	WJF		
WFR,	RFW		

Student A1 (High School Junior)
    WJFR, WJ, WF, RJF
    WJF, JR, JF, FR

Student A2 (Harold O'Keefe—Age 20)

WJFR	RJF	JF	F
WJF		RJ	J
WJ		R	

Student A3 (College Freshman)

WR	WRJ	RJ	
WJ	WJF	RF	WJFR

Student A4 (College Junior)

WR	WJ	WF	WRJ	RJF	
RJ	RF	JF	WRJF	W	R J

Student A5 (High School Freshman)
    WR, WJ, WF, RJ, RF, JF
    WRJ, WRF, WJF, RJF, WRJF
    W, R, J, F

Student A6 (Norma Kuhn, age 20)
    W, R, J, F, WRJF, WR, WJ, WF
    RJ, RF, FJ, WRJ, WRF, WJF, RJF

Student A7 (John Blake, age 16)

WRJF	RJF	JF	F	WJF
WRJ	RJ	J		WF
WRF	RF			WJ
WR	R			
W				

Student A5 (High School Freshman)
    WR, WJ, WF, RJ, RF, JF
    WRJ, WRF, WJF, RJF, WRJF
    W, R, J, F
Student A6 (Norma Kuhn, age 20)
    W, R, J, F, WRJF, WR, WJ, WF
    RJ, RF, FJ, WRJ, WRF, WJF, RJF
Student A7 (John Blake, age 16)
    WRJF   RJF   JF   F   WJF
    WRJ   RJ   J   WF
    WRF   RF   WJ
    WR   R
    W

On a quiz given in 1981, the UNL college student responses were:

No. of Possibilities Listed	No. of Students so Listing
15–	7
12–14	3
9–11	1
6–8	6
3–5	21
0–2	1
Total	39

Now consider the questions on the next page.

Questions

1. What similarities did you find among the responses of students A? Please record your analyses here.

2. What similarities did you find among the responses of students B? Please record your analyses here.

3. What difference did you find between A and B responses?

4. Looking back, did your own solution, perhaps in its initial stages, resemble any of the above? If so, how?

Now proceed to another puzzle or the self-check test page 18 of this chapter.

CONCLUDING REMARKS

We hope the activities in this chapter have alerted you to the types of reasoning patterns that your college students might use. Please complete this self check and then go on to chapter 2.

Chapter 1 Self Check

After you have studied the student responses to the puzzles in this chapter, please read the following responses and classify them as Type A or Type B. Compare your answers with ours (bottom of page).

Student X_1 (age 20) Islands Puzzle

1. Answer: Can't tell from the two clues
   Explanation: No information about flights between B and D.
2. Answer: Yes
   Explanation: Go from C to D and then to B.
3. Answer: Can't tell from the three clues.
   Explanation: Not possible to fly from B to A, and there is no mention of a direct flight between C and A.   Type_____

Student X_2 (age 20) Mealworm Puzzle

A) light but not moisture. "When the sunlight is at one end of the box it is dry, they all move to that one end."   Type_____

Student X_3 (age 21) Mr. Short/Mr. Tall Puzzle

Prediction for Mr. Tall: 15 paper clips high
    Explanation: "Guess, I'm really not sure how to do this."   Type_____

Student X_4 (age 23) Treasure Hunt Puzzle

W, WR, WJ, WF, WRJ, WRJF, WRF, WJF, R, J, F   Type_____

Our Answers: X_1 - A; X_2 - B; X_3 - B; X_4 - A

CHAPTER 2

CONCRETE AND FORMAL OPERATIONAL REASONING

INTRODUCTION

In the previous chapter you were invited to respond to four puzzles and examine the responses of students to those same puzzles. Observations of many children and adolescents attempting to perform similar tasks have led Jean Piaget and other psychologists to formulate theories concerning the mental processes individuals use to deal with problem situations. In this module, we shall introduce you to the idea of concrete and formal operational reasoning, a feature of Piaget's theory we consider important for college teachers. Chapters 3 and 4 will give you more details and examples to illustrate what we say here. The later modules will introduce you to other important ideas in Piaget's theory and help you to apply these ideas to your college teaching.

Objective of This Chapter

To enable you to identify and describe student behavior indicative of concrete and formal operational reasoning.

Procedure

Please begin by reading the essay, "Piaget's Theory in a Nutshell." After you read the essay, you are asked to revisit student responses to the zles in chapter 1.

Essay Piaget's Theory in a Nutshell

In reading the student responses to the puzzles in chapter 1, you undoubtedly recognized that type A answers were more complete, more consistent, and more systematic, in short, were better than type B answers. In fact, you may have been somewhat surprised to learn that many college students gave type B answers.

We suggest that each of the two types of answers demonstrates the use of either concrete or formal reasoning as described by the Swiss psychologist and epistemologist, Jean Piaget, in his theory of intellectual development. We shall, therefore, give you some general background regarding Piaget's theory and then apply it to the problem-solving and reasoning patterns used by students who responded to the puzzles in chapter 1.

Figure 2.1. Dr. Piaget, 1975, Philadelphia, PA.

Jean Piaget
(1895–1980)
Geneva, Switzerland
Three Periods of Work
1922–29 —Started at Binet's Lab
—Began semiclinical interviews
—Discovered and described "Children's Philosophies" e.g., "Sun Follows Me" Egocentrism
1929–40 —Studied his own three children
—Traced Origins of Child's Spontaneous Mental Growth to Infant Behavior e.g., Peek-a-Boo
Conservation reasoning
1940–80 —Development of Logical Thought in Children and Adolescents
—Child's Construction of His World. Mind is not a passive mirror
—Child can reason about things but not about propositions.

Table 2.1

Dr. Piaget began his inquiry into the origins of human knowledge early in the 20th century. He sought to understand how knowledge develops in the human minds, i.e. to understand the genesis of knowledge. He called himself a genetic epistemologist to emphasize his interest in both the development of knowledge in the human species and the development of knowledge by an individual. Dr. Piaget's life long work had several distinct phases as shown in Table 2.1. From the large collection of Piaget's work we are only selecting a few concepts.

The fundamental units of knowing, for Piaget, are schemes. A scheme is a class of physical or mental actions you can perform on the world. Notice, that in the Piagetian sense, knowledge is better described as knowing, as an active process. Hence, we will often use the term reasoning to indicate the active, systematic process by which you come to know, or solve, something.

Two concepts of Piaget that we believe are most helpful to college teachers are: (1) sequences or stages in the development of schemes and (2) self-regulation (equilibration). Schemes develop gradually and sequentially and always from less effective to more effective levels. We shall discuss important schemes below.

The second key idea, self-regulation, refers to a process whereby an individual's reasoning advances from one level to the next. This advance in reasoning is always from a less to a more integrated level. Piaget views this process of intellectual development as analogous to the differentiation and integration one sees in embryonic development. It is also seen as an adaptation analogous to the adaptation of evolving species. The process of self-regulation is discussed in a later chapter.

Piaget characterized human intellectual development in terms of four, sequential stages of reasoning (Inhelder & Piaget, 1958, p. 309). (See Table 2.2).

The first two, called sensory-motor and preoperational, are usually passed by the time a child is 7- or 8-years-old. The last two, however, are of particular interest to college teachers; they are called the stages of concrete operational reasoning and of formal operational reasoning. What follows are some schemes that constitute important aspects of concrete operational reasoning and formal operational reasoning.

Schemes That Constitute Important Aspects of Concrete Operational Reasoning:

C1 Class inclusion: An individual uses simple classifications and generalizations (e.g., all dogs are animals, only some animals are dogs.)

C2 Conservation: An individual applies conservation reasoning (e.g., if nothing is added or taken away, the amount, number, length, weight, etc. remains the same even though the appearance differs).

Table 2.2. Logical Knowledge Stages of Cognitive Development (Jean Piaget)

Stage	Characteristics	Approximate Age Range (Years)
Sensory-Motor	Preverbal Reasoning	0–2
Preoperational	No cause and effect reasoning. Uses verbal symbols, simple classifications, lacks conservation reasoning	1–8
Concrete operational	Reasoning is logical but concrete rather than abstract	8– ?
Formal operational	Hypothetico-deductive reasoning	11– (?)

C3 Serial Ordering: An individual arranges a set of objects or data in serial order and establishes a one-to-one correspondence (e.g., the youngest plants have the smallest leaves).

These basic reasoning patterns enable an individual to:

(a) use concepts and simple hypotheses that make a direct reference to familiar actions and objects, and can be explained in terms of simple association (e.g., the plants in this container are taller because they get more fertilizer);
(b) follow step-by-step instructions as in a recipe, provided each step is completely specified (e.g., can identify organisms with the use of a taxonomic key, or find an element in a chemical solution using a standard procedure);
(c) relate one's own viewpoint to that of another in a simple situation (e.g., a girl is aware that she is her sister's sister).

However, individuals whose schemes have not developed beyond the concrete operational stage have certain limitations in reasoning ability. These limitations are demonstrated as the individual:

(d) searches for and identifies some variables influencing a phenomenon, but does so unsystematically (e.g., investigates the effects of one variable but does not necessarily hold the others constant);
(e) makes observations and draws inferences from them, but does not consider all possibilities;
(f) responds to difficult problems by applying a related but not necessarily correct algorithm;

(g) processes information but is not spontaneously aware of one's own reasoning (e.g. does not check one's own conclusions against the given data or other experience).

The above characteristics typify concrete operational reasoning.

Schemes That Constitute Important Aspects of Formal Operational Reasoning:

F1 Combinatorial Reasoning: An individual systematically considers all possible relations of experimental or theoretical conditions, even though some may not be realized in nature (recall the Treasure Hunt Puzzle from chapter 1).

F2 Separation and Control of Variables: In testing the validity of a relationship, an individual recognizes the necessity of taking into consideration all the known variables and designing a test that controls all variables but the one being investigated (e.g., in the Mealworm Puzzle in chapter 1, recognizes the inadequacy of the setup using Box 1).

F3 Proportional Reasoning: The individual recognizes and interprets relationships in situations described by observable or abstract variables (e.g., the rate of diffusion of a molecule through a semipermeable membrane is inversely proportional to the square root of its molecular weight. In the Mr. Short/Mr. Tall Puzzle in chapter 1, Mr. Tall was six buttons tall and Mr. Short was 4 buttons tall, therefore, Mr. Tall must be one and a half times bigger than Mr. Short in any system of measurement.)

F4 Probabilistic Reasoning: An individual recognizes the fact that natural phenomena themselves are probabilistic in character, that any conclusions or explanatory model must involve probabilistic considerations, and that useful quantitative relationships can be derived, for example, the ratio of actual events to the total number possible (e.g., in the Frog Puzzle, given at the end of this chapter, the ability to assess the probability of certain assumptions holding true such as: the frogs mingled thoroughly, no new frogs were born, the bands did not increase the death or predation rate of the banded frogs, and use of the ratio of 1 to 6).

F5 Correlational Reasoning: In spite of random fluctuations, an individual is able to recognize causes or relations in the phenomenon under study by comparing the number of confirming and disconfirming cases (e.g to establish a correlation of say, blond hair with blue eyes and brunette hair with brown eyes, the number of blue-eyed blonds and brown-eyed brunettes minus the number of brown-eyed blonds and blue-eyed brunettes is compared to the total number of subjects).

These schemes, taken in concert, enable an individual to accept hypothesized statements (assumptions) as the starting point for reasoning about a situation. One is able to reason hypothetico-deductively. In other words, one is able to image all possible relations of factors, deduce the consequences of these relations, then empirically verify which of those consequences, in fact occurs. For example, in the Island Puzzle in chapter 1, such an individual could explain "If there were a plane route between Island A and C, then people could get from A to B but that is forbidden."

At the concrete operational stage, some formal schemes may be absent or they are only intuitively understood. Hence they are applied only in familiar situations and only partially and unsystematically. One can be said to be reasoning at the formal operational level when formal operational schemes have become explicit and useful as general problem-solving procedures. We consider the concrete/formal dichotomy a useful heuristic to guide us in our classroom activities. It is NOT a new system of pigeon holes into which you place students. This dichotomy can serve as another perspective by which you can more clearly view the reasoning used by your students.

In Table 2.3, we summarize some differences between concrete and formal operational reasoning.

Teachers who are interested in applying these ideas in their teaching should be aware that many theoretical and experimental issues relating to Piaget's work are still being investigated. Piaget's original notion was that all persons progress through the major stages in the same, invariant sequence, though not necessarily at the same rate. Recent studies suggest

Table 2.3. Characteristics of Concrete and Formal Operational Reasoning

Concrete Reasoning	*Formal Reasoning*
Needs reference to familiar actions, objects, and observable properties.	Can reason with concepts, relationships, abstract properties, axioms, and theories; uses symbols to express ideas.
Uses concrete schemes C1–C3. Schemes F1–F5 are either not used, or used only partially, unsystematically, and only in familiar contexts.	Uses formal schemes F1–F5 as well as C1–C3.
Needs step-by-step instructions in a lengthy procedure.	Can plan a lengthy procedure given certain overall goals and resources.
Limited awareness of one's own reasoning. May be oblivious to inconsistencies among various statements one makes, or contradictions with other known facts.	Is aware and critical of one's own reasoning; actively checks conclusions by appealing to other known information.

strongly that, although almost everyone becomes able to use concrete schemes, many people do not come to use the same formal operational schemes effectively. (See chapter 12.)

Piaget's research has been a very rich resource for ideas about the construction of knowledge. A number of scholars around the world, known by the label "constructivists," are continuing to study the implications of Piaget's epistemology for education and learning. For example, the original version of this essay was written by Dr. Robert Karplus, a physicist and science educator at the University of California-Berkeley, who developed an elementary school (K–6) science curriculum (*Science Curriculum Improvement Study,* 1964) based on Piaget's ideas.

Since the above patterns of reasoning that have been described as formal operational represent extremely worthwhile educational aims and indeed are fundamental to developing meaningful understanding of theoretical and complex disciplines, the finding that many college students do not effectively employ formal operations on a great many content tasks presents a real challenge to college teachers.

In addition to this finding, five further points regarding concrete and formal operational reasoning should be kept in mind by teachers:

- First, formal operational reasoning is more than this or that specific behavior. It is also an orientation towards approaching and attempting to solve problems. For this reason, a person who is confident and experienced in one area may reason hypothetico-deductively (formally) in that area, but may be unwilling to unable to generate hypotheses and reason flexibly in a threatening or unfamiliar area.
- Second, a person's ability to effectively deal with problems using formal knowing is really open-ended in that one may deepen and broaden one's understanding in a particular domain, and/or add new intellectual areas within which one can reason formally.
- Third, many persons demonstrate the use of reasoning patterns which seem to be a mixture of concrete and formal operational schemes when solving particular problems. This type of reasoning can perhaps best be termed transitional.
- Fourth, a person develops formal operational schemes from concrete operational schemes through the process of self-regulation. Concrete schemes involving class inclusion, serial ordering, and conservation about real objects, events, and situations are the valuable *prerequisites* for the development of formal operational schemes.

- Fifth, sometimes by applying memorized formulae, words or phrases, students can appear to be using formal operational schemes and/or be comprehending formal subject matter, when they are in fact not.

Although this essay has not touched on many aspects of Piagetian theory, we will briefly mention its major implications for college teaching. These ideas will be expanded upon in later chapters.

The Theory's Main Implications for College Teaching Are:

1. Reasoning is an active, constructing process that must engage your students in developing more adequate schemes.
2. Be aware that some of your students may sometimes use predominantly concrete schemes.
3. Be aware that many of the topics and concepts you teach require formal operational reasoning. You should figure out which topics these are.
4. Try to arrange your subject matter so it follows the developmental progression of familiar, directly observable to less familiar, less observable, and more theoretical.
5. Demonstrate to your students a questioning, dynamic, and active attitude towards the course you teach. Generate hypotheses, discuss alternative explanations and encourage your students to do the same. Turn your classroom into a laboratory where real problems are investigated and knowing is derived from acting on evidence that is produced. Rewarding this type of activity by your students helps students
    (i) realize that many hypotheses are constructed,
    (ii) reflect upon the meaning of hypotheses,
    (iii) examine alternative hypotheses,
    (iv) examine evidence and its meaning, and
    (v) construct formal operational schemes.

Analysis of Student Responses in Chapter 1

Now we would like you to reexamine a few student responses to the puzzles from chapter 1. This time, try to apply ideas from the essay "Piaget's Theory in a Nutshell" to classify these responses into the following more descriptive categories, rather than the A/B designation that we employed.,

> PC = Preconcrete, acausal, "off-the-wall" explanation
> C = Concrete operational
> Tr = Transitional (mixed concrete and formal operational characteristics)
> F = Formal operational
> ? = Not possible to classify without more information

First select one student and reread and classify his or her responses to each of the puzzles. Record your classification of those responses thus making a "profile" of schemes used by this student. Follow this procedure for at least four students (see Table 2.4).

Now look at the results of your analysis. What can you conclude about the schemes any student may use at any time on any specific task?

We have prepared a general analysis of responses to each puzzle, including the Frog Puzzle and the Student Population Puzzle, given at the end of this chapter, that you may want to give to some of your own students. We have found these, and other similar puzzles, very useful as we have tried to evaluate the reasoning patterns typically used by our students.

Puzzle Analysis Addendum

To give you some specific illustrations of how the reasoning patterns used by students can be related to Piaget's theory we have prepared the following general analysis of responses to the puzzles in chapter 1 and to the Frog and Student Population Puzzles.

Table 2.4. Your Classification of Student Responses

Student (Age)	Scheme Classification			
	Island	Mealworm	Short/Tall	Treasure Hunt
Delores Johnson (19)				
Barbara Downing (21)				
David Kenting (19)				
Harold O'Keefe (20)				
Norma Kuhn (20)				
John Blake (16)				

Islands Puzzle

Formal Operational Reasoning (Type A): On Question 2, the trip from Island B to Island C is conceptualized as possibly achieved by a change of planes or stop over at Island D. In other words, the clues about plane routes are not only evaluated in terms of the direct information they provide, but also in terms of the inferences that are possible by using the general rules about connections that were stated in the introduction of the puzzle. On Question 3, a student using reasoning can imagine all possible routes from Island A to Island C in order to bring to bear the information available in the clues. In particular, one must hypothesize that air travel is possible and evaluate this hypothesis for consistency with the data. Note that most of the Type A responses quoted in Module 1 did not make use of the formal approach to Question 3, but did on Question 2. This mixture of procedures is often observed in practice and indicates transitional reasoning, a reflection of the fact that the stages of Piaget's theory are idealizations which help one to classify observed behavior, but should not be used to classify people superficially.

Concrete Operational Reasoning (Type B): Since the clues do not give the answers to the questions directly, the concrete thinker either can't tell, selects certain details from the map (geographical placement, island separation) or postulates properties of each island to explain his ideas. The properties of a single island (size, topography) used in this approach are conceptually simpler to manipulate than the plane routes, which represent relationships between islands. This approach also eliminates the need to make use of the rules for combining plane routes.

Mealworm Puzzle

Formal Operational Reasoning (Type A): Variables are held constant while only one is allowed to change. All possible causal factors are examined in turn to test the hypotheses that light or moisture or both are responsible for the distribution of the mealworms. The answer will be derived in a systematic manner with each possible conclusion being tested. Probabilistic reasoning is also evidenced by the student's ability to ignore the few mealworms in the "wrong" ends of boxes I, II, and IV.

Concrete Operational Reasoning (Type B): An individual using concrete reasoning will fix on one variable to the exclusion of others. One does not detect the logic of the experiment which allows for variables to be separated and isolated, so that they can be dealt with as casual agents. One sees the one-to-one correspondence where one factor causes one response in one of the boxes.

Mr. Short/Mr. Tall Puzzle

Formal Operational Reasoning (Type A): Each button corresponds to a certain number of paper clips, an intermediate quantity not stated in the puzzle nor asked for. Once this conversion ratio is known, the answer is found by multiplication. Alternatively, the student might conceptualize the height ratio, another intermediate abstraction, and then reason that this ratio must be invariant with respect to the units of measurement.

Concrete Operational Reasoning (Type B): Since the height of Mr. Short measures more paper clips than buttons, simply add the extra amount to the height of Mr. Tall. Even though the arithmetic difference in units is not stated or asked for: it is a much more direct measure of the qualitative difference than is the ratio, which comes from making a correspondence between each individual button and paper clip. Another concrete approach make use of the height difference in buttons of the two figures, and associates that directly with the same difference in paper clips. Note that extra buttons are equated to extra paper clips, in contradiction to the fact that the four buttons measuring Mr. Short are equal to six and not four paper clips. This inconsistency is not noticed at the stage of concrete reasoning but would be noticed at the formal stage and would lead the students who had originally made this mistake to reexamine their procedures, to self-regulate.

Treasure Hunt Puzzle

Formal Operational Reasoning (Type A): The student analyzes the problem as a combinatorial one. All the search parties are merely combinations of different characters from none, one alone, combinations of two, combinations of three, and one combination of four. The solution of all the possible (16) combinations (including none) is arrived at in a systematic way. Formal reasoning results in a tidiness, where combinations are not duplicated and are orderly arranged. Student reasoning in this way can generate all the possibilities. This is a hallmark of formal thought—one hypothesizes what *could be* instead of *what is.*

Concrete Operational Reasoning (Type B): Combinations of character are generated by unsystematically and perhaps only in doubles and singles. Pieces of a combinatorial reasoning system are evident. However, the full system is not developed. This leads to an unsystematic and inexhaustive series of combinations.

SUMMARY

Table 2.5 depicts a chart in which we have applied the above considerations to the responses of six students who attempted the four puzzles in Module 1. In looking at these responses you can see that not one subject gave all formal responses. This indicates that students are at varying levels in various subject areas. We would not expect college students to think formally in every content area. The transition from concrete to formal thinking depends a great deal on the kinds of experiences that a person has had in a particular field of study. If a student is a formal operational rather than a concrete operational reasoner in one area, however, the student is more likely to make the transition to formal reasoning in another area when the student is given suitable intellectual stimulation. How does this compare with your classifications?

The Frog and the Student Population Puzzles

We have used the Frog and Student Population Puzzles, on the following pages, with a wide variety of college students, from students in a freshmen English course to students in a general physics class. We have found the written student responses to the puzzles to be very helpful in revealing typical student reasoning patterns. We invite you to use them with your students. We developed the Student Population Puzzle, based on the Frog Puzzle (Figure 2.2) developed at the Lawrence Hall of Science at the University of California Berkeley, because we thought that students who did not think the person could really estimate the number of frogs in the pond might be swayed by the fact that, according to the story, a male professor was going to try to do it. So we invented another version in which a female first year college student was trying to do the same reasoning task. As you might expect, many more students say that she can not do it and offer a wide variety of reasons why that is so. One of our favorites is "Wearing armbands might become trendy."

Table 2.5. College Students' Responses

Student (age)	Island	Mealworm	Short/Tall	Treasure Hunt
Delores Johnson (19)	Tr	F	Tr-F	C
Barbara Downing (21)	F	Tr	F	C
David Kenting (19)	Tr	F	C	C
Harold O'Keefe (20)	C	C	C	Tr
Norma Kuhn (20)	Tr	C	C	F
John Blake (16)	Tr	F	F	F

Figure 2.2. The Frog Puzzle. ©1975 The Regents of the University of California, Lawrence Hall of Science.

THE STUDENT POPULATION PUZZLE

Amy Inquist, a first year student, wondered how many students were attending her college. Everyone she asked gave her a different answer, so she decided to conduct an experiment to see if she could determine the student population of her college. Since she could not get all of them together at once, she decided to interview a few students and get them to wear blue armbands for one week. A week later she interviewed some students and noted how many of them were wearing blue armbands. Figure 2.3 shows Amy Inquist's data:

First set of interviews:
She talked to 45 students and they all agreed to wear blue armbands for a week.

A week later
Second set of interviews:
She talked to 72 students and of those 9 were wearing blue armbands.

Figure 2.3. The Population Puzzle. ©1980. ADAPT, University of Nebraska Lincoln.

Amy assumed that the students wearing armbands mixed thoroughly and randomly with the students not wearing blue armbands, then she tried to approximate the number of students attending her college.

From Her Data:

Can Amy compute the approximate number of students at her college? Explain your answer.

If so, what number do you think she would get?

Explain the *reasoning* behind the answer or answers you give:

College Teaching and the Development of Reasoning   33

We hope you will use one of these puzzles with your students and then classify the reasoning patterns your students used in solving the puzzle. Please try to keep your classification to four categories.

> PC –   Preconcrete, acausal, "off-the-wall," explanation
> C –   Concrete operational
> Tr –   Transitional
> F –   Formal operational

What percentage of your students do you find in each category? You may want to compare your results to the results discussed in chapter 5.

Below are some general comments that you may find helpful in your classification-of-responses process.

Frog Puzzle:

Concrete Operational Reasoning: Differences are focused on rather than ratios. This student assumes constancy of differences and thus reasons as follows: there were 60 more unbanded frogs in the recapture sample, so there are 60 more frogs in the pond as a whole; 60 + 55 = 115. How would a person using concrete reasoning apply his reasoning to the following problem? "In a new recapture sample of 50 frogs, how many do you think are banded?" We have observed these responses: (1) Impossible to do; (2) 10; and (3) -10!!

Formal Operational Reasoning: Probabilistic reasoning is used. Starting with the relative frequency of banded frogs in the recapture sample, this student reasons that this ratio is an estimate of the relative frequency of banded frogs in the pond. After setting 12/72 equal to 55/x, the answer follows easily. This student is undisturbed by the uncertainty associated with a statistical estimate and realizes that, as an estimation, this procedure is valid.

Student Population Puzzle:

Concrete Operational Reasoning: Differences are focused on rather than ratios. This student assumes constancy of differences and thus reasons as follows: there were 63 more students without arm bands frogs in the second sample, so there are 63 more students in the college as a whole; 63 + 45 = 108. We have had some students who used this technique to add a comment such as "This seems like a very small college." That is a step towards thinking about one's own thinking

Formal Operational Reasoning: Probabilistic reasoning is used. Starting with the relative frequency of students with arm bands in the second sample, this student reasons that this ratio is an estimate of the relative frequency of students wearing arm bands in the whole college. After computing 72/9 they then compute the total student population to be 360 students. This student is undisturbed by the uncertainty associated with a statistical estimate and realizes that, as an estimation, this procedure is valid.

CONCLUDING REMARKS

In the chapters 3 and 4 we will introduce you to some actual transcripts of semiclinical interviews of students. We hope those two chapters will increase your understanding of the concrete operational and formal operational reasoning patterns used by students.

CHAPTER 3

FORMAL OPERATIONAL REASONING PATTERNS

INTRODUCTION

In Piaget's (1958) theory, concrete operational reasoning is characterized by patterns of reasoning including: serial ordering, simple classification, conservation, and other operations applied to objects that can be observed or manipulate directly. Formal operational reasoning patterns include these operations but go beyond them to utilize other processes in situations where one does not deal with tangible objects. Formal patterns often involve proportional reasoning, separation of variables, and combinatorial reasoning.

Dr. Robert Karplus and Dr. Rita Peterson (1976) created a film *Formal Reasoning Patterns* in which they interviewed secondary school students who exhibit concrete or formal operational reasoning patterns while responding to four Piagetian tasks. The young people appearing in this film were enrolled in Berkeley's High Potential program for secondary school students. They were above average in showing talent in some areas of accomplishment, not necessarily in academic achievement.

The students' performances were completely unrehearsed—none of them had prepared for the interview or knew in advance what would be required. The scenes in the film were selected to illustrate the concrete and formal operational reasoning patterns described in chapter 2.

Though not representative of a random sample of secondary school students, the film demonstrates that a diverse group of such students—a typical high school class, for instance, is likely to reveal both types of reasoning patterns.

Objective of this Chapter

To assist you in describing and/or identifying responses that indicate concrete or formal operational reasoning patterns in response to Piagetian tasks.

Procedure

Below is a transcript of selected portions of the Karplus/Peterson (1976) film. Reading these transcripts is a poor substitute from watching the film. We hope you will have a chance to borrow the film and watch it.

Notes on the Film, *Formal Reasoning Patterns,* by Robert Karplus and Rita Peterson (1976)

In the film, Drs. Rita Peterson and Robert Karplus, use the probing clinical interview technique employed by developmental psychologists. They are trying to encourage *the students to express their thoughts but NOT to teach them how to solve the tasks.* The references provided at the end of the chapter contain more complete descriptions of each task and the responses of larger numbers of young people.

TRANSCRIPTIONS OF PARTS OF THE *FORMAL REASONING PATTERNS* FILM

Proportional Reasoning (Mr. Short/Mr. Tall Puzzle—Karplus, Karplus, & Wollman, 1974)

The Mr. Short/Mr. Tall Puzzle introduced in chapter 1 is used as part of an individual interview. The student is shown pictures of Mr. Short and Mr. Tall, and a chain of large paper clips to measure the height of each. The student is then given a chain of #1 paper clips ("smallies") and is asked to measure the height of Mr. Short using these, and finally predicts the height of Mr. Tall measured in "smallies." Mr. Tall measures six paper clips in height with paper clips that measure Mr. Small to be four paper clips in height.

The young people in the film illustrate both (formal operational) proportional reasoning and (concrete operational) additive reasoning applied to this task.

Dr. Karplus shows the student a large, about 12" by 18", white card with drawings of Mr. Short and Mr. Tall on the opposite sides of the card:

Dr. Karplus: "OK Janet, here we have a problem, we have Mr. Short on this side of the card, and Mr. Tall, a bigger fellow on the other side. So, let me show you how to work on this project. Here we have Mr. Short, and I have some paper clips here. Some biggie paper clips and we will measure Mr. Short. How tall is he?"
Janet: "1, 2, 3, 4 paper clips."
Dr. Karplus: "4 paper clips in Mr. Short."

The junior high school student showing here with Dr. Karplus is working on a task developed to reveal proportional reasoning. A reasoning pattern contribution to formal thought as identified by Jean Piaget.

Dr. Karplus: "Here we have Mr. Tall on the back side who is measured as 6 biggies talk. We called them biggies, because in my other pocket, I have paper clips, smallies. And now would you like to measure Mr. Short using the smallies? Go ahead."
Janet: "1, 2, 3, 4, 5, 6½."
Dr. Karplus: "It's about 6½, very good, and now can you predict the height of Mr. Tall if you were to measure him with smallies?"
Janet: "... Using mathematics?"
Dr. Karplus: "Whatever, whatever method you would like to use. Even if you would like a paper and pencil, I can give you that and you can write the numbers down."
Janet: "Okay, can I have a paper and pencil please? Mr. Small, he was 4 paper clips, 4 big ones."

According to Piaget's developmental theory, thinking processes change during adolescence as formal operational reasoning patterns become established and supplement the concrete operational reasoning patterns that arose during earlier years. Concrete operational reasoning patterns include: serial ordering, simple classification, conservation, and other processes applied to objects and real events. Formal operational reasoning patterns involve these and other mental operations applied to hypothetical objects or events, relationships, and concepts.

> Janet: "I think you should divide 6½ by 4 or 4 by 6½, which ever it is, it doesn't matter, and you get 13/8 and so, maybe that is more than one whole. That's 1 and 5/8. so if you take 1 5/8 of 6, OK, so I multiply 6 x 13/8, which is 78/8, and 8 into 78 = 9 and 6/8 or ¾. I think it might be 9 paper clips and ¾ of one.

Janet used proportional reasoning, a formal reasoning pattern, when predicting Mr. Tall's height successfully in this task where she was prevented from comparing the figures, or paper clips, directly. She calculated the ratio of the two measurements of Mr. Short and then used this ratio to scale up the measurement of Mr. Tall. Many students who do not use this reasoning pattern focus on the difference rather than the ratio of measurements and make the prediction that Mr. Tall is about 8½ smallies high. Peter approaches the same task with confidence

> Dr. Karplus: "Now can you predict how high Mr. Tall would be when measured with these small paper clips?"
> Peter: "It will be about ... 8½."

His first response appears to focus on the difference.

> Peter: "He is 4 tall in the biggies ones and 6 tall in the other ones. And 4 is 2/3 of 6, so I multiply the 6 that he was in the big clips by three halves to get what I thought it would be, he should be 9."

When explaining his prediction, however, he finds and uses the ratio of measurements thus displaying the formal reasoning pattern.

Katie interviewed here, by Dr. Peterson makes use of concrete reasoning patterns consistently in her predictions and explanations.

> Dr. Peterson: "Now I would like you to predict, how tall you think Mr. Tall is in smallies?"
> Katie: "Let me see. He is about 8½ or so?"
> Dr. Peterson: "And how did you figure out your prediction?"
> Katie: "Because this was 4 before, and then it was 2½ more of the little ones."
> Katie: "So before it was 6 and 2½ more would be 8½."

We have found secondary school students divided in their use of concrete and formal reasoning patterns on the task in proportional reasoning.

Using the small paper clips, (Robert) finds Mr. Short to be six smallies high, what would you expect for him to predict for Mr. Tall's height?

Robert: "Uh, it would be 8."
Dr. Peterson: "Ok and how did you figure out your prediction?"
Robert: "Uh, well you know 4 is to 6 and 6 is to 8? Is that it?"
Dr. Peterson: "Ok. Would you like to measure it?"
Robert: "Yeah."

The actual measurement startled Robert but he did not propose a new explanation.

Robert: "Ten."
Dr. Peterson: "Ten. Do you want to reconsider how you do it?"
Robert: "No."

Separation and Control of Variables (Flexible Rods—Inhelder & Piaget, 1958)

The task shown in the film makes use of a device consisting of six thin rods clamped horizontally (see Figure 3.1). The rods bend when one, two, or three washers are attached.

This apparatus permits the adjustment and controlled investigation of four variables: length of the rod, thickness of the rod, material of rods, and weight, or number, of washers placed on a rod.

To verify the effects of length, for instance, the student must use one rod and a fixed number of washers, and slide the rod in its holder to vary the length. To determine the effect of material, the same number of washers must be placed on the two thin rods of different materials extended to the same length. The effect of thickness can be investigated by using two brass rods of different thickness, since this pair is made of the same material.

As you will see in later chapters, the formal operational reasoning pattern of controlling variables is critical for understanding many college assignments and textbook explanations because most phenomena depend on several variables. Often this reasoning is taken for granted and inadequate explanations are furnished to students who do not yet apply it.

Dr. Karplus: "Here is a road going by the lake and these are some piers that go out where people can go fishing. We have

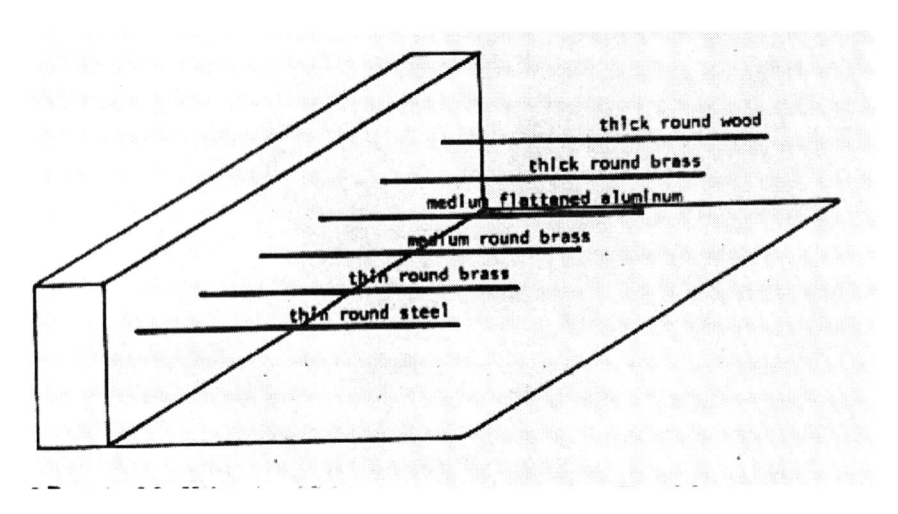

Figure 3.1. Flexibility of rods apparatus.

> 3 men, a little guy, a middle guy, and a big guy who want to go out fishing, and they want to go out to the end of the pier and they want to get close to the water. Just their feet touching the water, but not getting dunked all the way. Would you like to find how these 3 men might go to the end of the piers for their fishing?"

Here Jocelyn is introduced to a task requiring the separation and control of variables. After Jocelyn explores properties of the rods and their interaction with the weights, she identifies the variables that affect how much the rods bend.

> Dr. Karplus: "Would you tell me what properties of the piers. What about the piers that makes them bend different amounts."
> Jocelyn: "This one is thinner."
> Dr. Karplus: "Uh huh ... their thickness and thinness. What other things about the piers, or the men, makes them bend different amounts?"
> Jocelyn: "Some weigh more."
> Dr. Karplus: "The men weigh more, uh huh. Any other things?"
> Jocelyn: "Different types of metal?"
> Dr. Karplus: "Uh hah, different metals. Any other things about the piers that would make a difference in how far they bend."

Jocelyn:	"How far out they are."
Dr. Karplus:	"How far out they are. Very good. Anything else?"
Jocelyn:	"um …"
Dr. Karplus:	"Well that's four things that can make a difference, you were able to pick them, right. So the men can be each in a place where can do their fishing."

Asking students to do an experiment that proves the affect of a single variable, however, poses a problem that can not be handled by concrete reasoning patterns.

Dr. Karplus:	"Could you think of an experiment that could prove the material the piers is made of make a difference in how far in bends?"
Rhonda:	"um yeah, you could …"
Dr. Karplus:	"Go ahead …"
Rhonda:	"Oh you mean … with these three?"
Dr. Karplus:	"With what you have there and the piers, how could you do an experiment to prove that the material makes a difference."
Rhonda:	"Um well, first, this one, when it was on this one, it almost touched."
Dr. Karplus:	"Mmm hmm."
Rhonda:	"And if I put it on this one. It doesn't touch at all."
Dr. Karplus:	"Mmm hmm."
Rhonda:	"And if I put it on this one. Its umm, well this one was closer in weight, so its closer, and …"
Dr. Karplus:	"What does that prove now?"
Rhonda:	"That proves that umm … because this one was thinner."
Dr. Karplus:	"Mmm hmm."
Rhonda:	"This one went down farther because it's the weigh of this makes the man to get down to the water and as each one became progressively umm stronger, the man came up more."
Dr. Karplus:	"Oh, he did not go so far."

Rhonda for example, realized how she might make the rod bend a greater or smaller amount but the rods she chose differed with respect to several variables. To prove the affect of material, Rhonda should have used rods of the same length and thickness. The need to control these variables escaped her.

Monica has similar difficulties.

Dr. Peterson: "Could you do an experiment to shows that what it's made of really makes a difference. OK, now on that one..."
Monica: "It goes all the way down."
Dr. Peterson: "Ok …"
Monica: "This one is not …"

Monica, like Rhonda varies length, thickness, and material.

Monica: "How thick or thin the rods are and what its made of makes difference in how far they'll bend."
Dr. Peterson: "Ok, and on this last experiment, now here you compared a wooden rod with a metal thin one, so you proved that it does make a difference what material it's made out of?"

Some students, like Jocelyn, at first overlooked the need to control variables, but modified their procedure after this fact is called to their attention.

Dr. Karplus: "Now the first one you mention how thin they are makes a difference, could you do an experiment to prove that? What are you going to do? Why don't you tell me while you do it. So I know what is coming up?"
Jocelyn: "Well, if this one is thick, so its stronger and this one is thin, so its kinda weak."
Dr. Karplus: "Uh huh … and that proves that the thickness makes a difference. Suppose somebody else had done you know, just like you did here and it hardly bends. And you had used this other pier, and it hardly bends either. Thickness doesn't make a difference."
Jocelyn: "It's farther back."
Dr. Karplus: "Uh ho … and so that is not a fair experiment?"

Jocelyn's actions and explanations give evidence that she does apply a formal reasoning pattern to the task.

Greg spontaneously separates and controls variables indicating his use of this formal reasoning pattern.

Dr. Peterson: "Ok now, its there anything you can do to show me that weight makes a difference."

Greg: "Well if you put a single weight on that one there, it stays above water, but if you put double weight on there, it just about hits the water as you put a triple on there, it hits the water."

Dr. Peterson: "Ok, well that is pretty convincing evidence."

Combinatorial Reasoning (Chemical Mixtures—Inhelder & Piaget, 1958)

The "coloring liquids" task shown in the film requires the student to identify the role of each of the four liquids combining with a fifth to form a brown color, the color of iodine. The five liquids are:

1 = dilute sulfuric acid; 2 = water; 3 = hydrogen peroxide solution; 4 = sodium thiosulfate solution and G = sodium iodide solution

Liquids 1 and 3 are necessary to form the brown color with G by oxidizing the iodide to iodine. Liquid 2 has no effect—it may be added or omitted. Liquid 4 prevents the brown color from forming or eliminates it (when present) by reducing the iodine.

The students working on this task illustrate the difference between (1) formal operational reasoning which goes through the full range of possibilities and (2) the concrete operational approach of trying combinations unsystematically and incompletely.

This task requires students to use combinatorial reasoning as they recognize that several ingredients may produce an effect only in certain combinations which includes some liquids and omit others.

Dr. Karplus: "… I have over here a little bit of liquid taken from these bottles. And now when I take some from G and drop it in."

Greg also uses formal reasoning patterns, when he identifies the combination of liquids required to produce to the dark brown color.

Dr. Karplus: "It turned brown and the other one didn't. And your problem now it to figure out how these liquids can be used to make the brown color, when G is put in. Go ahead."

Greg also uses formal reasoning patterns, when he identifies the combination of liquids required to produce to the dark brown color. He systematically tries one of each and G, then combinations of pairs of liquids and G, and then combinations of three liquids and G, and finally all four and G.

Dr. Karplus: "What do you think of it now? You think it's reasonably close?"
Greg: "It is pretty close. I'll see what happens if I add four because last time it cleared it up."
Dr. Karplus: "Oh what did it do this time?"
Greg: "it made it lighter, I'll add a little more and see if it clears up. When you mix all 3 in 1 2 3 and G. It makes it brown. But when you add 4, it clears it up."

Robert like Greg approaches this task with a formal reasoning pattern.

Dr. Karplus: "Well what did you find out from that?"
Robert: "That, that uh, G mixed with any one of them doesn't make a reaction. So it's a combination of all."
Dr. Karplus: "What are you going to do next?"
Robert: "Uh … mix two of them, well let see. All right."

His systematic approach ultimately leads to success.

Robert: "There it is."
Dr. Karplus: "Oh, what do you know now?"
Robert: "That uh, the 3 together will do it but uh individually they won't. you know. It's just a certain combination, I guess."

Katie, who has not yet developed this formal reasoning pattern tries many combinations but does not choose them systematically. And cannot remember what she has tried.

Katie: "Uh, what have I done? 2, 3 and G."
Dr. Peterson: "Uh huh, and G. ok."
Katie: Hope this is it. This better be it. Oh my gosh,
Dr. Peterson: Clear again right?
Katie: right, that is very strange.

Each of three tasks shown in the film emphasized one formal reasoning pattern: proportional reasoning, separation and control of variables, or combinatorial logic.

Application of Proportional Reasoning and Separation of Variables (Equal Arm Balance—Inhelder & Piaget, 1958)

The last task in the film, balancing the beam, requires students to apply proportional reasoning while separating the variables of weight and distance. There are twenty notches for hanging weights on each side of the fulcrum, with a mark at the 10th notch but no numbering. The weights provided are 3, 5, 7, and 10 units made of the same washers as were used in the flexible rods task.

At the beginning of each interview, the student was shown the beam in balance, with 10 unit weights at the distance of 10 notches on each side of the arm. The following four tasks were then posited.

1. Use a 7-weight and a 3-weight to balance a 10-weight placed *10* units from the fulcrum.
2. Use a 5-weight to balance a 10-weight placed at *10* units from the fulcrum.
3. Use a 7-weight to balance a 10-weight placed *14* units from the fulcrum.
4. Use a 7-weight to balance a 5-weight placed *7* units from the fulcrum.

Students using concrete operational reasoning patterns have a general idea that increased distance on one arm compensates for increased weight on the other arm. They may reason qualitatively or use weight differences rather than ratios in all but the simplest cases of 2:1 comparisons. Formal operational reasoning patterns are in evidence when the more complicated weight comparisons in tasks 3 and 4, listed above, are treated by ratios.

The last task, balancing the beam requires students to apply proportional reasoning and separation of variables to a more difficult problem. Jocelyn has just predicted and found that one 10 unit weight balances another 10 unit weight placed at the same distance of support.

Dr. Karplus: "Here is the seven, and the three. Could you hang them on your side and weigh that it will balance again. And could you tell me why you predict that it will balance?"
Jocelyn: "the 7 and 3 is 10."
Dr. Karplus: "Uh huh."
Jocelyn: "And they are both on this side, and it equals to 10 and the other side is 10." (She hangs the 2 weights from the

	same notch so she has 10 weights hanging from the 10 notch.)
Dr. Karplus:	"Very good. Ok, could you take them down again? And we will make it harder to still. Now here is a five. Could you figure out a way to hang the 5 on your side of the bean to balance my 10 over here." (Dr. Karplus has the 10 weight hanging from a notch 10 units from the pivot point. Jocelyn has been handed a 5 weight.)
Jocelyn:	"I don't know …"
Dr. Karplus:	"You don't feel quite as sure as before?"
Jocelyn:	"No."
Dr. Karplus:	"And why did you hang it over at that spot? Can you explain that? I noticed you were counting?"
Jocelyn:	"Five from five is…. Umm, I am not sure."
Dr. Karplus:	"Now, what about the fives?"
Jocelyn:	"Five to five from five…." (She places the 5 weight out 5 notches, at 15 from the pivot point.)
Dr. Karplus:	"Oh, you went five out farther. I see. And why did you pick five to go out."
Jocelyn:	"Cuz this was 10. And this weigh is 5."

She had only a qualitative notion that increased distance compensates for decreased weight, but used the weight difference and not the ratio to make her prediction.

Robert has no difficulty applying proportional reasoning to the same problem.

Dr. Karplus:	"Could you hang up this one 5 unit weight on that side to balance the 10 hanging over here at the 10 mark? Where would you put that?"
Robert:	"On the end (the 20 mark)."
Dr. Karplus:	"Way out on the end?"
Robert:	"Yeah, that's right."
Dr. Karplus:	"Why would you put it there?"
Robert:	"Because it's only half the weight of this one. Well, ok then I guess. They should balance."
Dr. Karplus:	"It does, very good. Can you take it off again? And could you, lets move this. (Ten weight to the 14 mark) Move it over here, uh, could you take this 7 weight and balance the 10 when it hangs there (at 14)."
Robert:	"Hmm. Lets hang it up here."
Dr. Karplus:	"And why did you hang it at that place?"

Robert: "Let me think ... it can't be uh, let see. I'm not sure, I just felt like that it's the place it should be. "

But he did not apply proportional reasoning to the balancing of 7 against 10, students in the process of forming more advanced reasoning patterns can often apply them to simple examples but are unable to generalize their procedure.

Dr. Karplus: "Could you give me an explanation, or it this a guess."
Robert: "Yes this is a guess."

For Vladimir, who has mastered proportional reasoning, the same weight ratio of 7 to 19 presents no obstacle.

Dr. Karplus: "How do you figure that?"
Vladimir: "Umm well, I'm taking the uh.... The ratio of this weigh to that, and ..."
Dr. Karplus: "Uh huh.... Very good."
Vladimir: "Um, using ..."
Dr. Karplus: "Where do you come out then?"
Vladimir: "Um, let see. This 10 sevenths, 7 times, I need 10 out."
Dr. Karplus: "Is that your prediction, should we make a test?"
Vladimir: "Is it 10 out?"
Dr. Karplus: "It is, fabulous."

The four tasks presented in the film revealed the use of reasoning patterns that span the range of concrete operations to formal thought.

Children who have not yet developed concrete operational reasoning patterns would approach these tasks haphazardly and through guessing without awareness of cause effect relationships. Such behavior is rare among secondary school students and was not shown in the film. Still, the student using primarily concrete operational reasoning patterns does not have a comprehensive system for organizing his or her data, and maybe overwhelmed by their number and variety.

The student applying concrete operational reasoning patterns is limited to what he or she does and observes and frequently answers a different question than asked when confronted with a multiple cause and effect relationship.

Sometimes, a student uses a mathematical formula and obtains an incorrect result. Can he evaluate his own work in the light of his experience? Moon here finds himself in this predicament when he attempts to explain his placement of the 7 unit weight balancing the 10 unit weight placed at 14 notches from the pivot point.

Dr. Karplus:	"I am going to ask you to explain why you think that's the place?"
Moon:	"I made an approximate ratio."
Dr. Karplus:	"Yes, could you tell me how you made the approximate ratio?"
Moon:	"Ten, 14 notches over 10 is equal to x which is the unknown, over 7 which is the weight."
Dr. Karplus:	"I see."
Moon:	"Ten, 10 ... I am not very good in math."
Dr. Karplus:	"Would you like to use a piece of paper?"

He then changes his procedure.

Moon:	"Here is 10 over 7, equal to x over 14. and solve for x to get 20."
Dr. Karplus:	"Now let's try that."

The film shows examples of young people applying concrete and formal operational reasoning patterns. A person may use one or the other of these depending on the nature and familiarity of the problem situation. Among the participants in this film, there was no clear progression of reasoning patterns with age. Teachers can identify the reasoning of their students by observing their approaches to problems and listening carefully to their explanations, their justifications. If that is to be done successfully, however, the possible effects of motivation, interest, and anxiety have to be taken into account also.

Adolescence is a turbulent period for many young people. The additional insights into intellectual development afforded by Piaget's theory and the identification of reasoning patterns can help teachers make this a period of productive growth.

CONCLUDING REMARKS

Our emphasis in this book is on the development of reasoning. Many other factors, such as motivation, interest and anxiety, also influence student performance. Even though we do not discuss these factors in detail, we have kept them in mind. We believe that the situations you provide in student learning can help your students develop their reasoning. In some later chapters we will offer some suggestions for teaching that are intended to help you provide opportunities for your students to develop their reasoning, but our suggestions may also increase motivation and allay anxiety.

REFERENCES

Inhelder, B., & Piaget, J. (1958). *The growth of logical thinking from childhood to adolescence.* New York: Basic Books.

Karplus, E. F., Karplus, R., & Wollman, W. (1974). Intellectual development beyond elementary school IV: Ratio, the influence of cognitive style. *School Science and Mathematics, 75*(6), 476–482.

Karplus, R., & Peterson, R. (Producers). (1976). *Formal reasoning patterns* [Motion picture] Davis, CA: Davidson Films. (Available as videocassette or 16mm film.)

Viewers of the film find Karplus and myself taking turns interacting one-to-one with each student. The film reveals Bob's very compelling enthusiasm for solving problems and watching students discover new relationships. Playfully Bob challenges Vladimir, Jocelyn, Robert, and Monica on film: "Very good! You have found out how tall Mr. Short and Mr. Tall are in small paper clips. Now let's see if you can measure Mr. Small in big paper clips and then predict—without measuring—how tall Mr. Tall would be in big paper clips!" As students worked through this and other puzzles, Bob continues to encourage and challenge each student. Later in the film, viewers see Karplus present students with another problem and say, "Ah-ha! So now you have discovered how to balance two equal weights on each side of the balance beam. Now let's see what you can discover about balancing unequal weights!" Thousands of people by now have watched Robert Karplus on this film in the decades that have followed its release, and have witnessed his enthusiasm for the act of discovery itself, and his desire to share that enjoyment with the students we met on film.

Everyone who has watched to film has some of favorite bits. One viewer's favorite is Bob's questioning of the girl who starts to explain how to control variables on the rods task, and Bob says "Can you show me?" The girl says something like, "Oh, you mean here?" and proceeds to show that she does not separate and control variables.... Another favorite is the boy near the end of the film who tells Bob he solved the equal arm balance task by making "an approximate ratio." Bob asks "Can you explain how you made an approximate ratio?" and the boy does so. The film is filled with good examples of Bob's keen interest in discovering how students reason.

—Rita Peterson (2002)

CHAPTER 4

INTERVIEWS OF COLLEGE STUDENTS

INTRODUCTION

In Piaget's theory, concrete operational thought is characterized by serial ordering, simple classification, and conservation logic applied directly to objects. A person using concrete operational reasoning doing a Piagetian task must be able to observe objects and/or manipulate them. Formal operational thought involves proportional reasoning, separations of variables, elimination of contradictions, and class inclusion or exclusion operations. A person using formal operational reasoning is able to work in situations where one does not deal directly with tangible objects. A person using formal operational reasoning can apply concrete operations and can go beyond these operations when solving problems.

A videotape developed at Illinois Central College by Dr. Thomas Campbell (physics) and Mr. Phil McGill (mathematics) illustrates the thinking strategy used by beginning college students who are responding to the Mealworm Puzzle as described in chapter 1, the Frog Puzzle as described in chapter 2 and the Algae Puzzle given in this chapter. The Algae Puzzle is a task requiring combinatorial logic and was a part of the original Lawrence Hall of Science workshop materials. It is the reasoning analog to the Treasure Hunt puzzle we showed you in chapter 1.

College Teaching and the Development of Reasoning, pp. 51–62
Copyright © 2009 by Information Age Publishing
All rights of reproduction in any form reserved.

52   R. G. FULLER ET AL.

You may find it helpful to review these puzzles before you read the transcriptions of the interviews with these college students.

The interviews demonstrate that a college population typically includes students who approach certain tasks with concrete operational reasoning patterns, while others apply formal operational reasoning. Students selected for the interviews were freshmen enrolled in the Piagetian program called DOORS (Development Of Operational Reasoning Skills) developed at Illinois Central College in 1977. Students volunteered to participate in the interviews outside of class time. The original videotape ran about 26 minutes.

Objective of This Chapter

To assist you in describing and identifying responses that indicate concrete or formal operational reasoning as applied to different tasks.

Procedure

As you read the transcript of these interviews, try to identify the clues in each student's reasoning that indicate the use of concrete or formal operational reasoning patterns.

Ask a teaching colleague to read the transcript and identify the concrete or formal operational reasoning patterns in the student responses. Then share your thoughts and discuss your findings.

Of course, actually watching the video is much better than just reading the transcription, so we have made it available through the UNL Digital Commons Web site under a link at http://digitalcommons.unl.edu/adaptworkshopmodule4/.

ILLINOIS CENTRAL COLLEGE STUDENTS DOING ALGAE, FROG AND MEALWORM PUZZLES

Interview Setting

The student volunteer was introduced to the puzzle that was written out on a large sheet of bulletin board paper. The puzzle was read aloud to the student and the interviewer tried to make sure that the student clearly understood the questions being asked by the puzzle. The puzzle was visible to the student at all times during the interview. The student was asked to work out a response to the puzzle, writing on a blackboard with a piece of chalk. What the student was writing as well as the student's comments were available on the videotape.

In this transcription we have provided the words of the students and the interviewers and a description of what the student was writing on the blackboard when that is important for you to be able to understand how the student is thinking about the puzzle.

THE ALGAE PUZZLE

Dr. Campbell: There are four kinds of algae that are present along the seashore which these crabs feed on. Ok, and they've all been out eating, and they come back now. We have collected some of those and we like to predict what combinations of algae that we might find in those stomachs. What I like you to do is pick up a piece of chalk and could you make a list on the board, and I like you to use Y for yellow, R for red, G for green, and B for brown.

[Bob writes YRGB, YR, YG, YB, then, in another column he writes RY, RG, RB on the board.]

Bob:	[*pause*] I am kinda lost here.
Dr. Campbell:	How many combinations do you have there?
Bob:	I've got seven.
Dr. Campbell:	Seven combinations. Ok.

The Algae Puzzle

A population of crabs which eats algae lives on a seashore. On the seashore there are four kinds of algae: yellow, red, brown, and green algae.

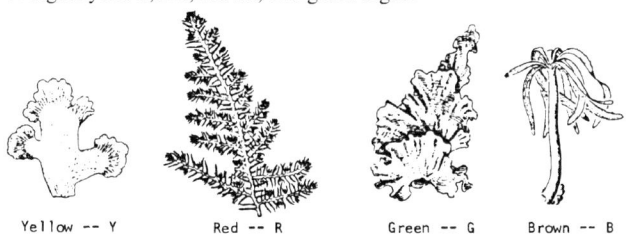

Yellow -- Y   Red -- R   Green -- G   Brown -- B

Dr. Saltspray, a biologist, is interested in determining which of the types of algae are actually eaten by the crabs. He plans to find out by examining the stomach contents of the crabs. Before he does his investigation he lists every interesting possibility he thinks he may find in the stomachs.

Write down every possibility he can find.
Use letters Y, R, G, and B to save space.

Figure 4.1. The Algae Puzzle as shown to the student. © 1975 The Regents of the University of California, Lawrence Hall of Science.

Bob:	I got one out of order, it doesn't matter what order. *[Erases RY, adds the combination GB]*
Dr. Campbell:	Can you think of anymore?
Bob:	*[long pause]*
Dr. Campbell:	Can you show me how it is that those might be possible? Did you do any ordering to help you decide that those were combinations?
Bob:	I thought I'd go YR, YG, YB.
Dr. Campbell:	Ok, those are the ones are over there.
Bob:	Yeah, I was gonna to go RY, RG, RB, but RY, we've already got here, it doesn't matter the order.
Dr. Campbell:	Then over here you have RG, RB and then you've got GB Ok.
Bob:	GB, yes.
Dr. Campbell:	I see that. Can you think of anymore, or it's that all of them.
Student:	*[long pause]* That's all I can think of.
Dr. Campbell:	Ok.

Steve:	[writes combinations: YRGB, BGRY, GBRY, BYGR on the board.]
Mr. McGill:	As you go along, could you explain a bit of what you are thinking? By what you are doing there Steve, please.
Steve:	Well, I was alternating: alternating the series, not in any particular order but with this next series. I started with the last letter. Then I went from right to left. And that, I think is a third of the possible combination. *[Adds combinations RGBY, GBYK.]*
Mr. McGill:	Now this represents what you would find in each crab's stomach, right?
Steve:	Uh hmm. I suppose that it's the order that the crab eats the algae.
Mr. McGill:	Ok.
Steve:	*[adds BYRG]* Gotta repeat.
Mr. McGill:	How many are there total? Do you have any idea?
Steve:	16, There are 16. There are 16 different possibilities.
Mr. McGill:	16, and how do you figure that? How did you compute that?
Steve:	Umm ... well there are four different items, and there are four different ways each item can be placed in a certain order. I just ah ... *[long pause]*.

Mr. McGill: Ok. I think, you know it's quite good, Steve. I have one other question. Each time you're finding four types of algae in the stomach. Is that the only possibility?

Steve: For the algae?

Mr. McGill: Right.

Steve: It could be entirely one type, or percentage wise, it could be 10% of the yellow, 20% of the red.

Mr. McGill: Ok, disregarding the percentage type. Can you think of combinations other than four algae at one time?

Steve: If the algae's type I see here it's strictly the diet, it should be only four different types.

Jim: *[writes in one column; Y, R, G, B, he is makes a second column of YR, YG, YB, the a third column of RG, RB, GB on the board]*

Mr. McGill: Those are the two kinds of findings?

Jim: Yeah. *[Then he makes a third column of YRG, YRB, RGB, YGB, and adds YRGB in a forth column on the board]*

Mr. McGill: It looks like you have some kind of pattern there, could you explain the pattern of how you arrange things.

Jim: Well the first one, it's the possibility of each one alone I picked the first one and I mixed it with the others, and uh, the second one and mixed in with the others, and these two should already be covered, and I picked the first one and mixed the with the next two, and the first one with the last two.

Mr. McGill: And then the last one it's all of them. Ok.

Jim: Yeah. Something like that.

Mr. McGill: Ok, fine, very good Jim.

THE FROG PUZZLE

Mr. McGill: Ok Jim, I have a frog puzzle now that I'd like you to consider. It's the following; a biologist would like to estimate the number of frogs in a pond. He goes and takes a trip to the pond and he captures 55 frogs. He bands each frog and release the frogs back into the pond. One week later, he makes the second trip to the pond, he captures at that time 72 frogs. But of those 72, he finds 12 of them has already been banded from the first time. Based on the information here, he would like to try and esti-

> **THE FROG PUZZLE**
>
> Professor Thistlebush, an ecologist, conducted an experiment to determine the number of frogs that live in a pond near the field station. Since he could not catch all of the frogs he caught as many as he could, put a white band around their left hind legs, and then put them back in the pond. A week later he returned to the pond and again caught as many frogs as he could. Here are the Professor's data.
>
> **First trip to the pond**
>
> 55 frogs caught and banded
>
> **Second trip to the pond**
>
> 72 frogs caught, of those 72 frogs 12 were found to be banded
>
> The Professor assumed that the banded frogs had mixed thoroughly with the unbanded frogs, and from his data he was able to approximate the number of frogs that live in the pond. If you can compute this number, please do so. Write it in the space below. Explain in words how you calculated your results.

Figure 4.2. The Frog Puzzle as shown to the student. © 1975 The Regents of the University of California, Lawrence Hall of Science.

mate the total number of frogs in the pond. Do you have any idea how to work that problem?

Jim:	You mean with just what they have right there?
Mr. McGill:	From the information right here, yes.
Jim:	*[He writes 55 on the board]* 55 he caught the first trip, he banded them all. And these were threw back to the same pond.
Mr. McGill:	Yes, threw all the frogs back.
Jim:	Caught 72 and 12 were banded. *[He writes 72 on the board with 12 below it and subtracts the 12 from the 72 to get 60 Then he writes the 60 below the 55 and draws a line and writes 115 below it.]* That's what I think the total would be. *[He has 55 + 60 = 115, 72 − 12 = 60 written on the board.]*
Mr. McGill:	The total would be 115. Ok, very good. Thank you.

Steve:	I don't see any way of computing the total number of frogs in the pond without knowing the area that we are dealing with.

College Teaching and the Development of Reasoning 57

Mr. McGill: So you would have to know the total area. How would you use that total area?

Steve: Well I would, ah, find out the likelihood and various populations that are very serious in that climate. And make a prediction of what type of populations to expect, and possibly determine the age of these frogs and perhaps, take that percentage and compute the younger and the older populations.

Mr. McGill: suppose I told you that of the 55, there were some adult frogs, and some young frogs, and that in general those frogs were evenly distributed throughout the pond. Would that be of any value?

Steve: Well with that you could determine the pond size and the kind of population to expect from that biosystem.

Mr. McGill: Could you write something down to help me out. I am not quite sure I understand everything you are saying.

Steve: Ok. *[He writes Pond Size = ?, on another line he writes Expected Population = ?]*

Mr. McGill: And now you write the pond size question mark. I really am mostly interested in the total number of frogs, but that is part of knowing the pond size. Is that correct?

Steve: Well with an expected population, a certain biosystem could sustain a certain number of frogs along with the other symbiotic organisms in the things. And you can generalize and say 20% of the biosystem of that pond could be frogs. Of that we found in one trip in so much time, we found so many frogs each time. And we could generalize and say whether 20% of that would be x number of frogs.

Mr. McGill: Ok, well there's really no place we can go to get the total number without that?

Steve: To get an actual and a virtual account, I don't think so.

Mr. McGill: What about an estimation of it?

Steve: This should be the way to arrive at estimation. *[After more questioning, he writes 72-12 = 60 and 60 + 55 = 115.]* We could do it this way, 60, ah, 12 minus the second trip, 12 less than the number caught plus the 55 of the original first trip and the number of actual frogs found is a 100 and 115 actually found. With that whatever the pond size is, we would have an expected value, and we could put this over the expected value

58 R. G. FULLER ET AL.

	times 100 and see if we actually come up with an acceptable value from that.
Mr. McGill:	Ok, very good.

Craig:	For the second trip to the pond, he caught 12, banded out of 72, that gives 1/6 of the frogs caught have been banded, *[He writes 12/72 = 1/6 on the board.]* so reversing that philosophy, he banded 1/6 of the frogs in the pond the first time. So 55 frogs banned, and if they were a 1/6 of that, there would have been, *[He writes 55 x 6 on the board = 330]* The total would be 330 frogs in the pond.
Mr. McGill:	Excellent. Very good job.

THE MEALWORM PUZZLE

Mr. McGill: The next puzzle, Craig, its call the mealworm puzzle (see Figure 4.3). In this puzzle, we have mealworms in a container, in fact we have indicated, mealworms by the little dots. They are found in four separate containers. The bottom of each container is dry and wet for the first case. And the second case, the entire bottom is dry. The third case, you have the dry-wet mode, and then the last case, the bottom is entirely dry. Added to this, we have one other thing to consider and that's a light, there is a light source, for the first two cases, the light is on the left. For the last two cases, the light is on the right. Now this diagram shows that mealworms respond in some way to these modes, what I like you to do, if you could, tell me if they respond to A. Light but not moisture, B. Moisture but not light, C. Both light and moisture, or D. Neither light nor moisture. And I wish you would please explain why you choose the particular response.

Craig:	Ok. I would say they respond to C. To both light and moisture. The reason I say that is in this example. They go to the light and also to where it's dry. Where here, they are responding to the light, and there is one more staying where is wet. Maybe he got stuck in the mud I don't know. But where you have the light on the wet side. Most of them will staying in the dry rather than going to the light and getting wet. And for that reason, well when its wet and wet since they're

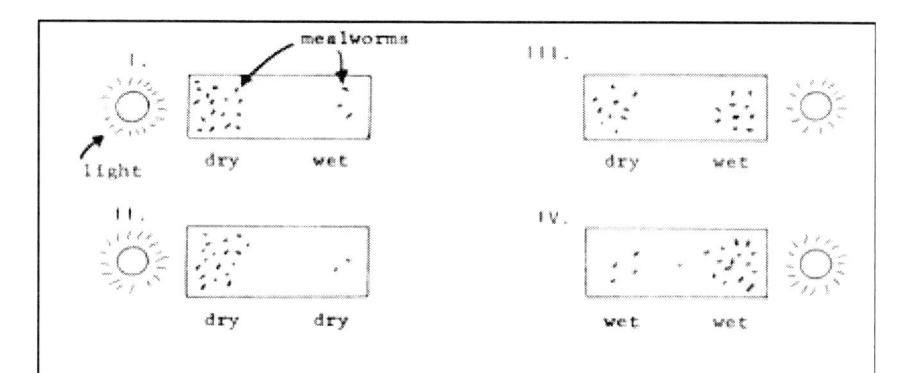

College Teaching and the Development of Reasoning 59

> What can you conclude from these diagrams? The diagrams show that mealworms respond to (response means move toward or away from):
> A. light but not moisture
> B) moisture but not light
> C) both light and moisture
> D) neither light nor moisture
> Please explain your choice.

Figure 4.3. The Mealworm Puzzle. © 1975 The Regents of the University of California, Lawrence Hall of Science.

	already wet, they go to the light. So I'd say they like the light and they like it to be dry.
Instructor:	So light and moisture in a negative sense.
Craig:	Right.
Mr. McGill:	Ok.

Alicia:	Well, they respond to light and yeah, I think they respond to light in all of them, like here and here. And here some.
Dr. Campbell:	They respond to light. What do you mean?
Alicia:	They respond, they move toward it.
Dr. Campbell:	They move toward the light. Ok.
Alicia:	Yeah, they move toward the light. Mm, I don't think it matters whether it's wet or not. Because in here it's dry and they move over here, and still it's wet and they moved over here. So I say light but not moisture.

60 R. G. FULLER ET AL.

Dr. Campbell: Ok, light but not moisture, so you pick A. Ok, do you think this was a good test to whether they respond that way or not.

Alicia: They should have tried it with one variable ... mm, It's an alright test. I guess you could just try it with the wetness without the light.

Dr. Campbell: Can you think of a way they could have done that?

Alicia: Umm ... just put them in darkness, in complete darkness you know. Without a choice of light to see if they move from dryness to wetness. Or wet ... you know from where they stay. You could try like that or have it in a complete light situation. And still try to dryness and wet. Cuz, this is an alright test, you know. But it still could have added a fifth and a sixth box. You know what I mean?

Dr. Campbell: Right.

Alicia: That's about it.

Dr. Campbell: So you think this would have helped the conclusion here that you have reached.

Alicia: Yes.

Dr. Campbell: Ok, good, thank you very much.

Alicia: Thanks.

———

Bob: Now one of these [*solutions*] has to pertain all four of these.

Dr. Campbell: These are four different experimental setups that were setup to find out the response. He had a box that was dry on one end and wet on the other end. That had light expose to this end of the box, and this is what the mealworms stayed in.

Bob: Ok, so this is at four different situations.

Dr. Campbell: This is four different situations that occurred in four different boxes.

Bob: Right, and from these, I am suppose to tell which one of these.[*Select the correct solution*].

Dr. Campbell: What I am asking you is what can you tell me about the responses of mealworms to light and moisture.

Bob: From that data?

Dr. Campbell: Yes, four pieces of data. What can you tell me about those two variables?

Bob: Ah. *[Long pause while he looks at the big card.]*

Dr. Campbell: Suppose you take the first one, light but not moisture.

Bob:	Ok.
Dr. Campbell:	Now look at the data and see if you can find any rationale for that, in other words, the mealworms respond to that means they move or away toward light but they do not move toward or away from moisture. Do you see any data here that might indicate the correct response.
Bob:	Umm. *[Long pause.]* No I don't think that is the right response.
Dr. Campbell:	You don't think that is the right one? The next one says moisture but not light.
Bob:	Ok, umm that couldn't be the right one either, because there is moisture here, and light here. And they both go into it.
Dr. Campbell:	Ok, well what about [Answer C] both light and moisture.
Bob:	Ok, they respond to that, they go to that because it's wet here and they go to light.
Dr. Campbell:	Ok, can you tell me what they do to light. Do they like light or not?
Bob:	Yeah they like light. Because they are over here, and here, and here and here toward the light, except for I don't know why they are way over here.
Dr. Campbell:	But they definitely like light.
Bob:	Yeah.
Dr. Campbell:	The other thing here is about moisture. What can you tell me about moisture?
Bob:	The data looks kinda conflicting to me.
Dr. Campbell:	Can you explain that, what you mean?
Bob:	Well they like the wet and the light, and they like the dry and the light. Well they like the wet here and the wet here with light. And then here without the light, they don't like the wet or here.
Dr. Campbell:	What about just moisture. What would be your guess? Do mealworms like moisture or not?
Bob:	I'd say some do and some don't.

CONCLUDING REMARKS

We hope these examples of college student reasoning will pique your interest in the reasoning patterns used by your students. We hope you will use some puzzles, either the ones in this book or ones that you create yourself, to get your students to reveal their reasoning patterns to you. In the later chapters in this book we will offer you some teaching strategies that we think you can use to encourage your students to develop more advanced reasoning skills. Before going on to those chapters, in the next chapter we introduce you to the evaluation of college student reasoning that has been accumulated. You will see that the challenge of improving student reasoning is a wide spread. Nevertheless, we believe that if you will shape your college teaching goals to include encouraging your students to develop their reasoning in addition to mastering the content of your discipline, you will be amply rewarded.

REFERENCE

Interviews With Students. (1977). *DOORS Program*. East Peoria, IL: Illinois Central College. Retrieved from http://digitalcommons.unl.edu/adaptworkshopmodule4/

CHAPTER 5

COLLEGE STUDENT RESEARCH FINDINGS

INTRODUCTION

What is the performance of college students on reasoning tasks? Over the years there have been a number of investigations into the reasoning patterns of beginning college students. These investigations tend to support what you have already discovered in the previous chapters of this book.

College students do not consistently use formal operational reasoning when presented with new concepts. In fact, we have found that the most common feature of the reasoning of college students is variability. The context, setting, and details of a problem seem to have a large influence on how students search for a solution. The profound, universal, unifying concept, so obvious to a professor who writes the problem or question for the student, is often a hidden mystery to the student.

Objective of This Chapter

To present some research data on the responses of college students to various Piagetian-type reasoning tasks.

College Teaching and the Development of Reasoning, pp. 63–68
Copyright © 2009 by Information Age Publishing
All rights of reproduction in any form reserved.

Results

The original Piaget concept of stages of development suggests strong, consistent performance. This has not been found for college students and adults. Martorano (Dev. Psych. 1977, pp. 666–672) administered 10 traditional formal operations tasks and found that the percentage of students displaying formal operations depended on which task you looked at, ranging from 0% to 60% in sixth graders and from 15% to 95% in 12th graders. The widely cited 50% figure for college students may be misleading. The best way for you to understand the reasoning patterns of your students is to ask them to respond to one of the puzzles given in this book or cited in the literature. We believe once you see for yourself the kinds of reasoning your students use your approach to your college teaching will be transformed and we intend to show you how to do that in the rest of this book.

Procedure

Examine the research data on college student reasoning patterns on the next two pages and then consider the implications of these results for your own teaching of college students.

Table 5.1. Classification of College Students' Responses to Piagetian Type Tasks

Number of Students	Year in College	Number & Type of Task	Concrete	Transitional	Formal	Reference
25	1st	2-oral	10	60	30	1
30	Mixed	3-oral	20	40	40	2
60	1st	1-oral	|←	70 →|	30	3
71	1st & 2nd	4-oral	20	65	15	4
88	Mixed	3-written	20	30	50	5
95	1st & 2nd	2-written	35	30	35	6
131	1st	5-oral	50	25	25	7
185	1st	2-oral	30	30	40	8
215	1st & 2nd	2-written	40	30	30	9
2,455	Mixed	2-written	12	40	40	10
3,020	Mixed	2-written	10	40	49	11

*Classification (%)

*as interpreted by R. G. Fuller in the following references:

References

(1) Kolodiy, G. & Coll. J. (1975). *Sci. Teach. 6*, 20 .

(2) Keasey, C. T. (1972). *Dev. Psychology, 6*, 364 .

(3) Griffiths, D. (1976). *Am. J. Phys. 44*, 81 .

(4) Lawson, A., Nordland, F., Devito, A. J. (1976). *Res. Sci. Teach. 12*, 423.

(5) Keasey, C. T. (1975). See Module 11.

(6) Campbell, T. (1976). unpublished .

(7) McKinnon, J., &Renner, J. (1971). *Am. J. Phys. 39*, 1047.

(8) Renner, J., & Lawson, A. (1973). *Phys. Teach. 11*, 273.

(9) Campbell, T. (1976). unpublished .

(10) AAAS-NSF Chautauqua-type Short Course Participants C-7 (Midwest), 1976–77.

(11) AAAS-NSF Chautauqua-type Short Course Participants W-15 (West Coast), 1977–78. Thornton, M. C. & Fuller R. G. (1981). *How Do College Students Solve Proportion Problems? J. Res. Sci. Teach., 18*, 335.

A general review that will introduce you to the work of psychologists in this area is "Intellectual Development During Adolescence" by E. D. Neimark, Chapter 10 in Volume 4 of *Review of Childhood Development Research*, University of Chicago Press, 1975. More recent references are given below. More recent research confirms these earlier findings.

Table 5.2. Classification of College Students' Responses to Piagetian Type Tasks (Continued From Table 5.1)

Sample			[†]Classification (%)			
Number of Students	Year in College	Number & Type of Task	Concrete	Transitional	Formal	Reference
55	mixed	24-written[1]	40	38	22	12
642	mixed	13-written	13	37	50	13
604	mixed	13-written	21	70	9	14

[†] as interpreted by T. C. Campbell or R. G. Fuller from the given references.
[1] Lawson's Classroom Test for Scientific Reasoning: See the Appendix in Reference 12.

References:

(12) Coletta, V. P., & Phillips, J. A. (2005). Interpreting FCI scores: Normalized gain, pre-instruction scores, and scientific reasoning ability, *Am. J. Phys. 73*(12), 117 –1182.

Table continues on next page.

Table 5.2. Continued

References (continued):

(13) Lawson. A. E., Alkhoury, S., Benford, R., Clark, B. R., & Falconer, K. A. (2000). What kinds of scientific concepts exist? Concept Construction and intellectual development in college biology. *Journal of Research in Science Teaching, 37*, 996–1018.

(14) Lawson, A. E., Clark. B., Cramer-Meldrum, E., Falconer, K. A., Sequist, J. M., & Kwon, Y-J. (2000). Development of scientific reasoning in college biology: Do two levels of general hypothesis-testing skills exist? *Journal of Research in Science Teaching, 37*, 81–101.

Other Recent References:

Lawson, A. E. (2006). Developing scientific reasoning patterns in college biology, In J. J. Mintzes & W. H. Leonard (Eds.), *Handbook of College Science Teaching* (pp. 109-118). Arlington, VA: National Science Teacher's Association.

Moshman, D. (2005). *Adolescent psychological development: Rationality, morality, and identity* (2nd ed.). Mahwah, NJ: Erlbaum.

Kuhn, D., & Franklin, S. (2006). The second decade: What develops (and how)? In D. Kuhn & R. Siegler (Eds.), *Handbook of child psychology, Vol. 2: Cognition, perception, and language* (6th ed, pp. 953–993) (W. Damon & R. Lerner, series eds.). Hoboken, NJ: Wiley.

Moshman, D. (in press). Adolescence. In U. Müller, J. Carpendale, & L. Smith (Eds.), *Cambridge Companion to Piaget*. Cambridge, UK: Cambridge University Press.

CONCLUDING REMARKS

Many of us, when we first read, or heard, about such results for college students were sure that they did not apply to our students. Surely our students had a greater facility for formal operational reasoning than the students at these other colleges. Then we used some of these Piagetian-type tests, or puzzles, with our own students. Even using a single puzzle, such as the Frog Puzzle, or Student Population Puzzle, given in chapter 2, with our own students and paying special attention to the explanations our students wrote as they responded to the puzzle was enough to convince us that the consistent use of formal operational reasoning was a major struggle for many of our students.

In the next two chapters we hope you will learn how to use the Piagetian-based model to analyze the reasoning patterns that your examination questions and your textbooks require of your students. In later chapters you will be introduced to a classroom instructional strategy that we think will help your students improve their reasoning.

Before going on to the next chapter, please pause to consider the following questions:

Questions for You to Consider:

1. What do you think are the implications of these studies for your work as a teacher of college students?
2. In what ways do these results relate to your observations of students' performances in your introductory classes?

Neither of us had ever seen or heard students actually respond to the problems described by Piaget, even though we were familiar with Piaget's description of Swiss students' responses to the problems. As far as we knew, we were the first researchers in the United States to replicate Piaget's experiments. Our goal was to make a film that illustrated Piaget's clinical method of interviewing students, a process that entailed presenting problems to individual children and adolescents. Through his spontaneous interviews, Piaget described and interpreted students' unstated and previously unknown frames of reference, referred to as indicators of developmental stages in their logical or formal, abstract reasoning. Thus, it was critical that Bob [Karplus] and I gain some first-hand experience interviewing real students before we began filming ourselves conducting interviews, since there could be no safety-net provided by a detailed script.

Early the next morning Bob and I set up two card-tables in the foyer of the Lawrence Hall of Science where we attempted to entice students as they emerged from school busses, expecting to spend the day at the many exhibits at LHS. Our plan was to invite individual students to join us at our tables to solve new experimental science puzzles as each busload of students entered the foyer. One of the most memorable moments of those impromptu interviews occurred when a young adolescent girl with a distinctively European accent said, after she had responded to the equal arm balance problem, "You know, I have seen this very problem once before when I was a little girl in Switzerland. This very old man with white hair and twinkles in his eyes used to give us puzzles, and this was one of them!" I asked her if she knew the man's name and she responded quickly with reflective fondness, "Oh yes; I never forget his name. He is called Professor Piaget. He is a very important man in our city."

—Rita Peterson (2002)

CHAPTER 6

ANALYSIS OF TEST QUESTIONS

INTRODUCTION

You may be wondering how to apply the concept of developmental stages in your college teaching. To help you with this, we have prepared chapters dealing with different aspects of instruction. Chapter 6 concentrates on the analysis and writing of test questions. As you read the examples we have selected, keep in mind the characteristics of concrete and formal operational reasoning described in chapter 2. A matter that we find difficult to resolve concerns how to give all students, those using concrete operational reasoning and those using formal operational reasoning, practice in appropriate levels of problem solving. At the same time, evaluation through tests should give both groups an opportunity to show what they have learned, even though the students using formal reasoning will certainly demonstrate much more skill and elegance.

College Teaching and the Development of Reasoning, pp. 69–74
Copyright © 2009 by Information Age Publishing
All rights of reproduction in any form reserved.

Objectives of This Chapter

After you complete this chapter, you will be able to classify test questions as calling for primarily concrete operational or primarily formal operational reasoning on the part of the student.

After completing this chapter, you will be able to write questions that are "concrete" or "formal," as you wish.

Procedure

1. Select several exams or quizzes you have recently given to students enrolled in introductory college class where most students are freshman. Select several items from each of the tests which you feel a student thinking concrete operationally could answer. We shall call these "concrete" items. Likewise mark questions or problems which would require formal operational reasoning patterns to answer successfully. These we call "formal" items.
2. Consider the limitations of a student attempting each selected test item. Make notes on the parts of the question that would present no problems for a student using concrete operational reasoning patterns.
3. For the same test questions, consider how a student using formal operational reasoning patterns would approach the question or problem. What advantages are afforded a student using formal operational reasoning patterns over a student using concrete operational reasoning patterns?
4. After reviewing several test questions using this procedure, select an item which definitely requires formal operational reasoning. Consider how you might rewrite the question to require only concrete operational thought.
5. Select a question which requires only concrete operational reasoning. Consider how it might be rewritten to require formal operational reasoning.

From your test questions, list some characteristics of "concrete" items.

List some characteristics of "formal" items.

Now read the following essay on concrete and formal test items. Compare your list of concrete and formal characteristics with ours. Does our list change your categorization of your test items?

CHAPTER 6—ESSAY—"CONCRETE" AND "FORMAL" TEST ITEMS

We believe that test items can be classified as being "concrete" or "formal," according to the kinds of operational reasoning required to respond successfully without guessing. Using the patterns described in chapter 2 and restated below in somewhat different form, we categorized some items as "formal" and others as "concrete."

Items to which students using concrete operational reasoning patterns will be able to respond successfully include those which require them to:

1. recall or recognize information and statements (but not determine the criteria for their relevance);
2. establish one-to-one correspondence between two sets of data, serial order a set of observations, or classify observations into groups;
3. apply a memorized algorithm or formulas (but not judge its suitability);
4. use concepts defined only in terms of familiar objects, events, and situations;
5. process information and identify variables (but not systematically or completely).

We categorize items as "formal" if successful responses *require* the student to:

1. reason hypothetically, that is, with the form, if ... then ... therefore;
2. apply theories or idealized models to interpret data;
3. evaluate results of experiments and recognize ambiguous and unambiguous conditions, that is, to understand a general necessity for the control of variables and recognize hidden assumptions;

4. use combinatorial, proportional, or probabilistic reasoning;
5. understand and apply concepts that derive meaning through inferences from experience rather than through direct experience.

In our judgment, most questions in humanistic subjects require formal operational thinking for interesting answers. The obvious purely "concrete" questions likely to recur are those that ask for remembered information about matters such as names, dates and places. Such questions are useful both because they allow students using concrete operational reasoning patterns to experience success and because they tell the questioner whether the student possesses information useful in answering the interesting questions. Deciding which information is useful, however, requires formal operational thought.

For example, a reader aware of the role of cause-and-effect in narrative will see interest in the question: "In the novel *One Flew Over the Cuckoo's Nest* written by Ken Kesey, what was the cause of Cheswick's death?" The fact that Cheswick committed suicide is interesting because McMurphy has let Cheswick down and therefore feels guilty of Cheswick's death; his guilt-feelings in turn lead him to resume the course that leads to his own death at the novel's climactic ending.

The question, "What is the significance of Cheswick's death?" is formal if the student, to answer it successfully, must apply knowledge of causal relationships in novels to the case in hand. There are, however, ways of making such a question function as concrete; thereby, confusing the matter. Suppose a student has been told in detail the role that Cheswick's death plays in the causal sequence of the novel, and is then asked in a test to describe it. A later question about that role would then require primarily recall for an answer and would therefore be treated by most students as concrete. In our judgment, a student learns when asked to determine an answer by examining the work of literature, but does not learn when supplied with answers to memorize.

As if perversely to make the teacher's task still more difficult, some questions that appear to be concrete may actually be formal. Take the apparently simple "fact" of Cheswick's suicide. Good writers often allow the pleasure of inferring such facts by the use of "if … then … therefore" reasoning; as does Kesey in this case. The question, "How did Cheswick die?" may therefore be concrete if the student knows from hearing it that Cheswick committed suicide, or formal if the student is given the description from the novel and asked to infer the answer. To underscore the point: A question is "formal" or "concrete" depending on the type of reasoning a student must engage to answer it satisfactorily. One cannot tell simply from the question whether a formal or a concrete response is being requested.

Clues for Recognizing "Concrete" Questions:
Can one or more of the following questions about a question be answered affirmatively?

C1. Can a simple definition be used to find the answer?
C2. Does the solution deal with only clearly observable elements of a literary work?
C3. Can the solution be derived without rephrasing it in terms of a complex concept?
C4. Is the method for answering the question evident in the formulation of the question?

Clues for Recognizing "Formal" Questions:
Can one or more of the following questions about a question be answered affirmatively?

F1. Do I need to apply a familiar definition in an unfamiliar manner?
F2. Do I need to introduce or construct an intermediate step between the question and the answer?
F3. Do I need to select theoretical ground rules that govern the nature of my answer?
F4. Do I need to consider the possibility that the question may be answered correctly in more than one way, and should my answer incorporate more than one possible answer?
F5. Is a comprehensive analysis of the question required before a credible solution can be offered?

The clues that we have listed are of course rough-hewn indicators rather than precise rules for classification. For your own purposes you may want to refine one or another, or to make additions to either list.

In general, "concrete" questions appear to be those answerable through the application of an evident or memorized formula to directly observable material. "Formal" questions appear to be those answerable only after analysis of both question and data, theoretical improvisation, and awareness of method.

We believe that asking students to justify their answers can be an important part of a test, a part that particularly emphasizes the use of reasoning patterns in an identifiable way. Thus, we strongly urge you to include a few test items that require justification and for which you allow more time.

You may be familiar with Bloom's (1956) method of classifying test items. The relationship between Bloom's taxonomic levels and our "concrete" and "formal" classification scheme is of interest. Basically the

Bloom taxonomy allows one to classify items into one of six items: (1) Knowledge, (2) Comprehension, (3) Application, (4), Analysis, (5) Synthesis, and (6) Evaluation.

In general, any item at the Knowledge level of the taxonomy would require only pre-operational or concrete operational reasoning patterns for successful response (C1). Although items on this level may involve abstract theories or idealized models, students need only *recall* the names of such theories. They need not use them in a way that would imply that they are understood.

Items classified into the Comprehension or Application levels may require either concrete operational or formal operational thought depending upon the nature of the concept being assessed.

Test items on the Analysis, Synthesis and Evaluation levels, which require elements such as (a) recognizing unstated assumptions, (b) checking consistency of hypotheses with given information and assumptions, (c) comprehending interrelationships among ideas, and (d) comparing major theories and generalizations, all involve formal operational reasoning patterns.

CONCLUDING REMARKS

We hope you will use these concepts as you write and evaluate test questions. Now we invite you to go on to the next chapter in which we will consider what reasoning patterns are needed to understand typical textbooks.

REFERENCE

Bloom, B. S. (Ed.). (1956). *Taxonomy of educational objectives, the classification of educational goals, handbook I: Cognitive domain.* New York: David McKay.

CHAPTER 7

ANALYSIS OF TEXTBOOKS

INTRODUCTION

Probably you have had many students at the end of the semester tell you they could not read the textbook or else they read it and got nothing out of it. One cause of this could be a mismatch between the reasoning skills the student normally uses and the skills the textbook requires. As you read the text excerpts selected for your review, keep in mind the characteristics of concrete and formal operational reasoning as explained in chapter 2. Also, remember that even students using formal operational reasoning find it easier and probably understand in a more broadly-based way if they can progress through self-regulation from a concrete operational to a formal operational view of the subject.

Objective of This Chapter

To assist you in evaluating text passages in regard to their reasoning requirements.

Procedure

Please select a passage of a textbook that you are using with your introductory students. We want you to analyze it for its demands on student reasoning.

We have provided you with several selections from college textbooks about several different concepts in different disciplines. These analyses have been written by professors in the appropriate discipline. You will discover that different professors applied the analysis techniques in different ways. We hope this will illustrate for you that there are a variety of approaches you can use to analyze your own textbook. Remember, the fundamental goal is to try to figure out what reasoning is required of the novice learner in order to understand the textbook passage.

As you know the same concept can be treated by different authors to reach different students.

We have provided analyses by a variety of teachers of the following passages in the following content areas:

Biology—two passages, evolution and the work of Mendel
Chemistry—two passages, pressure
Economics—two passages, elasticity
English Composition—two passages, hypothesis/thesis
English Literature—two passages, symbolism
Mathematics—three passages, functions
Physics—three passages, kinetic energy
Psychology—two passages, scientific method

Please read the passages that are closest to your interest and then use our analyses as a model for you to conduct a reasoning analysis of a selected passage in one of the textbooks you are using with your students

Excerpt 1. From Biology: Living Systems, Oram R., Hummer, P. and Smoot, R., Charles E. Merrill Publishing Co., Columbus, 1973, pp. 656-658.

28:1 Evolution of a Forest

Usually the first stage in a succession of major importance involves very hardy organisms. They must be autotrophs which are capable of growing under adverse conditions. The first stage of succession is called the *pioneering stage*.

Consider the evolution of a community in New England. *A —* Community life may begin with lichens growing on bare rock. Lichens produce acids which begin to break the rock into small particles. As the lichens die, decomposers break them down. This decomposed organic material enriches the particles to make it a simple soil. Later more complex plants such as mosses, grasses, ferns, and shrubs appear. *B —* Their decay increases the humus content of the soil and makes it more complex and rich. Also, animals such as insects and worms add to the richness of the soil. *C —* Eventually trees such as pines or oaks occupy the area. As the community changes, the variety of animal life increases. As the soil continues to become richer, the pines and oaks are crowded out in the shade of beeches and maples.

D — Beeches and maples eventually dominate the community (Figure 28-1). They are known as the *dominant species*. This final stage in the evolution of the community is called the *climax community*.

Hardy organisms are the first to invade a new area.

Each stage of an ecological succession is characterized by a more complex set of plants and animals.

A climax community is stable and usually has a dominant plant species.

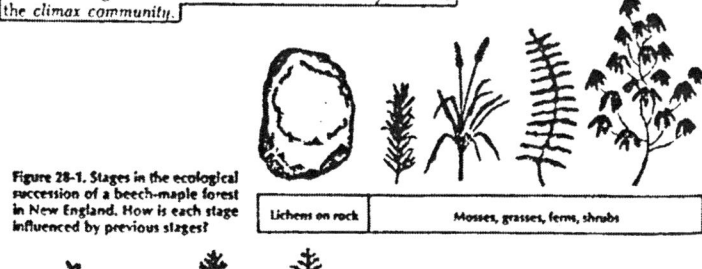

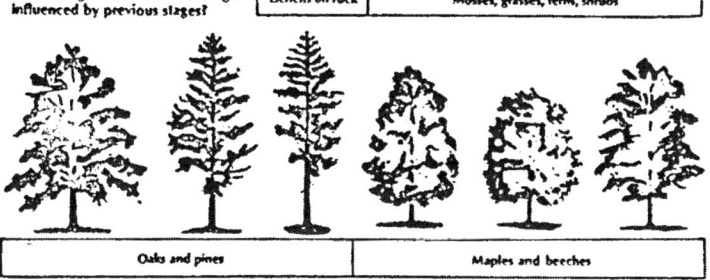

Figure 28-1. Stages in the ecological succession of a beech-maple forest in New England. How is each stage influenced by previous stages?

Lichens on rock | Mosses, grasses, ferns, shrubs

Oaks and pines | Maples and beeches

Figure 7.1. First Biology Textbook Analysis. © 1977, Regents of the University of California

Commentary

The reader is required to imagine a series of changing plant types that inhabit a particular area (A). Although there may be no immediate experiences available to demonstrate this succession, the examples used are familiar ones and imagining these changes through time does not demand formal reasoning. The concrete reasoning patterns of serial ordering (placing plant types into a series ranging from simple to complex) and classification are sufficient.

Notice, however, that the passage leaves a number of implied questions unanswered. For example, it is stated that decay of some plants enriches the soil (B) and eventually pines and oaks occupy the area (C). But why? Why doesn't this soil enrichment just make it possible for more mosses and grasses to live there? Clearly an answer requires more than description (concrete reasoning). This suggests that describing succession may only involve concrete reasoning, but understanding the process requires more.

Notice also that in the last paragraph (D) it is stated that Beeches and Maples eventually dominate the community and that this is the final stage in succession. But why don't some other trees replace the Beeches and Maples? Again, concrete reasoning is sufficient to describe the state of affairs, but formal reasoning would be needed to understand the subtle nature of the "final" conditions in which the organisms exist in a self-perpetuating equilibrium with the physical habitat.

Figure 7.2. First Biology Textbook Analysis, continued. © 1977, Regents of the University of California.

Excerpt 2. From the BSCS Yellow Version, 3rd Edition, Harcourt, Brace, Javanovich, New York, 1973, p. 611.

The Work of Mendel

Gregor Mendel (Figure 27-1) grew up in an agricultural district of what is today Czechoslovakia. Quite early he was attracted to the monastic life. He was ordained an Augustinian priest at the age of twenty-five. Later he took additional training at the University of Vienna and taught in the high school in the town of Brünn for some years. It was during these years that he kept a small garden plot at the monastery and carried out his experiments with garden peas. These were the experiments that threw the first clear light on the nature of heredity. His results were published in 1865.

27-1 Gregor Mendel. The rules that he discovered for the inheritance of traits in peas have been found to apply to many other organisms.

A — Mendel spent several years making sure that he had pure strains of pea plants. He did this by allowing plants with certain traits to produce seeds by self-pollination.
B — If the offspring always had the same trait he knew that they were *true-breeding* or *pure* for this trait.

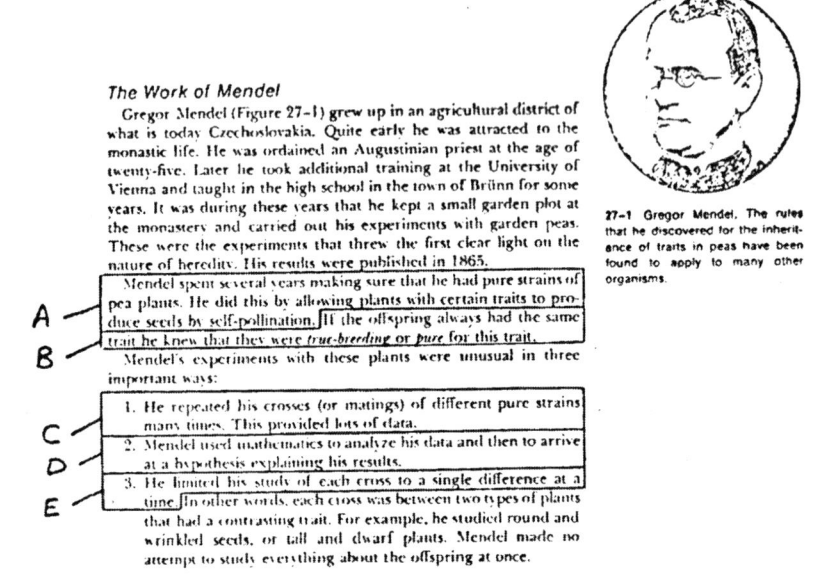

Mendel's experiments with these plants were unusual in three important ways:

C — 1. He repeated his crosses (or matings) of different pure strains many times. This provided lots of data.
D — 2. Mendel used mathematics to analyze his data and then to arrive at a hypothesis explaining his results.
E — 3. He limited his study of each cross to a single difference at a time. In other words, each cross was between two types of plants that had a contrasting trait. For example, he studied round and wrinkled seeds, or tall and dwarf plants. Mendel made no attempt to study everything about the offspring at once.

Figure 7.3. Second Biology Textbook Analysis. © 1977, Regents of the University of California. (*Figure continues on next page*)*98

> There is another point you should keep in mind. When Mendel began his experiments, biologists knew nothing of chromosomes or the processes of cell division. The principles Mendel established were based solely on the evidence from breeding experiments.
>
> Mendel chose garden peas for his experiments because he had found they have many desirable features. The plants are easy to cultivate and cross. Also, the length of a generation is reasonably short. Numerous varieties of pea plants were available, and the offspring of crosses between these different varieties are fertile. That is, the offspring are able to reproduce successfully. **F** — Of great importance, the pea flower is usually self-pollinating. It is not easily cross-pollinated by bees or other insects. Can you guess why this was important?

Figure 7.3. Second Biology Textbook Analysis, continued. © 1977, Regents of the University of California.

Commentary

In the second paragraph, the notion of "pure strains of pea plants" is presented in two ways, one requiring formal patterns, the other concrete. Formal patterns are required to understand why self-pollination results in the reappearance of a given trait (A), whereas only concrete patterns are required to grasp and to use the operational definition of offspring always having the same trait (B).

Also in (A), why did Mendel spend "several years making sure that he had pure strains?" Why not several days or several hours? Although concrete patterns would suffice to understand the answer to this question, they would not suffice for raising the question -- for going beyond the given statement.

In Item 1 (C) the reader would have to recognize the probabilistic nature of phenomena to appreciate the value of having lots of data. This requires formal reasoning. Referring to Item 2 (D), formal reasoning, would also be required to appreciate Mendel's use of mathematics as an explanatory model for his data. Further, the formal reasoning pattern underlying the control of variables would be needed to understand the necessity for Mendel to limit his study of each cross to a single difference at a time -- Item 3 (E).

At the end of the excerpt (F) the reader is to guess why it is important that the pea flower not be easily cross-pollinated by bees or other insects. Why is this important? Does correctly answering this question require formal reasoning?

Figure 7.4. Second Biology Textbook Analysis, continued. © 1977, Regents of the University of California

80 R. G. FULLER ET AL.

Excerpt 1. From Chemistry: Experimental Foundations, 2nd edition, R. Parry et. al., Prentice-Hall, Englewood Cliffs, 1975, p. 11.

> Most of us have seen small balls made of "super-rubber." When such balls are dropped to the floor, they rebound upward, rising *almost* to the height from which they were dropped. When thrown directly against the wall in a small room, the ball bounces back and forth between the walls many times before gradually slowing down and stopping. —A Could there be a connection between the motion of the rubber balls and the air in the balloon?
>
> A collection of bouncing balls is a *relatively simple system* for experimental study and can be described in quantitative terms. As such, it might be a good model system for representing the gas in the balloon. Suppose we picture air, or any other gas, as a collection of miniature balls bouncing around and colliding with the walls of the container. When a ball strikes the container, it pushes against it. But the wall pushes back with an equal force, and the ball leaves the wall going in a different direction. If there were an enormous number of particles, there would be many such collisions per second. Such a model could account for the "*push*" of the gas on the balloon wall. The "push" —B acting on a given area of wall surface (say, a square this big: ☐) is called the gas pressure. We could say that the collisions of the balls with the balloon wall account for the observed pressure of the gas. If more gas is added to the balloon, there will be more particles, hence —C more wall collisions per second. This means more "push" per unit of wall area, hence higher pressure. As the pressure (*push per unit of area*) on the balloon wall increases, the rubber walls will stretch outward —D exposing *more wall area*. This process continues until the push per unit of area is only slightly larger than it was before. In short, the balloon grows bigger if more gas is added and the pressure of gas in the balloon increases only slightly.

Commentary

   Although this was only meant to be an introductory account as much concerned with the concept of a model per se as with gas pressure (treatedd mathematically in a later chapter), the treatment is rather formal. Bouncing super-rubber and exerting a push (A) are concrete enough, but formal reasoning is required to infer pressure from a time-averaged superposition of the minute effects of very many tiny unobserved super-balls (implied by B). The qualitative effect of more gas giving rise to a greater push is also concrete (C). Yet the new equilibrium state of the balloon is described in a manner (D) which requires much inference, hence formal reasoning, and which even conceals these inferences (What are they?).

   This account of gas pressure could only be fully comprehended by the use of formal reasoning patterns applied with a great deal of facility since the information is so compact. A student limited to concrete reasoning patterns would appreciate the discussion to a slight extent--for instance, more particles means more collisions and more force. This and some other isolated relationships are inadequate to make the excerpt comprehensible or to stimulate the development of formal reasoning patterns.

© 1977, Regents of Univ. of Cal.

Figure 7.5.   First Chemistry Textbook Analysis.

Excerpt 2. From *Chemistry: An Investigative Approach*, F. Cotton and L. Lynch, Houghton Mifflin Co., New York, 1968, p. 51.

How Relative Molecular Weights Are Determined

3-5 Pressure-Volume Relationship of Gases; Avogadro's Hypothesis

A — Boyle's Law was deduced from pressure-volume data for oxygen gas (Table 3-1). Similar experiments with other gases show that Boyle's Law applies to all of them, that is, for all of them $PV = $ a constant. The value of the constant for each gas, however, will be proportional to the weight of gas used: if the weight of gas is doubled, the magnitude of PV will be doubled. So if the pressure-volume behavior of one gas is to be compared accurately with that of another, the weights of the gases used must be specified. It would seem that the simplest thing to do would be to use the same weight of each gas. (Care must be taken to measure the PV products of all the gases at the same temperature, since temperature, as you will see later, also influences the magnitude of PV.)

B —

The data given earlier for oxygen were obtained using 32 grams of gas and a temperature of 0°C. Particular conditions were chosen for definite reasons which will become clear later. For the present, however, they

C —

may be considered arbitrary and our only concern is to measure the PV product for other gases using the same weight and the same temperature.

Two of these other gases can be hydrogen chloride and ammonia. Using 32 g of each gas at 0°, the following results are obtained:

Oxygen $\qquad PV = 22.4$ liter atm
Hydrogen chloride $\quad PV = 19.6$ atm
Ammonia $\qquad PV = 42.1$ liter atm

Each gas follows Boyle's Law, but 32 g of each one gives a different "constant." — D

Commentary

At the beginning of the excerpt (A), formal reasoning patterns are demanded since numerical data are modeled by mathematical rather than qualitative relationships. Proportions require formal patterns and so does the very abstract notion of "pressure - volume behavior," all the more the idea of accurately comparing such behaviors.

Notice that the second paragraph admits the arbitrariness of the preceding description, but asks the reader to accept the authors' judgment without question until "later" (C). Accepting such information as a working hypothesis requires formal reasoning.

Consider the following questions in relation to the excerpt:

(A) What is the reasoning pattern applied in (B)?

(B) What significance does the conclusion (D), the different "constant" in the empirical relationships for PV, have for the reader of this passage?

(C). 1977, Regents of the Univ. of Cal.

Figure 7.6. Second Chemistry Textbook Analysis.

ELASTICITY OF DEMAND

You already know that when the price goes down, people will buy more. That's the "law of demand." The .... of demand answers the question: "How much more?" You already know that if it is "a lot more," that means the demand has a *lot* of elasticity. If it is "only a *little* more" then the demand has only a little elasticity.

If the price goes down a little and a great deal more is bought, then we say that the demand is "highly elastic." If the price goes down a lot and only a very little bit more is bought, we say the demand is "highly inelastic" (meaning "very little elasticity"). What we are talking about is the .... *elasticity* of demand—the sensitivity, or responsiveness of buyers to *price* changes.

Economists like to be precise about things. It makes us nervous to talk about "a lot more" and "a little more"—or to say that the quantity people demand is "very responsive" or "not very responsive" to price changes. We need more precise ways of measuring and expressing elasticity of demand. So we developed some.

Elasticity Depends on Percentage Changes

We say it this way: If a 1 percent change in price would cause a *larger* percentage change (say, a 2 percent change) in the quantity people would buy, the demand is relatively elastic. "Relatively elastic" demand means the *percentage change in the quantity bought* would be greater than the *percentage change in the price*. It means the quantity bought is highly responsive to price changes—that is, the quantity people would buy "stretches a lot" when the price goes down and "shrinks a lot" when the price goes up. That's all it means. We also use the term *price elastic* to mean the same thing.

If the 1 percent change in price would cause a *smaller* percentage change (say, a .5 percent change) in the quantity bought, we say that the demand is relatively inelastic. "Relatively inelastic" demand means the *quantity* changes by a *smaller percentage* than the *price* changes. The quantity people would buy isn't very responsive to price changes—that is, it doesn't "stretch" (or "shrink") very much if the price goes down (or up). We also use the term *price inelastic* to mean the same thing.

Elastic, Inelastic, Unitary. Suppose it happens that the one percent change in price causes an exactly equal percentage change in the quantity bought. Then we say: "the elasticity of demand is unitary." Why unitary? Because if you *divide the percentage change in*

EXCERPT A

This introduction of the idea of elasticity is presented in terms of student experience. It is a non-rigorous intuitive explanation.

These two paragraphs make good use of "experiential" terms—"stretches", "shrinks"—but lack a good concrete example. Among other things, an example would serve to remind students what "percent" involves.

The error in this paragraph wouldn't help the student. And, if what was meant was a .5 percent change, that might be equally confusing for the concrete thinker. The transformation from decimals to percent often presents problems; to use them together is to ask for trouble.

Figure 7.7. First Economics Textbook Analysis. © 1977, ADAPT, UNL.

price (1 percent) into the percentage change in quantity (1 percent) what do you get? You get one, which is *unity*, of course!

If you got a number *larger* than one you would know the demand was *relatively elastic*. The "quantity response" was *greater* than the price change. If you got a number smaller than one you would know the demand was *relatively inelastic*. The "quantity response" was *less* than the price change. Why *relatively* inelastic? Relative to what? Relative to *unitary elasticity!* Of course. Here's an example.

A "Percentage Change" Example. Suppose American Airlines decides to offer a 25 percent reduction in air fares for students. Following the announcement of the reduced fare, suppose twice as many students start buying tickets and flying American. The demand turned out to be relatively elastic—highly elastic, in fact. A 25 percent price cut brought a 100 percent increase in "quantity bought." The elasticity of demand would be 4. The 100 percent quantity increase, divided by the 25 percent price decrease, equals 4 (100% ÷ 25% = 4).

What if there had been only a 15 percent increase in ticket sales to students? Then we would say the demand was relatively inelastic (elasticity of less than one). The elasticity of demand would be .6 (15% ÷ 25% = .6). What if the student ticket sales increased by exactly 25 percent? Well, unitary elasticity, of course! (25% ÷ 25% = 1.)

Elasticity Affects the Amount Spent

Another way of looking at "elasticity of demand" is to see whether or not people spend more money on something after the price goes down (or up). Suppose you like bananas. When the price is 15 cents a pound you usually buy two pounds every week. You spend 30 cents a week on bananas.

Now suppose the price of bananas comes down to 10 cents a pound. What will you do? If you *spend more* than 30 cents a week for bananas (buy more than 3 pounds @ 10¢), your "banana demand" is "relatively elastic." If you *spend the same amount* (buy 3 pounds @ 10¢) your "banana demand" has "unit elasticity." If you *spend less* than 30 cents (buy *less than* 3 pounds @ 10¢) then your demand for bananas is "relatively inelastic."

We can summarize it this way. When the price of something goes down, people will buy more. But will they spend more money? Or not? The lower price saves them some money. But the greater quantity costs them some money. Which one will win out? The price change? Or the quantity change? It all depends on how much the quantity changes in response to the price change. Right?

Suppose the quantity doesn't change at all. That means the demand is absolutely inelastic. Then, if the price went down, total spending for that good would go down for sure! If the price went up, total spending for that good would have to go up. Why? Because the quantity doesn't change to offset the "expenditure effect" of the price change.

> This final paragraph is difficult because it asks for an hypothesis which the student may view as "contrary to fact". Quantity doesn't change? "That does not compute." The Law of Demand says it will change.

> These paragraphs are helpful because they do provide an example; but they would be much more helpful if they carefully started with raw data and step-by-step carried out the calculation to arrive at 25 percent or 100 percent. The examples would then be more concrete.

> I think this section portrays a good example of a bad trait—moving beyond the ability of the concrete thinker. Notice the leap in logic from amount spent to elasticity. The concrete thinker will not understand the connection without developing and working through the intervening steps.

Economics: The Science of Common Sense by Elbert V. Bowden. South-western Publishing Co., Cincinnati, Second Edition, 1977. pp. 322-323.

Figure 7.8. First Economics Textbook Analysis, continued. © 1977, ADAPT, UNL.

84 R. G. FULLER ET AL.

ELASTICITY OF DEMAND

The preceding sections say the most important things about consumer demands as signals to producers. But demand for individual products vary widely, and it is useful to be able to describe some of these differences precisely in analyzing how well the economic system responds to changing consumer demands.

Consider salt. Suppose ordinary table salt sells for 10 cents a pound and you use about a pound a month. If the price goes up to 15 cents, how much less salt will you use? Probably no less at all. Unsalted beans and potatoes don't taste very good, and the fraction of a cent saved each day by not salting your food is trivial compared with the better taste of flavored cooking.

This is a case where quantity bought responds very little, or not at all, to price changes. A higher price doesn't weed out very many buyers. Plotted on a graph, the demand curve for table salt at the local grocery store would be substantially vertical over the 10- to 15-cent price range. We say that the demand for table salt is very "inelastic" over this price range. Quantity bought changes very little in response to a change in price.

At the other extreme, take your demand for steak at the local A&P if you are substantially indifferent about whether you eat beef or pork. Suppose the price of beef jumps 10 percent. The chances are that you will cut back your steak purchases sharply and substitute pork. Here your demand for steak would be highly "elastic." You would cut your purchases a lot in response to an increase in price.

"Elasticity" is a measure that tells how much the quantity bought will change in response to a change in price. Thus, elasticity of demand is a measure of the responsiveness of quantity bought to changes in price. (It is defined precisely on page 59.) Elasticity is one characteristic of any given demand curve or schedule. To say a given demand is elastic or inelastic is merely to describe it, just as you might describe your next-door neighbor as tall or short.

[Mathematical Appendix I at the end of the book provides a precise mathematical statement of demand elasticity, which may be helpful to students who think readily in mathematical terms.]

[Strictly, we should call this concept "price elasticity of demand." There is a related concept, "income elasticity of demand," that measures the response of quantity bought to a change in income received. However, throughout this book we shall use "elasticity" to mean "price elasticity." At a more advanced level, we can also speak of "cross-elasticity" of demand. This is the percentage change in the amount of product J that will be bought in response to a given percentage change in the price of product K.]

EXCERPT B

These introductory paragraphs are a good start; they provide a familiar, concrete example.

But notice the reference to how the demand curve would look on a graph. This reference, I fear, would be beyond the transformational capabilities of the concrete thinker; show him.

This definition of elasticity seems accessible to the concrete thinker. It is not presented symbolically.

Note the author's awareness of different levels of intellectual demand.

Economics: An Introduction to Analysis and Policy by George Leland Bach. Prentice-Hall, Inc., Englewood Cliffs, N. J., 9th Edition, 1977. pp. 57-58.

Figure 7.9. Second Economics Textbook Analysis. © 1977, ADAPT, UNL.

Total revenue and elasticity of demand

The concept of demand elasticity helps us predict what effect price changes will have on total expenditure for a commodity. Look at the last column of Table 5-3. Suppose the grocer cuts the price of sugar 25 percent, from 20 to 15 cents a pound. Sales jump from six to ten pounds per week, a 67 percent increase, and his total revenue from sugar goes up from $1.20 to $1.50 per week. The increase in quantity sold more than offsets the decrease in price. Looking at what happens to total expenditures (revenue) gives us a precise measure of elasticity. If demand is elastic, total expenditures will change in the opposite direction from a change in price. If demand is inelastic, total expenditures on a commodity will change in the same direction as a change in price. Examine the reasoning.

1. *Elastic demand—total revenue moves in the opposite direction from price.* This is the sugar case just described. Although the storekeeper gets 25 percent less per pound, he sells 67 percent more pounds, and total revenue increases. Demand is elastic. Reverse the process over the same price range and you will see again that total revenue moves in the opposite direction from price.

2. *Inelastic demand—total revenue moves in the same direction as price.* Now observe what happens when the grocer cuts the price from 10 to 5 cents. He gets 50 percent less for each pound of sugar, but he sells only 13 percent more pounds. The volume increase, with inelastic demand, is not great enough to offset the lower price per pound sold. Total revenue drops with a cut in price. Demand is inelastic. Now reverse the process over the same price range. Total revenue will rise if he raises the price from 5 to 10 cents.

3. *Unit elasticity—total revenue is unaffected by price changes.* The borderline case between elastic and inelastic demand is called "unit" elasticity. This occurs where an upward or downward shift of price is just offset by a proportional change in quantity bought, so that total revenue remains unchanged. The crossroads demand for sugar between 10 and 15 cents is a case in point. Total expenditure on sugar is identical at either price, since the shift in amount bought just offsets the change in price.

A warning: Note that the same demand curve may be elastic in some price ranges and inelastic in others. In most cases, it is not correct to speak of one demand curve as elastic or inelastic as a whole. You need to specify at what price.

I believe this section would be a problem for the concrete thinker. The author indicates awareness of reasoning demands (he urges students to "examine the reasoning"—but can they?). While all the necessary information is presented either in the text or in the table, a "recipe" on exactly how to use the information to relate elasticity to total revenue is missing.

In addition, the first paragraph in this section seems to assume that students have a precise definition of elasticity which allows them to judge "elastic" or "inelastic".

These instructions to "reverse the the process" would leave the concrete thinker bewildered. What is "the process"? How can it be "reversed"? These are mental games which need to be detailed.

This paragraph is much too cryptic for the concrete thinker. It would need examples, and even then the concept may be beyond the reach of some students.

Table 5-3
Crossroads demand for sugar

Price per pound	PURCHASES PER WEEK BY: A	B	C	All three	Expenditures	Demand
20 cents	3 lb	1 lb	2 lb	6 lb	$1.20	Elastic
15 cents	4 lb	2 lb	4 lb	10 lb	1.50	Unitary
10 cents	6 lb	3 lb	6 lb	15 lb	1.50	Inelastic
5 cents	6 lb	4 lb	7 lb	17 lb	.85	

Figure 7.10. Second Economics Textbook Analysis, continued.

A. X. J. Kennedy, <u>An Introduction to Poetry</u>, 3rd edition (1974). ******ENGLISH**
Ch. 12 "Symbol and Allegory," pp. 203-205. ****COMPOSITION***,**

Excerpt A

SYMBOL

The national flag is supposed to bestir our patriotic feelings. When a black cat crosses his path, a superstitious man shivers, foreseeing bad luck. To each of these, by custom, our society expects a standard response. A flag, a black cat's crossing one's path — each is a **symbol:** a visible object or action that suggests some further meaning in addition to itself. In literature, a symbol might be the word *flag* or the words *a black cat crossed his path* or every description of flag or cat in an entire novel, story, play, or poem.

A flag and the crossing of a black cat may be called **conventional symbols,** since they can have a conventional or customary effect on us. Conventional symbols are also part of the language of poetry, as we know when we meet the red rose, emblem of love, in a lyric, or the Christian cross in the devotional poems of George Herbert. More often, however, symbols in literature have no conventional, long-established meaning, but particular meanings of their own. In Melville's novel *Moby Dick,* to take a rich example, whatever we associate with the great white whale is *not* attached unmistakably to white whales by custom. Though Melville tells us that men have long regarded whales with awe and relates Moby Dick to the celebrated fish that swallowed Jonah, the reader's response is to one particular whale, the creature of Herman Melville. Only the experience of reading the novel in its entirety can give Moby Dick his particular meaning.

We should say *meanings,* for as Eudora Welty has observed, it is a good thing Melville made Moby Dick a whale, a creature large enough to contain all that critics have found in him. A symbol in literature, if not conventional, has more than just one meaning. In "The Raven," by Edgar Allan Poe, the appearance of a strange black bird in the narrator's study is sinister; and indeed, if we take the poem seriously, we may even respond with a sympathetic shiver of dread. Does the bird mean death, fate, melancholy, the loss of a loved one, knowledge in the service of evil? All these, perhaps. Like any well-chosen symbol, Poe's raven sets going within the reader an unending train of feelings and associations.

We miss the value of a symbol, however, if we think it can mean absolutely anything we wish. If a poet has any control over our reactions, his poem will guide our responses in a certain direction.

T. S. Eliot (1888-1965)
THE BOSTON EVENING TRANSCRIPT

The readers of the *Boston Evening Transcript*
Sway in the wind like a field of ripe corn.

When evening quickens faintly in the street,
Wakening the appetites of life in some
And to others bringing the *Boston Evening Transcript,*
I mount the steps and ring the bell, turning
Wearily, as one would turn to nod good-bye to La Rochefoucauld,
If the street were time and he at the end of the street,
And I say, "Cousin Harriet, here is the *Boston Evening Transcript.*"

The newspaper, whose name Eliot purposely repeats so monotonously, indicates what this poem is about. Now defunct, the *Transcript* covered in detail the slightest activity of Boston's leading families and

---

Two familiar examples of symbols

A single line definition referring back to the examples.

Common conventional symbols in poetry compared to special symbolism. Example: Moby-Dick.

Discusses multiple meanings of symbols, using examples of Moby Dick and "The Raven."

The poet's control over our reactions, illustrated by analysis of a poem.

Figure 7.11. First English Textbook Analysis. ©1977, ADAPT, UNL.

Excerpt A --continued-- *** ENGLISH COMPOSITION(con't)****

was noted for the great length of its obituaries. Eliot, then, uses the newspaper as a symbol for an existence of boredom, fatigue (*Wearily*), petty and unvarying routine (since an evening newspaper, like night, arrives on schedule). The *Transcript* evokes a way of life without zest or passion, for, opposed to people who read it, Eliot sets people who do not: those whose desires revive, not expire, when the working day is through. Suggestions abound in the ironic comparison of the *Transcript*'s readers to a cornfield late in summer. To mention only a few: the readers sway because they are sleepy; they vegetate; they are drying up; each makes a rattling sound when turning his page. It is not necessary that we know the remote and similarly disillusioned friend to whom the speaker might nod: La Rochefoucauld, whose cynical *Maxims* entertained Parisian society under Louis XIV (sample: "All of us have enough strength to endure the misfortunes of others"). We understand that the nod is symbolic of an immense weariness of spirit. We know nothing about Cousin Harriet, whom the speaker addresses, but imagine from the greeting she inspires that she is probably a bore.

If Eliot wishes to say that certain Bostonians lead lives of sterile boredom, why does he couch his meaning in symbols? Why doesn't he tell us directly what he means? These questions imply two assumptions not necessarily true: first, that Eliot has a message to impart; second, that he is concealing it. We have reason to think that Eliot did not usually have a message in mind when beginning a poem, for as he once told a critic: "The conscious problems with which one is concerned in the actual writing are more those of a quasi musical nature . . . than of a conscious exposition of ideas." A poet sometimes discovers what he has to say while in the act of saying it. And it may be that in his *Transcript* poem, Eliot is saying exactly what he means. By communicating his meaning through symbols instead of statements, he may be choosing the only kind of language appropriate to an idea of great subtlety and complexity. (The paraphrase "Certain Bostonians are bored" hardly begins to describe the poem in all its possible meaning.) And by his use of symbolism, Eliot affords us the pleasure of finding our own entrances to his poem. Another great strength of a symbol is that, like some figures of speech, it renders the abstract in concrete terms, and, like any other image, refers to what we can perceive — an object like a newspaper, a gesture like a nod. Eliot might, like Robert Frost, have called himself a "synecdochist." Frost explained: "Always a larger significance. A little thing touches a larger thing."

This power of suggestion that a symbol contains is, perhaps, its greatest advantage.

Discusses how symbols convey meaning, using the poem as example, and quoting Robert Frost.

Figure 7.12. First English Textbook Analysis, continued. ©1977, ADAPT, UNL.

88   R. G. FULLER ET AL.

*****ENGLISH COMPOSITION****

B. J. Paul Hunter, Ed., <u>The Norton Introduction to Literature: Poetry</u> (1973). "The Elements of Poetry, pp. 520-521.

A symbol is many things to many people, and often it means no more than that the person using the term is dealing with something he doesn't know how to describe or think about precisely. The term is difficult to define and be precise about, but it can be used quite sensibly. A symbol is, put simply, something which stands for something else. The everyday world is full of simple examples; a flag, a peace sign, a star, or a skull and crossbones all suggest things beyond themselves, and everyone is likely to understand what their display is meant to signify, even though the viewer may not necessarily share the commitment which the object represents. In common usage a prison is a symbol of confinement, constriction, and loss of freedom, and in specialized traditional usage a cross may symbolize oppression, cruelty,

Figurative Language   521

suffering, death, resurrection, triumph, or the intersection of two separate things, traditions, ideas, etc. The specific symbolic significance is controlled by the context; a reader may often decide by looking at contiguous details in the poem and by examining the poem's attitude toward a particular tradition or body of beliefs; a star means one kind of thing to a Jewish poet and something else to a Christian poet, still something else to a Nazi or to someone whose religion is surfing. Too easy categorization, though, is dangerous. For a Christian poet may use the star of David in a traditional Jewish way (as in Marianne Moore's *The Hero*, p. 292), and a nonbeliever may draw upon the fund of traditional symbolic values without implying commitment to a particular religious system that lies behind them.

In a very literal sense, words themselves are all symbols (they stand for an object, action, or quality, not just for letters or sounds), but symbols in poetry are said to be those words and groups of words which have a range of reference beyond their literal denotation. The word "rose" simply denotes a kind of flower, but in poetry over the years it has come to symbolize youth, beauty, perfection, and shortness of youth and life. When a poem pervasively uses symbols as a major strategy and when the poem is more committed to the things which the symbols represent than to everyday reality, it is called a **symbolic poem** and is said to use **symbolism**. Poems, like everyday conversation, may use symbols occasionally and casually without being called symbolic.

Excerpt B

A warning that the concept is vague and imprecise; yet can be used "sensibly."

A single-line definition.

Several everyday examples showing dependence of meaning on those using the symbols.

Examples of the same object meaning different things to different kinds of people.

Special use of the word in poetry to refer to words or groups of words that have a range of reference beyond their literal denotation. Difference between a symbolic poem and a poem that uses symbols.

Figure 7.13.   Second English Textbook Analysis. ©1977, ADAPT, UNL.

*****ENGLISH COMPOSITION*****

Summary:

Even though Excerpts A and B cover almost the same ground, they go about doing so in quite different ways. Excerpt A moves quickly from symbols used in everyday life to the literary use of symbols. It attempts to explain the nature of literary symbols in some detail, using complex literary examples that have little connection with the student's everyday experience. He has probably heard about <u>Moby Dick</u> but he probably has not read it, or understood it if he has. He will probably be intimidated by the T. S. Eliot poem, since even experienced readers find it difficult. The defense of the use of symbols may leave the student impressed, but since he himself either has or has not experienced their value, we wonder how much it increases his understanding.

Excerpt B, on the other hand, though brief, spends one third of its length discussing common symbols as used in everyday experience, and when introducing symbolism in poetry refers to poets of different religious beliefs, a matter familiar to students from their own experience. It then goes on to distinguish literary symbolism from everyday symbolism and to distinguish symbolic poems from poems that use symbols "occasionally and casually" as in everyday conversation.

We do not think that either of these excerpts will give much help to a beginning student of poetry who does not already have a good idea from his own experience of what they are talking about. We fear, however, that by pretending to explain symbolism in so much detail, Excerpt A misrepresents the difficulty of the concept and misleads the student. By emphasizing what the student already knows about symbolism, Excerpt B gives him a better idea of what he has yet to learn when he extends his knowledge into poetic symbolism, and implies pretty clearly that that knowledge must come from the experience of poems. Therefore, we prefer Excerpt B.

Figure 7.14. Summary of First and Second English Textbook Analyses. ©1977, ADAPT, UNL.

*****ENGLSIH LITERATURE*****

Excerpts C and D: Hypothesis/Thesis

We have chosen the next two excerpts to illustrate two extremely different approaches to the problem of teaching students to write. The difference is indicated even in the titles of the books. Excerpt C focuses on the paper, and assumes that the problem for the student is how to present his thoughts; whereas Excerpt D focuses on finding something to say, assuming that lack of something to say is what is handicapping the student.

There is general agreement that if one is to learn to write well, one must write; but writing is not done in a vacuum and there is also agreement that one learns something by studying the writing of others and by thinking about the rules of writing. About what aspects of writing one should study or what the rules are that one should concentrate on, there is disagreement. Since writing is the process of creating unified structures out of words, the formal thinker who is able to grasp complex relationships of many variables should have an advantage over the concrete thinker who can control fewer relationships. We wish to raise two difficult questions: 1) What does each passage offer to each type of thinker? and 2) Will what is offered help each type of thinker become a better writer?

In the chart below we have identified items that are pertinent to the developmental stage of the reader. Refer to the chart while reading the excerpts.

Item (marked in text)	Excerpt C	Excerpt D
(1) Subject	Advises spending time before hand thinking about thoughts and feelings, and then continuing the process while you write.	States that finding a subject is a matter of "invention" and comes first, but is only the beginning. Some subjects are assigned, some are freely chosen.
(2) The writing process	Talks about discovering things to say as one writes and the importance of making the writing sound real.	Not discussed.
(3) The prewriting process	Talks about when to think about a paper, when to write down ideas. Suggests three topics to think about that the chapter will cover: subject, thesis, and purpose.	Discusses turning a subject into a proposition, gives an illustration of the difference, suggests a three-question formula, and gives an example of its use.
(4) The audience-speaker relationship	Refers to later exercises that help overcome artificiality; gives examples of specific audiences and specific roles for a writer.	Not discussed.

Figure 7.15. Third and Fourth English Textbook Analyses. ©1977, ADAPT, UNL.

Excerpt C

****ENGLISH LITERATURE*****
(continued)

Discovery

(1) Writing is *discovery*—of feeling, of thought, of the means of communicating real messages to real people. For good writers the process of writing *is* an act of discovery. As they put down words—playing the game of selecting, enjoying, rejecting—they *discover* words that fit exactly the thoughts and feelings they are trying to communicate. If you have trouble getting started, it is probably because you aren't letting this discovery process work for you. Or you may not be allowing enough time to play with your feelings and thoughts and the words that fit them. Last-minute, one-shot writing lacks this sense of play, of discovery; it carries with it, instead, a feeling of fumbling, of false starts hastily covered up with uncomfortable words, of fuzzy thought in worn-out language. If you are a fumbler or a last-minute writer, learn to discover your exact thoughts and feelings before you try to set them down—that's what getting started is all about. Then continue this discovery process as you write your paper.

(2) As you write, new ideas will come to you. Like the more experienced writer, you should discover that the writing process itself generates ideas, adding to those you've already decided on. Don't hesitate to include these new thoughts, for they are an important part of the creative process of writing. Equally important, however, is an additional discovery you should make—that your in-class papers must somehow become those "real messages" and that you and your teacher are the "real people" involved.

(4) Some of the exercises you will be asked to do in a later section of this book are designed to make you more aware of this person-to-person relationship in writing and to help you overcome the artificiality which often creeps into classroom themes. For example, you may be asked to write for a specific audience (a close friend, your parents, your teacher in a friendly mood, someone younger than you, an old person, someone in Congress). Or you may be asked to play a role, writing as if you were someone very specific (yourself in a disguised mood, your mother, a city official, a sports writer, a television newscaster). You should discover new things to say and new ways of saying the things you already know; you should discover that language and thoughts and people are always part of the writing equation.

(3) How much time you take to think and write will depend on the difficulty of the subject, your knowledge of the subject, and your experience with it. The good writer always takes the prewriting time he needs—hours, days, perhaps weeks—before choosing a specific idea and the writing strategy to go with it. You may not have as much time, but you probably have more thinking time available than you are aware of—while eating, showering, or shaving, combing your hair, brushing your teeth, or walking to class. And you must set aside some thinking or reading time specifically for this discovery process, for jotting down ideas that occur to you. Because the aim of this chapter is to get you started quickly and efficiently, you will be asked to think about and to practice solving the following problems: (1) the specific, limited subject you are going to write about; (2) the precise main point (or thesis) you are going to establish; and (3) the exact purpose of your paper.

Figure 7.16.   Third English Textbook Analysis. ©1977, ADAPT, UNL.

*****ENGLISH LITERATURE*****
(continued)

Excerpt D

DISCOVERY OF ARGUMENTS

Formulating a Thesis

(1) The beginning of all discourse is a subject. Subject is the *res* of the *res-verba* combination that rhetoricians talked about. *Res* (*what* is said) was the province of rhetoric called "invention." *Verba* (*how* it is said) was the concern of two other parts of rhetoric, "style" and "delivery." Obviously, no decisions about expression can be made until one's subject matter has been clearly defined.

Frequently, our subject matter is assigned to us. The teacher announces in class, "For next Friday I want you to write a 500-word letter to the editor of the school newspaper, giving your views on the proposed increase in tuition." Or the editor of a magazine writes to one of his authors and asks him whether he will do a 3000-word piece on the civil rights demonstrations in his community. Or the president of a corporation asks one of his junior executives to prepare a report for the next business meeting on the success of the latest advertising campaign. In such instances, our subject is given to us. At other times, of course, an author chooses his own subject.

(3) But the choice or designation of a subject is only a beginning; in fact, it can be a dead-end if something further is not done to define the subject. It is not enough to decide that one is going to write on "democracy." Before "democracy" can become a real subject for a discourse, something must be *predicated* of it. The subject must be converted into a theme; it must, to use a term from logic, be stated in the form of a *proposition*. So our vague subject "democracy" must become something like "Democracy is the form of government which best allows a man to realize his potentialities as a human being" or "Democracy functions best when the people are educated." Now we have a theme; now we have a more precise notion of what we are going to write about.

Figure 7.17. Fourth English Textbook Analysis. ©1977, ADAPT, UNL.

Excerpt D continued:

*****ENGLISH LITERATURE*****
(continued)

FORMULATING A THESIS 35

(3)

John Henry Newman, in a section called "Elementary Studies" in his *Idea of a University*, points out the importance of stating a subject in the form of a proposition. His fictitious Mr. Black is commenting on a composition written by a boy named Robert:

> "Now look here," Mr. Black says, "the subject is '*Fortes fortuna adjuvat*' [Fortune favors the brave]; now this is a *proposition;* it states a certain general principle, and this is just what an ordinary boy would be sure to miss, and Robert does miss it. He goes off at once on the word '*fortuna.*' '*Fortuna*' was not his subject; the thesis was intended to *guide* him, for his own good; he refuses to be put into leading strings; he breaks loose, and runs off in his own fashion on the broad field and in wild chase of 'fortune,' instead of closing with a subject, which, as being definite, would have supported him.
>
> "It would have been very cruel to have told a boy to write on 'fortune'; it would have been like asking him his opinion 'of things in general.' Fortune is 'good,' 'bad,' 'capricious,' 'unexpected,' ten thousand things all at once (you see them all in the Gradus), and one of them as much as the other. Ten thousand things may be said of it: give me *one* of them, and I will write upon it; I cannot write on more than one; Robert prefers to write upon all."

(3)

Hundreds of Roberts are defeated every year in their composition classes because they will not or cannot define their subject. The Latin rhetoricians used a formula for determining the point of issue in a court trial that might help students decide on a thesis. The formula consisted of three questions that were asked about the subject of dispute or discussion:

An sit (whether a thing is)—a question of fact
Quid sit (what it is)—a question of definition
Quale sit (what kind it is)—a question of quality

In a murder trial, for instance, the case for the prosecution and the defense could turn on one of three issues:

1. Did Brutus, as has been alleged, kill Caesar? (whether a thing is)
2. If it is granted that Brutus *did* kill Caesar, was the act murder or self-defense? (what it is)
3. If it was in fact murder, was Brutus justified in murdering Caesar? (what kind it is)

The application of this formula settles the issue in a trial and in turn suggests the topics that the lawyers resort to in arguing their case.

The use of this formula will not establish the thesis of a discourse, but it can help the student determine what aspect of the subject he is going to treat, and then he is in a position to formulate a thesis.

SUMMARY:

Excerpt C stresses the continuity of the thinking and writing process and emphasizes the complexity of the activity by referring to a number of the considerations that must be in the writer's mind. Excerpt D immediately isolates the task of formulating a thesis and proceeds swiftly to the suggestion of a helpful general formula. Which is better? The formal thinker will be impatient with the general exhortations of Excerpt C, and will prefer the practical formula supplied in Excerpt D. Will the concrete thinker profit from either one? We are uncertain. Does it not depend on whether he can connect them with specific problems he has actually isolated in his own writing. Our general feeling is that reading about writing will be of little help to the concrete thinker.

7-22

Figure 7.18. Fourth English Textbook Analysis, continued. ©1977, ADAPT, UNL.

Excerpt A

2.1 THE DEFINITION OF A FUNCTION

When the value of a real number y is somehow unambiguously determined by a value being assigned to a real number x, we usually say that y is a function of x. For example, consider the following:

(a) $y = x^2$
(b) $y = |x| + 1$
(c) $y = \begin{cases} 2x, \text{ if } x \geq 0 \\ 3x + 1, \text{ if } x < 0 \end{cases}$

Excerpt A ← — 1.

In (a), (b) and (c), once a value for x has been chosen, the value for y is determined. In fact (a), (b), and (c) provide specific *rules* for assigning to each real number x another real number y as follows: — 2.

(a') rule f: given a real number, square it!
(b') rule g: given a real number, take its absolute value and add 1!
(c') rule h: given a real number, $\begin{cases} \text{if it is non-negative, double it!} \\ \text{if it is negative, multiply it by 3} \\ \text{and add 1!} \end{cases}$

3.

4.

Abstracting from these examples, we arrive at the following *provisional* definition of function.

A *function* is a *rule* (or *correspondence*) which to any given number assigns (unambiguously) another number.   (1)

— 5.

Although this provisional concept of function would be adequate for a while, sooner or later calculus (not to mention physics, chemistry, economics, etc.) requires a broader outlook. To give a simple illustration, consider the surface S of a hot-plate which may be regarded as a subset of 2-space (Fig. 2.1A). We may consider the rule:

6.

To a point $P(x, y) \in S$, assign the real number t which is the temperature at P.   (2)

Now, since (2) gives a rule which assigns to each point $P \in S$ a real number t, we certainly would like to call (2) a function and refer to t as a function of P (that is, temperature is a function of position). If we extend our provisional definition of function, we can accomplish this and much more.

2.1A Definition of function

A *function* f is a *rule* (or *correspondence*) which assigns (unambiguously) to each element of a set A a *single* element of a set B. The set A is called the *domain* of f and the set B the *range* of f.

Notation. The symbol $f: A \to B$ will denote a function f with domain A and range B. Note that this does not give the rule. The rule must be given separately. If $a \in A$, $f(a)$ will denote that element of B assigned to the element a by f. We refer to $f(a)$ as the *image* of a under f, and write $f: a \to f(a)$, or simply $a \to f(a)$. Note that this does not give the domain explicitly.

Example 1. The rule (2) defines a function $f: S \to R$ from the set S consisting of points

Figure 7.19. First Mathematics Textbook Analysis. © 1977, ADAPT, UNL.

1. The selection begins with three examples which are probably close to the experience most students had in previous courses.

2. This might even be how some students think of these functions.

3. Here the meaning of "unambiguously" may not be clear to everybody.

4. The hotplate example is qualitatively different than the others. The picture is very helpful in visualizing the physical situation. This example provides good motivation for considering the domain to be more than the reals in the definition following.

5. The rule or correspondence notion of a function seems to be reasonably well motivated via the examples from the students' experience.

6. Note that a distinction is made between the name for a function and its value at some point.

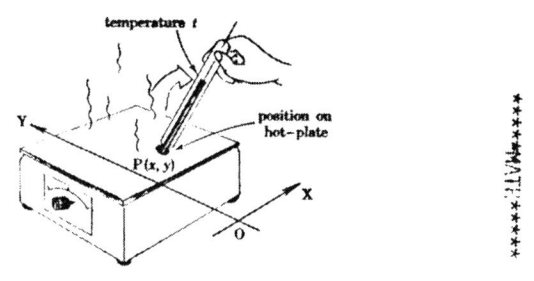

Fig. 2.1A. Temperature as a function of position.

Excerpt A:
Calculus by E. R. Fadell and A. G. Fadell, (c) 1964 Litton Educational Publishing, Inc. Permission of D. Van Nostrand Company.

Figure 7.20. First Mathematics Textbook Analysis, continued. © 1977, ADAPT, UNL.

96   R. G. FULLER ET AL.

Excerpt B

> **1.4. FUNCTIONS**
>
> A *function* (or *mapping*) f from a set A to a set B is a relation from A to B such that:
>
> (a) For each $x \in A$, there is a $y \in B$ such that $(x,y) \in f$.
> (b) If $(x,y) \in f$ and $(x,z) \in f$, then $y = z$.
>
> The notation $f: A \to B$ will indicate that f is a function from A to B. The set A is called the *domain* of f and B is called the *range* of f.
>
> It is customary to write $y = f(x)$ instead of $(x,y) \in f$ and to call y the *value* of the function f at x. Conditions (a) and (b) together assert that for each $x \in A$ there is a unique $y \in B$ such that $y = f(x)$, that is, such that y is the value of f at x.
>
> An alternate and more traditional approach to the notion of function can be given in terms of the "rule" definition. In this version, a function from A to B is a rule that assigns to each $x \in A$ a unique $y \in B$ where $y = f(x)$ is written to denote the correspondence. This is essentially the same as the definition given above since the term "rule" is to be interpreted in such a way that each rule f determines the relation $\{(x,y) \in A \times B : y = f(x)\}$, and conversely. We shall discuss these two approaches to the definition of function from a pedagogical point of view in the Remarks and References section at the end of this chapter.
>
> Some other examples of functions will now be considered.
>
> **Example 1.9.** Suppose that R is the set of all real numbers. For each $x \in R$, define $G(x)$ to be the *greatest integer in* x; that is, $G(x) = k$ where k is the integer satisfying $k \leq x < k + 1$. (For example, $G(\frac{1}{2}) = 0$, $G(\pi) = 3$, $G(-7.1) = -8$.) The rule that assigns to each real number x the greatest integer $G(x)$ in x defines a function $G: R \to R$. In terms of relations, we can write
>
> $$G = \{(x,y) \in R \times R : y = G(x)\}.$$
>
> **Example 1.10.** Suppose that T is the set of all plane triangles and that B is the set of all positive real numbers. Define
>
> $$f = \{(t,a) \in T \times B : a = \text{area of } t\}.$$
>
> Then f is a function from T to B, namely, the function determined by the rule that assigns to each triangle t its area a.

1.
2.
3.
4.
5.

Figure 7.21.   Second Mathematics Textbook Analysis. © 1977, ADAPT, UNL.

1. The definition is unmotivated and highly symbolic. Understanding the existential statement (a) and the implication (b) both require formal thought operations. For students well grounded in set theory this should be a very compact and satisfying definition. Note this definition assumes knowledge of what a relation is. This was given several pages earlier.

2. Understanding this last sentence requires a bit of deductive reasoning.

3. Again, the "conversely" requires some formal operations to completely understand.

4. The greatest integer function may be new to many students. A graph of this would be particularly useful to make it understandable.

5. To think of the set of ALL triangles or ALL positive numbers again requires formal thought.

Any student not at least in a transitional stage would encounter great difficulties with this passage. Simple, concrete examples before the definition might be necessary for some students.

Excerpt B:

<u>Topics and Modern Mathematics for Teachers</u> by A. L. Peressini and D. R. Sherbert, Holt, Rinehart, & Winston, New York, 1971. pp. 24 and 25.

Figure 7.22. Second Mathematics Textbook Analysis, continued. © 1977, ADAPT, UNL.

3. FUNCTIONS. FUNCTIONAL NOTATION

Excerpt C

In mathematics and many of the physical sciences, simple formulas occur repeatedly. For example, if r is the radius of a circle and A is its area, then

$$A = \pi r^2.$$

⟵ 1.

If heat is added to an ideal gas in a container of fixed volume, the pressure p and the temperature T satisfy the relation

$$p = a + cT$$

⟵ 2.

where a and c are fixed numbers with values depending on the properties of the gas, the units used, and so forth.

The relationships expressed by these formulas are simple examples of the concept of function, to be defined precisely later. However, it is not essential that a function be associated with a particular formula. As an example, we consider the cost C in cents of mailing a first-class letter which weighs x ounces. Since postal regulations state that the cost is "6¢ per ounce or fraction thereof," we can construct the following table.

3.

Table 1

Weight x in ounces	$0 < x \leq 1$	$1 < x \leq 2$	$2 < x \leq 3$	$3 < x \leq 4$	$4 < x \leq 5$
Cost C in cents	6	12	18	24	30

4.

This table could be continued until $x = 320$, the maximum weight permitted by postal regulations. To each value of x between 0 and 320 there corresponds a precise cost C. We have here an example of a function relating x and C.

5.

It frequently happens that an experimenter finds by measurement that the numerical value y of some quantity depends in a *unique* way on the measured value x of some other quantity. It is usually the case that no known formula expresses the relationship between x and y. All we have is the set of ordered pairs (x, y). In such circumstances, the entire interconnection between x and y is determined by the ordered pairs. We are led to the following definition.

Definition. *A* **function** *is a set of ordered pairs (x, y) of real numbers in which no two pairs have the same first element. In other words, to each value of x (the first member of the pair) there corresponds exactly one value of y (the second member). The set of all values of x which occur is called the* **domain** *of the function, and the set of all y which occur is called the* **range** *of the function.*

An example of a function is given by the set of all pairs (r, A) obtained from the formula $A = \pi r^2$ when $r > 0$. The domain of this function is the half-infinite interval $(0, \infty)$. The range is $(0, \infty)$.

Figure 7.23. Third Mathematics Textbook Analysis.

College Teaching and the Development of Reasoning 99

1. This example should touch most student's experience although the number π may still be mysterious to some.

2. This is a concrete example in the sense it is given by an easy, specific formula. It is quite beyond experience in the sense that few have ever seen a fixed volume and measured the temperature and pressure, and no one has ever found an "ideal gas".

3. The Post Office function is very close to the greatest integer function in Excerpt B. Note how much nearer to experience this description is (except for the 6¢/ounce). This gives an excellent example of how the same mathematical notion can be presented in a concrete and a formal manner.

4. This definition is given only for real numbers and so is more restrictive than that of Excerpt A or B. Compare the "uniqueness of image" part of this definition with (b) of Excerpt B and "unambiguously" of Excerpt A.

5. Some students would be helpd by saying "$(2,4\pi)$, $(3,9\pi)$, $(10,100\pi)$, $(r,\pi r^2)$, etc." instead of "all pairs (r,A)".

Excerpt C:

College Calculus With Analytic Geometry by M. H. Protter and C. B. Morrey, Jr., Addison Wesley, Reading, Mass. 1970. p. 24.

Figure 7.24. Third Mathematics Textbook Analysis, continued. © 1977, ADAPT, UNL.

****PHYSICS*****

<u>Introductory Physics: A Model Approach</u>, Robert Karplus, W. A. Benjamin, Inc., N.Y. 1969

Excerpt A:

14·6 Kinetic energy

You probably have learned that the distance required to stop a car increases fourfold when its speed doubles. Have you ever wondered why? When a bicycle rider approaches a hill, he usually pedals as fast as he can so that he will get to the top of the hill more easily. Just how far up will his speed carry him? In both these examples, there is a transfer of energy from kinetic energy to another type: thermal energy of the brakes, or gravitational field energy of the bicycle, rider, and earth system.

As we have said in Chapter 4, kinetic energy is the energy stored in moving objects. Thus, the kinetic energy of the car determines how far it will advance as the brakes bring it to a stop. The bicyclist maximizes his kinetic energy as he approaches the hill.

When a force acts on a particle, its velocity or momentum changes, and usually its energy changes also. In this section we will derive a mathematical model for the relation of kinetic energy to speed. We will show how this relation can be used in conjunction with the law of conservation of energy to predict the motion of objects under many circumstances, such as the car coming to a stop and the bicycle moving uphill.

Derivation. Instead of constructing the model in the light of experimental results, we will derive it from Newton's theory. Imagine a particle at rest (zero speed, zero kinetic energy) that is acted upon by a constant net force until it is moving with the velocity v. The kinetic energy of the particle is, according to the law of conservation of energy, equal to the work done by the net force (Eq. 14·16). To find the work, we have to calculate the distance through which the particle moved while it was being accelerated by the action of the force.

This problem is very similar to the problem of free fall solved in Section 14·4. There, too, a constant force speeded up a particle that was initially at rest. The principal differences between that and the present tasks are that now the force can be any force (not only the force of gravity), and the motion can occur in any direction (not only vertically). Still, the motion and the force are in the same direction, because the particle starts from rest (Fig. 14·20).

The relative position of the particle is equal to one half of the velocity times the time (Eq. 14·17 from Eq. 14·10). The net force also can be related to the actual velocity (equal to the change of velocity) and to the elapsed time (Eq. 14·18 from Eq. 14·5). Since the force, the velocity, and the relative position are all in the same direction, the component of the displacement along the force direction is equal to the magnitude of the relative position (Eq. 14·19). When the formulas are combined to calculate the work and therefore the kinetic energy, we obtain a mathematical model (Eq. 14·20).

Equation 14·16

kinetic energy	KE
work	W
net force	F
displacement component along the force direction	Δs_F

$KE = W = |F| \Delta s_F$

Equation 14·17

position relative to starting point	s
velocity	v
elapsed time	t

$s = \frac{1}{2} v t$

Equation 14·18

mass	M

$F = M \frac{v}{t}$

Equation 14·19

speed v
$\Delta s_F = |s| = \frac{1}{2} v t$

Equation 14·20

$KE = |F| \Delta s_F = M \frac{|v|}{t} \times \frac{1}{2} v t$

$= \frac{1}{2} M v^2$

Figure 14·20 The kinetic energy of a particle is equal to the work done by a constant force that accelerates the particle from zero velocity to its actual velocity. The force required and the position relative to the starting point reached by the particle are related to the velocity by Eqs. 14·17 and 14·18.

<u>Introduction:</u>

Two familiar examples, described with reference to kinetic energy

<u>Feedback:</u>

The concept of kinetic energy has evidently been introduced earlier, though not related to the mass and speed of the moving body

<u>Introduction of a net force:</u>

Anticipation of relation between kinetic energy and speed

<u>Selection of a constant force:</u>

Reference to Newton's theory, but no rationale for constant force.

<u>Introduction of work:</u>

Reference to energy conservation

<u>Algebraic derivation:</u>

Leans on earlier treatment of free fall from rest which was illustrated with stroboscopic photographs and tables of time-distance data; the discussion paraphrases the equations very concisely and without new examples; keeps direction of motion general

<u>Final Conclusion:</u>

The specific form of the speed-kinetic energy relation is exhibited

Figure 7.25. First Physics Textbook Analysis. ©1975, AAPT.

Physics, Part I, David Halliday and Robert Resnick, John Wiley & Sons, Inc., N.Y., 1966

******PHYSICS******

EXCERPT B:

7-5 Kinetic Energy and the Work-Energy Theorem

In our previous examples of work done by forces, we dealt with *unaccelerated* objects. In such cases the *resultant force* acting on the object is zero. Let us suppose now that the *resultant force* acting on an object is *not zero*, so that the object is *accelerated*. The conditions are the same in all respects to those that exist when a single unbalanced force acts on the object.

The simplest situation to consider is that of a *constant resultant force* F. Such a force, acting on a particle of mass m, will produce a constant acceleration a. Let us choose the x-axis to be in the common direction of F and a. What is the work done by this force on the particle in causing a displacement x? We have (for constant acceleration) the relations

$$a = \frac{v - v_0}{t}$$

and

$$x = \frac{v + v_0}{2} \cdot t,$$

which are Eqs. 3-12 and 3-14 respectively (in which we have dropped the subscript x, for convenience, and chosen $x_0 = 0$ in the last equation). Here v_0 is the particle's speed at $t = 0$ and v its speed at the time t. Then the work done is

$$W = Fx = max$$
$$= m\left(\frac{v - v_0}{t}\right)\left(\frac{v + v_0}{2}\right)t = \tfrac{1}{2}mv^2 - \tfrac{1}{2}mv_0^2 \quad (7\text{-}11)$$

We call one-half the product of the mass of a body and the square of its speed the kinetic energy of the body. If we represent kinetic energy by the symbol K, then

$$K = \tfrac{1}{2}mv^2. \quad (7\text{-}12)$$

We may then state Eq. 7-11 this way: *The work done by the resultant force acting on a particle is equal to the change in the kinetic energy of the particle.*

Introduction:

Completely abstract statement about forces, objects, and accelerations.

Feedback:

Reminder of behavior of unaccelerated objects to set the stage for now doing something else.

Introduction of a net force:

Reminder of relation between force and acceleration

Selection of a constant force:

Implied reference to Newton's law, but no rationale for constant force.

Introduction of work concept:

No rationale for suddenly asking about work

Algebraic derivation:

Quotes results from motion in one dimension with constant acceleration which was illustrated with time-distance and time-speed graphs; specializes to x-axis, but drops subscript.

Final conclusion:

The formula resulting from the algebraic operations is used to define the kinetic energy.

In our opinion, the first half of Excerpt A can be understood by the use of concrete patterns of reasoning and will therefore give all readers a better understanding (gut-feeling) of energy relationships. In spite of being intended for very different readers than Excerpt B, the remainder of Excerpt A is discouragingly similar to B. Still, the reader of A can omit the section entitled "Derivation" and come to grips with kinetic energy in a qualitative way; the reader of B gains at best a very formula-based notion of kinetic energy, with no idea how this "energy" is related to the energy he has met in his every-day life, chemistry courses, etc.

Figure 7.26. Second Physics Textbook Analysis. ©1975, AAPT.

****PHYSICS****

Physics Including Human Applications, H.Q Fuller, R.M.Fuller, and R.G. Fuller, Harper and Row Publishers, Inc., N.Y. 1978.

Excerpt C:

5.4 Kinetic Energy

In the introduction of this chapter we considered an example of a toy car responding to a push. The energy imparted to the car by a push increased the speed of the car.

The energy of motion of a body is called kinetic energy.

Think of some examples of kinetic energy.

If a body has a velocity, it must be decelerated to bring it to rest. There is then a force acting on it. For simplicity let us assume the deceleration is constant and consequently the force is constant. The force will act through a distance s in bringing the body to rest. In this case *work is done* on the body by the braking force, and the kinetic energy of the body decreases. If a body is at rest and it is accelerated by a force to a constant velocity, *work is done* on the body by the accelerating force, and the kinetic energy of the body increases.

Suppose a cyclist starts from rest and accelerates at a constant rate until reaching a speed v. We wish to find the work done by the cyclist to produce the kinetic energy possessed at speed v. Let the total mass of the cyclist and cycle be m. The magnitude of the accelerating force is given by Newton's second law: $F = ma$, but $a = v/t$, where t is the time required to reach velocity v. In this same time the cyclist moves a distance s which is equal to the product of the average velocity and the time:

$$s = \frac{v}{2} t$$

where $v/2$ is the average velocity for this case. The work done by the accelerating force of the cyclist is given by the product of the magnitude of the force times the distance through which it acts

$$W = Fs = mas = M\frac{v}{t} \times \frac{v}{2} t = \frac{1}{2} mv^2 = \text{kinetic energy at speed } v \quad (5.2)$$

The work done by the cyclist to reach speed v is used to define his kinetic energy at speed v.

Consider the braking of the cyclist reducing speed from v to v' in time t. The magnitude of the braking force F (assumed constant) produces a deceleration given by Newton's second law as

$$F = ma' \quad \text{where} \quad a' = \frac{v' - v}{t}$$

and the braking distance s' is given by

$$s' = \frac{v' + v}{2} t$$

Thus the work done by the braking force is given by Equation 5.1 as:

$$w' = Fs' = m\left(\frac{v'-v}{t}\right)\left(\frac{v'+v}{2}\right)t$$

$$w' = \tfrac{1}{2} mv'^2 - \tfrac{1}{2} mv^2 = \Delta KE \quad (5.3)$$

The work done is equal to the change in the kinetic energy of the cyclist. Note that in this case since kinetic energy decreases, the work done is negative. This sign convention is used throughout physics. Positive work on a system increases the energy of the system. Negative work is work by a system that reduces its energy.

EXAMPLE

What is the kinetic energy of a 50-kg girl running at 4 m/sec?

$KE = \tfrac{1}{2} mv^2 = \tfrac{1}{2} \times 50 \times 4^2 = 400$ J

This represents the work that must be done to stop the girl.

Introduction:
Recalls specific example of a moving toy car previously discussed.
Gives a word definition for kinetic energy.

Introduction of a Force:
Uses general discussion of changes in velocity, i.e. the ideas of Newton's Second Law, to introduce work. Uses simplicity argument for chosing constant acceleration and force.

Work and Energy:
Uses the work done as a way to compute kinetic energy for a specific case, cyclist starting from rest.

Algebraic Derivation:
Relies upon the work done in the kinematics section without much further explanation. Distinction between (5.2) and (5.3) not made clear.

Conclusion:
States a version of the work-energy theorem and introduces a sign convention for work.
Offers a final numerical calculation of the kinetic energy of a person.

Our analysis:
This excerpt falls between excerpts A and B. It begins with concrete examples, but ends with a derivation very similar to Excerpt B and offers only a numerical calculation at the end. It seems unlikely that students using concrete reasoning could follow much of this discussion after the first few sentences. Such students might get a general feeling about how moving objects have some kind of energy.

© 1977, ADAPT

Figure 7.27. Third Physics Textbook Analysis.

EXCERPT A

Note: This passage comes in a chapter on <u>Measurement</u> after some cursory remarks and examples on "probability" and on types of "scales" -- i.e., "Ratio and Interval Scales"; "Ordinal and Nominal Scales". After this passage are sections on "the Normal curve of distribution","Descriptive Statistics", "Inferential Statistics" and "Mathematical Computations".

is psychological measurement valid?

Since psychology is forced to rely on ordinal and nominal scales rather than the much more sensitive interval and ratio scales, the psychologist is handicapped much as a physicist would be if he had no ratio scale of weights and could say only that something is very heavy, heavy, not so heavy, only slightly heavy, or not heavy at all. (Or as a cook would be if recipes could only recommend a lot of this, a medium amount of that, and a small amount of the other.) This is a continuing problem in the science. Many investigators are trying to devise more adequate scales, and at least modest progress in psychological measurement is being made every year. But any discussion of psychological measurement must contain a warning that the scales on which we must now rely leave a great deal to be desired. We must not overestimate the accuracy of the numbers we use, and we must be cautious about the conclusions that we draw from them.

It should also be pointed out, however, that no form of measurement is completely accurate. Even the measurements used in the physical sciences are subject to error. At what point, for example, does 99 degrees Fahrenheit cease to be 99 degrees and become 100? Or, if we are trying to make finer distinctions, at what point does 99.9 degrees become 100? At what point does a person cease to weigh 120 pounds and begin to weigh 121, and at what point does an automobile cease to travel thirty-five miles an hour and begin to travel thirty-six? (In cooking, how level is a "level teaspoon," and how heaping is a "heaping tablespoon"?) An engineer using the measurements of physical science may feel that he has a reasonably accurate idea of weights, tensile strengths, and possible loads, but he builds the bridge two or three times stronger anyway, to allow for possible errors.

We have to apply psychological measurements with caution—much more caution than is called for in using a yardstick or a thermometer. We must not fall into the error of thinking that our statistical analysis of the measurements is sacred just because it can be put into numbers and mathematical equations. But we have to try to measure psychological traits as best we can if we are to study and understand them. And statistical analysis, used with proper humility, is an invaluable tool in helping us comprehend the meaning of our figures and avoid generalizations that are too sweeping or mathematically false. *

A Concrete Operational reader will be made quite <u>uncomfortable by this</u>.
It will be difficult for him to distinguish between the "kinds" of scales referred to -- he tends to believe all measures are built-in to the things being measured -- "height" is simply a property of the object for which there is <u>one</u> correct expression.
Being unable to generate ratios for himself, he relies upon <u>rules</u> he has learned for handling the problems. He will probably understand "ratio scales" in the same terms.
Developing flexibility in using a variety of scales will be very difficult for the con. op. student. The idea of the relative adequacy of scales will be liable to be seen as involving a problem like that of how clear to make one's glasses so as to see <u>what is out there</u> -- and not as involving problems of interpretation of the measurer's own activities.

These examples are very good -- they refer to scales with which the con. op. student is probably quite familiar. A short "lab" would help in which students were forced to develop and refine measuring standards for themselves without access to the usual scales. After such an experience, they should be made aware of the points at which their own arbitrary decisions, the outcomes they expected, and the properties or behavior of the material to be measured played key roles and have important bearing on how they interpret their results.

* Excerpt from Kagan, Jerome and E. Havemann's <u>Psychology: An Introduction</u>, Second Edition; Harcourt, Brace, Jovanovich, Inc. (1972) NY pp.439-40

Figure 7.28. First Psychology Textbook Analysis. © 1977, ADAPT, UNL.

EXCERPT B

Note: This passage occurs in an early section entitled, "How does a psychologist apply the scientific method?". This preceeds sections on "Experimental Method", "Experimental and Control Groups" and "Systematic Observation and Nature's Experiments" --setting the stage for introduction of statistical methods, etc.

The early part of this section has terms, "hypothesis" and "theory", introduced in a fairly simple way -- in each case, after introduction of the term, a brief example is given, in which other common terms in psych are used. e.g., "variables", "conditions", "data", "phenomena", etc.

Unlike the layman, the scientist systematically tests his hypotheses and theories to determine whether or not they are valid. He does not rely on opinion but he looks for facts based on the data he collects. He accepts or rejects his hypothesis on the basis of systematic empirical evidence derived from careful and objective observation. Quantitative, precise measurements are used wherever possible. Experiments are conducted and observations made very carefully, so that they can be repeated, and thus verified, by other psychologists.

Hypotheses must be stated in testable form. This means the broad general problems often have to be restated and formulated so that they are capable of scientific solution. Thus the question "Does frustration increase aggression?" is too broad and must be rephrased in more precise terms so that everyone knows exactly what is meant. This is accomplished by means of *operational definitions*: each term in the hypothesis is defined objectively as an observable response or a measurement. Thus in the investigation of the relationship between "frustration" and "aggression," frustration could be defined operationally as preventing someone from doing something he wants to do—for example, preventing young children from playing with attractive toys. Aggression could be defined in terms of overt responses such as hitting or arguing.

Note how the question has changed. It now reads, in operational terms, "Does preventing young children from playing with attractive toys increase the number of hitting or arguing responses?" This question can be answered by careful observation.

Once he has defined his terms operationally, the researcher can proceed with his investigation. The preferred method of research in many areas of psychology, as in most scientific fields, is the laboratory experiment. We will therefore take this up first and will later consider objective, nonexperimental research methods. *

Some of these terms are loaded so that the way in which the con. op. student will be able to give them meaning will lack some important psychological sense.

"Systematically tests his hypothesis," and "valid" re: a hypothesis are expressions with which the con. op. student will have little experience to hook up. Con. op. children typically lack system and see no difference between "valid" and "good".

If he were allowed to observe someone's behavior, first to see what he was able to observe, and next to determine what was "systematic" about it, even the con. op. student may be able to appreciate the aspects of "systematic testing" of which science is made. A similar experience with questioning the "validity" of one's ideas would be a way into the meaning of "valid" re: psychological studies.

This introduction of "operational definition" may be brushed over on the way to the example on investigating a relationship between "frustration" and "aggression" without seeing how operational definition is supposed to be different from any "definition". The example of operational definition of "frustration" as _____, and "aggression" as _____, is not apt to be seen as clearly different from their own off-hand "definition" of these terms.

Concrete experience of observing some interactive behavior and having to decide exactly what to call "aggression" and "frustration" --where one countable act of "aggression" will be said to stop and another piece of behavior begins, etc. -- for the purpose of giving concrete sense to the operational definition of terms and the assignment of quantity for "measurement".

* Excerpt from Mussen, Paul and Rosenzweig, M.R., *Psychology, An Introduction* D. C. Heath and Co. (1973) MA pp. 27-8

Figure 7.29. Second Psychology Textbook Analysis. © 1977, ADAPT, UNL.

Textbook Analysis Activities

After reading this chapter, please go back to your selected textbook passage and analyze it in the light of the ideas in this book.

Consider how your textual passage could be made appropriate for all of your students. Make specific point by point suggestions. As you analyze your passage, keep the following questions in mind:

(a) How does the passage introduce its content? How does it progress from the concrete operational, real to the formal operational, theoretical?
(b) How is the rationale for the sequence of ideas in the passage developed? In what ways does the rationale grow out of familiar experiences? Out of a hypothetical framework?
(c) What kinds of idealizations are made in the passage? What details are likely to confuse a neophyte?
(d) How much of the passage is based upon the manipulation of concepts, rules, or formulae? Upon the use of definitions, operations, or experiences?
(e) What models, or mental constructs, are essential for the understanding of this passage? What evidence do you have that your students have already constructed, or are now ready to construct, these models?

CONCLUDING REMARKS

By now you may be thinking, "OK, I get it. Some of my students will be using reasoning patterns that make it very difficult for them to understand what I am trying to teach them. What can I do about that?"

In the following chapters we will introduce you in more detail to the essential aspects of developing reasoning as proposed by Dr. Piaget. In addition, we will suggest some classroom teaching strategies that we think will encourage your students to engage their minds in the process of developing their reasoning skills. You may find it a bit of a steep learning curve, but we think you are up to the task. First, please be prepared to be a little bit confused by the first part of the next chapter. We hope it will put you in touch with the experiences that some of your students have in your courses.

Just as William Perry said about teaching, "Every student in my class has a different teacher," we say about a required textbook for a course that every student in the course is reading a different textbook.

—Fuller and Dykstra (2009)

CHAPTER 8

SELF-REGULATION

INTRODUCTION

How can students be made more aware of their own reasoning? This question identifies one aspect of formal operational thought. It must be answered if students are to proceed to formal operational thought by *self-regulation*, the process whereby an individual advances from one stage of development to the next. We have alluded to *self-regulation* in several of the earlier chapters but concentrated on the characteristic reasoning patterns associated with each stage. In this chapter we shall describe *self-regulation* in detail.

Objective of this Chapter

To assist you in describing *self-regulation*.

Procedure

1. This chapter begins with an activity, *Petals Around A Rose*
2. After completion of this activity, please read the essay on *self-regulation*.

College Teaching and the Development of Reasoning, pp. 107–114
Copyright © 2009 by Information Age Publishing
All rights of reproduction in any form reserved.

Petals Around A Rose

In an attempt to simulate the intellectual and emotional experience of a student using only concrete operational reasoning patterns in a class that requires formal operational reasoning, we have chosen a dice game called the *Petals Around A Rose*. Our purpose in introducing this activity to you is to encourage you to have a learning experience that may serve as background for Piaget's second key concept, *self-regulation*. To this end, as you complete this exercise please note your reasoning processes.

The dice game *Petals Around A Rose* is very simple but seems quite baffling to some college teachers. It has only two basic directions.

1. the name of the game tells you what the rule is.
2. No one is EVER TOLD what the rule is. Everyone must discover the rule for one's self.

In a workshop setting to begin the game, someone who knows the rule will roll several dice (we will start with six) and will tell you how many *petals around a rose* are showing for that roll. This procedure will be repeated as often as necessary for workshop participants to discover what the rule is which determines the number of *petals* showing on a roll. The same rule will work for any number of dice.

Since you are reading a book and not participating in a workshop, we will show you a variety of the tops of dice as may have been rolled by a leader. We will tell you the number of petals showing with each roll. As you participate in this activity, if you have a conjecture about what the rule is, write it down. Then test your conjecture by looking at another throw of the dice and see if you properly predicted how many petals are showing. Once you have a conjecture about the rule which consistently gives the correct number of petals (direction (1) above) then you have won the game. If you wish to see more throws of the dice, please turn to Appendix C. Each of the pages there reduces the number of dice being used until on the last page there is only one die.

Thinking About Your Thinking

How did your thinking patterns change as you obtained more information and experience?

What errors persisted in spite of your best efforts?
When and what made order out of confusion?
What would have made this game easier? Harder?
How could you best teach this game to your students?

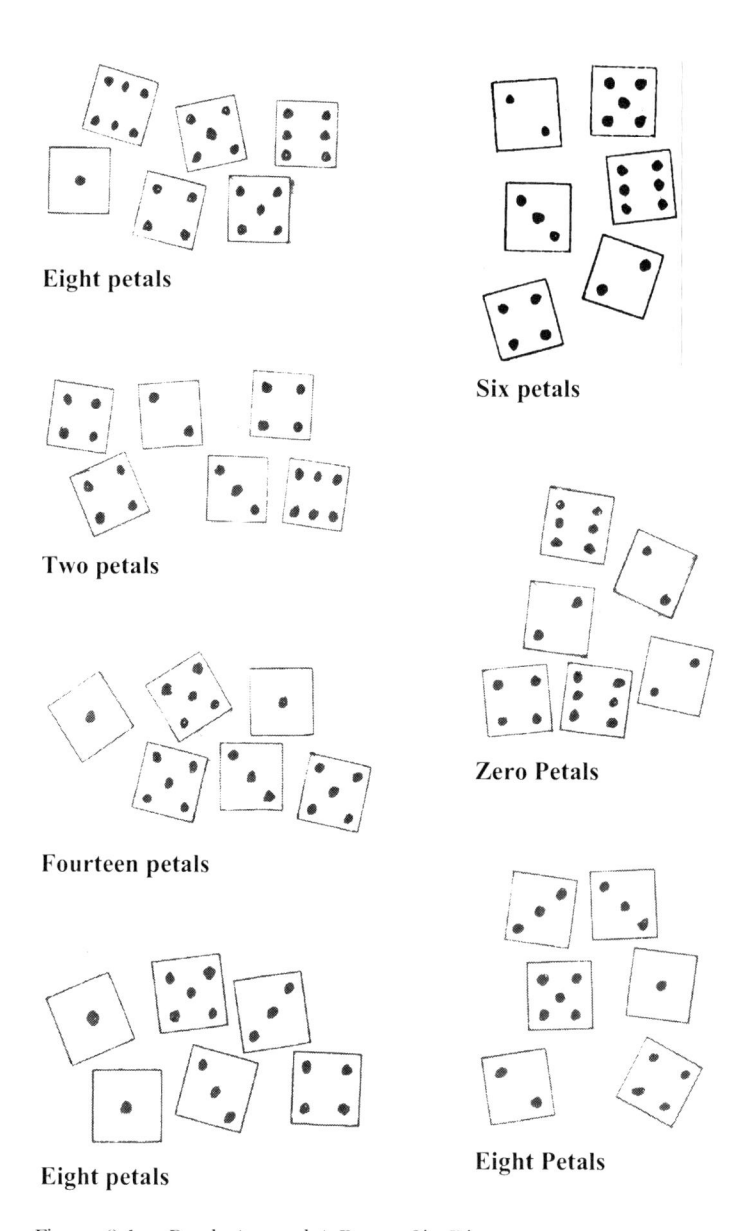

College Teaching and the Development of Reasoning   109

Eight petals

Two petals

Fourteen petals

Eight petals

Six petals

Zero Petals

Eight Petals

Figure 8.1.   Petals Around A Rose—Six Dice.

We believe that the optimal time for intellectual growth occurs when one's experiences contradict one's mental expectations. During the time of confusion, which Piaget labels as disequilibration, one's mind is actively searching for a way to make sense out of the experiences that did not fit into one's existing mental schemes. This mismatch between experience and reason is the driving force of the process of intellectual growth which Piaget called *self-regulation*.

We hope that your experience with *Petals Around A Rose* provided you will the opportunity to experience disequilibration. Disequilibration is the response when one realizes that there is something that does not match between one's expectations and one's experience. Now, we hope, you are prepared to read our essay about *self-regulation*.

Essay on *Self-Regulation*

Self-regulation is Piaget's all-encompassing term for describing how people gradually change their patterns of reasoning and advance from one level of understanding to another. In the present context, it can be paraphrased as "setting one's intellectual house in order" or restoring equilibrium between one's schemes for knowing the world and one's experience with the world. The process is one in which a person actively searches for relationships and patterns to resolve contradictions and to bring coherence to a new set of experiences within one's schemes for explaining the world. Implicit in this notion is the image of a relatively autonomous individual, or, at least, a decision-making individual not under the constant guidance and control of a teacher or strict precedent.

In order to be more explicit about how *self-regulation* operates, we need to look in somewhat more detail at (a) the nature of schemes, (b) the processes of assimilation and accommodation involved in the functioning of schemes, and (c) the process of self-regulation by which old schemes are coordinated and transformed into new schemes.

As we indicated in chapter 2, the fundamental units of knowing, for Piaget, are schemes. Schemes may express themselves as actions either physical, which one can in principle at least perform on the physical world, or mental which, in general, one cannot perform on the physical world. These actions or schemes are the way we know the world. Our conceptions involve actions or potential actions and are how we think the world works. We apply a conception to a situation to which we believe the conception applies in order to generate an expected outcome when some hypothetical change is made.

When a scheme "does its thing," we say that the individual is (a) assimilating reality to that scheme, and (b) simultaneously accommodating the scheme to reality. As we experience things we are applying schemes, some of the time apparently unconsciously, in order to "make sense of," or know, the experience. This process is called assimilation. But, since no two experiences are exactly alike, we are also making adjustments to our schemes in order that they better fit the experiences. This adjusting of the schemes is called accommodation. For Piaget, our knowing dwells exclusively in our mind. We construct our worlds in our minds. As such, these constructs cannot be transmitted or received. They have no physical existence.

For example as you experience the first roll of the dice and the number of petals around the rose, you may think of your flower schemes or you may think of counting schemes, but neither of these fit the information about the number of petals around a rose—at least not as is. This lack of equilibrium, or fit, with existing schemes generally results in the experience called disequilibration. Since the counting scheme fails to fit the number of petals around a rose, maybe it involves some calculation, so you imagine some other schemes you have that you might use to modify the counting scheme. Maybe divide by the number of dice? No. This does not give the desired result of eight, so you try something else. As you see more examples, you accumulate more experience, but you also eliminate certain possibilities about the possible scheme. This searching around for adjustments to schemes or new schemes is the process of *self-regulation*. The process of *self-regulation* is the search for a scheme that fits, is in equilibrium with, the experience. In this case, one is developing and testing for a scheme that fits the view of the dice and the stated numbers of petals around a rose, in order to restore equilibrium between one's schemes and one's experiences. Since the whole process is triggered by the perception of disequilibrium between one's existing schemes and this new experience and because one's schemes are the only thing one can really change, then one accommodates schemes in order to restore equilibrium between one's schemes and one's experiences."

Knowing, then, for Piaget, also involves assimilating reality to the schemes one brings to the situation and a corresponding accommodation of those schemes to the thing-to-be-known.

Piaget, operating from what he calls a constructivist view of knowing, argues that knowledge is not preformed either in the mind or in the environment, but rather is constructed. Thus, intelligent knowing consists not of a primacy of either assimilation or accommodation, but rather of balance between the two. True understanding, for Piaget, consists of neither assimilation nor accommodation in isolation, but rather of a dynamic balancing of both that makes it possible to assimilate reality without distorting it and simultaneously to accommodate to that reality without compromising the integrity of the fit between cognitive structures and experience. Thus, for example, *self-regulation* with respect to the dice game maintains the integrity of both (a) the mental scheme of adding individual items to obtain a result and (b) the physical reality of the number of spots on the dice and their relation to the total number of petals showing.

Our daily lives are filled with disequilibrating experiences and the on going process of *self-regulation*. One of us likes to illustrate this daily process by his experience of returning to his home city airport via a small airline. The check-in desk attendant was out on the runway unloading the passenger's baggage and the airlines telephone rang. There was no one else around so he picked up the telephone and answered "Air Wisconsin," He immediately recognized the voice of his wife on the telephone. She asked, "Has the 7 P.M. flight arrived yet?" "Yes, it has." he answered. "I need to get a message to my husband. Our car had a flat tire and I will be late getting to the airport to meet him. Can you tell him that?" she asked. "What is his name?" he asked. "Robert Fuller," she said. "How do you spell that?" he asked. "F-U-L-L-E-R" she said. "What does he look like?" he asked. She began to describe her husband, but he could no longer keep up the ruse. He started to giggle. She immediately said, "Bob Fuller, what are you doing on the telephone?" Because the first scheme she was using was one for talking to an air travel employee about one of their passengers, her mind was not open to recognizing her husband's voice. At first she fit what she heard to her intended scheme, in effect ignoring—not recognizing—that she was hearing her husband. As the questions to her began to seem a bit fishy, her mind began to wonder about the person to whom she was talking. It was not until she accommodated by dropping the "talk to the airline employee" scheme and modified her "talk to Bob" scheme to include calling the airport phone number and actually talking to her husband that it all made sense. She had gone through a process of *self-regulation*.

The subtle but crucial concept of *self-regulation* provides the link between Piaget's views on how schemes function and his closely related views on how, during the course of their functioning, new schemes are constructed. *Self-regulation* is probably best understood when viewed within its biological context. Biologists have long understood that the functioning and development of an organism within its environment cannot be understood simply as the sum of the organism's effects on that environment (in Piaget's terms, its assimilation of the environment) and the environment's effect on the organism (that is, the organism's forced accommodations to the environment). Rather, it is the nature of living systems to maintain their internal coherence in the face of environmental intrusions via complex feedback mechanisms involving interaction between organism and environment. Piaget argues that cognition is another aspect of an organism's adaptation to its environment and thus involves analogous self-regulating mechanisms. In the face of new environmental demands, then the construction of new knowledge is not merely the accommodation of old schemes to the altered environment (as empiricists would have it), but the active construction of new schemes, often constructed out of existing more elemental schemes, putting them together in new ways, new schemes of schemes. This delicate dance between the assimilating and accommodating aspects of knowing is performed to restore equilibrium between one's system of schemes and one's experience.

It is through such self-regulation that the active thinking student finds a path between on the one extreme of automatically assimilating educational input to present schemes (and thus distorting it) and on the other extreme of passively accommodating to educational input (and thus merely imitating it). Only in this way can the integrity of a person as a living, knowing self-regulating system be maintained. The ideal for the educator is to provide input that will not force distorting assimilations or blind accommodations but rather will facilitate the ongoing self-regulating process.

CONCLUDING REMARKS

In what ways was the dice game a self-regulating experience for you?

How do you relate your experience with the dice game to the experiences students have in your classes?

Recall and interpret some of your previous learning experiences in terms of the *self-regulation* model. Try to relate the *self-regulation* concept with your experience as a teacher.

Now it is time for us to move on to a discussion of teaching strategies that may encourage your students to engage in the process of *self-regulation* as they struggle to become more and more comfortable using formal reasoning patterns.

These strategies are based on the curriculum work done by Robert Karplus and his colleagues (1974), at the Lawrence Hall of Science at the University of California Berkeley. They were adapted and used successfully in a variety of college programs as discussed in chapter 14 of this book.

REFERENCE

Karplus, R. (and colleagues). (1974). *SCIS Teacher's Handbook.* Berkely, CA: Lawrence Hall of Science.

The wonderful ideas that I refer to need not necessarily look wonderful to the outside world. I see no difference in kind between wonderful ideas that many other people have already had, and wonderful ideas that nobody has yet happened upon. That is, the nature of creative intellectual acts remains the same, whether it is an infant who for the first time makes the connection between seeing things and reaching for them, or a student who has the idea of putting straws in order of their length, or a musician who invents a harmonic sequence, or an astronomer who develops a new theory of the creation of the universe. In each case, new connections are being made among things already mastered. The more we help children to have their wonderful ideas and to feel good about themselves for having them, the more likely it is that they will some day happen upon wonderful ideas that no one else has happened upon before.

—Eleanor Duckworth (1996)

CHAPTER 9

THE LEARNING CYCLE

INTRODUCTION

What can we as college teachers do to help our students develop from using concrete reasoning to using formal reasoning? On the basis of a developmental theory, classroom activities may play a central role in the improvement of student reasoning while constructing new conceptions of the phenomena. Given the possible importance of classroom experiences, does it make any difference what kind of classroom exercises we ask students to perform? We have done some research on the cognitive development of college students in response to instructional experiences. We will suggest in this chapter some of the implications that we deduce from the work of Piaget and Karplus. You can use your classroom as an environment to promote and study the cognitive development of your students.

Indeed, it is quite clear in the research related to the work of Piaget that persons may need physical, empirical props. Gradually they develop greater facility in performing these mental operations and they are able to perform the same operations without relying upon props. In other words, "hands-on," "eyes-on" experiences are essential prerequisites for the development of advanced reasoning abilities.

On the basis of their efforts in the Science Curriculum Improvement Study to encourage the development of reasoning by students, Karplus

---

College Teaching and the Development of Reasoning, pp. 115–134
Copyright © 2009 by Information Age Publishing
All rights of reproduction in any form reserved.

and his team proposed a teaching strategy called a *Learning Cycle*. This chapter introduces you to that strategy.

Objectives of This Chapter

To enable you to describe a *Learning Cycle* approach to teaching.

To assist you in designing classroom activities that encourage *self-regulation*.

Procedure

We provide essays on the *Learning Cycle* teaching strategy and how it might be used in biology, chemistry, economics, English, mathematics, philosophy, and physics. Read the one, or ones, of your choice. The essays were written by different professionals in the various disciplines. You may find that some redundant statements follow each of the Learning Cycle examples. This is provided for the reader who reads only one, or two, of the examples.

Make a few notes to yourself as you consider the activities that make up the different phases of a *Learning Cycle*.

Essay	*The Learning Cycle*	*Biology*

Suppose you are beginning your biology course's section on evolution. How would you begin? Jot down what you would consider a useful beginning exercise.

Now consider the proposed exercises that follow. Rank them from most useful to least useful for your purposes.

___(a) Showing a film that traces the evolution of several modern organisms by reviewing fossil evidence, procedures of dating rock strata, and reconstructions of ancient forms of these organisms.

___(b) Arranging for a trip to a museum where students are free to select exhibits that enable them to observe fossils of ancient organisms, follow the geologic history of the earth, look for relationships between climate changes and changes in populations or organisms, and trace the evolutionary lines of the horse, Darwin's finches, or the skeleton of vertebrates.

___(c) Providing groups of students with chalk, meter sticks, and a list of important events in geological and archaeological time, as a challenge to construct a time line indicating the relative occurrence of these events on a time line.

___(d) Presenting an explanation of how biotic potential, limiting factors, variation, heredity, and natural selection interact over enormous spans of time to result in the changes in organisms now called evolution.

___(e) Providing a laboratory where students observe, draw, and classify—with the aid of a key—a variety of fossil specimens.

___(f) Presenting an explanation concerning the five basic processes recognized by the modern synthetic theory of evolution (gene mutation, changes in chromosome number and structure, genetic recombination, natural selection, and reproductive isolation) and diagramming how these interact to result in progressive change.

Certainly the resources available to you and the preparation of your students will influence your choice. Compare our comments below with yours and if possible, with those of another faculty colleague.

(a) Films are popular ways of introducing new topics. In this case the film presents observations the students might make in a museum or laboratory if they had access to the necessary materials. However, we would recommend the film be used after a museum visit. Films raise questions, provoke inquiry, or present contradictions less effectively than first hand experiences. Since paying attention to the film preempts their initiative, few students watching a film for the first time would think critically about what they observe. Furthermore, seeing a picture of an object or process does not carry the impact of seeing the object or influencing the process itself.

(b) We believe this approach to be very worthwhile as an introductory activity to the very difficult topic of evolution. The students have a great deal of freedom to examine and compare past life forms according to their own interests and curiosity. Their experience and discussions with one another will lead them to ask themselves how old life forms disappeared from the face of the earth while newer ones took their place. Seeking answers to this question becomes the aim of the remainder of the course's section on evolution. This gives the instructor an opportunity to gain insight in students' reasoning patterns.

(c) This activity can be very effective for getting students to appreciate the tremendous span of time during which natural selection operated. As described, it is open and allows students initiative, the possibility to make mistakes, and opportunities for self-regulation as they discover contradictions between their preconceived ideas and the lengths of time-line segments. Because of the narrower focus of this activity, it is not as good an introduction to the entire section as alternative (b).

(d) This rather theoretical approach would be highly inappropriate as the introduction of a new topic because it takes for granted that all students have a good grasp of the five rather difficult concepts.

(e) Use of keys for classifying objects can be worthwhile for elementary school pupils in that it involves class inclusion, a reasoning pattern many children of this age find challenging. Very few older students would be challenged by this activity, and most would not reexamine their reasoning patterns.

(f) Even though this approach, often taking the form of a lecture, provides a unified picture and appears very efficient, it is far too abstract for most students and does not provide them with any way by which they can judge the validity of a statement for themselves.

The recommended approach in (b) is an example of exploratory activity upon which later conceptual understandings can be built. It represents the *EXPLORATION* phase of a three-phase *Learning Cycle* based on current theories of learning and designed to encourage self-regulation. The three phases of an entire *Learning Cycle* are called *EXPLORATION, INVENTION,* and *APPLICATION.*

During *EXPLORATION*, the students learn through their own actions and reactions in a new situation. In this phase, they explore new materials and new ideas with minimal guidance or expectation of specific accomplishments. The new experience should raise questions that they cannot answer with their accustomed patterns of reasoning. Some of the students experience disequlibration. Having made an effort that was not completely successful, the students will be ready for *self-regulation*.

The second phase, *INVENTION*, starts with the invention of a new concept or principle—variation, natural selection, evolution—that leads the students to apply new patterns of reasoning to their experiences. The *Invention* phase should start with students speculating about possible explanations for the disequilibrating experiences in the exploration and then testing them against the evidence. The concept is invented in class discussion, based on the exploration activity, and reemphasized by the teacher. Subsequently, a textbook, a film, or another medium may be used to clarify the invented concept. *Invention*, which aids in *self-regulation*, should always follow *EXPLORATION* and relate to the exploration activities. The film in alternative (a) above or the lecture in alternative (d) could serve as CONCEPT *INVENTION* sessions following the laboratory activity (b). Students should be encouraged to develop as much of a new reasoning pattern as possible before it is explained to the class.

In the last phase of the *Learning Cycle*, *APPLICATION*, the students apply the new concept and/or reasoning pattern they have developed to additional examples. After the *Invention* of natural selection, for instance, *APPLICATION* might be concerned with plant and animal breeding, evolution of an organism in a hypothetical environment, industrial mechanism, or the founder principle. The film in alternative (e) could also serve as an *APPLICATION* activity. The *APPLICATION* phase is necessary to extend the range of applicability of the new concept. CONCEPT *APPLICATION* provides additional time and experiences for self-regulation and stabilizing the new reasoning patterns. Without a number and variety of *APPLICATIONs*, the concept meaning will remain restricted to the examples used during its *Invention*. Many students may fail to abstract it from the specific examples or generalize it to other situations. In addition, *APPLICATION* activities aid students whose conceptual reorganization takes place more slowly than average, or who did not adequately relate the invented explanation to their experiences. Individual conferences with these students to help identify and resolve their difficulties are especially helpful.

All of these phases, *Exploration*, *Invention* and *Application*, can contribute to self-regulation if students are allowed to benefit from each phase according to their individual abilities and needs. If a phase is eliminated or all students are expected to demonstrate specified uniform accomplishments after each one, then the overall effectiveness of the *Learning Cycle* will be compromised.

As another example of the *Learning Cycle*, we direct your attention to this essay. We did not begin with a definition of the *Learning Cycle*, but rather tried to place you in a situation of considering alternative strategies for teaching evolution according to your own experiences and preferences to be compared with our ideas. That served as *EXPLORATION*. Next we described the three-phase learning cycle, the *INVENTION* in this essay, with reference to the evolution example. Your *APPLICATION* activities in this essay began with a look at the essay itself. Finally, we should like you to examine, after the conclusion of this chapter, our entire book plan, from chapters 1 through 11, which is also formulated according to two *Learning Cycles*, one on concrete and formal operational reasoning and one on *self-regulation*. That examination will form an *APPLICATION* activity for you, we hope.

Essay	*The Learning Cycle*	*Chemistry*

Suppose you are about to start your chemistry course's section on solubility and solution equilibration. How would you begin? Jot down what you would consider a useful beginning exercise.

Now consider the proposed exercises that follow. Rank them from most useful to least useful for your purposes.

___(a) Presenting a film with scenes of crystals dissolving or being formed (time lapse), along with animated sequences showing the same phenomena at the atomic-molecular level, with the particles represented by small moving circles of various colors.

___(b) Arranging for a laboratory period in which your students could use water and alcohol to dissolve colorless and colorful substances, observe schlieren, compare optical densities of solution, and leave liquids to evaporate.

___(c) Providing your students with molecular model sets so they could assemble molecules, see their ionic constituents, and compare the models of electrolytes with models of non-electrolytes.

___(d) Presenting an explanation with demonstrations on the dynamic equilibrium involving solutions and excess solute, the changes that occur on the addition or evaporation of solvent, and the alterations in freezing and boiling temperatures of solutions compared to pure solvents.

___(e) Scheduling a laboratory in which students carefully measure the amounts of solvent and solute they allow to interact so as to determine the solubility of one or two substances at several temperatures.

Certainly the resources available to you and the preparation of your students will influence your choice. Compare our comments below with yours and, if possible, with those of another faculty colleague.

Continues on next page.

(a)	Films are popular ways of introducing new topics. In this case, the film combines observations the student might make in the laboratory with theoretical ideas derived from the kinetic theory. We would recommend that the film be used after a laboratory period if laboratory materials are available. Films raise questions, provide inquiry, or present contradictions less effectively than first-hand laboratory experiences. Since paying attention to the film preempts the viewers' initiative, few students watching the film for the first time would think critically about what they observe. Additionally, seeing a picture of an object or process does not carry the impact of handling the object or influencing the process oneself.
(b)	We would highly recommend an approach of this kind, where the students have a great deal of freedom to use their own judgment, try out their own ideas, and learn from their own mistakes as they gain practical experience with materials they will study theoretically later. The teacher can evaluate the reasoning patterns the students use and later provide more direction or extend the autonomous investigations as needed.
(c)	Even though this approach involves the students in concrete manipulations, they are dealing with idealized representations of atoms, not with the atoms themselves. Recognizing the way in which a model is faithful to nature and the ways in which it omits or oversimplifies details requires formal reasoning patterns that a newcomer to the topic is unlikely to possess.
(d)	This rather theoretical approach, often in the form of a lecture, would be completely inappropriate for the introduction of a new topic, because it takes for granted that the students have good grasp of concentration, equilibrium, temperature, and colligative properties. The teacher has no chance to evaluate the students' perceptions since the learners are passive.
(e)	This type of laboratory discourages students from asking their own questions and taking responsibility for satisfying their own curiosity. The reason for making the careful observations, waiting for equilibrium to be established, and varying the temperature will not be clear at this time either. Such a laboratory would be more appropriate at a later state of the teaching sequence, but even then it might focus some attention on the transient processes while equilibrium is being established.

The recommended approach in (b) is an example of exploratory activity upon which later conceptual understandings can be built. It represents the *EXPLORATION* phase of a three-phase *Learning Cycle* based on current theories of learning and designed to encourage self-regulation. The three phases of the entire learning cycle are called *EXPLORATION*, *INVENTION*, and *APPLICATION*.

During *EXPLORATION*, the students learn through their own actions and reactions in a new situation. In this phase they explore new materials and new ideas with minimal guidance or expectation of specific accomplishments. The new experience should raise questions that they cannot answer with their accustomed patterns of reasoning. Some of the students experience disequilibration. Having made an effort that was not completely successful, the students will be ready for *self-regulation*.

The second phase, *INVENTION*, starts with the invention of a new concept or principle—solubility, equilibrium, concentration—that leads the students to apply new patterns of reasoning to their experiences. The *Invention* phase should start with students speculating about possible explanations for the disequilibrating experiences in the *Exploration* and then testing them against the evidence. The concept is invented in class discussion, based on the exploration activity, and re-emphasized by the teacher. Subsequently, a textbook, a film, or another medium may be used to clarify the invented concept. This step, which aids in *self-regulation*, should always follow *EXPLORATION* and relate to the *EXPLORATION* activities. The film in alternative (a) above or the lecture in alternative (d) could serve as *INVENTION* sessions following the laboratory activity (b). Students should be encouraged to develop as much of a new reasoning pattern as possible before it is explained to the class, but expecting students to invent the complex ideas of modern science is unrealistic.

In the last phase of the *Learning Cycle*, APPLICATION, the students apply the new concept and/or reasoning pattern to additional examples. The measurement of solubility of various substances at several temperatures as in alternative (a) would be a good *APPLICATION* activity following the introduction of the solubility concept. Other *APPLICATION* activities might concern the effects of different solvents on the same solute and the relation of solubility to properties of the solute. The *APPLICATION* phase is necessary to extend the range of applicability of the new concept. *APPLICATION* provides additional time and experiences for self-regulation and stabilizing the new reasoning patterns. Without a number and variety of *APPLICATIONs*, the concept's meaning will remain restricted to the examples used during its definition. Many students may fail to abstract it from its specific examples or generalize it to other situations. In addition, *APPLICATION* activities aid students whose conceptual reorganization takes place more slowly than average, or who did not adequately relate the invented explanation to their experiences. Individual conferences with these students to help identify and resolve their difficulties are especially helpful.

All three of these phases, *Exploration, Invention and Application*, can contribute to self-regulation if students are allowed to benefit from each phase according to their individual abilities and needs. If a phase is eliminated or all students are expected to demonstrate specified uniform accomplishments after each one, then the overall effectiveness of the *Learning Cycle* will be compromised.

As another example of the *Learning Cycle*, we direct your attention to this essay. We did not begin with a definition of the *Learning Cycle*, but rather tried to place you in a situation of considering alternative teaching strategies for solubility and solution according to your own experiences and preferences, to be compared with our ideas. That served as *EXPLORATION*. Next we described the three-phase learning cycle, the

INVENTION in this essay, with reference to the solubility example. Your *APPLICATION* activities in this essay began with a look at the essay itself.

Finally, we should like you to examine, after the conclusion of this chapter, our entire book plan, from chapters 1 through 11, which is also formulated as two *Learning Cycles*, one on concrete and formal operational reasoning and one on *self-regulation*. That examination will form an *APPLICATION* activity for you, we hope.

Essay	*The Learning Cycle*	*Economics*

Suppose you are planning to begin your course's section on diminishing returns and marginal product. How would you begin? Jot down what you would consider a useful beginning exercise.

Now consider the proposed exercises that follow. Rank them from most useful to least useful for your purposes.

___(a) Drawing a production possibilities curve and explaining the significance of its curvature.

___(b) Assigning some arithmetical computation problems requiring the student to compute total product and marginal product as a production process expands.

___(c) Putting your students to work collating and stapling mimeographed materials into packets, requiring them to work in groups ranging from 1 to 10 students per given table space and asking them to record how quickly they completed 50 packets.

___(d) Discussing the labor market, the demand for labor, and income distribution.

___(e) Asking the students to imagine a typical agricultural example of a farmer applying more and more variable inputs (labor, fertilizer, water) to a given amount of a fixed resource (land).

___(f) Explaining a mathematical approach to this concept in which the marginal product of a resource is shown to be the first derivative of total product with respect to that resource.

Certainly, the time available to you as well as the level of students will influence your choice. Compare your reactions with our comments on the alternatives:

(a) This procedure is often used because of its "universality" and because of its reminder to the students of opportunity cost and trade-off. However, it seems to us to require rather sophisticated formal thought processes to comprehend this abstraction and to relate the real idea of output to the mathematical properties of the diagram.

(b) This is a more concrete approach, and could be very useful in cementing the concept after the foundation for the idea has been established. Its major drawback is that it is a purely computational approach with no experiential base.

(c) We would recommend an approach of this kind, where the student is asked to undertake an activity with no prior conception of what will happen, which generates its own data (which the student identifies and can trust), and which allows the concept to emerge from the student's world.

(d) This approach would be inappropriate at the beginning of the topic. Discussion of the topics mentioned seems to require as a prerequisite the concepts you are trying to teach in this unit.

College Teaching and the Development of Reasoning

(e) In the absence of an experiential project such as described in (c), we would recommend this approach to connect the new ideas with the students' previous experience.

(f) This approach is obviously highly formal and would present an impossible learning situation for a student using concrete reasoning.

The preferred approach in (c) or possibly (e) is an example of the *EXPLORATION* phase in a three-phase *Learning Cycle* which we recommend for the planning of teaching activities. The entire *Learning Cycle* consists of three phases what we call *EXPLORATION*, *INVENTION*, and *APPLICATION*. During *EXPLORATION* the students learn through their own more or less spontaneous reactions to a new situation. In this phase, they explore new materials or ideas with minimal guidance or expectation of specific achievements. Some of the students experience disequilibration. Their patterns of reasoning maybe inadequate to cope with the new data, and they may begin self-regulation.

During the *INVENTION* phase, you define a new concept, invent a new principle, or explain a new kind of *APPLICATION* to expand the students' knowledge, skills, or reasoning. This step should always follow *EXPLORATION* and relate to the *EXPLORATION* activities. It will thereby assist in your student's self-regulation. In the example of diminishing returns above, for instance, alternative (b) represents a possible *INVENTION* phase, particularly if the computations are based on the results of the classroom activity in (c). Do encourage students to "invent" part or all of a new idea for themselves, before you discuss it with the class.

The last phase of the *Learning Cycle* is *APPLICATION* during which a student finds new uses for the concepts or skills he has learned recently. Diminishing returns, for example, can be applied to other situations, or might even lead to a better understanding of concepts such as the production possibilities curve, diminishing marginal utility, and so forth. The *APPLICATION* phase provides additional time and experiences for self-regulation to take place. It also gives you the opportunity to introduce the new concept repeatedly to help students whose conceptual reorganization proceeds more slowly than average or who did not adequately relate tine invented explanation to their experiences. Individual conferences with these students to identify their difficulties are especially helpful.

All three of these phases, *Exploration, Invention and Application*, can contribute to self-regulation if students are allowed to benefit from each phase according to their individual abilities and needs. If a phase is eliminated or all students are expected to demonstrate specified uniform accomplishments after each one, then the overall effectiveness of the *Learning Cycle* will be compromised.

As another example of the *Learning Cycle*, we direct your attention to this essay. We did not begin it with a definition of the learning cycle, but rather tried to place you in a situation of considering alternative teaching strategies according to your own experience and preferences, to be compared with our thoughts. That served as *EXPLORATION*, the best we could think of in the context of this module. Next we described the three-phase *Learning Cycle*, the *INVENTION* in this essay, with references to your exploratory experience with diminishing returns. Finally, we should like you to examine, after the conclusion of this workshop, our entire workshop plan, which is also formulated according to two *Learning Cycles*, one on concrete and formal reasoning and one on *self-regulation*. That examination will form an *APPLICATION* activity for you, we hope.

Essay	*The Learning Cycle*	*English*

Suppose you are planning a section dealing with paragraphing for your freshman composition course. How would you begin? Jot down what you would consider a useful beginning exercise.

Now consider the proposed exercises that follow. Rank them from most useful to least useful for your purposes.

___(a) List the qualities on which good paragraphs are constructed. The qualities would include logical development of a complete idea, appropriate diction, integrity (both of speaker and of matter), coherence, and the like.

___(b) Arrange a class period in which groups of students jointly compose paragraphs on assigned subjects and discuss the paragraphs composed by other groups.

___(c) Remind your students of their everyday experiences with concrete objects that are constructed with order and coherence (example, a car). Invite them to suggest other such objects from their experience, and ask them to write a paragraph describing such an object and discuss with them the order they used in their paragraphs.

___(d) Describe various modes of paragraph structuring, comparison and contrast, chronological; spatial, inductive, deductive; enthememic, and so forth.

___(e) Divide the class into groups as in "b," but this time have them compose sentences as models, in miniature, of a "complete thought" such as the paragraph represents in greater magnitude. Topic sentences might receive special attention, as might introductory transitional or concluding sentences.

___(f) Provide a class in which each student is assigned to examine paragraphs for topic sentences, transitions, structural clues, and other such items.

Certainly many factors would influence your choice, factors too numerous and diverse to be fully accounted for here. But you might nevertheless compare your reactions to the foregoing materials with ours.

(a) This procedure is often used because of its "universality" and because of its reminder to the students of opportunity cost and trade-off. However, it seems to us to require rather sophisticated formal thought processes to comprehend this abstraction and to relate the real idea of output to the mathematical properties of the diagram.

(b) Of these procedures, this is the one we would recommend. Here students exercise considerable freedom of judgment and at the same time must consider the judgment of their peers. In most of the situations for which we are preparing students, writing is a social activity, so it is good for a student to have access to the thought processes of others. Approach (b) has the further advantage of providing the social context Piaget maintains is so vital to all learning. Learners are much more likely to experience disequilibrium when they face the disparate notions of their peers than when such notions are laid out by authority. Finally this approach has the advantage of promoting the free and spontaneous generation of materials which is a fundamental component of composition.

(c) This approach has the advantage of relating paragraphing to the students' previous experience. But it should be noted that it loses the spontaneity of (b) and is more directive.

(d) This approach would be less appropriate at the beginning of paragraph teaching because it is rather theoretical and because it highlights segments of paragraphing theory (i.e., how to construct one or another kind of paragraph) before the students consider actual paragraphs.

(e) Since sentences in one sense compose paragraphs, we would consider a task such as this useful, at least potentially. It has many of the social qualities of (b) but it also has some drawbacks. Unless more carefully modulated, such assignments are too theoretical to be useful. It is also too prescriptive to be useful at this sate.

(f) This exercise prevents students from asking their own questions and satisfying their own curiosity. Like (e) it is too restrictive and is more analytical than generative. All the concepts of paragraphing must have been properly assimilated before the students could successfully cope with this activity.

The preferred approach in (b) or (c) is an example of the *EXPLORATION* phase in the *Learning Cycle* which we recommend for the planning of teaching activities. The entire *Learning Cycle* consists of three phases that we call *EXPLORATION*, *INVENTION*, and *APPLICATION*. During *EXPLORATION* the students learn through their own more or less spontaneous reactions to a new situation. In this phase, they explore new materials or ideas with minimal guidance or expectation of specific achievements. Some of the students experience disequilibration. Their patterns of reasoning may be inadequate to cope with the new data, and they may begin *self-regulation*.

During the *INVENTION* phase, the students are looking for concepts, principles, and tactical tricks that will help them to solve the problems that have arisen during *EXPLORATION*. At this stage they should receive hints and suggestions from the teacher; such hints and suggestions, however, must be carefully designed to help them with the problems that they see and not the problems that the teacher sees. The *INVENTION* step should always follow *EXPLORATION* and relate to the *EXPLORATION* activities. In the example of the paragraphing exercise above, for instance, alternative (a) represents a possible *INVENTION* phase, perhaps introduced via (e) as an intermediate step to relate *EXPLORATION* and

INVENTION. Since students have been reading and writing paragraphs all their lives, it is better if the concepts are "invented" by the students, after which the teacher may introduce the conventional terms for them.

The last phase of the *Learning Cycle* is *APPLICATION*, during which a student finds new *APPLICATION*s for the concepts or skills he has INVENTED. Surely in a unit on paragraphing this means writing additional paragraphs but just as surely it does not mean writing done as a mechanical exercise. That is, the student must be set on a new task which he recognizes as calling for a new *EXPLORATION* phase leading to the *APPLICATION* of his new concepts or skills. Other *APPLICATION* activities could involve writing descriptions of paragraphs written by other students in the class, or by published authors.

The *APPLICATION* phase provides additional time and experiences for self-regulation to take place. It also gives you the opportunity to introduce the new concept repeatedly to help students whose conceptual reorganization proceeds more slowly than average, or who did not adequately relate your original explanation to their experiences. Individual conferences with these students to identify their difficulties are especially helpful.

All three of these phases, *Exploration, Invention and Application*, can contribute to self-regulation if students are allowed to benefit from each phase according to their individual abilities and needs. If a phase is eliminated or all students are expected to demonstrate specified uniform accomplishments after each one, then the overall effectiveness of the *Learning Cycle* will be compromised.

As another example of the *Learning Cycle*, we direct your attention to this essay. We did not begin it with a definition of the learning cycle, but rather tried to place you in a situation of considering alternative teaching strategies according to your own experiences and preferences, to be compared with our thoughts. That served as *EXPLORATION*. the best we could think of in the context of this chapter. Next we described the three-phase learning cycle, the *INVENTION* in this essay, with references to your exploratory experience with paragraphing. Finally, we should like you to examine, after the conclusion of this chapter, our entire book plan, from chapters 1 through 11, which is also formulated according to two *Learning Cycles*, one on concrete and formal reasoning and one on *self-regulation*. That examination will form an *APPLICATION* activity for you, we hope!

Essay	*The Learning Cycle*	*Mathematics*

What teaching strategy do you detect in following procedure used to discuss an algorithm for listing all subsets of a finite set?

Part I. (A) Give the class several easy combinatorial problems which use all subsets of, say, three elements. Examples: (1) how many ice cream sundaes can one make with apple, banana, and cherry topping? (2) Given a dime, penny, and dollar, what different donations could you make to the Salvation Army kettle at Christmas? Ask each student to solve these problems by listing the different possibilities on his paper.

(B) Have each student write the numbers zero to seven in a column using the binary number system: 0, 1, 10, 11, and so forth.

(C) Have students exchange papers or confer in small groups. Have them note any particular order of the answers in the combinatorial problems (1) and (2). Have them share with each other, if they don't remember, how to count in base two.

Part II. (A) Bring the class back together and list in a column the base two numbers zero to seven. Comment that in order to keep things straight and in the right columns you will write each as a three digit number, for example, 010 for 10 and 000 for 0.

(B) Pick a paper at random and record the answers to (1). For the apple-cherry sundae list that as "a0c" in the same row as "101" in the list of base two numbers. Again comment the 0 is to keep the rows straight. Continue to list all 8 possibilities. For ease of notation, write apples above the first column and change each a to a 1. Point out you consider 1 to mean present or yes and 0 to mean absent or no. By this time some the class will have noticed the one to one correspondence you wish them to understand.

(C) List the possible donations to the kettle in numerical order. Change from dollars to cents, and add zeros to have all three digit numbers.

(D) State as clearly as you can the correspondence between n-digit binary numbers and subsets of sets of n elements. If appropriate interpret as characteristic functions. Make certain all students understand the correspondence.

Part III. (A) Suggest some problems to see if they really understand the algorithm. Have them list all subsets of two or of our elements in the order given by the binary numbers.

(B) Propose some new problems: (1) By just having your fingers up or down, how far can you count on one hand? (2) Can you write all six digit binary numbers in a column by giving all the left most digits first, then second to left, and so forth?

One could consider Part I as an example of the *EXPLORATION* phase in the *Learning Cycle* which we recommend for the planning of teaching activities. The entire *Learning Cycle* consists of three phases that we call *EXPLORATION*, *INVENTION*, and *APPLICATION*. During *EXPLORATION* the students are working with some fairly concrete ideas and they gather some information when they share their answers with their classmates. They will have in their minds several problems but may not be aware that they are mathematically the same. They maybe a bit puzzled by the apparent lack of order or by the indefinite order of some of the answers. Some of the students experience disequlibration.

Part II was to invite students to notice the one to one correspondence which is the basis for the algorithm. Many students will notice this correspondence in these cases, but it should be explicitly stated for all to apply in other cases. This stating of the correspondence we will call the *INVENTION* stage. Here the instructor is suggesting a new way of viewing the experiences in the *EXPLORATION* phase. In essence the instructor is proposing anew structure which will account for the experiences of *EXPLORATION*.

Part III can be called *APPLICATIONs* or *APPLICATION* of new ways of using the *INVENTION*. These *APPLICATION* experiences should serve to reinforce, refine, and enlarge the content of the *INVENTION*. It's a good chance to check that all students understand the INVENTION before moving on.

All three of these phases, *Exploration, Invention and Application*, can contribute to self-regulation if students are allowed to benefit from each phase according to their individual abilities and needs. If a phase is eliminated or all students are expected to demonstrate specified uniform accomplishments after each one, then the overall effectiveness of the *Learning Cycle* will be compromised.

As another example of a *Learning Cycle*, we direct your attention to this essay. We did not begin it with a definition of the learning cycle, but rather tried to place you in a situation of considering teaching strategies to be compared with our thoughts. That served as *EXPLORATION*, the best we could think of in the context of this chapter. Next we described the three phase learning cycle and gave it a specific name. This was the *INVENTION* in this essay and it referred to your exploratory experience. At the conclusion of this chapter, we should like you to examine the entire book plan, chapter 1 through 11, which was formulated as two *Learning Cycles*, one on concrete and formal reasoning and one on *self-regulation*. Hopefully that will be an *APPLICATION* activity for you.

Logic and Language	*Learning Cycle*	*Philosophy*

Suppose you are responsible for teaching a course in Elementary Logic in which you want students to be able to translate ordinary language arguments into the symbolic language used in your text materials. The students should begin this exercise with the ability to determine what strings of words to consider as "propositions" and what strings not to count as "propositions." Now they need to learn to distinguish between the kinds of expressions used to show logical relationships between propositions so that they will be able to determine what "operator" to use in their symbolic formulae for various forms of argument.

What would you consider to be a useful exercise for introduction to the logical operations? Rank the following from the most useful to the least useful.

College Teaching and the Development of Reasoning

___(a) Present the students a list of the operations you are going to work with (e.g., implication, disjunction, conjunction, negation, etc.) along with a definition of each operation in terms of the possible truth-values of the component propositions in each operation. Have them memorize the definitions and do exercises in applying them to a variety of passages containing argument.

___(b) Present the list, as in (a) above, along with examples of ordinary expressions that fit the definitions of each operation. Then have students expand those examples to include most of the ordinary language expressions that they are likely to encounter.

___(c) Have the students produce a list of English expressions that they think are used to show relationships between whole propositions. Have them work in small groups to classify those expressions according to the kind of relationship they indicate. Then have them characterize those "kinds" in the form of some sort of definition and provide a class-heading for each kind. After they have completed this, have them compare their groupings and their "definitions" with each other's and with that presented in their text materials.

___(d) Present the students a list of about a dozen most common expressions which sort readily into two or three operational "kinds" and have them sort and "define" as in (c) above, but as a *whole classroom*, while you write the groupings they suggest on the board. Then compare these with that presented in the text material.

___(e) Present students with examples of sentences showing the prepositional relations and tell the students which ones are alike and how you can characterize the relationships in terms of truth-values. (Make sure your groupings and definitions are similar to those presented in the text material.)

Certainly many factors would influence your choices in ranking these ways of proceeding. Compare our comments below with yours and, if possible, with those of another teacher.

(a) This procedure is probably used in most textbooks and thus is likely most used by teachers. However, it prevents the students from asking their own questions and, thus, from feeling the real usefulness of the definitional categories other than that they are what's "given in the book". Commonly the students are not encouraged to ask "why it's given that way?" Hence they have little opportunity to judge different methods of classification presented in different texts, and so forth. Against such a background, applying the definitions to specific passages is likely to become an algorithmic exercise with success resting primarily on the students' ability to memorize a list of expressions for each operator. It relies on rote memory, rather than on understanding. Encountering relational expressions which were not included in the lists will present a difficult problem to students.

(b) Although this has most of the same limitations as (a) above, the addition of the procedure of having students expand the lists of expressions that exemplify the defined operations is a significant advantage. By way of this exercise, students will be actively engaged in building at least portions of the categories themselves and, in a format in which they must explain their additions, it would afford the teacher helpful access to the students' reasoning. How much of an advantage over (a) this would be would depend a great deal on how much in-class time was devoted to this part of the exercise - too little time to afford the students peer and teacher feedback about their reasoning in classifying could make it a relatively useless and very frustrating exercise. Enough time must be afforded to allow all students—but especially concrete operational students—to explore expressions of their ordinary language for nuances of various relationships to find sense in classifying them.

Continued on next page.

(c) We prefer this way of proceeding, providing there is adequate time to allow the students to do the initial sorting and to get some sort of characterization that is acceptable in their groups and to gain the feedback from comparing with other groups. The fact that students generate their own list of expressions to sort has the advantage of providing a greater variety of expressions for them to consider. Although the sorting will take more time, they will be more likely to formulate useful definitions having contrastive, as well as comparative, features. The operation of sorting and defining can be extremely helpful for students if they are required to formulate rationale for each sort they do. (c), therefore, has the advantage over (d), because working in small groups, rather than as a whole classroom, several students can be gaining experience at the same time. Also, the tendency to submit to the teacher's characterizations and valuations of suggestions is not liable to get in the way of the students' own reasoning activities, when their major confrontations are with their peers in the small groups. Teachers, of course, can eavesdrop on the groups to get access to the students' reasonings.

(d) In the face of serious limitations on in-class time, making (c) impractical, this is the procedure we recommend next. By limiting the variety with which students must deal in their in-class sorting, they can complete the groupings in a relatively short time. But their characterizations of the "kinds" are liable to be in more general terms, since there will be fewer kinds with which they have had to contrast each group. As a means of promoting flexibility in handling a greater variety of expressions, one might assign "Revise your system" tasks to be done out of class time, but it will be less helpful to those who have no access to classmates outside the class, because they will lack important opportunities for self-regulation provided by working with others.

(e) This approach relates the operations which the student must learn to the example-sentences. The students may relate these sentences to their own experiences with their language. Its disadvantage is that the students are left to find their own rationale for the groupings and for the definitions. The teacher has no way of getting access to the students' reasoning. It offers no adequate way for the teacher to be sure that the students understand the principles is sufficient for them to handle a variety of problems for themselves.

In our preferred approach (c) you can allow for the experiences necessary to learn new concepts while you gain data on the students' reasoning processes along the way.

The exercise of sorting out expressions of relationships between propositions focuses the student attention on a part of their language behavior that has become automatic to them. Since it engages them in *exploring* purposefully parts of their language that they use with confidence, they are likely to share their expertise in small group work with their peers. There they can gain the feedback they need for *self-regulation* when they propound something that doesn't work well for others.

As each word is compared to others, similarity and differences in their uses are considered and their importance is weighed. Then the *INVENTION* of classifications of uses which are definable by the student requires at least advanced concrete operational thought. The ability to invent criteria by which to sort consistently and systematically an indefinite number of expressions requires formal operations.

Once the initial list of words has been classified and the criteria for those groups formulated, the *APPLICATION* phase of the *Learning Cycle* is undertaken with the presentation of more expressions, including some which do not readily fit into the established groups.

All three of these phases, *Exploration, Invention and Application*, can contribute to self-regulation if students are allowed to benefit from each phase according to their individual abilities and needs. If a phase is eliminated or all students are expected to demonstrate specified uniform accomplishments after each one, then the overall effectiveness of the *Learning Cycle* will be compromised.

As another example of the *Learning Cycle*, we direct your attention to this essay. We did not begin it with a definition of the *Learning Cycle*, but rather tried to place you in a situation of considering alternative teaching strategies according to your own experience and preferences, to be compared with our thoughts. That served as *EXPLORATION*, the best we could think of in the context of this chapter. Next we described the three-phase learning cycle, the *INVENTION* in this essay, with references to your exploratory experience with logic and language. Finally, we would like you to examine, after the conclusion of this chapter, our entire chapter plan, from Chapters 1 through 11, which was formulated as two *Learning Cycles*, one on concrete and formal reasoning and one on *self-regulation*. That examination will form an *APPLICATION* activity for you, we hope.

Essay	*The Learning Cycle*	*Physics*

Suppose you are planning to begin your course's section on geometrical optics. How would you begin? Jot down what you would consider a useful beginning exercise.

Now consider the proposed exercises that follow. Rank them from most useful to least useful for your purposes.

___(a) List the assumptions of the ray model for light, from which the results of geometrical optics can be derived.

___(b) Arrange for a laboratory period in which your students could assemble light sources, lenses, mirrors, plastic blocks, and glasses of water into optical system to observe image formation under various conditions.

___(c) Remind your students of their everyday experiences with light and invite them to describe some of the properties of light that are revealed by their observations.

___(d) Describe the transfer of energy by means of electromagnetic radiation of various frequencies, and then specializing to the visible part of the spectrum.

___(e) Provide a laboratory as in (b), but making certain that your students could work with "pencils" of light, as emitted by a laser or a source with a good collimator.

___(f) Provide a laboratory where your students are assigned to measure accurately the focal lengths of convergent and divergent mirrors and their lenses on a carefully aligned optical bench.

Certainly, the resources available to you and the level of students will influence your choice. Compare your reactions with our comments on the alternatives:

(a) This procedure is frequently used because of its conciseness but it is likely to be difficult for your students, especially those using concrete reasoning patterns, to assimilate. They do not know the basis of the assumptions and therefore cannot evaluate them when these are to be used.

(b) We would recommend an approach of this kind, where the students have a great deal of freedom to use their own judgment and try out their own ideas as they gain practical experience with the objects they will study theoretically later. See also (e).

(c) In the absence of laboratory materials, we would recommend this approach to connect the new ideas about light propagation with the student's previous experience; demonstrations with student participation would help.

(d) This rather theoretical approach would be inappropriate at the beginning of the topic, because it highlights the wave nature of light which is disregarded in geometrical optics except insofar as it limits the applications.

(e) Since light "rays" play an important part in geometrical optics, we would consider this a very helpful addition to the lab. An ordinary comb with coarse teeth can be used very effectively to make a bundle of light "rays" whose behavior can be followed.

(f) This type of laboratory prevents the students from asking their own questions and satisfying their own curiosity. The concept of focal length needs to be defined and understood before this lab can be worthwhile. At a later time in the course it might be quite appropriate, though we favor a more open approach.

The preferred approach in (b) or (e) is an example of the *EXPLORATION* phase in the *Learning Cycle* which we recommend for the planning of teaching activities. The entire learning cycle consists of three phases that we call *EXPLORATION*, *INVENTION*, and *APPLICATION*. During *EXPLORATION* the students learn through their own more or less spontaneous reactions to a new situation. In this phase, they explore new materials or ideas with minimal guidance or expectation of specific achievements. Some of the students experience disequilibration. Their pattern of reasoning may be inadequate to cope with the new data, and they may begin self-regulation. The exercise opening this essay gave you an *EXPLORATION* experience.

During the *INVENTION* phase, a new concept is defined or a new principle invented or to expand the students' knowledge, skills, or reasoning. This step should always follow *EXPLORATION* and relate to the *EXPLORATION* activities. It will thereby assist in your students' self-regulation. In the example of geometrical optics above, for instance, alternative (a) represents a possible *INVENTION* phase, perhaps introduced via (c) as an intermediate step to relate *EXPLORATION* and *INVENTION*. Do encourage individual students to "invent" part or all of a new idea for themselves, before you discuss it with the class.

During the last phase of the *Learning Cycle*, *APPLICATION*, a student finds new uses for the concepts or skills he has invented earlier. The measurement of focal lengths of a variety of optical systems (single and multiple lenses, glasses of water) would be an appropriate *APPLICATION* activity to follow the introduction of geometrical optics. Other *APPLICATION* activities could involve the theoretical analysis of various optical elements and systems for object-image relationships. The *APPLICATION* phase provides additional time and experiences for self-regulation to take place. It also gives you the opportunity to introduce the new concept repeatedly to help students whose conceptual reorganization proceeds more slowly than average, or who did not adequately relate the invented explanation to their experiences. Individual conferences with these students to identify their difficulties are especially helpful.

All three of these phases, *Exploration, Invention and Application*, can contribute to self-regulation if students are allowed to benefit from each phase according to their individual abilities and needs. If a phase is eliminated or all students are expected to demonstrate specified uniform accomplishments after each one, then the overall effectiveness of the *Learning Cycle* will be compromised.

As another example of the *Learning Cycle*, we direct your attention to this essay. We did not begin it with a definition of the *Learning Cycle*, but rather tried to place you in a situation of considering alternative teaching strategies according got your own experience and preferences, to be compared with our thoughts. That served as *EXPLORATION*, the best we could think of in the context of this chapter. Next we described the three-phase learning cycle, the *INVENTION* in this essay, with references to your exploratory experience with the optics example. Finally, we should like you to examine, after the conclusion of this chapter, our entire book plan, from chapters 1 through 11, was formulated as two *Learning Cycles*, one on concrete and formal reasoning and one on *self-regulation*. That examination will form an *APPLICATION* activity for you, we hope.

CONCLUDING ACTIVITIES

1. Make a list of the characteristics of each phase of a **Learning Cycle: Exploration, Invention** and **Application**.
2. Consider how you could introduce your students to a concept using a **Learning Cycle**.
3. Now practice creating a **Learning Cycle**. Select a concept from a class you teach on a regular basis. How could you structure teaching this concept using a **Learning Cycle**?
4. Try it with your students. After you have actually tried creating and using a **Learning Cycle** we hope our essay **DESIGNING ACTIVE LEARNING BASED UPON THE WORK OF PIAGET AND KARPLUS,** which we provide in Chapter 10, will be meaningful and helpful to you.

It is most important that Piaget's ideas can and should be used actively for instructional improvement and should not be interpreted as implying that education must wait until development has occurred spontaneously. Piaget (1973) has described the interaction between education and development in these words: "Thus education is … a necessary formative condition toward natural development itself." Of course, theory will not solve all educational problems but it can help those aspects of concept development and understanding which make science courses especially difficult for many students.

—Robert Karplus (1977)

CHAPTER 10

TEACHING GOALS AND STRATEGIES

INTRODUCTION

At this time you may be wondering how you can begin to use the ideas of stages of reasoning and self-regulation immediately, without writing your own textbook or developing all new laboratory activities. Even though the teaching materials have a strong influence on your course, your own personal actions and approaches to the students can be very important as well. In this chapter we shall describe procedures that will enable you to make your teaching more effective in stimulating your students to use their existing reasoning patterns and to develop new ones by self-regulation. We shall also ask you to consider how you might balance course goals directed towards course content with other goals directed towards advancing your student's reasoning patterns. At this point we reemphasize that Piaget views intellectual development as an internal, personal construction. In other words, the formation of new reasoning patterns is really the product of the individual student's mind - hence the term self-regulation.

We believe that the teaching approaches suggested by application of Piaget's theory and described in this chapter are compatible with other theories of teaching and learning. They can best be used as part of an instructional program that also stresses creativity, development of self-worth, self-reliance, and respect for the opinions of others.

Objectives of This Chapter

To give you practice in designing a *Learning Cycle* in your discipline

To assist you in selecting and utilizing a teaching strategy that will encourage self-regulation on the part of your students

To assist you in balancing course goals aimed at content with those aimed at improved reasoning

Procedure

Select a topic in your discipline. Design *EXPLORATION*, *INVENTION* and *APPLICATION* activities for that topic. Attached is an essay *Designing Active Learning Based On The Work of Piaget and Karplus*.

Summarize your *Learning Cycle* for sharing with the other teachers in your discipline.

DESIGNING ACTIVE LEARNING: BASED UPON THE WORK OF PIAGET AND KARPLUS

A Piagetian-based classroom instruction strategy to assist students in the development of logical thought was developed by Robert Karplus. He called it a *Learning Cycle*. The Karplus *Learning Cycle* has been modified for college instruction by the ADAPT faculty.

An ADAPT Learning Cycle is divided into three major phases known as *EXPLORATION*, *INVENTION*, and *APPLICATION*. The general characteristics of each phase of an ADAPT *Learning Cycle* are given below. We have discovered two things about designing *Learning Cycles* for use in the ADAPT program.

1. Since much of our class work is focused on specific aspects of our discipline, we usually design our *Learning Cycles* by starting with *INVENTION* and/or *APPLICATION* activities. Frequently we have a task we want our students to be able to do, for example, write an essay on the significance of a poem or determine the density of materials of various sizes and shapes. Then we try to design an *EXPLORATION* activity, or puzzle, which can be resolved by that *INVENTION* and/or *APPLICATION*.

2. We find it very helpful to try out our *Learning Cycles* on other faculty members (not in our discipline) before using them with students.

As you design your *Learning Cycle* you may want to consider the following attributes of the three phases of a *Learning Cycle*.

EXPLORATION—Following a brief statement of topic and direction, students are encouraged to learn through their own experience. Activities are supplied or suggested by the instructor which will help the students to recall (and share) past concrete experiences and to assimilate new "hands-on," "eyes-on" experiences helpful for later *INVENTION* and/or *APPLICATION* activities. During *EXPLORATION* the students receive only minimal guidance from their instructor and examine new ideas in a spontaneous fashion.

Emphasis—"hands-on," "eyes-on" experiences with familiar objects and systems.

Focus—Open-ended student activity

Function—Student experience is joined with appropriate environmental options not previously considered by the student.

1. This phase of the *Learning Cycle* provides students with reinforcement of previous "hands-on," "eyes-on" experiences and/or introduces them to new "hands-on," "eyes-on" experiences to be related to the later *INVENTION* phase.
2. *EXPLORATION* allows for open-ended considerations, encouraging students to use concrete experiences to consider new ideas.
3. During *EXPLORATION* the instructor supplies encouragement, provides challenges, asks questions, and suggests alternatives. The instructor should encourage students to try a variety of experiments.
4. Student behavior during *EXPLORATION* provides information for the teacher about the student's ability to deal with the concepts and/or skills being introduced. The students will reveal the reasoning skills which they evoke in search for the solution to a problem.

Questioning Skills and Strategies—Open-ended questions are asked to broaden an area of study by generating multiple possibilities. The instructor uses extended wait-time, that is, the time one waits for students to give a response to a question one has asked, for example, quietly count to 10, and may even expect no answer at all (Rowe, 1986).

INVENTION—In this phase the "hands-on," "eyes-on" experiences of the *EXPLORATION* are used as the basis for generalizing a concept or for inventing a principle. Student and instructor roles in this activity may vary depending upon the nature of the content. Generally, students are asked to invent the relationship for themselves with the instructor supplying encouragement and challenges when needed. This procedure allows the students to gain confidence with the conceptions they have invented. This confidence comes from the fact that they have tested possibilities and kept those features that enabled concepts to fit with the experiences.

Emphasis—Generalization of "hands-on," "eyes-on" experiences and *INVENTION* of hypothetical possibilities.

Focus—Student's active involvement with instructor for generalization.

Function—Students become familiar with generalized concepts and/or skills. During this time students are encouraged to formulate relationships which generalize their new ideas and concrete experiences.

Questioning Skills and Strategies—Focusing and valuing questions are asked to encourage the transformation of information and the determination of appropriateness of results. Such questions require a long wait time, perhaps 5 seconds or more. Some direct information questions are usually asked so that factual information can be broadly shared.

APPLICATION—The *APPLICATION* phase allows each student an opportunity to directly apply the concepts or skills learned during the *INVENTION* activities. *APPLICATION* provides the students with additional broadening experiences. They use the invented concepts in different specific settings. The *Learning Cycle* allows each student the opportunity to think for one's self. The instructor is present as an overseer of the activity. Yet the instructor must guard against overplaying the role as director and facilitator. The instructor must provide an open classroom atmosphere within a well-defined boundary.

Emphasis—Relevant use of generalized concepts and/or skills.

Focus—Directed student activity

Function—Further use of generalized concepts in other systems.

1. To begin the *APPLICATION*, the students and the instructor may interact in planning an activity for applying the invented concept and/or skill. The activity should provide a new or unique concrete situation.
2. Students are asked to complete the designed activity to the satisfaction of the instructor. The activities should provide further experi-

ence which will act as broadening and stabilizing experiences related to the new skills or concepts.

Questioning Skills and Strategies—Goal-oriented questions are asked that may require directed activity on the part of the students. These are questions that may set the students to work on a common task.

Below is an essay on teaching strategies for self-regulation. We have included a brief summary of the major ideas proposed in this book. You may find it helpful to discuss, with some of your colleagues, the relevance of these ideas to your teaching.

Essay: Teaching Strategies for Self-Regulation

Here are several procedures we have found useful for encouraging self-regulation with our students. You will find that some can be used with very little effort, while others require substantial planning and preparation. Work together with other faculty in your college and community to try these approaches so you can share any necessary work, discuss student reactions, and learn from one another's experiences.

Introducing a New Topic

1. Arrange your teaching sequence so you can begin with concepts defined operationally through demonstrations, examples and actions. Present more formal definitions of these concrete concepts and any other concepts only at a later time.

2. Use EXPLORATION activities at the beginning of a new topic or before introducing a new concept. At this time and on other occasions, give your students opportunities to work with objects and make observations in an environment that allows them to ask their own questions and follow their own interests.

3. Begin class discussions with simple demonstrations and challenge your students to raise questions or predict the outcome of experiments. Then use the actual results for initiating an examination of unexpressed assumptions or expectations.

Following Through

4. Encourage students to interact with one another during discussions, laboratories and problem-solving sessions. By learning about the view points of others, they will become more aware of their reasoning. Students using formal operational reasoning patterns will serve as role models for the more concrete operational thinkers. The latter, because of their more limited understanding, will chal-

lenge their advanced colleague's short-cuts in reasoning, thus making them rethink their ideas. Furthermore, students are more likely to reveal weaknesses by asking apparently off-the-wall questions of one another, when the teacher cannot hear. Conceptual difficulties that might never have been revealed can then be dealt with by peers. Often, these conceptual issues are indications of aspects of their thinking about the phenomenon about which you are unaware. If you listen and try to understand their conceptions in this context, instead of trying to get them back "on track," you can deepen your own understanding of their conceptions. Armed with this new construction of your own about their conceptions, you will be in a position to design more effective explorations, either on the spot or for next time.

5. Allow students time and opportunities for abundant and repeated experiences. Material covered in your course may have to decrease. The resulting deeper understanding constructed by the students as a result yields far more capable students—less material, but deeper understanding of fundamental issues. Alternative ways of perceiving relationships help students to resolve contradictions and become aware of their own reasoning. You should ask them to justify their conclusions, predictions, and inferences regardless of whether these are correct or incorrect. "What makes you sure of that?" "What is the evidence?" "How could you explain that to me?" "What are some other ways of thinking about that problem?" are questions that might be asked of a group or of an individual student.

6. Though you may feel strange at first, allow your students more control of their behavior so they may become aware and critical of their own reasoning. Recognize that many of them are accustomed to teaching that delivers information without challenging reasoning. *EXPLORATION* activities or open-ended questions are likely to seem strange to them, because they must take responsibility rather than having their teacher decide what is right or wrong.

7. Reason out loud in your discussions with students. Reveal how you consider alternative possibilities and may at times be unsure how to proceed. Propose hypotheses, make inferences, compare them with other data, and examine evidence. Invite the class to join you in this activity by commenting on your ideas, proposing others, and evaluating their adequacy. Leave some questions unanswered even if you know the answers. Answer students questions with questions designed to focus their thinking. Model the reasoning behavior you hope to foster.

8. Try to be as receptive as possible to apparently off-the-track ideas or hypotheses. Don't squelch a timid first attempt, but encourage it to draw attention to its good points and possibly unusual point of view. Suggest a laboratory activity, further reading, or discussion to help the student reexamine an inadequate reasoning pattern or preconception. Emphasize the reasons behind an answer rather than the "right answer" itself.

Using the Laboratory

9. Use the *Learning Cycle* to organize laboratory activities. Always begin with 20 to 30 minutes (or more) of *EXPLORATION* during which the students use the equipment with only a very general goal statement. Encourage students to make discoveries, even those that do not fit your plans for the outcome of the sessions. After *EXPLORATION*, be clear and explicit in the *Invention* of the new idea or relationship at the focus of the laboratory.

10. As an introduction to a laboratory activity, invite your students to identify the variables that might affect the phenomenon being studied. Then give them a written list of their ideas and encourage them to design experiments for testing their ideas. By examining the outcomes of an inadequate procedure and the list of variables, your students may learn to recognize their shortcomings and control variables more effectively.

11. Before making an assignment from your text, read the selection carefully as we have suggested in chapter 7. Identify the demands for formal reasoning it presents and possibly supplement it with short explanations that will help students using concrete reasoning patterns. Note also the clarity of the illustrations and whether they help communicate the message of the text.

12. Assign specially constructed problems that encourage students to evaluate their own reasoning allowing several answers, each justifiable on a different basis. An example might be this:

> Two cities are located along a river. Johnstown is five miles up the river from Lafayette. During a strike in Johnstown, thousands of gallons of raw sewage were released into the river. This alarmed the officials of Lafayette as the river was used for swimming. To prevent infection, they dumped large quantities of a strong antiseptic into the river. For some weeks after the antiseptic had washed away, the river was brown and murky and filled with small pieces of plant materials. City officials in Lafayette blamed those in Johnstown for the state of the river. Officials in Johnstown blamed those in Lafayette for

dumping antiseptic into the river. Who do you think is to blame? Explain your conclusion.

Managing Small Groups

13. An important characteristic of the *Learning Cycle* as implemented in the ADAPT program is the use of small groups of students working together on the tasks set for them. Ample evidence exists on the value of using small groups of students for cooperative learning. This strategy, coupled with an understanding of how students learn based on Piaget's theory of cognitive equilibration, forms the basis of the *Learning Cycle*.

   To achieve the full benefit to the students of a cooperative learning environment, you need to do more than just turn a group of students loose on a task. Your design of the task should be based on an understanding of how students learn. (That is what this book is all about. This point is sometimes missed by proponents of cooperative learning.) The task needs to be designed to foster the necessary cooperation among the members of the group and the students need to learn how to work cooperatively.

Testing

14. When you select items for a test, keep in mind that it makes demands on subject knowledge and on reasoning. Avoid problems in which ingenious reasoning overshadows the subject - use these only in supplementary materials for gifted students. Also avoid exam items that rely solely on memorizable statements.

15. Include test items on which you ask students to justify their answers so you can assess their reasoning patterns as well as their knowledge. Chapter 6 has more detailed suggestions on this topic.

Course Goals, Content or Reasoning?

16. The teacher who intends to explore new material must expect to allow for self-regulation if he wishes the students to construct a good working understanding of new ideas. How much time will be needed depends on the level of the course and preparation of the students. Less time will be needed in an advanced placement course where most students reason formal operationally and have a background of experience and understanding the subject. More time will be needed in the lower levels and high schools where students are less experienced and may reason predominantly with concrete operational patterns.

In view of these considerations, we would like to rephrase the question in the title above to *Course Goals: Content With or Without Reasoning?* since the reasoning patterns are closely related to the subject matter you select. Usually teachers define course goals exclusively according to the major topics covered, with a great deal of freedom for the individual teacher as regards emphasis and elaboration of details. Now you may wish to consider including goals related to your students' reasoning. Are these compatible with all the content goals? Are the topics in your course sequenced in order of increasing use of formal operational reasoning patterns? Is there sufficient opportunity for experience in the laboratory? Are there provisions for making students aware of their own reasoning and disequilibration so that they can initiate self-regulation?

SUMMARY OF MAJOR IDEAS

1. Piaget's theory describes two major stages of logical, operational reasoning in human intellectual development, the stage of concrete operational reasoning and the stage of formal operational reasoning. Earlier stages identifiable in the behavior of young children may be called preoperational.
2. Each of these two major stages is characterized by certain reasoning patterns, used by individuals to classify observations, interpret data, draw conclusions, and make predictions (see Table 10.1).
3. The formal operational stage is an idealization in that most persons after age 12 use formal operational reasoning patterns under some conditions and concrete operational reasoning patterns under others. The latter is likely to occur whenever the subject matter is unfamiliar, as is the case for a student beginning work in a new area. The former is likely to be the case for an experienced worker in the field.
4. The process of self-regulation plays a vital role when an individual advances from the use of concrete operational reasoning patterns to the use of formal operational reasoning patterns. Self-regulation begins with one's awareness that the concrete operational reasoning patterns, or their conceptions of a phenomenon, are inadequate; disequilibration. It proceeds through direct experience with

phenomena supplemented by the construction and testing of related organizing principles and major concepts.

5. A person who uses only concrete operational reasoning patterns is likely to proceed through self-regulation in a new subject much more slowly than a person who reasons formal operationally in connection with other subjects. The latter individual benefits from the possibility of transferring formal reasoning patterns to the new area, especially if the new and old are closely related as is the case with mathematics and science.

6. Some students who are required to learn formal operational-level material in a subject in which they so far have only used concrete operational reasoning may go through self-regulation spontaneously. Other students, with less experience or self-awareness, are not likely to experience the necessary self-regulation; instead, they will memorize certain prominent words, phrases, formulas, and procedures, but will apply these with little understanding unless the teaching program takes their specific needs into account.

7. Tests should be designed to evaluate the students' reasoning and also help them engage in self-regulation.

8. The *Learning Cycle* can be an effective strategy in classes where some students display concrete operational reasoning patterns and some formal operational reasoning patterns.

Table 10.1. Characteristics of Concrete and Formal Operational Reasoning

Concrete Operational Reasoning	*Formal Operational Reasoning*
Individuals—	Individual—
(a) Need reference to familiar actions, objects, and observable properties.	(a) Can reason with concepts, relationships, abstract properties axioms, and theories; use symbols to express ideas
(b) Use classification, conservation, and seriation reasoning patterns in relation to concrete items (a) above. Have limited and intuitive understanding of formal reasoning patterns.	(b) Apply classification, conservation, seriation, combinatorial, proportional, probabilistic, correlational, and controlling variables reasoning in abstract items (a) above.
(c) Need step-by-step instructions in a lengthy procedure	(c) Can plan a lengthy procedure given certain overall goals and resources
(d) Are not aware of their own reasoning, or inconsistencies among various statements they make, or contradictions with other known facts	(d) Are aware and critical of their own reasoning, actively seek checks on the validity of their conclusions by appealing to other known information

CONCLUDING REMARKS

We hope these chapters have given you some insight and impetus to examine your college teaching and consider student reasoning as an important aspect of your role as a mentor for students.

In the following chapters we provide you with some additional references on this topic, a link between this earlier work and more recent work, an overview of college teaching and learning as well as a review of the earlier Piagetian-based college programs. Finally, in the Appendices we have provided some additional readings as well as a partial copy of the original *Physics Teaching and Development of Reasoning Workshop* materials by Robert Karplus et al. from 1975. The complete copy of that workshop is available in a downloadable PDF file from the UNL Digital Commons Web site: http://digitalcommons.unl.edu/adapt/.

The next chapter, chapter 11, concludes the contents of the original ADAPT workshops, with the exception of the readings.

REFERENCE

Rowe, B. M. (1986). Wait time: Slowing down may be a way of speeding up! *Journal of Teacher Education, 37*(1), 43–50.

Our school system, as much under left-wing as under right-wing regimes, has been constructed by conservatives (from the pedagogic point of view) who were thinking much more in terms of fitting our rising generation into the molds of traditional learning than in terms of training inventive and critical minds. From the point of view of society's present needs, it is apparent that those old molds are cracking in order to make way for broader, more flexible systems and more active methods. But from the point of view of the teachers and their social situation, those old educational conceptions, having made the teachers in to mere transmitters of elementary or only slightly more than elementary general knowledge, without allowing them any opportunity for initiative and even less for research and discovery, have thereby imprisoned them in their present lowly status. And now, at the moment when we are witnessing an educational revolution of great historical importance, since it is centered on the child and the adolescent, and on precisely those qualities they possess that will be most useful to tomorrow's society, the teachers in our various schools can command neither a science of education sufficiently advanced to permit personal efforts on their part that would contribute to the further progress of that discipline, nor the solid [respect] that would be attached to such a scientific, practical, and socially essential form of activity.

From every point of view then, the problem of teacher training constitutes the key problem upon whose solution those of all the other questions examined until now depend.

—Jean Piaget (1965)

CHAPTER 11

IMPLEMENTATION AND SUGGESTED READINGS

The ADAPT Manifesto:

The principal goal of education is to create people who are capable of doing new things, not simply repeating what other generations have done— people who are creators, inventors, and discoverers.

    The second goal of education is to form minds which can be critical, can verify, and do not accept everything they are offered. The great danger today is from slogans, collective opinions, ready-made trends of thought. We have to be able to resist individually, to criticize, to distinguish between what is proven and what is not. So we need students who are active, who learn early to find out by themselves, partly by their own spontaneous activity and partly through materials we set up for them; who learn early to tell what is verifiable and what is simply the first idea to come to them.

—Jean Piaget (1964)

INTRODUCTION

Now is the time for you to take the ideas from this book and apply them to your college teaching. We have offered you a mental construct to help you understand the reasoning patterns used by your students. We have suggested a classroom strategy that we have found helpful in encouraging students to develop more mature reasoning patterns. We believe that the college years can be years of positive intellectual growth for all students and you can play an important role in their development of reasoning.

Objective of This Chapter

To apply the ideas and instructional techniques presented in this book to your own teaching.

Procedure

1. You are encouraged to evaluate the reasoning patterns used by your students. Do the concrete/formal operational ideas seem useful in explaining student performance?
2. In what ways do the Piagetian notions enable you to anticipate student reasoning difficulties?
3. Review the teaching strategies for self-regulation suggested in chapter 10. Try to apply them in your teaching. Do they help improve student reasoning?
4. Design a Learning Cycle for use in one of your classes. Expect it not to go well. Students tend to resist exploration activities when they are used to teacher-directed work.
5. Try to organize a discussion group with like-minded teachers. It is difficult to stand against a world of rote-learning, algorithmic thinking students by yourself. You will need a supportive community if you seriously try to change the way you understand your teaching.
6. Continue to read articles on the development of reasoning to provide for your own intellectual growth with these ideas. To assist you with this we have provided a set of readings and an annotated bibliography.

Additional Readings—Appendix A

In Appendix A, Additional Readings, we have provided you with a collection of articles that we have found helpful. They represent an application of Piagetian ideas in a variety of disciplines as well as an article by Piaget himself. We present first the two articles that created the "continental divide" in college and university physics curriculum improvements as discussed in Introduction and Rationale.

- Arons, A. B., & Karplus, R. (1976). Implications of accumulating data on levels of intellectual development. *Amer. J. Phys., 44,* 396.
- Fuller, R. G., Karplus, R., & Lawson, A. E. (1977). Can physics develop reasoning? *Physics Today, 30*(2), 23–28.
- Arons, A. B. (1976). Cultivating the capacity for formal reasoning: Objectives and procedures in an introductory physical science course. *Amer. J. of Phys., 44,* 834–388.
- Carpenter, E. T. (1977). *Self-regulation in reading a story.*
- Copes, L. (1975). *Can college students reason?* Contact copes@edmath.org
- Piaget, J. (1972). *Problems of equilibration.* Jean Piaget Society.

Sources for the Original Faculty Development and Media Materials:
These materials serve as the basis of the idea for this book and provide much of its content.

1. *Science Teaching and the Development of Reasoning*, Lawrence Hall of Science, University of California, Berkeley, CA 94720. © 1975. Various parts of these materials are included in this book and are referenced by the © Board of Regents note at the bottom of the first page of the materials. Most of these materials were modified over the years by the ADAPT program at the University of Nebraska.
2. Workshop on *Physics Teaching and the Development of Reasoning*. American Association of Physics Teachers, One Physics Ellipse, College Park, MD 20740. © 1975. Some of these materials are included in Appendix B in their original form.

EPILOGUE

Straight Scoop on Piagetian Books by Robert G. Fuller

I. David Elkind

He is my American hero as an interpreter of the work of Jean Piaget. I always recommend you start with him.

1. David Elkind (1974). *Childen and adolescence; Interpretive essays on Jean Piaget* (2nd ed.). New York: Oxford University Press.

2. David Elkind (1976). *Child development and education, A Piagetian perspective*. New York: Oxford University Press. A more advanced book with a good discussion of Piaget's ideas and their educational implications. Mostly in an elementary school setting but easily transformed into a college environment by formal operational faculty.

II. Eleanor Duckworth

She is the foremost translator of Piaget's spoken French into English. Every college teacher owes oneself the joy of reading the opening essay in her book on teaching and learning.

3. Eleanor Duckworth (1996). *The having of wonderful ideas & Other essays on teaching and learning* (2nd ed.) New York: Teachers College Press.

III. Jean Himself

No Piagetian neophyte can be protected forever from his own writings. I suggest you begin gently.

4. Jean Piaget (1976). *To understand is to invent: The future of education*. New York: Penguin Books. A general interest book prepared for common folk. Several excellent quotable sections, for example, pp. 19–20, pp. 105–106.

5. Barbel Inhelder & Jean Piaget (1958). *The growth of logical thinking from childhood to adolescence*. New York: Basic Books. This is it! Very interesting first half of each chapter. Perhaps skip the last half of each chapter to avoid disequilibration. Back around pp. 309—there are pages that summarize Piaget's ideas on formal thought. You may want to prepare yourself for this book by reading my 50 year review of the book published in 2008: *Can One Book Really Transform Your Career?* (2008, Sept–Oct). *Journal of Applied Developmental Psychology, 29*(5), 412–414.

IV. Others

6. H. G. Furth and M. Wachs (1974). *THINKING Goes to School*. New York: Oxford University Press. The sections, pp. 12–30 and 40–47, provide good practical insights into the applications of Piaget's concepts to teaching. Again the setting is elementary school but is readily generalized to college.

7. P. G. Richmond (1971). *An introduction to Piaget*. New York: Basic Books. Near the end of this book there is a discussion of applications

to education. I thought pp. 106–109 contained ideas for college teaching.

8. Howard E. and J. Jacques Voneche (1976). *The essential Piaget: An interpretive reference and guide*. New York: Basic Books. The heavy weight of Piaget's books. A super compilation of all kinds of Piaget's articles and books. Reading this lifts you out of the neophyte stage of Piagetian development.

9. Brian Rotman (1977). *Jean Piaget: Psychologist of the real*. Ithaca, NY: Cornell University Press. This book allows a gradually transition from neophyte to Piagetian amateur. Sets the work of Piaget in the broad perspective of Western culture. After reading this you can answer questions such as this: Asked by a Frenchman, "What is the relationship between Piaget and Popper?" if you care to answer that, read this book.

****

ADDENDA BY MELVIN C. THORNTON

1. *Journal of Research in Science Teaching*, 2(3), 1964. The entire issue is titled " 'Piaget Rediscovered': Selected papers from a report of the Conference on Cognitive Studies and Curriculum Development, March 1964." Piaget's important "Development and Learning" paper comes from this issue. Also included are articles by Karplus, Duckworth and one by David P. Ausubel called "The Transition from Concrete to Abstract Cognitive Functioning: Theoretical Issues and Implications for Education."

2. Herbert Ginsburg and Sylvia Opper (1969). *Piaget's theory of intellectual development, an introduction*. Prentice Hall, paperback. This is a very basic introduction for teachers. The first chapter gives a biography of Piaget and a good summary of his basic ideas. The last chapter considers implications for education.

In ordinary daily work, our understanding of how students see, whether we agree or not, legitimizes their being as makers of sense. If they make overly simple sense, we must ask them to look further. But by acknowledging that making sense as they used to do was legitimate in its own time, and even a necessary step, we empower them to learn new and better sense. Our recognition is most encouraging in moments when the student is moving from one level of sense-making to another. When the transition happens right in front of us, we will see the eager realization and then, perhaps very shortly, the shadow of the cloud. We say something like, "Yes, you've got the point all right … but we do wish it made things simpler." The most heartening leaven for the mind can come from just such a brief acknowledgment as this.

—William G. Perry, Jr. (1985)

CHAPTER 12

PROGRESS SINCE 1978

INTRODUCTION

The work of Robert Karplus and Jean Piaget, which forms the basis for the first 11 chapters of this book, was the foundation for the development of research in the physics education community. Arnold B. Arons and Karplus were prominent research physicists who turned their professional attention to problems in science education. Their work led to the acceptance of research in physics education by several university physics departments where PhDs in research in physics education became acceptable. This is in contrast to several other disciplines where the study of how people come to understand a particular subject was largely ignored by the professionals in the disciplines and left to researchers in colleges of education to examine.[1] The reverse tends to be true in physics. The wide array of results from physics education research done in physics departments is largely ignored by educational research professionals in colleges of education.[2]

The strong interest of Arons and Karplus in the intellectual development of students, well supported by the work and theory of Piaget, led to detailed studies of students' conceptions as well as attempts to measure students' conceptual learning. The attempts to put these ideas into practice in science classrooms lead to a variety of interactive engagement learning strategies. In this chapter we are going to focus our attention on these two different trends in the research in physics education movement.

College Teaching and the Development of Reasoning, pp. 153–182
Copyright © 2009 by Information Age Publishing
All rights of reproduction in any form reserved.

We believe they are broadly applicable to the other disciplines in higher education. First, we will discuss recent work in conceptual learning and its basis in cognitive science and physics education research. Second, we will turn our attention to a variety on approaches to interactive learning with special emphasis on the use of computers and educational games.

CONCEPTUAL LEARNING

We describe here a number of developments of instructional materials and practices, which have grown out of physics education research (PER). Because they are derived from the results of PER, sometimes PER conducted by the groups themselves, sometimes results of PER conducted by other groups, they are all influenced by Jean Piaget's work and its introduction to the physics community by Robert Karplus. These projects and programs were not all developed with Piagetian principles in mind, nor do the investigator-developers all acknowledge agreement with the substance of Piaget's theory[3] and the nature of knowledge at its foundation. In fact, in some cases, the nature of knowledge in Piaget's theory has been explicitly rejected by some of the investigator-developers. Nonetheless, because in each project or program, students' conceptions are explicitly a central issue, the work can be understood in Piagetian terms and seen as influenced by Piaget's work which led to the development of the PER community.

A Test of Scientific Reasoning

The work that most closely builds upon the work of Robert Karplus and Piaget is the body of work done by Anton E. Lawson at Arizona State University. Dr. Lawson worked as a post-doctoral fellow with Professor Karplus at the Lawrence Hall of Science in Berkeley. When he took a faculty position at Arizona State University, he developed a written test instrument to measure a variety of formal operational reasoning patterns and published that instrument as a Test of Scientific Reasoning (Lawson, 1978). He has continued his concern with ways that classroom instruction can be used to enable students to develop more advanced reasoning skills. He has published a large number of articles in this area of research and we encourage every college faculty member to become familiar with the work of Dr. Lawson. We provide you with a list of just a few of his publications dealing with the development of reasoning by students in science courses. (Lawson, 1985, 1995, 2000a, 2000b, 2005, 2007).

The Force and Motion Conceptual Evaluation, Tools for Scientific Thinking[4] and Real-Time Physics[5]

In 1980 articles reporting the results of physics education research investigations of students conceptions concerning motion began to be published. (Trowbridge & McDermott, 1980, 1981) This work, in addition to playing a central role in the development of *Physics by Inquiry*, a curriculum development of the Physics Education Group at the University of Washington described below, influenced the thinking of many others in physics education research. This was also the time during which microcomputers began to be available. In 1986 microcomputer-based laboratory (MBL) equipment was introduced at the Summer meeting of the American Association of Physics Teachers in Flagstaff, Arizona (Mokros & Tinker, 1987).

Traditionally science laboratory instruction, physics in particular, involves much time collecting, recording, and usually graphing data. These activities occupy most of the time available for labs. Very little time is left to directly experience the phenomenon, usually just once near the beginning of lab to generate the data, and very little time is left to consider the meaning or develop understanding of the phenomenon, usually just at the very end of lab once the graphs have been completed. The paucity of time to experience the phenomenon or to try to understand what is going on in the phenomenon, coupled with the very long delay and cognitive distraction of all the manipulations involved in constructing the graphs, results in little change in understanding of the phenomenon as a result of these laboratory experiences. The use of MBL equipment in the lab makes it possible for graphs to be produced with only fractional second delays as the phenomenon unfolds, all of this without the major cognitive distraction of rendering data and constructing graphs.

Early on it was demonstrated that this nearly real-time graphing of a person's individual motion was crucial to the learning results that can be demonstrated with MBL. Brasell (1987) demonstrated that a 20–30 second delay in presenting the graph on the screen in the same activities eliminated the substantial learning results in junior high students. Students who experienced the delayed-MBL showed learning results hardly different than students who experienced no MBL at all.

Because a new graph of another example of the phenomenon can be produced in essentially the time it takes to make another run, many example graphs can be produced during the lab, instead of just one set of graphs of one run being produced in a typical lab period. With MBL a majority of the typical lab period can be spent experiencing a phenomenon and its variations, drawing correlations between this experience and graphical representation of the phenomenon, and developing deeper conceptual understanding of the phenomenon being studied. Since the late 1980s, Thornton and Sokoloff (1990) have been engaged in capitalizing on this affordance of MBL applied to the work on students' conceptions in physics (e.g., Trowbridge & McDermott, 1980, 1981) and how their conceptions apparently change.

From these early days of research in physics education, college and university faculty demonstrated a remarkable resistance to change in their teaching practices in the face of findings from the research. Thornton and Sokoloff launched a strategy of introducing the affordances of MBL and a focus on developing conceptual understanding of the phenomena, which requires minimal change in the standard lecture-lab format of introductory courses and no change in the standard lectures. The strategy is to provide laboratory curriculum materials using MBL equipment in the labs. The labs are generally taught by teaching assistants and not attended by the lecturer. The first such laboratory curriculum was the Tools for Scientific Thinking (TST) Project. (Thornton & Sokoloff, 1998).

TST follows a typical sequence of topics in kinematics and force. This facilitates its fit with an otherwise conventional course in introductory physics. As lab activities, the materials are very different than standard labs, not only because essentially no time is devoted to constructing graphs by hand, but because of the engagement strategies used. In contrast to the standard *inform* (lecture & text), *verify* (laboratory), *practice* (homework problems), TST lab materials do not focus on verification of what has been presented in lecture and text. Instead TST lab materials engage students in examining their own conceptions concerning the phenomena and graphical representations of the phenomena, in encountering examples where their conceptions do not fit the outcomes, and in constructing new conceptions to better fit the experiential outcomes in lab. This is all driven by knowledge of students' conceptions from both the published literature and ongoing experience developing the activities, trying them out with real students. This basic TST strategy using the MBL equipment has been shown to work very well with college and high school students by Thornton and Sokoloff (1998). It also works effectively with students as young as fourth grade (Brasell, 1987; Dykstra & Sweet, 2009)

The focus on students' conceptions and conceptual change leads to a kind of assessment or diagnostic orientation, for example, what is the nature of the students' understandings of a phenomenon, instead of an evaluation orientation, for example, can the students give the intended right answers. This factor, coupled with the scientific orientation, really just common good sense practice, of principled measurement of change, leads in the case of the work of Thornton and Sokoloff (1998) to the development of an assessment tool. The Force and Motion Conceptual Evaluation (FMCE) was developed and is deployed using pre- and post-administrations to detect evidence of change in students' conceptions of motion and force. From patterns of responses to the items in the FMCE one can discern a spectrum of conceptions and details of conceptions students might display concerning motion and its relationship to force. With results of the FMCE one can say much more than merely the extent to which students are answering consistently with a Newtonian point-of-view (Dykstra, 2005; Thornton, 1997)

The TST materials treat motion and force and heat and temperature and were essentially conceptual. They involve very little mathematics. While the resulting conceptual development is essential to the learning results demonstrated via the use of these materials, Thornton and Sokoloff used what they learned from TST, included more quantitative skill development and expanded to a wider range of topics. The result is Real-Time Physics (RTP) (Sokoloff, 2004).

RTP uses the same strategies as TST to promote conceptual development. It continues the same goal of being a set of materials suitable for laboratories in standard lecture-lab courses. While some calculus-level introductory physics instructors might shy away from the nearly totally qualitative TST materials, the RTP materials accomplish the same qualitative conceptual development coupled with additional quantitative skills. The result is materials that are adopted in calculus-level introductory physics courses.

The TST/RTP materials can be seen as having a modified learning cycle structure. They focus on students engaging in conceptual change. The exploration phase generally has gone on previous to a particular activity in the materials. This exploration consists of life experience and the previous activities in the materials. As a result, students come to the course with already formed conceptions of the phenomena, or at least a ready tool set of conceptual elements to apply to any situation. The central focus in the materials is on the concept invention phase. Frequently, the invention is driven by a disequilibration. The students' previously constructed conceptions lead them to make predictions that do not work out when tried. Recognition of this discrepancy between their conceptions and their experience of what happens triggers the disequilibration. The details of the discrepancy are generally used by the students as clues for the reconstruction of the original conception, now seen as having failed. Trial new conceptions are checked against evidence and further tests of the conception are often the next activity in the materials. Eventually, successful new conceptions are applied in subsequent activities. This latter is the application phase when compared to the learning cycle.

Interactive Lecture Demonstrations

Once the TST materials were developed and tested until Sokoloff and Thornton with their colleagues had a good idea what was happening and the assessment evidence showed they work spectacularly compared to even good, well-executed standard instructional practices, Sokoloff began considering a situation at his institution which exists at many others. TST materials are designed and work in settings of lab sections, typically around 24 students, but not many more. A question that arises and Sokoloff was considering is what about settings in which one does not have access to students in lab section sized groups, but where one must work in a kind of lecture hall with groups much larger than 24. In other words is the approach only useful in small sections divided into lab groups with an apparatus set-up for each lab group?

Sokoloff decided that since this small group arrangement was not possible for all students in his situation,[6] he would develop a version of the approach for what might be called a group of the whole, demonstration mode in large classes at his institution. The result is what he named Interactive Lecture Demonstrations (ILDs). One way of thinking about ILDs is they are a similar set of activities to the TST activities or RTP activities, but done together with the whole class and one set of apparatus with the computer display projected so everyone can see it.

The challenge here is engagement of everyone in class. A number of strategies are used during the process to make engagement more likely: handouts, parts of which have to be returned, on which predictions can be recorded and outcomes or results can be recorded; asking members of the class to describe their predictions; asking members of the class to describe the actual graphical results; asking members of the class to assist making the motions, and so forth, Sokoloff and Thornton (1997, p. 340) worked out a set of steps to be applied to each individual ILD activity:

1. Instructor describes the demonstration and does it for the class without MBL measurements.
2. Students record their names and individual predictions on a Prediction Sheet, which will be collected. (Students are assured that these predictions will not be graded, although some course credit is usually awarded for attendance at these ILD sessions.)
3. Students engage in small-group discussions with their one or two nearest neighbors.

4. Students record their final predictions on the Prediction Sheet.
5. Instructor elicits common student predictions from the whole class.
6. nstructor, sometimes with students, carries out demonstration with MBL measurements suitably displayed (using multiple monitors, LCD, panel or computer projector).
7. A few students describe the results and discuss them in the context of the demonstration. Option: Students fill out Results Sheet, identical to Prediction Sheet, to take with them.
8. Instructor discusses analogous physical situation(s) with different "surface" features—that is, different physical situation(s) based on the same concept(s).

There are two crucial aspects of the ILDs. One is this series of steps to be applied to each activity. These steps are designed to maximize engagement throughout the class. The other equally important aspect is the nature of the issues and questions in each activity. This aspect had already been worked out in the TST project. There needs to be focus on aspects of the phenomenon and/or the graphs of the phenomenon that the students do not expect. They need to be asked for predictions and explanations for those predictions. Once the graphs have come out, focus needs to be on the differences between the predictions and the outcomes and the implications of these differences on the explanations originally posed. Time needs to be available for students to construct adjustments to the original explanations or new explanations altogether. This latter is not always carried out in class during an ILD, but it needs to be followed up in subsequent ILDs. These two aspects combined in the use of ILDs during lecture meetings of a course result in significant change in student conceptions, far beyond that typically seen from good lecture-lab (*inform-verify-practice*) courses, regardless of level of students and regardless of instructor (Sokoloff & Thornton, 1997). Cummings has written: "introduction of research-based techniques and activities does have clear beneficial effects. Interactive Lecture Demonstrations generated significant gains in conceptual understanding with remarkably little instructional time" (Cummings et al., 1999).

Because the ILD approach comes out of a vast amount of experience with TST and RTP, the underlying cognitive strategy is essentially the same, but applied to the large group setting details are specified to make it more likely more students are engaged than would be in a normal lecture or demonstration in the lecture hall. The ILD can be viewed as a learning cycle with the emphasis in class on the concept invention phase as with the TST and the RTP materials.

Powerful Ideas in Physical Science[8]

In the early 1990s Don Kirwan of the American Institute of Physics submitted a successful grant proposal to the National Science Foundation titled: Physical Science Instruction for Pre-service Elementary Teachers (PSI-PET). The plan was to bring together a team who could apply the latest findings from research in physics education to produce a kind of manual for physics professors who found themselves with the task of teaching physical science topics to elementary school teacher candidates. Since courses specializing in teaching just these students are fairly rare, the project was expanded to include conceptual physics courses for non-science majors in college. Often such courses are the only setting on a campus in which elementary school teacher candidates experience instruction in these topics.

The development team developed a kind of model course as a guide or example in which to explain and showcase instructional practices and information from research in physics education. Example student materials were written and tested by the team at their own institutions, then extensive instructor notes and explanations were developed to enable physics professors to intelligently customize the materials for use in their own courses.

One of the challenges in generating such materials is the fact that at many institutions, courses for which these materials are intended to be a guide, are often taught with large lecture classes accompanied by multiple sections of laboratory. Only a few of the development team have the luxury of small classes. The materials are designed to be used in either setting, small classes or large courses with lecture and lab. Engaging students in constructing new conceptions and development of reasoning can be successful regardless of the size of a course.

The original materials included four units: The nature of matter, Heat and Energy, Electric Circuits, Light and Color. Later because of demand, two additional units were developed, one on Motion and the other on the nature of force. The package of materials: student handouts, instructor notes, etc. is published by the American Association of Physics Teachers under the name, Powerful Ideas in Physical Science—a model course, PIPS for short.

The format of the student materials used in all of the PIPS units is designed to engage students in examining their own conceptions in comparison with the phenomena and in constructing and testing new or modified conceptions for fit with the phenomena. The units consist of multiple investigations, each composed of activities. Each activity is titled by a question. The questions are intended to engage the students in a prediction. The point of the prediction is not to guess "the truth" or what actually happens, but to use the prediction to examine one's own conception of what is going on in the phenomenon, how it works.

The materials can be seen as learning cycles nested in learning cycles. Each activity, a kind of learning cycle, has four steps to facilitate this process. The first two steps are: (1) What do you think? and (2) What does your group think? Students work in groups of 4. These first two steps are a kind of exploration; an exploration of one's own previous experience and sense or conception of the phenomenon and an exploration of other students' conceptions applied to the situation being asked about.

The second two steps are: (3) Making observations and (4) Making sense. In the "Making sense" step students are explicitly comparing their predictions with the actual outcome. The focus here is not who guessed right or what actually happens, but instead it is on the experience as a test of the original conception. If the outcome is that the original conception fits this example, then we move on. If the outcome is that the original conception leads to a prediction that does not fit, then disequilibration is the result.

The Making sense step in an activity supports the start of self-regulation. Subsequent activities continue to support and drive the self-regulation process. In this manner the concept invention phase is a central feature of the activities. The application phase occurs as the students begin to test new, still forming, conceptions in subsequent activities in the materials.

In each activity the exploration is primarily an exploration of one's own conceptions and those of others. The concept invention is an ongoing process that is initiated via disequilibration when the predictions do not match the outcome. It is important to note that these activities in the materials, each a learning cycle, are generally not stand-alone. They do not result in closure at the end of the activity. Instead, the individual activities, until toward the end of a unit, lead to new elements of disequilibration. The successive disequilibrations result in partial resolutions being constructed which are then applied in the initial prediction steps of the next activity to a new situation. Working with each other, the students formulate increasingly useful new conceptions of the phenomenon being studied. Likewise, the collections of activities, called investigations, are also learning cycles. Earlier investigations serve as explorations for subsequent investigations in which larger scale conceptions of a phenomenon are constructed invented and applied to the phenomenon.

Cognitive Acceleration

Michael Shayer and Philip Adey (1990) at King's College London introduced an instructional strategy they call cognitive acceleration (CA) in a series of papers in the early 1990s. They demonstrated that students who had experienced this strategy in science class not only scored about one grade level better in a standardized science test, but they also improved similarly in a standardized math and a standardized English test, too, when compared to students who had not experienced the CA science lessons.

CA activities have a structure that can be seen in terms of the learning cycle. An introduction which sets the scene serves as an exploration. In this introduction links are made to existing experience. The concept invention is triggered by a puzzle or challenge—something that doesn't work the way the students expect. The concept invention is continued in group work in which the students discuss the situation and share possible solutions. When the groups have solutions to the puzzle or challenge, then they present their solutions in a kind of plenary with discussion of the whole class. This plenary results in successful solutions to the puzzle or challenge. Once the invented concept is established, then there is metacognitive discussion about the lines of thinking the various groups used to develop their solutions. The students are engaged in discussing their own thinking. Finally, there is a session in which the newly developed solutions are applied to previous experiences and examples from everyday life. This latter is an application phase.

Shayer and Adey (2002) continue the work in CA. Their first project was Cognitive Acceleration through Science Education (CASE). They have developed with Cognitive Acceleration through Maths Education (CAME) and Cognitive Acceleration through Technology Education (CATE). In their work Shayer and Adey acknowledge the influence of both Piaget and Vygotsky (Shayer, 2002).

Physics Education Group: University of Washington

In the years since the original Physics Teaching and the Development of Reasoning workshop, a number of studies and teaching methods have built on the basic notions of the *Learning Cycle*, learner's construction of knowledge, and the importance of conceptual knowledge. Notable among these is the work by the Physics Education Group (PEG) at the University of Washington. Under the direction of Lillian McDermott, the PEG has investigated the student as a learner since 1973.[8] Housed in the Department of Physics, the PEG is one of the first disciplined-based education research programs (McDermott, 2001). This work focuses on student understanding of physics, rather than general educational theory or methods. This work has identified many conceptions held by physics students and the ineffectiveness of standard lecture methods (teaching by telling). In case after case, the PEG has found that students in traditional physics courses perform no better after the course on qualitative questions than they had before the course. In other words, while they may have been able to solve mathematical physics problems, they did not understand the underlying physical concepts on which the mathematics is based.

These revelations led to two major curriculum development projects: *Physics by Inquiry* and *Tutorials in Introductory Physics*. In parallel to the *Learning Cycle*, *Physics by Inquiry* creates learning experiences that seek to elicit student conceptions by creating a situation where known, common errors are confronted (Exploration); after students recognize the inadequacy of their existing models, they are lead through the reasoning needed to resolve their models (Invention); and finally students are given the opportunity to apply and generalize their newly acquired knowledge (Application). The PEG refers to this cycle as *elicit, confront, resolve, apply*.

The PEG describes features and effectiveness of *Physics by Inquiry* (PbI) through its structure causing students to go:

> ... step-by-step through the reasoning needed to overcome conceptual hurdles and build a consistent coherent framework. There are also other features that we think are important. Collaborative learning and peer instruction are integrated into PBI. Students work with partners and in larger groups. Guided by the questions and exercises, they conduct open-ended explorations, perform simple experiments, discuss their findings, compare their interpretations, and collaborate in constructing qualitative models that can help them account for observations and make predictions. Great stress is placed on explanations of reasoning, both orally and in writing. The instructor does not lecture but poses questions that motivate students to think critically about the material. The appropriate response to most questions by students is not a direct answer but a question to help them arrive at their own answers. (McDermott, 2001)

Investigative Science Learning Environment

Investigative Science Learning Environment (ISLE), is a teaching method

> ... that helps students learn physics by engaging in processes that mirror the activities of physicists when they construct and apply knowledge. These processes involve observing, finding patterns, building and testing explanations of the patterns, and using multiple representations to reason about physical phenomena.

One feature involves students' development of their own ideas by

(a) observing phenomena and looking for patterns,
(b) developing explanations for these patterns,
(c) using these explanations to make predictions about the outcomes of testing experiments,
(d) deciding if the outcomes of the testing experiments are consistent with the predictions, and
(e) revising the explanations if necessary.

Another key feature is encouraging students to represent physical processes in multiple ways, thus helping them develop productive representations for qualitative reasoning and for problem solving. (Etkina, 2007)

Again, in parallel to the *Learning Cycle* ISLE has three main phases, *Observational experiment; Testing experiment,* and *Application Experiment* (see Figure 12.1). In the *Observational experiment*, students do just what the name applies, observe a new phenomenon. Subsequently, students create explanations of the phenomenon (Exploration). During the *Testing experiment*, students conduct an experiment to see if their theory is correct (Invention). Finally, the *Application experiment* extends the theory to new areas (Application). (Etkina, 2002).

ISLE's parallels to the *Learning Cycle* become even more apparent when Etkina explains its key features in terms of a constructivist approach to cognition:

- Students are not told about physics concepts but construct them actively.
- Observational experiments that start every conceptual cycle are chosen in a way that students are able to describe them in their own words, thus connecting them to prior knowledge.
- Students use their prior knowledge to generate explanations for observed phenomena.
- Students undergo conceptual change when they design and conduct testing experiments for their explanations and when they use new ideas to explain real-life phenomena. (Etkina, 2007)

Force Concept Inventory and Modeling Instruction

Another effort to identify student understanding and misunderstanding of standard physics concepts is the Force Concept Inventory (FCI) (Hestenes, 1992). The FCI represents a list of students' conceptions, such as students' failure to discriminate between position and velocity or between velocity and acceleration and acceleration implies increasing force.

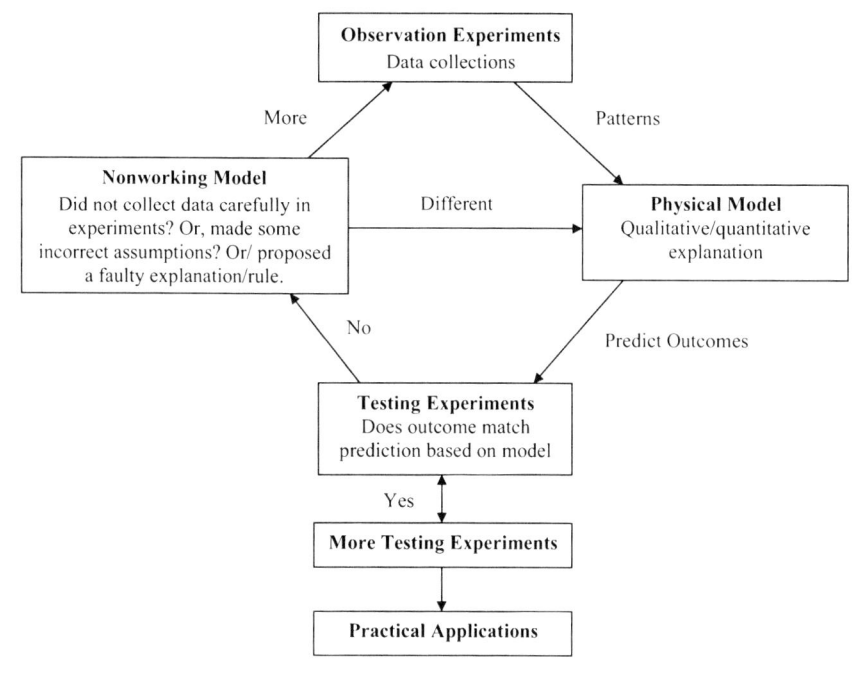

College Teaching and the Development of Reasoning 165

```
                    ┌─────────────────────────┐
                    │ Observation Experiments │
                    │     Data collections    │
                    └─────────────────────────┘
                        ↗               ↘
                    More                  Patterns
                   ↗                         ↘
┌──────────────────────────┐           ┌──────────────────────┐
│    Nonworking Model      │ Different │    Physical Model    │
│ Did not collect data     │──────────▶│Qualitative/quantitative│
│ carefully in experiments?│           │      explanation     │
│ Or, made some incorrect  │           └──────────────────────┘
│ assumptions? Or/ proposed│                      │
│ a faulty explanation/rule│                 Predict Outcomes
└──────────────────────────┘                      ↓
              ▲              No          ┌──────────────────┐
              └────────────────────────── │ Testing Experiments│
                                         │ Does outcome match │
                                         │prediction based on model│
                                         └──────────────────┘
                                                  │ Yes
                                                  ▼
                                    ┌──────────────────────────┐
                                    │  More Testing Experiments │
                                    └──────────────────────────┘
                                                  │
                                                  ▼
                                    ┌──────────────────────────┐
                                    │   Practical Applications  │
                                    └──────────────────────────┘
```

Figure 12.1. The Investigative Science Learning Environment (ISLE) Cycle.

Hestenes states:

> ... it has been established that (1) commonsense beliefs about motion and force are incompatible with Newtonian concepts in most respects, (2) conventional physics instruction produces little change in these beliefs, and (3) this result is independent of the instructor and the mode of [standard] instruction ... students have evidently not learned the most basic Newtonian concepts.... They have been forced to cope with the subject by rote memorization of isolated fragments and by carrying out meaningless tasks. (Hestenes, 1992)

In overcoming the limitations of traditional instruction Hestenes, with Wells and others, has developed Modeling Instruction. Modeling instruction aims:

> ... to organize course content around *scientific models* as coherent units of structured knowledge; to engage students in *making and using models* to describe, explain, predict, design, and control physical phenomena; to involve students in *using computers as scientific* tools for collecting, organizing, analyzing, visualizing, and modeling real data; [and] to *assess student understanding* in more meaningful ways. (Hestenes, 1987; Jackson, 2008)

In a parallel to the *Learning Cycle*, Modeling Instruction is based on phases. The first phase is model development demonstrations and discussions (Exploration). During the second phase students form a model of the phenomenon under investigation (Invention). In the model deployment phase students apply their newly discovered model to new situations (Application). Like the *Learning Cycle*, Modeling Instruction changes the role of the teacher from provider of knowledge to that of a facilitator, guiding students to construct their own knowledge. And as in Piagetian theory, Modeling Instruction is based on the belief that students' misunderstandings of concepts presented are due to 'filtering' new experiences through existing mental structures.

Cognitive Studies' Impact on Physics Teaching

In the early 1990s Edward Redish described "cognitive studies" as opposed to cognitive science feeling that,

> ... little in cognitive science satisfies the scientific criteria we are used to in physics of being precisely stated and well-tested experimentally, as well as useful. (Redish, 1994)

Cognitive studies was an apt term at the time. And although the discipline of cognitive science has advanced in the ensuing years, cognitive studies still describes much of the field. This is not to disparage the field or minimize its influence on our understanding of student learning. It is more to remind us that cognition and learning are not rooted in formal logic. Rather thinking is fuzzy and often inconsistent, ill-formed, contradictory models are often simultaneously maintained by individuals.

After reflecting on numerous cognitive studies by researchers including Arons, Inhelder, and Piaget, Redish identified four broad principles:

1. The Construction Principle
2. The Assimilation Principle
3. The Accommodation Principle
4. The Individuality Principle (Redish, 1994)

The Construction Principle states that people organize their experiences into mental models. Mental models may be made up of images, rules, procedures. There may be contradictory and incomplete elements. There are no well-defined boundaries between model elements, which means different, but similar models may get confused. Finally, models function to minimize mental effort. This frequently causes people to go to considerable lengths to fit experiences into their existing mental models.

The Assimilation Principle states that it is easy to learn something that closely matches or expands existing mental models. Conversely, it is difficult to learn something for which we do not have an existing, closely related mental model. This means, new information should be put in the context familiar to the learner. In communications studies this is called the "given-new principle" and implies that much learning is done by analogy.

The Accommodation Principle states that it is difficult to change existing mental models significantly,[9] yet for learning to take place, changes to mental models must occur. In order to change a mental model, predictions based on the existing mental model are in strong conflict with new experience and the new, replacement model must be intelligible, plausible, and fruitful. (Hewson & Lemberger, 2000; Posner et al., 1982).

The Individuality Principle states that each individual creates his or her personal mental "ecology." Therefore, different students have different mental models for physical phenomena as well as different models for learning. This implies that there is no best way to teach a concept and our own experiences cannot tell us what to do for others. Further, it suggests that the goal of teaching is to have students build proper mental models that are coherent, organized and accessible.

The focus on student development and reasoning that was pioneered by Arons and Karplus in the 1970s has spawned in addition a wide variety of efforts that make student mental activity and conceptual development, instead of just content mastery, a focus of instructors' efforts. These efforts include such disparate works as Laws' Workshop Physics (1991), Hake's Socratic dialogue (Hake, 1987), Mazur's Peer Instruction (Mazur, 1997), Kalman's Hermeneutical Circles (Kalman, 2008, 2009) and Dykstra's student understanding-driven instruction (Dykstra, 2005).

Interactive Learning

I believe that the motion picture is destined to revolutionize our educational system and that in a few years it will supplant largely, if not entirely, the use of textbooks.

—Thomas Edison (1922)

At the time of its creation more than 50 years ago, instructional television (ITV) was regarded as a means of increasing the quality of teaching by replacing the traditional classroom teacher.

—Hendry (2001)

So much for predictions. Still, there are technologies that are disruptive. That is, they make major changes in business and society. Personal computers have been available since the mid-70s. But it was not until the Internet reached the home that that the impact of information technology was transformative. Newspapers are closing as more and more people get there news from alternative sources like the Internet. Wikipedia has been shown to be as reliable as a professional written encyclopedia. Social networks like Facebook transform personal communications.

These changes are possible because the vast majority of homes have a computer and broadband Internet. Until every student has their own computer in their classroom, in-school education will not see the same impact. Undoubtedly, that day will come. If you consider smart phones, which contain microprocessors, that day is almost here. Certainly computers and the Internet have transformed how students learn and do homework and research at home. Some would argue, not necessarily for the better. Nonetheless, this is one genie that will not return to the bottle.

Games as Entertainment

A recent study found that 97 percent of American youth play video games (Lenhart, 2008). The study used a nationally representative sample of 1,102 young people, ages 12 to 17, and their parents, finding 99% of boys and 94% of girls play video games, with little difference in the percentages among various racial and ethnic groups and incomes. A recent article on designing games (vonAhn, 2008) notes with citations that more than 200 million hours are spent each day playing computer and video games in the United States, and that by age 21, the average American will have spent more than 10,000 hours playing such games. Games are clearly entertaining as judged by their use, but what if they had educational benefits?

While studies have shown that through exploring some virtual worlds children develop scientific methods (Steinkuehler 2008), few would argue that American youth learn science from their game play. Here we focuses not on general computer and video games, but on educational games, and for this we turn to a theory of intrinsically motivating instruction based on a rigorous study of educational computer games by Thomas Malone (1981). The foundation for Malone's work was Piaget's theories of how learners construct knowledge. His work and much recent work (Aldrich, 2004; Gee, 2003; Squire, 2004) has shown learning and fun are far from mutually exclusive. As Marshall McLuhan famously said: "Those who draw a distinction between education and entertainment don't know the first thing about either."

Educational Games

There have been a number of studies on the role of visual fidelity in computer-based systems on learning. More than twenty years ago, it was shown that with added realism in a simulated experimental device, students improved in their physics learning (Stevens, 1985). Visual fidelity and frame rate were shown to both increase retention and create a more positive attitude about the subject being studied by students (Christel, 1994). In this study, students presented with higher frame rate video actually retained more facts. More recently, a 3D virtual world was built with a commercial game engine for elementary students to explore ecological environments. A study of fourth grade students found that visual fidelity and navigational freedom had beneficial effects on learning, activity in-situ, and emotional reactions (Harrington, 2006).

Like the difference between viewing images of a film one at a time and seeing them presented at 24 frames per second, there is a threshold where the experience is fundamentally different. These studies have shown that subtle, not consciously perceived differences affect learning. Unfortunately, most developers assume that visual fidelity and frame rate have little effect on user experiences and certainly none on learning. These assumptions, along with the complexity of creating 3D environments, have led to the development of 2D simulations that are often low in resolution, frame rates, and fidelity having unintended, negative consequences for learners.

Here we ask:

What makes games fun?

Can physics games be fun?

How can purpose be designed into games?

Can games have an educational purpose?

How can interest, engagement, and creativity across a diverse audience of male and female users be stimulated with respect to new concepts?

Games With a Purpose

In the context of physics instruction, the recognition that teenagers were devoting significant time to arcade games for entertainment, and that the appeal of games could be leveraged for better multimedia physics instruction (at the time, computer-controlled videodiscs), dates back to early 1980s work by Robert Fuller and Dean Zollman (Fuller, 1985). Fuller noted the popularity of the first videodisc arcade game "Dragon's Lair" and reflected that students interactively learn through such games while physics instruction has traditionally been locked into a batch, lecture-based mode. In the 1980s the University of Nebraska Computer Learning Experiment began applying Malone's theory of intrinsically motivating instruction to physics simulations. The first such game was so successful that from then on the project created no computer-based materials in any format other than a game (Fuller, 1985), and went on to win the First National EdGame Challenge with *The Benjamin Franklin Computer Game of Electric Charges and Fields* (Fuller, 1983). Considering the success of these games and interactive videodiscs, it may seem surprising how little has been done in the intervening years. Much of this early work was funded by the NSF and other foundations and was quite costly, while publishers have little economic incentive to create educational games. And to date they are very difficult to develop.

A Theory of Educational Games

Experiences that are fun/captivating fall into two broad categories. Those that use a story and those that do not. They are different things that are designed differently. Entertainment experiences that do not require a traditional story may be purely fun, video games, or they may have a learning component, Oregon Trail type games. On the other hand, story has been part of human culture for thousands of years. The combination of game mechanics and story in support of learning is creating powerful learning environments in all disciplines.

Malone's work in educational computing looked at what makes games so captivating. His research identified a number of motivating factors including challenge (goals with uncertain outcomes), curiosity (sensory and cognitive), and fantasies (especially intrinsic fantasies where the fantasy depends crucially on the task). Fuller described Malone's theory and how it could be applied to the development of educational physics games (Fuller, 1985).

Challenge

An educational game is challenging if it provides a goal that is uncertain to attain. A good goal is one the learner can personally identify with, is obvious, and easily understood. The educational game must provide performance feedback so learners know how well they are doing in attaining the goals of the experience. Uncertainty can derive from several factors. Levels of difficulty is one factor. A higher-level goal can depend on the successful completion of a lower-level goal. It can also depend on the performance in the lower level goal, that is, how fast it was completed or how few errors were made. In an educational game, the difficulty of levels can be automatically determined based on past performance, chosen by the learners to match their perceived abilities, or determined by the skill of an opponent. Also, uncertain goals can be achieved by hiding information from learners, which is something that provokes curiosity. Randomness has also been shown to heighten interest. Challenge can be generated by playing against an opponent, either the computer or another student. It can be as simple as who completes a task first, or as complex as requiring cooperative problem solving. Challenge is captivating because it engages the learner's self-esteem. Success in challenging educational experiences makes students feel better about themselves and motivates them to take on further educational challenges.

Curiosity

Malone showed that learning environments evoke curiosity by providing an optimal level of complex information. The experience should be novel and surprising while still within the abilities of the learner. The experience should not be too complicated nor too simple with respect to the learner's existing knowledge. Cognitive curiosity stems from the desire to bring one's knowledge structures in line with experience. Learners want their knowledge to be complete, consistent, and parsimonious.

This suggests that educational games that reveal the learners' knowledge to be incomplete, inconsistent, or confused will engage their curiosity. In an optimally complex educational game, a learner will know enough to have expectations about what will occur, but where these expectations are sometimes not met. Thus, an educational game should sometimes be surprising but also constructive in helping the learner remove the misconceptions that caused them to be surprised in the first place.

Sensory curiosity involves the attention-attracting value of changes in light, sound, or other sensory stimuli. Educational games provide a myriad of possible visual and auditory sensory provoking effects that can be used to enhance the fantasy, as a reward, and as a representation system that may be more effective than words. With new input devices in consumer game consoles haptic and kinesthetic sensory curiosity can be added to computer learning experiences.

Fantasy

Learning experiences can be made more fun and interesting through the use of fantasy. Physics education already uses fantasies such as frictionless surfaces and point particles, but these are not fantasies that evoke students' interest. An easy way to increase the fun of learning is to overlay a fantasy on an existing lesson. The fantasy should cause the learner to progress toward a goal or avoid a catastrophe. An *extrinsic fantasy* is where the fantasy depends on the skill but not vice versa. For example, in the classic game "Hangman" the fantasy could just as easily be used to teach arithmetic as it is for spelling problems, so this classic game makes use of extrinsic fantasy.

In the best design, the fantasy depends on the knowledge being used and new knowledge grows from the fantasy. Malone called such a model *intrinsic fantasy*. Here the fantasy not only depends on the skill, but the skill relies on the fantasy. This means that problems are presented in terms of fantasy-world elements and learners receive a natural, constructive feedback. Malone showed that intrinsic fantasies add beneficial cognitive and emotional aspects to learning and help students apply old knowledge to new situations.

The vivid images of a fantasy world can help students remember what they have learned while satisfying some emotional needs. For example, what is more likely to motivate and interest a student: a bare vector addition numeric problem or a game of finding buried treasure that happens to need the use of vector addition?

As another example, when studying electric fields typically students are given the location and size of electric charges and asked to calculate the field at some other point. Fuller turned this into an intrinsic fantasy game where the task is to search for hidden charges in a cloud (Fuller 1985). The student becomes Ben Franklin and places a kite in the sky to try and find hidden charges. The game computes the field and displays it as an arrow with numerical values at the bottom of the screen. Unfortunately for Ben, a high force destroys his kite and he must buy a new one. Fortunately, he gets paid a sum of money from a local physicist for every charge he correctly identifies as to sign and magnitude. Formal studies of the game showed that students found the game exceptionally enjoyable, spending up to two hours to complete the game.

Fuller noted that space adventures are excellent fantasies for physics problems. Students have grown up with *Star Trek* and *Star Wars,* easily imaging zero gravity, zero resistance environments. Even an experiment that investigates density lends lends itself to a space fantasy, shown in Figure 12.2 as described in (Fuller, 1985):

The Planet Puzzle (from Fuller, 1985)

A starship visited four planets in the Greekon system where they collected representative samples of material from each planet. The samples were cut into rectangular parallelepipeds and covered with a protective coating. Unfortunately, proper codes were not placed on the samples.

You are given a sack containing 13 of these samples. Without damaging the coating, separate these samples into four classes which you think represent the material of each planet.

What are the properties that you can use to classify them?

Figure 12.2. Example of space fantasy to motivate physics problem solving.

The fantasies in educational games should also respect *Theatrical Convention* and *Aesthetic Distance:* the unwritten contract between audience member and actor, that allows the audience to "bridge the gap" between their physical location and the actual happenings upon the stage, in the film, or in the educational game. The audience will accept that Cleopatra is speaking English, but not that she would use a cell phone.

When Harder is Better

Laboratories have been defined as contrived learning experiences in which students interact with materials to observe phenomena (Hofstein, 1982). In the educational videodisc, The Puzzle of the Tacoma Narrows Bridge Collapse a laboratory experiment in the physics of standing waves on strings is simulated. Students are to observe phenomena related to standing waves. In addition they are to manipulate variables affecting the phenomena under study and use the data collected to deduce relationships between the variables. How students manipulate the variables in order to separate and control them is central to formal thinking.

In the traditional laboratory students use an electric vibrator, various strings, and a set of weights to test study standing waves (see Figure next page).

Like Hofstein's definition of traditional laboratories, "The Puzzle of the Tacoma Narrows Bridge Collapse" (TNB) videodisc laboratory is also

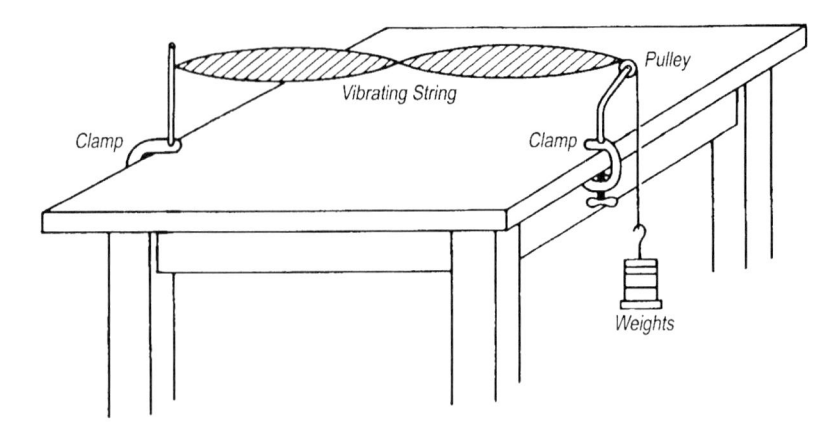

Figure 12.3. Laboratory setup for standing wave experiment.

a contrived learning experience in which students interact with materials to observe phenomena (see Figure 12.4). In the videodisc laboratory the students interact with videodisc images through the computer keyboard and a joystick. Student had complete freedom over the manipulation of the variables. Like the traditional laboratory, the videodisc laboratory (see Figure 12.4) allowed the students to add weights to the string, change the length of the string, and change the string itself (the linear mass density of the string).

Unlike the traditional laboratory, it is just as easy to change the string as it is to change the length or the weight. Students choose the values of the variables from a three-by-three matrix (see Figure 12.5). Students took data on the effect that changing independent variables had on a dependent variable. Students in the traditional laboratory used a systematic approach to investigating the effect of these variables, holding two of the variables constant while they change the third. This process is repeated for each of the independent variables. Students in the virtual laboratory used a non-systematic approach characterized by frequently changing more than one variable at a time (Stevens, 1985).

Students at the concrete stage of development do not think in abstract terms. The variable selection matrix is clearly an abstract representation of the operations of: putting strings on vibrators; adjusting their length; and adding weights to the strings. Rather than viewing the items in the variable selection matrix as representing physical operations, concrete thinkers view these items as the objects of interest.

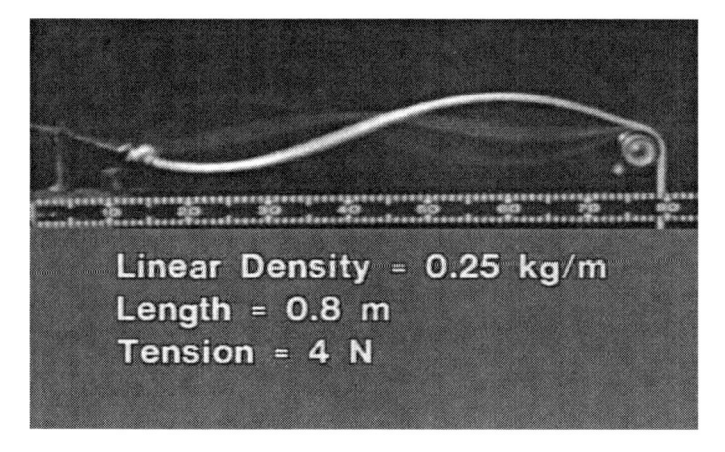

Figure 12.4. TNB video laboratory.

Linear Density	Length	Tension
High	High	High
Medium	Medium	Medium
Low	Low	Low

Figure 12.5. Variable Selection Matrix.

Symmetry abounds in the everyday world. Some theories of vision suggest that symmetry plays an important role in visual recognition (Marr, 1982; Rock, 1984). In the variable selection matrix, students highlighted symmetric patterns at a statistically significant higher rate compared to non-symmetric patterns. This indicates that students treated the visual objects in the variable selection matrix as primary objects of interest, not representations of objects in the video.

This work has led to the following design guidelines for educational games (Stevens, 2009):

> Educational game designers should analyze the way objects are used in real-world situations.
>
> The user interface should allow the user to manipulate simulated objects directly, making the user manipulate the simulated objects as they would real objects.
>
> The overall educational game design should direct the general approach to inquiry while concurrently allowing the users the flexibility to explore on their own.

The experience requires the user to analyze the situation while they are involved with it.

Finally, the design requires the user to use the objects and concepts in new and different ways.

Educational game designers must understand the phrase, "I am not the user." They must not design for themselves, but for the target learner.

Game Design

In his groundbreaking book, Schell (2008) identified 100 "lenses" through which developers view game design. Many of these resonate with Malone. The lens of endogenous value examines what is valuable inside a game and notes that they only have value inside the game. For example, Monopoly money only has meaning within the game of Monopoly and only has high value while playing the game. The game has given it meaning. It has no value outside the game. This idea guides the determination of how compelling a game might be. For example, the game of roulette does not have to be played with real money; it could use tokens or play money like Monopoly. But people will only play roulette when real money is at stake, because it is not a compelling game.

To design for endogenous value, Schell (2008) asks about players' feelings about items, objects, and scores in the game. What is valuable to the players and how can you make things more valuable? What is the relationship between value in the game and players' motivations? Think about what users care about and why.

Schell lists 10 qualities of games:

1. Games are entered willfully.
2. Games have goals.
3. Games have conflict.
4. Games have rules.
5. Games can be won and lost.
6. Games are interactive.
7. Games have challenge.
8. Games can create their own internal value.
9. Games engage players.
10. Games are closed formal systems.

Schell (2008) likens our educational system to a game. Students (players) are given a series of assignments (goals) that must be handed in (accomplished) by certain due dates (time limits). They receive grades (scores) as feedback repeatedly as assignments (challenges) get harder and harder until the end of the course when they are faced with a final exam (boss monster), which they can only pass (defeat) if they have mastered all the skills in the course (game). Schell's Lenses show why traditional education does not feel like a game. Most educational methods lack surprise, lack pleasure, and lack community.

Lectures, books, and video are all linear, and linear media are poor at conveying complex systems. The best way to understand a complex system is to *play* with it, getting a holistic sense of how parts are connected. Some systems that are best learned through simulations such as the human circulatory system and nuclear reactors. In physics, demonstrations and laboratories are all simulations, traditionally with physical objects, apparatus, and measuring devices.

Based on the foundations laid my Malone, Fuller, Schell and others, the hypothesis is that immersive 3D simulations and games incorporating surprise and building community will captivate students in a way that no tabletop lab exercise or textbook problem can. Consider that physics teachers have used trips to amusement parks as a motivational tool for over 30 years (Reno, 1995; Roeder, 1975; Natale, 1985). Obviously this is at best a once a year event for a select few. Three D worlds provide the ability for all students to experience amusement park physics. Figure 12.6a shows a typical lab setup to study energy transformation. Contemporary simulations (PhET, 2008) are flat 2D experiences (see Figure 12.6b). Which would motivate students more, a traditional lab, a 2D simulation reminiscent of a 1980s game, or a high-fidelity 3D roller coaster simulation (see Figure 12.6c) that permitted students to manipulate the course and study the effects of various designs, while measuring kinetic and potential energy throughout the course as they "ride" on the coaster?

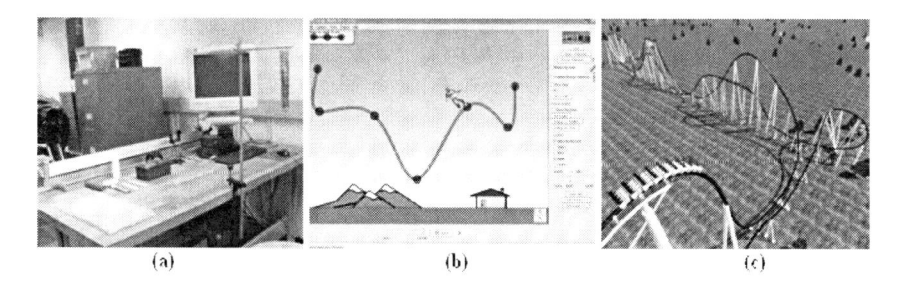

Figure 12.6. The study of energy transformations with (a) traditional lab apparatus; (b) 2D simulation; and (c) a hypothetical roller coaster interactive simulation with routing and other factors under user control.

But creating pedagogically sound, fun educational environments is difficult.

The challenges to educational game designers and developers are:

How to make entertainment and learning fun?

How to design interactive experiences in ways that captivate and intrigue people, illicit emotions, cause them to reflect, and educate them?

In addition an effective educational game should be *Realistic, Believable, Enjoyable,* and *Engaging* plus:

Interactions must be meaningful. Interactions must effect the experience. Fantasies (stories) must be intrinsic. Interfaces (worlds) must be intrinsic

CONCLUDING REMARKS

A common theme in this book is that an essential property of being human is the desire to understand ones environment. There are fundamental, intrinsic rewards to learning that naturally encourage humans to want to learn more. Intrinsically motivated, play-like activities are essential for many kinds of deep learning. So people are engineered to like them. They are fun. We need to know what a character in a game will find around the next corner. If a game design is based on what we know is intrinsically motivating to users, they will spend more time in the activity, they will learn more, and they will have more fun in the experience.

NOTES

1. That the issues of learning and teaching appear to be ignored by many in the disciplines can be attributed to a kind of folk theory of teaching. In this folk theory, teaching is the presentation of established canonical knowledge and learning of it is a matter of innate mental capacity and hard work on the part of the students. Neither the teaching nor the learning in this folk theory are particularly problematic or challenging and neither require specialized knowledge in the discipline, hence teaching and learning issues can be delegated to those in the College of Education. More on this folk theory can be found in chapter 13
2. Working under this folk theory of teaching, it is also no surprise that many non-discipline-based education research professionals might find the work on students' conceptions and reasoning of little interest.
3. We have an additional discussion of Piaget's theory in chapter 13.

4. Tools for Scientific Thinking materials are available from Vernier Software & Technology (http://www.vernier.com).
5. Real-Time Physics materials are available from John Wiley & Sons, Inc. (http://he-cda.wiley.com/WileyCDA/)
6. Some students at his institution in the introductory physics courses are not required by their degree programs to take the accompanying lab course. They do not attend the labs associated with the lecture course.
7. *Powerful Ideas in Physical Science—A Model Course* is available from the American Association of Physics Teachers.
8. Although Lillian McDermott remains active at this writing, she has retired. Paula Heron directs the activities of PEG now.
9. It should be noted that students' conceptions were frequently stated to be extremely resistant to change in the early days of physics education research (PER) in the 1970s and 80s. Since then, as alternative teaching strategies were developed, some based on Piagetian principles, evidence of conceptual change for major percentages of all types of students has been found. We know now that the apparent extreme resistance to change was more a result of the instruction than it is of the conceptions themselves. This is not to say that conceptual change is not a challenge for students, but even that is largely due to their over-training in the ways of traditional instruction. We will say more about this in the next chapter.

REFERENCES

Aldrich, C. (2004) *Simulations and the Future of Learning*. San Francisco: Pfeiffer.

Brasell, H. (1987). The effect of real-time laboratory graphing on learning graphic representations of distance and velocity. *J. Res. Sci. Teach*, 24(4), 385–395.

Christel, M. (1994). The role of visual fidelity in computer-based instruction. *Human-Computer Interaction*, 9, 183–223.

Cummings, K., Marx, J., Thornton, R., & Kuhl, D. (1999). Evaluating innovations in studio physics. *American Journal of Physics*, 67, S38–S44.

Dykstra, D. I., Jr. (2005). Against realist instruction: Superficial success masking catastrophic failure and an alternative. *Constructivist Foundations*, 1(1), 49–60. Retrieved from, http://www.univie.ac.at/constructivism/journal/

Dykstra, D. I., Jr., & Sweet, D. R. (2009). Conceptual development about motion and force in elementary and middle school students. *American Journal of Physics*, 77(5), 468–476.

Etkina, E., Van Heuvelen, A., Brookes, D., & Mills, D. (2002). Role of experiments in physics instruction—A process approach. *The Physics Teacher*, 40, 351–355.

Etkina, E., & Van Heuvelen, A. (2007). Investigative science learning environment—A science process approach to learning physics. *Reviews in Physics Education Research*, 1, 1–48.

Fuller, R. G., Winch, D. M., Stevens, S. M., & Bettis, C. L. (1983). *The Benjamin Franklin computer game of electric charges and fields*. Lincoln, NE: University of Nebraska Computer Learning Experiment.

Fuller, R.G. (1985, January-February) From the Dragon's Lair to the Tacoma Bridge. *Videodisc and Optical Disk*, 37–51.

Gee, J. (2003). *What video games have to teach us about learning and literacy*. New York: Palgrave Macmillan.

Hake, R. R. (1987) Promoting student crossover to the Newtonian world, *American Journal of Physics* 55(10), 878–884.

Harrington, M. (2006, July 30–August 3). Situational learning in real and virtual space: Lessons learned and future directions. In *Proc. ACM SIGGRAPH'06*, Boston.

Hendry, D. (2001, May/June). Instructional television's changing role in the classroom. *The Technology Source*. Retrieved from http://technologysource.org/article/instructional_televisions_changing_role_in_the_classroom/

Hestenes, D. (1987). Toward a modeling theory of physics instruction. *American Journal of Physics*, 55, 440–454.

Hestenes, D., Wells, M., & Swackhamer, G. (1992). Force concept inventory. *The Physics Teacher*, 30, 141–158.

Hewson, P. W., & Lemberger, J. (2000) Status as the hallmark of conceptual learning. In R. Millar, J. Leach, & J. Osborne (Eds.), *Improving Science education: The contribution of research* (pp. 110–125.) Open University Press: Buckingham.

Hofstein, A., & Lunetta, V. (1982). The role of the laboratory in science teaching: Neglected aspects of research. *Review of Educational Research*, 50(2), 201–217.

Jackson, J., Dukerich, L., & Hestenes, D. (2008, Spring). Modeling instruction: An Effective model for science education. *Science Educator*, 17, 10–17.

Judson, E., & Lawson, A. E. (2007). What is the role of constructivist teachers within faculty communication networks? *Journal of Research in Science Teaching*, 44(3), 490–505.

Kalman, C. (2008). *Successful science and engineering teaching: theoretical and learning perspectives (Innovation and change in professional education)*. New York: Springer.

Kalman, C. (2009). The need to emphasize epistemology in teaching and research. *Science & Education*, 18, 325- 348.

Laws, P. (1991). Calculus-based physics without lectures. *Physics Today*, 44(12), 24–31.

Lawson, A. E. (1978). The development and validation of a classroom test of formal reasoning. *Journal of Research in Science Teaching*, 15(1), 11–24.

Lawson, A. E. (1985). A review of research on formal reasoning and science teaching, *Journal of Research in Science Teaching*, 22(7), 569–617.

Lawson, A. E. (1987). Classroom test of scientific reasoning: Revised pencil and paper version. Retrieved from http://www.public.asu.edu/~anton1/LawsonAssessments.htm

Lawson, A. E. (1995). *Science teaching and the development of thinking*. Belmont, CA: Wadsworth.

Lawson, A. E. (2005). What is The Role of Induction and Deduction in Reasoning and Scientific Inquiry? *Journal of Research in Science Teaching*, 42(6), 716–740.

Lawson, A. E., Alkhoury, S., Benford, R., Clark, B., & Falconer, K. A. (2000a). What kinds of scientific concepts exist? Concept construction and intellectual development in college biology. *Journal of Research in Science Teaching*, 37(9), 996–1018.

Lawson, A. E., Clark, B., Cramer-Meldrum, E., Falconer, K. A., Kwon, Y. J., & Sequist, J. M. (2000b). The development of reasoning skills in college biology: Do two levels of general hypothesis-testing skills exist? *Journal of Research in Science Teaching*, 37(1), 81–101.

Lenhart, A., Kahne, J., Middaugh, E., Macgill, A., Evans, C., & Vitak, J. (2008, September) *Teens, video games, and civics*. Washington, DC: Pew Internet & American Life Project.

Malone, T. W. (1981). Toward a Theory of Intrinsically Motivating Instruction. *Cognitive Science*, 4, 333–369.

Marr, D. (1982). *Vision*. San Francisco: W.H. Freeman.

Mazur, E. (1997) *Peer Instruction: A User's Manual*, Prentice Hall: Upper Saddle River, NJ.

McDermott, L. (2001). Oersted Medal Lecture 2001: Physics education research—The key to student learning. *American Journal of Physics*, 69, 1127–1137.

Mokros, J. R., & Tinker, R. F. (1987). The impact of microcomputer-based labs on children's ability to interpret graphs. *Journal of Research in Science Teaching*, 24(4), 369–383.

PhET. (2008). *Physics Education technology*. Boulder: University of Colorado. Retrieved from http://phet.colorado.edu/index.php

Posner, G., Strike, K., Hewson, P., & Gertzog, W. (1982). Accommodation of a scientific conception: Toward a theory of conceptual change, *Science Education*, 66, 211–227.

Redish, E. (1994). Implications of cognitive studies for teaching physics, *American Journal of Physics*, 62, 796–803.

Rock, I. (1984). *Perception*, New York: Scientific American Library.

Schell, J. (2008). *The art of game design: A book of lenses*. Burlington, MA: Morgan Kaufmann.

Shayer, M. (2002). Not just Piaget, not just Vygotsky, and certainly not Vygotsky as an alternative to Piaget. In M. Shayer & P. Adey (Eds.), *Learning intelligence: Cognitive acceleration across the curriculum from 5 to 15 years 9* (pp. 179–195.) Open University Press.

Shayer, M., & Adey, P. (Eds.). (2002) *Learning intelligence: Cognitive acceleration across the curriculum from 5 to 15 years*. Milton Keynes: Open University Press

Shayer, M. & Adey, P. (1990). Accelerating the development of formal thinking in middle and high school students. *Journal of Research in Science Teaching*, 27(3), 267–285.

Sokoloff, D. R. (2004) *Real-time physics*. New York: Wiley.

Sokoloff, D. R., & Thornton, R. K. (1997) Using Interactive Lecture Demonstrations to Create an Active Learning Environment, *The Physics Teacher*, 35, 340–347.

Sokoloff, D. R., Thornton, R. K., & Laws, P. W. (1994). *Real-time physics mechanics* (V. 1.40). Portland, OR: Vernier Software.

Stevens, S. (2009). *Designing Serious Games For Deep Conceptual Learning*. Pittsburgh, PA: ETC Press.

Stevens, S. M. (1985). Interactive Computer/Videodisc Lessons and Their Effect on Students' Understanding of Science, National Association for Research in Science Teaching. In *Proc. 58th Annual NARST Conference*, Columbus, OH.

Thornton, R. K. (1997). Conceptual dynamics: Changing student views of force & motion. In E. F. Redish & J. S. Rigden (Eds.), *The changing role of physics departments in modern universities. Proceedings of the International Conference on Undergraduate Physics Education* (pp. 241–266). New York: Wiley.

Thornton, R. K.. & Sokoloff, D. R. (1990) Learning motion concepts using real-time microcomputer-based laboratory tools. *American Journal of Physics, 58*, 858–867.

Thornton, R. K. & Sokoloff, D. R. (1992). *Tools for scientific thinking—Motions and Force curriculum and teachers' guide* (2nd ed.). Portland, OR: Vernier Software.

Thornton, R. K., & Sokoloff, D. R. (1998). Assessing student learning of Newton's laws: The Force and Motion Conceptual Evaluation and the Evaluation of Active learning Laboratory and Lecture Curricula. *American Journal of Physics, 66*(4), 338–352.

Trowbridge, D. E., & McDermott, L. C. (1980). Investigation of student understanding of the concept of velocity in one dimension. *American Journal of Physics, 48*(12), 1020–1028

Trowbridge, D. E., & McDermott, L. C. (1981). Investigation of student understanding of the concept of acceleration in one dimension. *American Journal of Physics, 49*(3), 242–253.

von Ahn, L., & Dabbish, L. (2008). Designing games with a purpose. *Communications of the ACM, 51*(8), 58–67.

CHAPTER 13

THEORETICAL FOUNDATIONS FOR COLLEGE LEARNING—

Piaget and Vygotsky: Sorting Fact From Fiction

PIAGET'S THEORY OF COGNITIVE EQUILIBRATION

In previous chapters (1 & 2), we have illustrated how students' responses to problematic situations and puzzles can be grouped by apparent reasoning strategies. Piaget and his colleagues developed this grouping to describe the vast quantity of transcript data and observation records they collected over 6 decades of study at the Center for Genetic Epistemology in Geneva and elsewhere. The groupings are clearly influenced by the fact that Piaget and his colleagues were studying the development of knowledge in human beings. As in any science, there is an interplay between theory being developed and how the observational data is organized. The descriptions of the stages of reasoning are necessarily influenced by the theoretical explanation being developed, but they are not the theory itself.[1]

In chapter 8, we described a process called self-regulation. This self-regulation process is central to Piaget's theory of cognitive equilibration. Piaget and his colleagues describe the origins and development of knowledge in human beings in terms of successive equilibria between a person's schemes for understanding the world (the person's knowledge) and the person's experience with the world. Self-regulation can be described as how a person achieves a new equilibrium when the existing one breaks down.

As with the schemes described in the Petals Around A Rose exercise in chapter 8, one develops schemes to fit one's experiences, sometimes without being particularly aware of the process. When new experiences are encountered, existing schemes of understanding might or might not fit. When the schemes do not fit the experience, a disequilibration between schemes of understanding and experience is realized. When one experiences such a disequilibration, there are two basic possibilities. One is to avoid it and hope it does not happen again, keeping to the existing schemes. Alternatively, one can abandon the existing schemes, draw near the new experience and attempt to modify and test revisions of existing schemes or completely new schemes, until a new equilibrium is established. This latter process is called self-regulation.

While this self-regulation process is the central factor in cognitive equilibration, Piaget suggests there are three factors that influence cognitive development. First, is maturation. As a human being develops, sense making, sensory and physical and social manipulation abilities develop. The second factor is experience. This includes physical experiences with the world, social experiences in the world in interaction with others and 'inner' experiences with one's own thinking. The third factor, according to Piaget, is equilibration or self-regulation. Equilibration results in new or modified schemes. As schemes and systems of schemes evolve or change to fit new experience, cognitive development occurs (Piaget, 1964). This change or adjustment in the schemes, Piaget called accommodation.

Human behavior with respect to knowing the world, Piaget and his colleagues suggest, can be described as a striving for equilibrium between these cognitive schemes of understanding and experience. This cognitive development is not toward a particular equilibrium involving particular schemes, but toward any set of schemes that are determined to fit the experiences of a person by that person. This may seem unduly arbitrary, but it is not. There is a crucial limitation on the range of possible schemes. The criterion of fit between mental schemes and experiences, both physical and social, limits the range of schemes that can satisfy the goal of equilibrium between mental schemes and experience in human beings.

An important concept here, which differs from the usual notion of knowledge, is these schemes, and schemes composed of multiple other schemes, that compose our understanding, our knowledge of the world, fit our experience with the world. There is more than one scheme that can fit our experience with the world. Some of these schemes we have yet to imagine. Because our criterion for these schemes, our understanding, is fit to the experiences, we cannot claim a scheme is a true, or nearly true, description of the world as it really is. Our schemes of understanding are not a match or picture of reality.

This "not about truth" status of our explanatory knowledge or schemes may seem alien to science, but no less personages than Max Jammer and Albert Einstein have expressed the same idea about the status of our knowledge in science. Jammer wrote about this issue, originally in 1957, and refers to Einstein in so doing. Jammer, winner of the 2007 American Institute of Physics Abraham Pais Prize in the History of Physics, begins with a description of scientific knowledge:

> As a result of modern research in physics, the ambition and hope, still cherished by most authorities of the last century, that physical science could offer a photographic picture and true image of reality had to be abandoned. Science, as understood today, has a more restricted objective: its two major assignments are the description of certain phenomena in the world of experience and the establishment of general principles for their prediction and what might be called their "explanation." (Jammer, 1957/1999, p. 2)

Jammer (1957/1999) divides scientific knowledge into two categories: experiential knowledge, "description of certain phenomena in the world of experience," and explanatory knowledge, "general principles for their prediction." But, he goes on to write that to accomplish these two assignments, science employs a conceptual, explanatory apparatus consisting of two parts:

> (1) a system of concepts, definitions, axioms, and theorems, forming a hypothetico-deductive system, as exemplified in mathematics by Euclidean geometry; (2) a set of relations [rules of interpretation] linking certain concepts of the hypothetico-deductive system with certain data of sensory experience. (Jammer, 1957/1999, p. 2)

The consequence is a kind of ambiguity in explanatory knowledge in science:

> The adoption of rules of interpretation introduces, to some extent, an arbitrariness in the construction of the system as a whole by allowing for certain predilections in the choice of concepts to be employed. In other words, arbitrary modifications in the formation of the conceptual counterparts to given sensory impressions can be compensated by appropriate changes in the epistemic correlations [rules of interpretation] without necessarily destroying the correspondence [fit] with physical reality. In consequence of this

arbitrariness, scientific concepts "are free creations of the human mind and are not, however it may seem, uniquely determined by the external world." (Einstein & Infeld, 1938; Jammer, 1957/1999, p. 3)

Thus, by way of Jammer and Einstein, we have a description of science, which describes the nature of knowledge in the same way as Piaget's theory of cognitive equilibration. Knowledge is divided into two categories, experiential and explanatory. The explanatory knowledge must fit the experiential knowledge and enable prediction of this knowledge. Yet, the criterion is fit to the experiential knowledge, not match reality. The resulting explanatory knowledge is "not, however it may seem, uniquely determined by the external world" (Einstein & Infeld, 1938). The same can be said of knowledge in any field attempting to construct rational explanation of specified sets of experiential knowledge.

This status of our knowledge can free us, and our students, from a kind of totalitarian oppression from truth claims about the world. It also places on each of our students and us a responsibility for the understandings we construct to fit experience. This responsibility is distributed among all of us individually and collectively, instead of being the sole province of authority. As such, different notions of the roles of teachers and students are called for than with the traditional, realist view of knowledge.

In contrast, with the realist notion of knowledge, our understanding of the world is a match to the world and we can know the extent to which it is a match to the world. This understanding is taken to be as true a statement of the actual nature of the world as possible at present. In this view of the nature of knowledge, it is natural for the truth of understanding as being a match to reality to be the province of authority. The commonly understood roles of teacher and student in society today are a natural outcome of this view of knowledge: teacher as authority, student as the recipient of the presented truth, as it is presently known. The student has no responsibility or capacity for the creation of the knowledge. Consequently, the student is not engaged in developing skills to construct new knowledge in standard instruction.

Piaget's Theory and Implications for Teaching

Frequently the notion of teaching is expressed as "passing the accumulated knowledge of previous generations on to the next generation." In more operational terms, it can be stated as the presentation of the established canon by approved methods for the benefit of those capable and ready. This notion is a folk theory because (1) it is accepted by all, but (2) rarely if ever itself critically examined. This folk theory of teaching is the apparent basis for the design of teacher preparation programs and for the nature of efforts to evaluate teaching at all levels.

Piaget's work can be viewed from the point of view of this traditional notion of teaching. In this view, Piaget's description of stages of development of reasoning can serve to explain why many students do not 'get' what has been presented.[2] If what is presented requires a stage of development of reasoning a student has not as yet achieved, then the meaning of what is presented will not be accessible to the student. The student is not yet capable or ready. Logically then the instructor needs to adjust what is presented or how it is presented to match the stages of reasoning of the students or influence the students to advance in their stages of reasoning or both.

Both tasks, adjusting the level of reasoning of what is presented and engaging students in advancing their stages of reasoning, are challenging. Can the level of reasoning for a particular element of the canon be adjusted? Is this adjusted version of the canon appropriate to the rest of the curriculum for the present course? Can the stages of reasoning of the students be advanced to the required level for the expected elements of the canon to be presented? To meet the demands for coverage in the curriculum is it also possible to influence the development of students' stages of reasoning in the time available? Some instructors have addressed these challenges with positive results. Their teaching practices have become permanently changed. Many others are unaware of this perspective or have determined these challenges cannot be met. Their teaching practices still match the time-honoured traditions of the folk theory of teaching.

Let us go deeper beyond the stages of reasoning into the implications of Piaget's theory of cognitive equilibration for learning and therefore teaching. Because Piaget called his work, genetic epistemology, it is best characterized as experimental philosophy. He investigated, and his colleagues still investigate, the origins and development of knowledge in human beings. Necessarily, then the nature of human knowledge is a central issue. Piaget stated in several places in direct terms that his view of the nature of human knowledge is distinctly different from the view of knowledge based on realism. The realist view of the nature of knowledge has been stated as:

> ... we postulate the objective existence of physical reality that can be known to our minds ... with an ever growing precision by the subtle play of theory and experiment. (de la Torre & Zamorano, 2001, p. 103)

The metaphysical realist *looks* for knowledge that *matches* reality in the same sense as you might look for paint to match the color that is already on the wall you have to repair. In the epistemologist's case it is, of course, not color that concerns him, but some kind of "homomorphism," which is to say, an equivalence of relations, a sequence, or a characteristic structure—something, in other words, the he can consider *the same*, because only then could he say that his knowledge is *of* the world. (Glasersfeld, 1984, *emphasis* in the original, pp. 20–21)

The folk theory of teaching is entirely consistent with this realist view of knowledge.

In contrast Piaget and his colleagues take a very different view of the nature of human knowledge as their starting point:

Knowledge is not a copy of reality. To know an object, to know an event, is not simply to look at it and make a mental copy or image of it. To know an object is to act on it. (Piaget, 1964, p. 171)

It is clear there is an undeniable role played by experience in cognitive development; however, the influence of experience has not resulted in a conception of knowledge as a simple copy of outside reality. (Piaget, 1972, p. 8)

To understand is to invent. (Piaget, 1976)

This decidedly non-realist view of the nature of human knowledge makes Piaget's theory of cognitive equilibration fundamentally constructivist in nature and not particularly consistent with the folk theory of teaching.

In the folk theory knowledge is a kind of commodity which exists outside the minds of people. This type of knowledge can be put or transmitted into a person's mind by appropriate methods. When the transmission into a recipient's mind appears to have failed, in the folk theory, the knowledge was either poorly transmitted or the recipient was not capable nor ready to receive this knowledge. Since this knowledge can be stated so as to be presented, then to check to see if a student has received it, the teacher asks the student to present it back in some way. The focus is on specified words and specified actions. The student "gets" these words and actions or not as evidenced by how reliably they are recited back.

In contrast, in a view of teaching based on Piaget's theory of cognitive equilibration, coming to know the world is a construction of cognitive schemes *by the student*. The schemes cannot be told to the students and cannot themselves be directly observed. The role of the teacher becomes not that of master presenter and authority, but that of one who engages students in examining the fit between their existing schemes and new experiences and then in constructing and testing new schemes for fit, when existing schemes appear not to fit these experiences. Evidence of new schemes, new knowledge, can only be discerned in changes of behavior, predictions, expectations by the students. It is not a recitation of what has been seen or heard.

In a Piagetian or constructivist teaching practice, the focus is not on a canon of knowledge and not on presenting something. Instead, the central object of manipulation is the students' cognitive schemes of understanding or conceptions of the phenomena. Only the students can modify or reconstruct their own cognitive schemes. Because the motivation to change existing schemes is the students' perception of disequilibration, then if there is to be change in existing schemes, students must encounter experiences that do not fit their explanatory schemes. Students need to disequilibrate to some degree.

The teacher's basic tools then become understanding the students' conceptual schemes about a phenomenon and knowing a wide variety of experiences with the phenomenon that can be produced in class or lab. The teacher must deploy methods of engaging students in examining their own conceptual schemes in comparison with experiences that do not fit their schemes in order to maximize the possibility for disequilibration. Sometimes these experiences are physical, as in a study of forces on moving objects.[3] Sometimes these experiences are social, as in the example of discussion surrounding a stationary book on a table.[4] Either way and often as a result of responses to both kinds of experience, students refine and test possible conceptual schemes until ones that fit, both these new experiences and previous experience, are found. The modification and testing of schemes is carried out in a social setting and the criteria of fit are checked in physical interaction with the examples of the phenomenon at hand. As a result, students who have participated in this process know which plausible ideas do not work and which do work and they can point out specific examples they have tested of both.

This description of an entirely different practice of teaching, not driven by a canon, initially can appear to be essentially laissez-faire and have no place in the context of "subject matter teaching." However, if we ask ourselves a question such as: What is physics?[5] One way to think about the division of the turf of experience is to see physics as the investigation of particular aspects of the world in particular ways. Each science has its own slice of the pie. There are overlaps, but there are large areas of non-overlap. Hence, what makes a physics course physics is the aspects of the world studied and the questions asked in the course of these investigations.

The Piagetian or constructivist teaching practice briefly described in the previous paragraph is well suited to investigating aspects of the physical world. (Dykstra et al., 1992; Dykstra, 2005) Under such a teaching practice, students engaged in constructing for themselves new understandings of motion and the nature of force, for example, are seen to develop for themselves what any physicist would agree can be called Newtonian conceptions of the nature of motion and its relationship to force. In fact, a much greater percentage of students accomplish this under these circumstances than typically do in courses taught folk theory teaching practices. (Dykstra & Sweet, 2009; Dykstra, in press A, in press B) Yet, in this instructional practice, Newton's laws of motion are never presented either in text or in class.

Delving Deeper Into Piaget's Theory

Over the years there has been much debate over Piaget's ideas and evidence. Lourenco and Machado (1996) conducted a very thorough analysis and response to criticisms of Piaget's theory. They point out that most of the criticisms of Piaget's theory are based in misunderstandings of the theory. This is a challenge also faced by those holding views in which knowledge holds a similar status to that supported in Piaget's theory. (Dykstra, 2007)

Piaget's work spanned about 60 years. Piaget and his colleagues generated a very large body of published work in that time, not all of it in English and some not well translated into English. Chapman (1988) produced a detailed exposition and explanation of Piaget's ideas and their development. It covers Piaget's work from 1918 until his death in 1980.

Claims

Since the latter half of the twentieth century, two names have figured prominently in the attention of those interested in learning in classrooms. These two names are Jean Piaget and Lev Vygotsky.

In the early 1970s Piaget, already known among early childhood educators, was introduced into science education through Robert Karplus' work with the early childhood educators in the Science Curriculum Improvement Study (SCIS), funded by the National Science Foundation in the United States. This book documents the initial introduction by Karplus and colleagues of Piaget's ideas into the physics teaching community and the science teaching community in higher education and beyond. Some of the writing of Piaget and his group was available in English at the time. More of this writing has become available over time, but not all of it is available in English even at the time of the publication of this book.

Later in the 1980s the English-speaking science education community became aware Vygotsky's ideas (Pines & West, 1986). Vygotsky's ideas applied to learning has come to have a strong following not only in science education, but in other areas of education, as well. As we shall see, Vygotsky's ideas have strong appeal to those concerned with the effect of social interaction on learning (Otero, 2006).

Part of our effort in this chapter is to examine claims concerning the relationship between Piaget's ideas and Vygotsky's ideas. The first claim is that Piaget only concerned himself with the individual, whereas Vygotsky included the whole picture, which includes the social interactions or culture in the classroom. The second frequently made claim is that Vygotsky picked up where Piaget left off and expanded from the individual to the culture (Otero, 2006). The third claim is that Piaget and Vygotsky were both constructivists (Pass, 2004).

In what follows, we will compare and contrast the work of Piaget and Vygotsky. The status of these claims will become clear.

Piaget[6] and Vygotsky[7]

Jean Piaget was born in 1896 in Neuchâtel, Switzerland, a French-speaking region of Switzerland, the grandson of the originator of the Piaget watch company and son of a professor of medieval literature. Lev S. Vygotsky was born in 1896 in Belarus, Russia, the son of a local bank executive and community cultural leader. Vygotsky died in 1934 and Piaget in 1980. They were contemporaries of sorts, at least during Vygotsky's short life. However, Piaget was able to continue his work another 46 years. While Vygotsky apparently had access to Russian translations of Piaget's work from the 1920s, Piaget only had access to Vygotsky's work by word of mouth until the 1962 publication in English of Vygotsky's book, Thought and Language, originally published in Russian in 1934 (Vygotsky, 1962).

Vygotsky's focus as a psychologist was on the mediation of learning by culture. Among other examples, he observed such interactions as between parent and child and between teacher and students, established cultural practices. Piaget's focus as an experimental philosopher was the nature and development of reasoning and of conceptual schemes. He watched and listened to children interacting with their worlds; interacting with each other, making predictions, and explaining their experiences and predictions. Piaget was not studying established cultural practices.

These two very different foci of attention resulted in different views of the nature of knowledge and development. Vygotsky was able to see this because he had access to Piaget's publications from the 1920s. Chapter 2 in Vygotsky's book (1962) is titled, "Piaget's Theory of the Child's[8] Speech and Thought." On reading the chapter it becomes very clear, very quickly

Vygotsky is explaining what he views as fundamental errors in Piaget's theory.

Piaget was invited to respond to this chapter and parts of chapter 6, "The Development of Scientific[9] Concepts in Childhood: The Design of a Working Hypothesis," as well, in the English translation of Vygotsky's Thought and Language (1962). Piaget's response (2000)[10] was translated into English and included as a pamphlet tucked inside the cover of the original English edition of Vygotsky's book, not bound into the book. In responding Piaget faces the formidable task of a response 28 years later in the light of, as well as in spite of, his findings and changes in thinking during the same 28 years. Piaget writes in his response: "on certain points I find myself more in agreement with Vygotsky than I would have been in 1934, while on other points I believe I now have better arguments for answering him." Then, he discusses similarities and differences in their views of egocentric speech and the role it plays in development.

Later after describing how the normal order of introduction of aspects of geometry in school is opposite the order in which children appear to construct their geometric knowledge as they experience the world, Piaget (2000) writes:

> From such examples, which could be multiplied, it becomes easy to answer Vygotsky's comment. In the first place, he reproaches me for viewing school learning as not essentially related to the child's spontaneous development. Yet it should be clear that to my mind it is not the child that should be blamed for the eventual conflicts, but the school, unaware as it is of the use it could make of the child's spontaneous development, which it should reinforce by adequate methods instead of inhibiting it as it often does. In the second place—and this is Vygotsky's main error in his interpretation of my work—he believes that according to my theory adult thought, after various compromises, gradually "supplants" child thought, through some sort of "mechanical abolition" of the latter. Actually, today I am more often blamed for interpreting spontaneous development as tending of its own toward the logico-mathematical structures of the adult as its predetermined ideal!

Piaget goes on to address the issue of the interaction between spontaneous and nonspontaneous concepts. In Vygotskian literature in English the nonspontaneous concepts are named scientific concepts, but this is intended to mean concepts from the culture to be learned in school, what has been called established canon earlier in the present chapter or concepts from culture to be taught to students. In Vygotskian literature, by those other than Vygotsky as well, the interpretation seems to be that at least some of the spontaneous knowledge is at odds with the learning of "scientific," nonspontaneous concepts (Pines & West, 1986). On this issue Piaget suggests: "Vygotsky in fact misunderstands me when he thinks that from my point of view the child's spontaneous thought must be known by educators only as an enemy must be known to be fought successfully." Piaget (2000) goes on to describe the difference between himself and Vygotsky where these two types of concepts are concerned:

> This interaction is more complex than Vygotsky believes. In some cases, what is transmitted by instruction is well assimilated by the child because it represents in fact an extension of some spontaneous constructions of his own. In such cases, his development is accelerated. *But in other cases, the gifts of instruction are presented too soon or too late, or in a manner that precludes assimilation because it does not fit in with the child's spontaneous constructions. Then the child's development is impeded, or even deflected into barrenness, as so often happens in the teaching of the exact sciences.* Therefore I do not believe, as Vygotsky seems to do, that new concepts, even at school level, are always acquired through adult didactic intervention. This may occur, but there is a much more productive form of instruction: the so-called "active" schools endeavor to create situations that, while not "spontaneous" in themselves, evoke spontaneous elaboration on the part of the child,[11] if one manages both to spark his interest and to present the problem in such a way that it corresponds to the structures he had already formed himself. [emphasis added]

Piaget (2000) gives another distinction between his view and Vygotsky's:

> It would seem that, according to Vygotsky (though of course I do not know the rest of his work), the principal factor is to be sought in the "generalization of perceptions," the process of generalization being sufficient in itself to bring mental operations into consciousness. We, on the other hand, in studying the spontaneous development of scientific[12] notions, have come to view as the central factor the very process of constructing operations, which consists in interiorized actions becoming reversible and co-coordinating themselves into patterns of structures subject to well-defined laws. The progress of generalization is only the result of this elaboration of operational structures, and these structures derive not from perception but from the total action.

Of course, the description of differences between Piaget and Vygotsky from the Vygotskian point of view can be expected to be different in some way. Unfortunately, there is the popular version of distinctions between Piaget and Vygotsky often repeated and seen everywhere, a simplistic story in terms of mutually exclusive orientations, individual vs. culture. In such versions, Piaget saw knowledge as constructed by the individual and Vygotsky saw it as constructed socially. However, there is also the reasoned academic discussion of these differences found in rare instances. One such by Cole and Wertsch reveals that neither Piaget nor Vygotsky saw the origins of knowledge in such narrow ways. As with any serious academics, they state their case with reference directly to Piaget's works and the works of Vygotsky and those who worked directly with him. They summarize by writing:

> There is little doubt in our view that there is still much to be learned from both Piaget and Vygotsky, and in many cases the strengths of one theorist complement the weakness of the other. However, we believe that discussions of these two figures' accounts of mind and its boundaries are not well served by overly rehearsed debates about the primacy of the individual or the social. Instead, we have argued that the more interesting contrast between them concerns the role of cultural artifacts in constituting the two poles of the individual-social antimony. For Vygotsky, such artifacts play a central role in elaborating an account of what and where mind is. In pursuing this line of inquiry, he focused on a set of issues and phenomena that do not appear to have any clear counterpart in Piaget's thinking, and consequently may be more appropriately characterized as being different, rather than directly in conflict with those at the center of Piaget's project. (Cole & Wertsch, 1996)

Vygotsky in Brief

Vygotsky's focus being on cultural mediation, this mediation becomes the central, driving issue. A novice in a society first learns to repeat the words or skill of a "scientific" concept. With participation in culture repeating this concept or skill, the initial capacity is followed by the ability to use the words or skill of the concept in context. Finally, becoming an experienced member of society, as a result of the first two stages, the person comes to appropriate the concept, that is, take ownership of the concept, making it one's own by a kind of action on cultural experience and experience in culture. By this last stage, the individual has constructed an understanding of the concept with the culture.

In the cultural interactions that foster this development, there is interaction with culture in the form of more experienced members of the culture. At any given time during schooling for example, there is a range of cultural concepts and activities in which the novice can function competently independently. Just beyond this, there is a range of cultural concepts and activities in which the novice can only function competently in concert with or with the aid of a more experienced member of the culture. Beyond that is the range of cultural concepts and activities in which the novice cannot participate competently, even with aid. It is in the middle range, called the zone of proximal development that teachers should work with students. The students participating in concepts and activities with the teacher, then come to appropriate the concepts and activities moving toward full independent, competent participation in the culture. The result is that the inner range of independent competency expands and the zone of proximal development moves out into the range, as yet beyond competency.

The process of development described involves mediation, primarily in the form of language. For Vygotsky, language came to mean quite a wide range of means developed in the culture: speaking, writing, mathematics and its symbols, maps, diagrams, structured cultural environments, all sorts of artefacts developed in and by the culture. This approach to consideration of "language" is now known as semiotics. Development of mind, that is learning and development of higher mental functions, then occurs as the novice comes to appropriate more and more of the artifacts of the culture. As such, development of mind is culturally mediated, made possible by culture.

Cultural mediation involves not a direct action on the world, but action that takes place through the agency of these cultural artefacts as one gains mastery of them. Hence, one comes to know the world only indirectly through and with the aid of the cultural artefacts. Previous generations of the culture, whose mental work resulted in the artefacts as they are now, thus mediate the development of the future generations in the culture. One consequence is that mind is not just in the head according to the Vygotskian view. Higher mental functions are the result of the biological individual, through cultural artefacts, interacting with the world. Mind is distributed in the biological individual and the culture with its artefacts.

Piaget in Contrast: A View From a Teaching Perspective

For Vygotsky, it seems culture and its artefacts, what they are and mean to the culture, exist independently of the person. This is a kind of exterior perspective, exterior to a person. What the artefacts are and mean to the culture exist externally to a person and are impressed on the person who appropriates them to become a competent member in the culture. For Piaget, the focus was not culture and its artefacts impressing their meaning on the person from outside. Instead for Piaget, the person makes meaning by constructing it to fit experience, physical and social.

For Piaget, meaning exists in the mind, constructed within the mind. Meaning does not exist outside the mind in something physical or sociocultural, independently of minds. The existence of other minds, other persons, for a person is a construction by the person to fit experience, called social experience with culture, socio-cultural experience. The nature of and meaning content imputed to other minds is constructed by the person to fit the person's social experience

The Piagetian person constructs and tests schemes of understanding to fit both physical and social experiences in the same way. Such constructions of social experiences, that is, constructions of culture by the person, have no more truth status than any other such constructions, because the only criterion one can apply is fit to the evidence. One has no other way of knowing the meaning of another; hence one has to construct one's own meaning of the meaning of others (Glasersfeld, 2007).

For the instructor whose goal is for students to leave a course having developed new, deeper, more powerful understandings of the phenomena studied, the challenge is how to engage them in accomplishing this. We see from science education research, the consequence of assuming meaning, what things really are, can be impressed on students is essentially a spectacular failure in terms of any evidence of conceptual change (Duit, 2008). We also see as Piaget (2000) points out: "the child's development is impeded, or even deflected into barrenness, as so often happens in the teaching of the exact sciences."

These null and negative results are primarily due to efforts to impress knowledge as truth on students as though it can come from outside, well meaning and sincere though these efforts may be. The idea that meaning exists outside the mind in things and can be impressed on or into the mind is a basic tenet of a realist view of knowledge, as opposed to a Piagetian or constructivist view of knowledge. In the realist view, the truth-value of the knowledge justifies the pressing of the knowledge on students' minds. The negative consequences are then rationalized by the notion that not all students are capable or work hard enough, blaming the victims for the failures. But, it can be demonstrated that students so assessed, when participating in an entirely different Piagetian or constructivist teaching practice, do develop new, deeper understanding of the phenomena. It is not the students, but the teaching practice, which is at fault.

The Vygotskian notion that mind exists beyond the biological person, including the biological person and culture, strongly begs a realist-type view of knowledge. It is certainly easier for a realist to adopt a Vygotskian view without having to threaten one's realist tenets concerning knowledge, than it is to take Piaget's view of knowledge, which cannot be done without letting go of realism. When one adopts ideas from Vygotsky, Piaget or both, but without change to a basic realist view of the nature of knowledge, the result is generally consistent with the folk theory of teaching with its attendant null and negative results. On the other hand, if one adopts ideas from Vygotsky, Piaget, or both, taking a Piagetian or constructivist view of the nature of knowledge in one's teaching practice, such null and negative results are not the outcome for students. It is possible to interpret the Vygotskian ideas on culture and its interaction with a member of that culture from a Piagetian point-of-view.

Fact From Fiction

Claim One: Piaget Only Concerned Himself With the Individual Without Concern for the Social and Vygotsky Only With the Social (Cultural). Piaget from early in his work, whenever he enumerated the factors that influence cognitive development, always included social interaction as one of these factors, as we have described above. It is the case that some of the publications of Piaget and his colleagues are not translated into English even yet.[13] Their work on social interactions was not translated into English and published until 1995 (Piaget, 1995). As a consequence, most of the famous English-speaking critics of Piaget were and remain unaware of this work on social interaction.

Those who may not have taken the opportunity to look at Piaget's work itself, who may only know Piaget's work from second-hand sources, might easily have this impression that Piaget did not concern himself with the social aspects. But, serious scholars, such as Michael Cole and James Wertsch, two of the most respected American scholars on and translators of Vygotsky have written the following (Cole & Wertsch, 1996):

> Standard discussions of the difference between Vygotsky and Piaget place a crucial difference in the proximal locus of cognitive development. According to the canonical story, for Piaget, individual children construct knowledge through their actions on the world: to understand is to invent. By contrast, the Vygotskian claim is said to be that understanding is social in origin.
>
> There are (at least) two difficulties with this story.
> **First** of all, in principle, Piaget did not deny the co-equal role of the social world in the construction of knowledge. It is possible to find plenty of places where he says that both individual and social are important.
>
> There are no more such things as societies qua beings than there are isolated individuals. There are only relations ... and the combinations formed by them, always incomplete, cannot be taken as permanent substances. (Piaget, 1932, p. 360)
>
> ... there is no longer any need to choose between the primacy of the social or that of the intellect: collective intellect is the social equilibrium resulting from the interplay of the operations that enter into all cooperation. (Piaget, 1970, p. 114)

Second, Vygotsky, contrary to another stereotype, insisted on the centrality of the active construction of knowledge. This insistence is reflected in passages such as the following, which, ironically, Vygotsky wrote as part of a review and critique of Piaget's account of egocentric speech: "Activity and practice: these are the new concepts that have allowed us to consider the function of egocentric speech from a new perspective, to consider it in its completeness.... But we have seen that where the child's egocentric speech is linked to his practical activity, where it is linked to his thinking, things really do operate on his mind and influence it. By the word things, we mean reality. However, what we have in mind is not reality as it is passively reflected in perception or abstractly cognized. We mean reality as it is encountered in practice." (Vygotsky, 1987, pp. 78–79)

Thus one can see that the canonical notion described by Cole and Wertsch, essentially claim one, is an over-simplification, which distorts understanding of both Piaget and Vygotsky. It is simply not the case that Piaget thought only in terms of the individual, not the social, or that Vygotsky thought only in terms of the social, not the individual.

Claim Two: Vygotsky Came Along After Piaget and Took Up Where Piaget Left Off. Clearly, Vygotsky did not come along after Piaget. They were contemporaries and Vygotsky died 46 years before Piaget. It is also clear from Vygotsky's (1964) writing about Piaget's work and Piaget's (2000) response to Vygotsky's criticisms that they were not on the same path, even as early as the 1920s. Their notions concerning the nature of knowledge were different, hence the essence of their theories is different. It is apparently the case that for most in the West, Piaget's work was introduced before Vygotsky's work, but this has little to do with what Piaget and Vygotsky actually did. Coupled with the negative conclusion concerning Claim one, it is not the case that Vygotsky picked up where Piaget left off.

Claim Three: Piaget and Vygotsky Were Both Constructivists. If the only criterion for constructivism is that people construct their own understanding, then one would have to agree with this claim. We need to examine these two constructivisms more closely, as has begun above in this chapter.

Piaget's constructivism is not simply that people construct their own understanding. As we have described, Piaget's constructivism is not rooted in the position of realism concerning the nature of knowledge. The construction in Piaget's view is necessitated by the more fundamental idea that knowledge only exists in the mind. It is not a match, or close match, to what is independent of mind, what gives rise to experience. Instead it fits experience; hence it is not a description of reality in the sense of the realists. Knowledge does not reside in the experiential world, which includes the social, as well as, the physical.

Vygotsky's ideas appear to include the notion that mind exists across the biological individual and the culture in which the individual dwells. This immediately differentiates the two positions and apparently the two constructivisms. The extent to which Vygotsky's ideas include the notion that knowledge is of the realities of meaning in the culture, which exist independently of the individual, this represents a fundamental difference between the constructivisms of Piaget and of Vygotsky. The extent to which cultural meaning perceived by the individual is a match or copy of that in the culture and its more experienced members, this also is a fundamental difference between the constructivisms of Piaget and Vygotsky. If these two extents do indeed effectively describe Vygotsky's ideas, then it appears Vygotsky's notions may be rooted in a version of realism. This makes Vygotsky's constructivism distinctly not the same as Piaget's constructivism. The claim that they were both constructivists obfuscates the important differences and allows one to remain comfortable in one's realism.

CONCLUDING REMARKS

These often repeated claims distract people from facing and surmounting the real challenges of understanding either Piaget's theory of cognitive equilibration or Vygotsky's theory of mind in society. Distracted, then people tend to see either in terms of a description of the world, as they already know it. Consequently, the world does not change for them nor does their teaching practice.

The problem with preservation of teaching practices is that standard folk-theory teaching does not impact students' understandings of the canon taught, but it does impact their self-images and how they categorize people. From folk-theory teaching most students learn that there are two types of people: those who are good at something and those who are not. In the case of folk-theory science teaching, most learn they are in the latter category. Yet, we know from physics education research that the "problem" is not that too few are good at science. Instead, the problem is the instructional practices. Substantial change in teaching practice, such as has been described above, can result in nearly every student making major changes in their understanding of the phenomena. Does this not lead to the moral and ethical necessity of changing teaching practices away from folk-theory methods?

The insights of Piaget and Vygotsky into the cognitive development of human beings are both challenging to everyday norms: Piaget because of his non-realist notions of the nature of knowledge and Vygotsky because of his notions of mind in culture. Both are different conceptions of mind and knowledge, but these are not reasons to walk away from their contributions. Every day we as college professors are faced in the classroom with students whose conceptions of such things as force or evolution or the nature of atoms are profoundly different than ours as scientists (Duit, 2008). This does not discourage us from being teachers. We should not let the challenges of understanding Piaget and Vygotsky allow us not to benefit from their theories (Kalman, 2008). Understanding them more deeply will assist us in our quest to help students understand their world and themselves more deeply and powerfully.

NOTES

1. An analogy here would be the observational fact that one needs to form a complete electrical circuit before the circuit "works" is not a theory of electricity in a circuit. This fact is an element of experiential knowledge that must be accounted for in any useful or practical theory of electricity explaining the operation of the circuit.
2. Since the late 1970s, strongly influenced by the introduction of Piaget's work and interview methods, the physics education research community has been examining evidence of students' conceptions of physical phenomena. The general finding is that very little change in students' conceptions occurs as a result of traditional, folk theory instruction. This work has expanded into the other sciences. An 8,400 entry bibliography of published work is being kept at the University of Kiel in Germany (Duit, 2008).
3. See for example Dykstra's work in the Appendix to Dykstra (1992).
4. See for example Minstrell's work in Minstrell, 1982. In this example students encounter a difference in view as to whether a table can exert a force upward on a book resting on it. The resolution is not possible by measurement. It comes from students understanding each other's points of view.
5. Or: What is chemistry?, What is biology?, What is geology? ... psychology, history, philosophy, and so forth?
6. A good link to material on Piaget: http://www.piaget.org/index.html
7. A good link to material on Vygotsky: http://www.massey.ac.nz/~alock/virtual/project2.htm
8. Both Piaget and Vygotsky were attempting to describe and explain the cognitive development of human beings. They primarily studied young people in the ages of most observable development, hence the references to the child and children. It should be noted that (1) the age range covered by the term "child" is not always the same for these and other authors in the field as is in everyday use in the United States and (2) Piaget's and Vygotsky's descriptions of development are intended to apply to human beings in general. As such, their ideas are applicable by college professors in their teaching.
9. The term "Scientific" in translations of Vygotsky's work does not refer to science. Instead, it refers to concepts that the child must learn from culture about which more can be found later in this chapter.

10. The original response was published as an extra pamphlet tucked into the back of Vygotsky's book and is not easily available in that form. Subsequently, it was made generally available in *New Ideas in Psychology* in 2000.
11. This description is very consistent with the description of a Piagetian or constructivist teaching practice described earlier in this chapter.
12. Here in responding to Vygotsky's work, Piaget is using the term "scientific" in the way Vygotsky does, as the formal concepts, which are presented in school and through other cultural means. In Piaget's theory this distinction does not really exist.
13. One such piece is on the development of conceptions of force, which would be particularly interesting to physicists.

REFERENCES

Chapman, M. (1988). *Constructive evolution.* Cambridge, England: Cambridge University Press.

Cole, M., & Wertsch, J. V. (1996). Beyond the individual-social antimony in discussions of Piaget and Vygotsky. In L. S. Vygotsky, M. Cole, A. Lock, & J. Wertsch (Eds.), *The virtual faculty's second project:* Retrieved from http://www.massey.ac.nz/~ALock/virtual/project2.htm

de la Torre, A. C. & Zamorano, R. (2001). Answer to Question #31. Does any piece of mathematics exist for which there is no application whatsoever in physics? *American Journal of Physics,* 69(1), 103.

Duit, R. (2008). *Students' and teachers' conceptions and science education.* Kiel, Germany: University of Kiel, Institute for Science Education. Retrieved from http://www.ipn.uni-kiel.de/aktuell/stcse/stcse.html

Dykstra, D. I., Jr. (2007). The challenge of understanding radical constructivism. *Constructivist Foundations, 2*(2&3), 50–57. Retrieved from http://www.constructivistfoundations.info/2.2

Dykstra, D. I., Jr. (2005). Teaching introductory physics to college students. In C. Fosnot (Ed,), *Constructivism, foundations, perspectives and practice* (2nd ed., pp. 182–204). New York: Teachers College Press.

Dykstra, D. I., Jr. (in press A). *Why teach kinematics?: An examination of the teaching of kinematics and force–I.* Submitted to Physical Review Special Topics: Physics Education Research. Retrieved from www.boisestate.edu/physics/dykstra/WTK1.pdf

Dykstra, D. I., Jr. (in press B). *Why teach kinematics?: An examination of the teaching of kinematics and force–II.* Submitted to Physical Review Special Topics: Physics Education Research. Retrieved from www.boisestate.edu/physics/dykstra/WTK2.pdf

Dykstra, D. I., Jr., Boyle, C. F., & Monarch, I. A. (1992). Studying conceptual change in learning physics. *Science Education,* 76(6), 615–652.

Dykstra, D. I., Jr., & Sweet, D. R. (2009). Conceptual development about motion and force in elementary and middle school students. *American Journal of Physics,* 77(5), 468–476.

Einstein, A., & Infeld, L. (1938). *The evolution of physics*. New York: Simon & Schuster.

Glasersfeld, E. V. (1984). An Introduction to Radical Constructivism. In P. Watzlawick (Ed.), *The invented reality* (pp. 17–40). New York: W. W. Norton.

Glasersfeld, E. V. (2007). The constructivist view of communication. In A Müller & K. H. Müller (Eds.), *An unfinished revolution* (pp. 351–360). Vienna: Edition Echoraum.

Jammer, M. (1999). *Concepts of force*. New York: Dover. (originally work published 1957).

Kalman, C. S. (2008). *Successful science and engineering teaching: Theoretical and learning perspectives*. New York: Springer.

Lourenco, O., & Machado, A. (1996). In defense of Piaget's theory: A reply to 10 common criticisms. *Psychological Review, 103*(1), 143–164.

Minstrell, J. (1982). Explaining the "at rest" condition of an object. *The Physics Teacher, 20*, 10-14.

Otero, V. (2006). *Benefits and limitations of Vygotsky's theory of concept formation*. Paper presented at the 2006 Summer Meeting of the American Association of Physics Teachers, Syracuse University in Syracuse, NY.

Pass, S. (2004). *Parallel paths to constructivism: Jean Piaget and Lev Vygotsky*. Charlotte, NC: Information Age.

Piaget, J. (2000). Commentary on Vygotsky's criticisms of Language and Thought of the child and judgments and reasoning in the child. *New Ideas in Psychology, 18*, 241–259.

Piaget, J. (1995). *Sociological studies*. New York: Routledge.

Piaget, J. (1976). *To understand is to invent: The future of education*. New York: Penguin.

Piaget, J. (1972). Problems of equilibration. In C. F. Nodine, J. M. Gallagher, & R. H. Humphreys (Eds.), *Piaget and Inhelder on equilibration* (pp. 1–20). Philadelphia: The Jean Piaget Society.

Piaget, J. (1970). *Structuralism*. New York: Basic Books.

Piaget, J. (1964). Part I: Cognitive development in children: Piaget development and learning. *Journal of Research in Science Teaching, 2*(3), 176–186.

Piaget, J. (1932). *The moral judgment of the child*. London: Routledge & Kegan Paul.

Pines, A. L., & West, L. H. T. (1986). Conceptual understanding and science learning: An interpretation of research with a sources-of-knowledge framework. *Science Education, 70*(5), 583–604.

Vygotsky, L. S. (1987). The collected works of L.S. Vygotsky Vol.1: Problems of general psychology. Including the volume Thinking and speech (N. Minick, Trans.). New York: Plenum.

Vygotsky, L. S. (1962). *Thought and language*. Cambridge, MA: MIT Press.

CHAPTER 14

COLLEGE PROGRAMS

INTRODUCTION

The original faculty workshop offered to the physics teaching community was utilized as the basis for an expanded version for all general education faculty. This new workshop was developed at the University of Nebraska-Lincoln (UNL) by the ADAPT faculty and was first offered on the UNL campus in March of 1975. The first off campus offering of the workshop was at Xavier University of Louisiana in January of 1976. Over the next decade, the College Teaching and Development of Reasoning workshop was offered at more than 100 different locations in the United States and Canada. Several hundreds of university and college faculty were participants in workshop experience lasting from one to three days. These experiences struck a resonant chord with many of these faculty. These materials were also used for graduate student teaching assistant and teacher-in-service training. The ADAPT Program became a de-facto national clearing house for information about college programs that focused on the development of student reasoning. There were three national conferences on college teaching for the development of reasoning, two in Denver hosted by Metropolitan State College and one in Boise hosted by Boise State University. By the year 1980 there were 14 such programs around the country.

This chapter will provide recent information about those programs which began in the late 1970s and continued into the 1980s.

Researching Programs

In the fall of 2008 we began to seek information about the cognitive development programs which were started in colleges around 1980. Some contact had been maintained with the ADAPT leadership over the years and this information provided a good starting point. Reestablishing contact with faculty after more than 30 years proved to be difficult. However, with the use of the Internet, at least one participant in almost all established programs was located. The results of these contacts are summarized below in a listing of programs existing in the 1970–1980 time period. The listing provides a reference to the source of external funding, the host college or university, and a partial listing of faculty and staff who were responsible for starting the program on each campus. The names of the persons involved in each program may be incomplete. The persons known to have been directors, principal investigators or coordinators are listed first. The others are in alphabetical order and represent different disciplines. Essays about each program that were written about 1982 are available in PDF versions from the University of Nebraska Lincoln Digital Commons Web site: http://digitalcommons.unl.edu/adaptessays/. The names and acronyms of these fourteen programs are given in Appendix D. These programs were not identical, but did share several similarities:

- The programs were all cognitive-based utilizing a constructivist, Piagetian-type model for developing formal operational thought and moving students from concrete to formal operational reasoning.
- All programs were offered to beginning college students.
- Many faculty initiating each project had attended a workshop on intellectual development.
- All programs were initiated during the late 1970's and most had ended by the early 1990s. The sole remaining program is the SOAR Program at Xavier University of Louisiana.
- All programs were multidisciplinary, including at least two disciplines, and program faculty worked together to discuss their lesson plans and integrate the classroom experiences for students enrolled in the program.

Table 14.1.

Program	Funding	College or University	People Originally Involved	Dates
ADAPT	Exxon Ed. Fund. $100,000	Univ. of Nebraska Lincoln, NE	Fuller, Thornton, Narveson, Bergstrom, Carpenter, Duly, McShane, Moshman, Peterson, Petr, Tomlinson-Keasey, Weinberg, Williams,	1975-1997
DOORS	FIPSE, $100,000	Illinois Central College, IL	Campbell, Thompson, McGill, Miller, Taylor, Teal	1976-78
COMPAS	FIPSE, $100,000. An umbrella Program for the following seven community college programs. Campbell, PI			1978-80
CREATE	FIPSE	Surry CC, NC	Stevens, Gupton, Reeves, Selby	1978-82
DOORS	FIPSE	Illinois Central College, IL	Campbell, Thompson, Miller, Taylor, McGill, Teal	1979-82
LIFT	FIPSE	CC of Allegheny Co., PA	Cunningham	1978-82
PATH	FIPSE	William Rainey Harper CC, IL	Windham, Butzen, Fojo, Kolzow, Smith, Waite	1978-82
RISE	FIPSE	Prairie State CC, IL	Schmitz, Alexander, Faulkner, Haywood, Herbach, Kephart, Moore, Uram	1978-82
STARS	FIPSE	Seminole CC, FL	Dickison, Coulter, Detwiler, Ek, Johnson, Jordon, Mason, McAdan, Morrison, Schermerhorn, Wilcox, Wright	1978-82
STEPPE	FIPSE	Joliet Jr. College, IL	Miner, Cooper, Hodgman, Nicoll, Piket, Schields, Warman	1978-82
DORIS	NSF	Cal. State Univ. Fullerton, CA	Collea	1980-83
FAR	NSF	College of Charleston, SC	Kubinec, Drake, Oberman-Soroka, Ohr, Prazak, Wiseman	1980-83
SOAR	Kenan Fund.	Xavier Univ. of LA	Carmichael, Hassell, Hunter, Jones	1976-2009
The 4th R	FIPSE	Piedmont Tech. College, SC	Miles, Allred, Mahaffey, Murphy, Rehg, Upchurch	1976-82
The Cognitive Program	internal	Essex County College, NJ	McMahon, Griffith, Halper	1977-81
STAR	internal	Metropolitan State College, CO	Warrick, Killian, Cohen, Farkas, Friot, Gingras, Hahs, Hoffman, Otto, Plachyu, Purchatzki, Williams, Wilson,	1976-82

- Nearly every program included a person tasked to evaluate the effectiveness of each program in achieving its goals.

The ADAPT Program

The ADAPT Program began in the fall of 1975 as the result of an Exxon Education Foundation funding for a Multidisciplinary Piagetian-based Program for College Freshmen. For its first 2 years the Program features two semesters of six courses, anthropology, economics, English, history, mathematics and physics. All of the students in the program were enrolled in all of the courses. Each student had earned 30 semester hours of credit towards graduation by the end of their year in the ADAPT program.

The reasoning patterns used by ADAPT students were extensively studied at the end of their ADAPT year. Their intellectual growth was compared to that of typical freshmen at the University of Nebraska Lincoln (UNL). Those evaluations showed ADAPT student demonstrated considerably more growth than other UNL freshmen (http://digitalcommons.unl.edu/adaptessays/31/)

At the end of its second year when released time funding to hire senior faculty to teach freshmen ADAPT courses was no longer available, the ADAPT program shifted to a program of three 3-credit courses that the students took as cohorts. Each cohort consisted of about 24 students who took the three courses together. The courses were usually anthropology, English and physics. On occasion other social science courses were substituted for anthropology. Those included history, sociology, economics and psychology. On occasion a one credit career development course was included in the ADAPT program. Frequently the Myers-Briggs personality inventory was used with the students as well.

The ADAPT Program was sustained by local funding until 1997. It grew to about three cohorts of students, about 72 students per year. In 1981 the second semester physics course was replaced by a Problem Solving Using Computers course, also taught by a physicist, in a computer laboratory setting.

The extensive evaluation of the ADAPT program diminished after 1980. (For a summary of the 5 years of evaluation (see http://digitalcommons.unl.edu/adaptessays/20/) The faculty teaching in the ADAPT program used their ADAPT teaching assignment as a replacement for another part of their usual teaching assignment. They kept coming back to the ADAPT program to share in the students Ah-ha experience in the *Learning Cycles* used in the ADAPT classes. A more complete history of the ADAPT program was published in *The Genetic Epistemologist, 26:2*

(1998) *and 27:3* (1999) and is available at http://digitalcommons.unl.edu/adaptessays/1/.

THE DOORS Program

As the ADAPT Program began in the fall of 1975 after a semester of planning, Thomas Campbell was visiting the University of Nebraska Lincoln. He had been awarded a sabbatical leave from Illinois Central College (ICC) to work at the university and pursue an advanced degree. While at UNL he was able to observe first hand the ADAPT faculty at work and to attend some of their classes.

Campbell's initial impressions were very positive and he immediately asked to be informed concerning the background, philosophy and psychology of the program. Because his higher education experience was with community colleges, his questions often centered on how this type of program would translate into an effective program for community college students. Throughout the 1975–76 academic year, Campbell participated in as many ADAPT activities as possible. He coupled this with the work on an advanced degree and shortly became knowledgeable of the fundamentals of the Piagetian model of intellectual development and the inter workings of the ADAPT program

Using the ADAPT experience as background, the DOORS project was born in the form of a grant from the Fund for the Improvement of Post Secondary Education (FIPSE). Campbell returned to ICC to begin the program in the fall of 1976.

The first task was to obtain administrative approval. This was easily accomplished because the grant form the U.S. Department of Education was supporting the project concept and underwriting the cost.

Next, Campbell selected five additional faculty to join him in the project. Campbell selected from the best general education faculty on staff at the time. The group added a professional counselor to assist with designing and implementing the student selection and advising components of the project. This proved to be a critical part of the success of the program because identifying and tracking each student entering the program was very time consuming. In addition, students in this type of program need to be provided special group activities and functions to help identify the group of students active in the program as a whole. This group identity was uncommon for community college students who often have difficulty forming and maintaining social groups.

In the Summer of 1976, the DOORS faculty began meeting together to plan the program. To begin, the faculty traveled to Lincoln, Nebraska to meet with the ADAPT faculty and to complete a 1-day intensive Piaget workshop. This activity provided a baseline of understanding concerning the psychological aspects of the Piagetian model for the development of reasoning. Time was also provided for the DOORS faculty to meet individually with members of the ADAPT faculty who taught similar disciplines. This one-on-one time was very valuable when coordinated with the workshop. ADAPT faculty were able to provide the DOORS faculty with specific examples of the classroom materials they had developed for use in the Nebraska program. This provided a quick infusion of ideas directly related to the task set before the DOORS faculty; creating classroom materials utilizing the *Learning Cycle* classroom as a classroom methodology for an entire 16-week class.

Upon returning to ICC, the DOORS faculty began meeting on a regular basis to discuss the development of new materials for the program. The faculty found this work to be challenging and time consuming. As the weeks went by, the process began to flow more smoothly. Initially, these faculty had lots of questions about teaching using this new methodology. These meetings became a regular part of the fall semester for the DOORS faculty. As faculty prepared learning cycle exercises, they presented them to the other DOORS faculty and received feedback. Looking back, this was an extremely effective faculty development opportunity, and provided an excellent format to encourage faculty from different disciplines to talk to one another about student learning and development. During these discussions many critical concerns dominated the discussion. They included:

- Most of the planned classroom activities would require extensive class time. How could the class objectives be met and all of the content covered while giving up class time for these activities?
- The very nature of the classroom activities encourage students to internalize the concepts rather than memorize content. How can the extent of their learning be measured, or evaluated?
- Participating students would be enrolled in several DOORS classes during the semester. How could the faculty best integrate these classes for the benefit of the program and the development of the students?

A semester of planning was hardly enough time to prepare for an entire semester of teaching. On average, participating faculty were able to develop materials for the first 4 weeks of teaching and share these plans with the other DOORS faculty. The remaining lessons would be prepared as needed during the 1977 spring semester as the classes were taught. Other considerations for the program would include defining a target audience of students, developing program enrollment requirements, developing a student intake process, defining evaluation criteria, and developing marketing materials that could be used to notify college and high school academic advisors, department chairs and other faculty of the program and its benefits.

The DOORS faculty decided that the audience would be beginning college students (no previous college credits earned), Students with undefined career goals, and students with average to just below average high school academic records, or older adult students who were returning to school to begin their college careers. Whereas the ADAPT program required students to enroll in the program for an entire year, the DOORS faculty determined that this model would be too restrictive for community college students.

Following considerable discussion, the program at ICC would be one semester in length, students would be required to enroll in both DOORS English and DOORS Mathematics, and then select at least two additional DOORS classes from the following: economics, sociology, history, and physics.

The DOORS program was first offered to students at Illinois Central College on a trial bases in the Spring of 1977. The new program initially attracted a small number of students. This slow start allowed project faculty an opportunity to experiment with the newly developed classroom materials.

During the summer of 1977, the DOORS faculty again met together to review and revise the curriculum materials. This effort proved to be very valuable. Faculty now had experience with the format and results of using the *Learning Cycle* teaching methodology. While faculty continued to be concerned with their failure to cover all of the content usually included in these general education classes, they agreed that the effort to strengthen students' cognitive skills was also an important goal. During these discussions the faculty also realized their efforts to integrate the classes via class content was not working. However, they realized the program classes were integrating the reasoning skills which were basic to the six disciplines. After isolating and describing the skills, they were arranged in a natural ascending order, and faculty agreed to present students with classroom experiences focused on these cognitive skills at the following prescribed time schedule (see Table 14.2 next page).

In the fall of 1977, DOORS classes were offered to thirty-two students. Each faculty member selected class content appropriate to the general education class they were teaching, but presented this content utilizing the cognitive skills outlined in the schedule above. The impact of this organization was immediately recognized by the attending students. They appreciated the work by cooperating faculty and were quick to comment on the relationship of the disciplines they were seeing as they attended DOORS classes.

Table 14.2. DOORS Cognitive Skills Time Table

Timeline	English/History/Sociology	Math/Econ/Physics
Week 1	Observation(identification of variables)	Observation(identification of variables)
Week 2	Description(describing variables)	Description(describing variables)
Week 3	Comparing & Relating (comparison and contrast)	Comparing & Relating (graphing)
Week 4	Comparing &Relating (comparison and contrast)	Inferring (graphing)
Week 5	Classification	Classification
Week 6	Classification	Separation and control of variables
Week 7	Summary	Hypotheses Statements
Week 8	Cause and Effect	Separation and control of variables
Week 9-15	More advanced use of skills	More advanced use of skills

Project COMPAS

Following 2 years of successful operation, the DOORS program was gaining momentum at Illinois Central College. Through the efforts of the DOORS and ADAPT faculty members, and the interest expressed by other community colleges in starting programs at their locations, the COMPAS PROGRAM (Consortia for the Operation and Management of the Piagetian Application of Skills) received funding from the U.S. Department of Education's FIPSE program.

This Program called for the development of DOORS-type programs at six additional community colleges starting in 1979. These included:

- CREATE at Surry Community College, Dobson, NC
- LIFT at the Community College of Allegheny County, West Mifflin, PA
- PATH at William Rainey Harper College, Palatine, IL
- RISE at Prairie State College, Chicago Heights, IL
- STARS at Seminole Community College, Sanford, FL
- STEPPE at Joliet Junior College, Joliet, IL

The 2-year FIPSE grant was approved in 1979 and work began on the project. Support was extended to the six selected community colleges for faculty to develop and teach core courses in a freshman program placing emphases on the development of basic reasoning skills. While some latitude was provided to encourage programs to be unique, each local site was to retain some of the fundamental features of the ADAPT and the DOORS programs, including:

- Class presentations were to be based on the Piagetian Model for enhancing reasoning skills, utilizing the *Learning Cycle*.
- Programs should be designed for entering college freshman
- Program courses selected at each site should include some of the DOORS content areas.

The consortium officially began in December of 1979 with a 2½ day workshop for all project personnel. The workshop materials were developed by the ADAPT faculty and modified by the DOORS faculty to meet the needs of community college faculty.

A unique feature of the workshop included an opportunity for faculty to meet in content area groupings to discuss ways to use the Piagetian Model in the teaching of college classes. Non-teaching personnel (counselors and evaluators) from each site met with DOORS personnel to discuss student selection, screening, and evaluation procedures.

Site coordinators began meeting with their program personnel in the spring of 1980. DOORS faculty visited each program site to assist with the development and to encourage program faculty.

Student feedback following participation in these unique programs was impressive. Students recognized a distinct difference between classes taught using the cognitive development techniques compared to other classes they attended.

When faculty teaching in the programs were asked to reflect on the student comments they had received, several consistent themes were expressed:

- Students recognized the interdisciplinary benefits and made connections between the classes taught in the program. Students noted the obvious collaboration among faculty in planning lessons and pacing class schedules.
- Students noted the class atmosphere of openness and encouragement building a rapport among students and between students and instructors.
- Students reported seeing a direct relationship between course content and the real world.
- Students were far less likely to drop program classes and student attrition approached zero.

- Students formed friendships with other students in the program, unlike typical community college students who have difficulty identifying social relationships.

When asked about program weaknesses, faculty pointed out a variety of complicating factors:

- Classroom material development was very time consuming.
- The problem of giving up class time for activities rather the covering of content was difficult to reconcile.
- The open-ended nature of the classroom activities produced a new level of anxiety for students and faculty.
- Finding and implementing appropriate forms of evaluation and measuring student progress was difficult.
- The student selection process developed for the programs proved difficult to administer.

As the funding for the programs was terminated, most of the colleges struggled with the logistics of continuing. Lead faculty and support staff drifted away from involvement as their careers advanced. Several of the programs altered their plans to accommodate these changes as best they could. As a result some remnants of most of the programs could be found 4 or 5 years later, but nearly all of the programs were gone by 1990.

Faculty Use of the *Learning Cycle*

The key ingredient of the cognitive programs was found in the *Learning Cycle* which was used in developing classroom activities and presentations. This unique methodology was developed to assure that students experienced the proper cognitive challenge to encourage the development of the formal operational characteristics described by Piaget.

As faculty members were challenged to follow this construct in developing classroom materials, many unique lessons resulted. As the authors attempted to locate and correspond with these pioneering faculty, they were asked to recall their experience and describe a *Learning Cycle* which stands out in their minds. The two examples of these reflections are offered in Appendices E and F.

COMPAS Program Evaluation

Because the COMPAS Program was FIPSE funded, an evaluation by an independent professional was required. Dr. Melvin Hall, Sangamon State University, Springfield, IL, was selected to complete this task. This effort was complicated by the complexity of several variables difficult to control or measure: student selection, student immersion in the program, the variation of programs between colleges, the impact of campus socialization and the lack of recognized assessment tools for measuring growth in cognitive skills. These difficulties were offset by the large number of students who were enrolled in the seven programs and the unique evaluation design utilized.

The programs were evaluated using measures that produced both qualitative and quantitative data.

Qualitative Data Results

"Of the many factors monitored during evaluation, the one which seemed to summarize the rest was immersion. The degree to which a student—

- felt a part of something different,
- was consistently exposed to *Learning Cycles*,
- was involved in a variety of program classes which had high percentages of program students, and,
- became involved in program activities.

These factors seemed to dictate performance on all preset criteria for program success. The type of student identified in program recruitment profiles, the type of faculty involved, the classroom atmosphere, reliance of Piaget's theory, and the program's focus of cognitive development all served as independent variables in an apparent causal chain where various measures of immersion became the dependent outcome" (Hall, 1982).

Quantitative Data Results

The quantitative data yielded results which lead to several conclusions. First, the cognitive scale constructed for this study was reliable and gave several indications of validity. This adds to the strength of the conclusions.

The major conclusion from the cognitive data is that the programs at the various schools were able to effect a change in cognitive performance, though the magnitude of the change differed between locations....any attempt to determine which students will benefit from the program on the basis of pre-enrollment scores is unwarranted. Additionally, there was no evidence that the cognitive measure, the placement tests or the ACT predict classroom performance.

At every institution, the movement of the students was toward formal operations. The schools which showed the most dramatic change...(in the qualitative change) also showed the most dramatic shift in percentages of students toward the higher level, the result one would predict. The most notable characteristics of the individual data were the change in the total sample from 65% formal operational on the pretest to 83% on the post-test and the fact that at the beginning of the study 31% of the subjects did not give evidence of being formal operational. The latter finding agrees with previous research which has suggested that a substantial percentage of college students has not achieved formal operations. (Hall, 1982)

Survival of Piagetian-Based Programs

Reflection has always provided keen insights. Our situation with the development and operation of these unique programs is no exception. Years later, we continue to have many questions about our effort and why the programs did not continue. Each of us constructs a view from the data and other outcome information we have now in hand, and places a value on the outcomes which have shaped our careers. What then can we understand from our efforts to construct and operate the Piagetian-based programs outlined in these pages? And what can we say about the their failure to continue?

After some 30+ years since the ADAPT program began in the Fall of 1975, very little remains from the 14 programs we have outlined. The majority became extinct shortly after external funding was eliminated. This is unfortunate and may point to the difficulty innovators face when developing, managing, and attempting to sustain programs outside the traditional curriculum boundary.

Looking back our construct is somewhat disappointing, but not all that surprising. We greatly enjoyed our efforts, and continue to believe we were positively impacting students in a unique and positive way. We did not find this sense of satisfaction from teaching in the traditional freshman college classroom. We still sense the positive aspects of using these instructional methodologies which allowed us to see students from a totally new and refreshing point of view. Piaget's model opened lines of communications between students and instructor we could never have imagined. From this vantage point we learned as much from our students as they learned from our classes.

Evaluation of student growth was conducted on a regular basis. This assessment was made difficult due to the unique outcomes we were attempting to foster. Measuring cognitive growth is not a traditionally recognized student outcome. Students are usually evaluated on knowledge and facts and their ability to demonstrate this knowledge on factual examinations. This is especially true in the freshman experience. We were required to utilize non-traditional evaluation methods to assess non-traditional outcomes. The traditional academic establishment had a difficult time understanding these outcomes much less accepting or embracing them. This situation was often frustrating and defeating. Faculty using the Piagetian approach could, however, sense the excitement of the student classroom experience.

In summary what common threads of evidence could shed some light on the diminishing record of the programs we have outlined in this publication? As we consider this question, we cannot help but wonder what common threads of evidence would capture the essence of the historical record which shows the disappearance of the 14 programs featured. Here is a summary of our thoughts.

Institutional Support

At the onset, externally funded programs are easily endorsed buy an institution. Fresh new ideas come with a certain grace period. In this stage, these new approaches are not well known and pose little threat to the mainstream academic community. Institutions give latitude to experiment with what is seen as "low-risk" and "not invented here" programs. Even the most critical "budget watch dogs" are pleased to see new dollars roll in on the wave of excitement. Looking back, we have the distinct feeling that the frontal institutional support for our programs, while initially genuine, was for the most part superficial and fleeting. The nature of the deeply rooted support was not there to carry our programs to the point that a real change in institutional culture could occur, and the new methodology could be recognized and adopted.

In retrospect, it seems obvious now that "institutional attention" to fundamental changes in teaching methodology and instructional philosophy are short lived. Eventually, attention turns toward the "newest" program to receive outside funding or recognition. Yesterday's innovation becomes past "lack luster" efforts, not totally understood or embraced for continuation.

At this point, institutions tend to turn back toward the basics of how the academic machine has always operated: placing major emphasis on lecture-recitation learning environments which are the most efficient methods for teaching facts and conveying knowledge. We acknowledge and embrace this as true,. However, in our experience, this only speaks to a portion of the equation when considering how students think and learn new concepts. Students need more than presentation of facts, they need a classroom environment that will engage them in learning activities that challenge and improve their cognitive skills. In our experience, no innovative instructional program, no matter how successful will be allowed to penetrate the institutional culture which places great value on the learning of facts and storing information.

We admit that these are strong statements and have been generalized from our experience with a finite number of programs. But, as we reflect on the experiences, we believe that our outcomes match the experience of countless other instructional innovations.

Assessment and Evaluations

Clearly, a shortfall of our efforts related to outcome assessment. We were challenged from the start to provide compelling data from our programs that would substantiate the impact of our instructional programs and clearly convey these to the institution. While we did a through job of evaluating, the results did not impress the traditionalist because the data revealed student progress in terms not valued by the mainstream. The result was a fundamental disconnect. Our instructional values embraced cognitive growth; the traditional institution valued the demonstration of facts learned. Without the assessment of improvement of facts and gained knowledge, our programs seemed doomed from the start.

Individual Commitment

Innovative instructional projects require a huge effort by a committed core of individuals. In retrospect, while we adequately prepared for the initial requirements to begin our projects, the long-term, year-after-year commitment was more than we anticipated. In part, this occurred due to the need for more institutional support as described above. In retrospect we misjudged the subtle building momentum from the traditional academic community to sidetrack our programs as either "not effective" or "too costly."

Also, during the waning years of our programs, individuals, once committed to the programs, began to leave looking for other challenges. This occurred at a critical time in the life of these programs when more effort was needed to maintain the program while fighting for continuance against mounting forces. While tired program organizers scramble to meet new institutional mandates, they begin to realize that efforts to re-think or re-track the program would not be successful. In the end, the institutions turned to known traditions and left the innovative programs behind.

In the final analysis, we believe our efforts were substantial and the methods are needed at most colleges and universities. The lasting part of our experience lives on in the way it has changed our view of the instructional process. Over the years since elimination of the programs, converted faculty have continued to influence students using the cognitive methods advocated by these initiatives.

This publication offers faculty an alternative perspective on student learning. The essence of the college classroom is seen to be active student minds constructing better and more adaptive mental schemes. When set against this dynamic view of a college classroom the traditional classroom methods seem weak. The fallacy of the "content autocrats" who control the goals of higher education is clear. We believe the faculty who become engaged in the ideas proposed in this publication will not be satisfied with traditional methods of teaching. If they turn their back on these concepts, we believe the Spirit of Piaget will come to them in the quiet of their nights and ask, "What are you doing to encourage your students to develop their own reasoning?"

REFERENCE

Hall, M. (1982). *Project COMPAS: A design for change.* Lora L. Schermerhorn, Lorraine D. Williams, & Alexander K. Dickison (Compilers and Editors) (pp. 51–74). Sanford, FL: Seminole Community College.

> ... what I am talking about is something that we have left out of our talk of promoting development: What do we do about the house we leave when we go to a new place? When we leave the way we saw the world, in which everything was just so and just as we thought, and we see it all differently, we move in to a world where all of what was solid and known is crumbling. And the new is untried. What do we do about the house we just sold out of? What do we do about the old simple world? It may be a great joy to discover a new and more complex way of thinking and seeing, but what do we do about all the hopes that we had invested and experienced in those simpler terms? When we leave those terms behind, are we to leave hope, too?
>
> Does the teacher have a responsibility here, not other to promote growth and development, but to help people to do something with the losses?
>
> —Perry (1978)

APPENDIX A

Bibliography[1]

Bringuier, J-C. (1980). *Conversations with Jean Piaget*. Chicago: University of Chicago Press:

Chapman, M. (1988) *Constructive evolution: Origins and development of Piaget's thought*. New York: Cambridge University Press.

Duit, R. (2008). *Students' and teachers' conceptions and science education*. Kiel, Germany: University of Kiel, Institute for Science Education. Retrieved from http://www.ipn.uni-kiel.de/aktuell/stcse/stcse.html

Furth, H. (1969). *Piaget and knowledge: Theoretical foundations*. Englewood Cliffs, NJ: Prentice Hall.

Inhelder, B., & Piaget, J. (1958). *The growth of logical thinking from childhood to adolescence: An essay on the construction of formal operational structures*. New York: Basic Books.

Inhelder, B., Sinclair, H., & Bovet, M. (1974). *Learning and the development of cognition* (S. Wedgwood, trans.). Cambridge, MA: Harvard University Press.

Karplus, R. (1964). The science curriculum improvement study. *Journal of Research in Science Teaching, 2*(4), 293–303.

Lourenço, O., & Machado, A. (1996). In defense of Piaget's theory: A reply to 10 common criticisms. *Psychological Review, 103*(1), 143–164.

Piaget, J. (2000). *The child's conception of physical causality*. New York: Transaction Publishers.

Piaget, J. (1985). *The equilibration of cognitive structures: The central problem of intellectual development* (T. Brown & K. J. Thampy, Trans.). Chicago: University of Chicago Press.

Piaget, J. (1981). *Intelligence and affectivity: Their relationship during child development* (T. A. Brown & C. E. Kaegi, Trans.) Palo Alto, CA: Annual Reviews.

Piaget, J. (1980). *Experiments in contradiction* (D. Coltman, Trans.). Chicago: University of Chicago Press.

Piaget, J. (1978). *Success and understanding* (A. J. Pomerans, Trans.). Cambridge, MA: Harvard University Press.

Piaget, J. (1975). *The development of thought: Equilibration of cognitive structures* (A. Rosin trans.). New York: The Viking Press.

Piaget, J., Inhelder, B., Furth, H., Stephens, W. B., & Gallagher, J. M. (1971). *Piaget and Inhelder on equilibration: Proceedings of the First Annual Symposium of the Jean Piaget Society.* E. Duckworth, C. F. Nodine, J. M. Gallagher & R. D. Humphreys (Trans., Eds.). Philadelphia: The Jean Piaget Society.

Piaget, J. (1964). Cognitive development in children: Development and learning (E. Duckworth, Trans.). *Journal of Research in Science Teaching, 2,* 176–186.

NOTE

1. Publications authored or coauthored by Piaget are listed by the date they were published in English, not by the date they were originally published in French.

Implications of accumulating data on levels of intellectual development

Arnold B. Arons
Department of Physics, University of Washington, Seattle, Washington 98195

Robert Karplus
Lawrence Hall of Science, University of California, Berkeley, California 94720
(Received 14 October 1975)

For several years data have been accumulating regarding the fraction of various population groups at various age levels that have made the transition from "concrete operations" to "formal operations" in accordance with the increasingly familiar and empirically documented Piagetian Taxonomy.[1]

Using various Piagetian tasks (or modifications thereof) involving such aspects as conservation reasoning, control of variables, syllogistic reasoning, recognition of inadequacy of information, arithmetical proportional reasoning, etc., investigators have examined school, college, and adult populations ranging in age from about 13–45 yr.[2-8] Although the various investigations are beginning to reveal significant and interesting differences between social and economic groups, the grand averages have been emerging, with very little variation throughout the age and school level spectrum: about one-third have made the transition to formal operations, about one-third can be regarded as in the process of transition, and about one-third use primarily concrete patterns of reasoning.

The accumulating data can undoubtedly be interpreted in a variety of ways depending on the orientation and predilections of the interpreter, but we feel compelled to underline the following possible very grave implication for our society: If it is indeed true that one-third of the school population is formal operational by the age of about 14 while one-third is still concrete and that these proportions do not change substantially from then on in spite of further schooling (including at least some university levels), then we face the implication that our educational system is not contributing significantly to intellectual development (abstract logical reasoning). The one-third who become formal operational may well be *sui generis*, making the transition on their own regardless of the educational system, while the remainder are not being helped to make the progress that should be a major objective of formal education.

This is not to say that the educational system fails to develop certain basic skills such as reading, writing, and reckoning and various compendia of necessary facts and information (albeit there is much argument and criticism of the adequacy with which even these aspects are cultivated); our concern here is over the levels of intellectual development the educational system appears to generate.

If perpetuation and advancement of a democratic society do indeed demand the broadest participation of a thinking–reasoning citizenry, if intelligent participation does involve abstract reasoning on matters such as, for example, what constitutes *enlightened* self interest, if more people must be counted on to engage in decision making when confronted with incomplete, "on the one hand . . . and on the other hand" evidence shorn of reliance on a "pat" answer from an ultimate "expert" (as cogently argued recently by David),[9] then we *must* gear our educational system to greater effectiveness in enhancing intellectual development than the incoming data show it to exert.

If our suggested inference is correct, it seems to us that explicit awareness of the problem, and measures to attack it, must begin in the colleges and universities. These institutions educate the teachers for the educational system with which we are concerned. They must provide leadership in converting it from a passive one that merely allows the *sui generis* development of a small fraction to one that actively assists the intellectual development of the far larger proportion of the population we have every reason to believe is fully capable of abstract logical reasoning. We recognize that a number of institutions and scattered clusters of faculty members have initiated attacks on this problem. We emphasize, however, that significant progress can only result from far broader and more explicit awareness and from far more massive and wide spread efforts than have yet been activated in the realm of higher education.

[1] J. Piaget and B. Inhelder, *Growth of Logical Thinking* (Basic Books, New York, 1958).
[2] J. W. McKinnon and J. W. Renner, Am. J. Phys. **39**, 1047 (1971).
[3] J. W. Renner and A. E. Lawson, Phys. Teach. **11**, 273 (1973).
[4] A. E. Lawson and A. J. D. Blake, AESOP report, Lawrence Hall of Science, University of California at Berkeley, 1974 (unpublished).
[5] R. Karplus, E. Karplus, M. Formisano, and A. C. Paulsen, AESOP Report No. ID-25, Lawrence Hall of Science, University of California at Berkeley, 1975 (unpublished).
[6] R. P. Bauman, in proceedings of the AAPT Summer Meeting at Boulder, CO, June 1975 (unpublished).
[7] D. Kuhn, J. Langer, L. Kohlberg, and N. S. Haan, J. Genet. Psychol. (to be published).
[8] A. Arons and J. Smith, Sci. Educ. **58** (3), 391 (1974).
[9] E. E. David, Science **189**, 679 (1975).

Can physics develop reasoning?

The findings of Swiss scholar Jean Piaget suggest that it can—
by helping people achieve a series of four distinct but overlapping stages
of intellectual growth as they search for patterns and relationships.

Robert G. Fuller, Robert Karplus and Anton E. Lawson

The life of every physicist is punctuated by events that lead him to discover that the way physicists see natural phenomena is different from the way nonphysicists see them. Certain patterns of reasoning appear to be more common among physicists than in other groups. These include:

▶ focussing on the important variables (such as the force that accelerates the apple, rather than the lump it makes on your head);
▶ propositional logic ("if heat were a liquid it would occupy space and a cannon barrel could only contain a limited amount of heat, but this is contrary to my observations, so..."), and
▶ proportional reasoning (for example, the restoring force of a spring increases linearly with its displacement from equilibrium).

In recent studies of the reasoning used by students we have discovered among them qualitative differences similar to those between the reasoning patterns of physicists and nonphysicists.

How can we understand these qualitative differences in reasoning? What role does physics play in the way reasoning develops in young people?

Along with a group of teachers in physics and other disciplines, we believe that some of the answers to these questions can be found in the work of developmental psychologists, especially that of

Robert G. Fuller is a visiting professor of physics at the University of California, Berkeley and a research physicist at the Lawrence Hall of Science while on leave from the University of Nebraska-Lincoln, where he is a professor of physics; Robert Karplus is the acting director of the Lawrence Hall of Science and President of the American Association of Physics Teachers, and Anton E. Lawson is a research associate at the Lawrence Hall of Science, University of California, Berkeley.

the Swiss scholar Jean Piaget. We have helped start a modest movement, accordingly, to inform others of the relevant findings and theories of these social scientists.

To do so we have extended the psychologists' original investigations by dealing with their implications for the presentation of subject matter at the secondary-school and college levels. Textbooks, laboratory procedures, homework assignments, test questions and films may all be examined from the developmental point of view.[1]

In this article we shall describe those ideas in Piaget's work that we have found most useful; you may judge for yourself how valid they are. We shall conclude by suggesting ways in which you can use your expertise in physics and your personal contacts—whether you teach physics or not—to encourage others to develop their reasoning through their observations and analyses of physical systems.

Student responses to puzzles

To study the differences in reasoning used by students, we have devised a number of paper-and-pencil puzzles and given them to high-school and college students. Let us examine the following typical student responses to two of these, the Ticker-Tape Puzzle and the Islands Puzzle,[2] and discuss the differences in reasoning displayed in them by the students.

The responses to the Ticker-Tape Puzzle (see the Box on page 25) were collected from engineering and science students in an introductory physics course. Some of them had completed the term covering newtonian mechanics, others had not. Here are samples:

Fred (had used ticker tape)
1 B—Dots are spaced equally.
2 C—Dots are closing together, cart is

going less distance in the same time.
3 A—Dots are getting farther apart, cart is moving farther in same time (accelerating).
4 D—Cart is falling through air; it has a rapid acceleration.

James (had not used ticker tape)
1 B—At constant speed, the same distance will be covered per unit time.
2 E—Deceleration means less velocity, so less distance per unit time.
3 D—Acceleration is exponential, ruling out A.
4 C—Assume a frictionless system, with brakes momentarily applied between dots five and six.

The responses to the Islands Puzzle (see the Box on page 26) were collected from a wide variety of adolescents and adults. These two are typical:

Deloris (College student, age 17)
1 "Yes, because the people can go north from Island D—because in the clue it could be made in both directions."
2 "No; I am presuming both directions doesn't include a 45° angle from B to C."
3 "Yes, because Island C is right below Island A."

Myrna (College student, age 17)
1 "Can't tell from the clues given. The two clues don't relate the upper islands to the lower ones."
2 "Yes; they can go from B to D, and then to C, even if there are no direct flights."
3 "No, if they could go from C to A, then the people on B could go first to D, then to C, and then on to A. But this contradicts the second clue, that they don't go by plane between B and A."

You will notice some similarities between the responses of Fred (to the Ticker-Tape Puzzle) and Deloris (to the Island Puzzle). They both focus on the specific details of the puzzle. Fred makes

The wheels are turning as these two students compare the angles of rotation of three intermeshing gears. Their search for numerical relationships will help them develop proportional reasoning and understand when to apply this pattern of thought. The ability to handle functional relationships such as proportionality is a characteristic of formal reasoning, the fourth of Piaget's stages of intellectual development.

direct correspondence between the arrangement of the dots and the physical examples given. Although he introduces the idea of "acceleration," he does not indicate that he has any more than a vague general idea of its meaning. In a similar way, Deloris concentrates on the spatial arrangement of the islands. Her explanations have more to do with her perception of the physical arrangement of the islands than with the clues given in the puzzle. Both Fred and Deloris appear limited in their reasoning to the specific details of a puzzle, and do not readily relate the facts of the puzzles to more general principles.

Consider, on the other hand, the responses of James and Myrna. Both of them have made conjectures to facilitate answering the questions. James, who had not previously used a ticker tape, begins his explanations with generalized concepts such as constant speed, deceleration, acceleration and a frictionless system. Even when his explanation is wrong ("acceleration is exponential") he demonstrates that he is reasoning within a system of deduction from hypotheses, in which a ticker tape can serve as one specific example representative of a more general principle.

Myrna, as she reasons about the Islands Puzzle, fits the clues into an overall scheme for explaining the air travel between the islands. She suggested a hypothetical trip, demonstrating the correctness of her answer by reasoning to a contradiction. James and Myrna display patterns of reasoning commonly used by physicists.

Even in the responses to these simple written puzzles, the qualitative differences in student reasoning are vividly displayed. For an understanding of these differences, let us turn to the work of Piaget.

The development of reasoning

Jean Piaget began his research on children in about 1920. The results of his work of primary concern to us are reported in the book, *The Growth of Logical Thinking from Childhood to Adolescence*.[3] In this book the responses of young people to various tasks concerning physical phenomena are described. These tasks included physics experiments such as those on the equality of the angles of incidence and reflection, the law of floating bodies, the flexibility of metal rods, the oscillation of a pendulum, the motion of bodies on an inclined plane, the conservation of momentum of a horizontal plane, the equilibrium of a balance and the projection of shadows.

On the basis of the responses, Piaget and his co-workers developed a theory for interpreting the development of what he considers to be universal patterns of reasoning. Pivotal to this theory is the concept of *stages of intellectual development*. The stages—there are four in the theory—are characterized by distinctive features in the patterns of a person's reasoning. It was hypothesized that each of Piaget's four stages serves as a precursor to all succeeding stages, so that reasoning develops sequentially, always from the less effective to the more effective stage, although not necessarily at the same rate for every individual.

Like a concept in any theory, a stage of intellectual development is a simplification that is helpful in analyzing and interpreting observations, somewhat like a point particle or a frictionless plane in mechanics. In this spirit, we should not expect that most people during their period of development will exhibit all the reasoning characteristics of, say, stage A for a certain period of time and then suddenly change to all the reasoning patterns appropriate to stage B. Rather, the development of a person's reasoning should be thought of as gradual, at a particular time showing the features of stage A on some problems while exhibiting certain features of stage B on others. The stage concept therefore may be more useful for classifying reasoning patterns than for describing the overall intellectual behavior of every particular person at a given time.

The first Piagetian stage is called *sensory-motor*. This stage is characteristic of children's thinking from birth to about two years of age. Piaget's work with infants provided an explanation for the humor of the "peek-a-boo" game: The young infant appears to think that the only objects that exist are the objects that can be seen. The sudden "creation" of a large person by removing a blanket covering him does seem to be a funny event. Subsequent experiences provide the child with the opportunity to develop an awareness of the permanence of material objects.

The concept of permanence provides the basis for the child's need for language. If objects do exist when they are out of sight, then it is useful to have symbols (or words) to represent them. So the sensory-motor stage serves as the precursor for the next, *pre-operational*, stage.

During the pre-operational period the child is learning words and trying to fit his experiences of the world together. The pre-operational child lives in a very per-

The ticker-tape puzzle

The puzzle below is a task designed to display the variety of student reasoning patterns used in a typical physics classroom activity. It is taken from materials for the workshop on Physics Teaching and the Development of Reasoning offered at the 1975 AAPT–APS meeting in Anaheim, California (reference 1).

```
Start                                                    End
A  [· · · · ·  ·    ·    ·     ·     ·      ·      ·   ]
B  [·   ·   ·   ·   ·   ·   ·   ·   ·   ·   ·   ·   ·  ]
C  [·    ·    ·    ·    ·   ·   ·   ·  ·  ·  · · · · · ]
D  [···· ·       ·       ·        ·         ·          ]
E  [·    ·    ·    ·    ·    ·    ·    ·    ·    ·    ·]
```

Many physics labs allow you to study motion by making timer tapes like the five illustrated above. These are strips of paper attached to a moving object and passing through a timing mechanism that makes a row of small dots by striking regularly at equal time intervals, usually five to ten times per second.
- Have you ever used or watched such a device?
- Identify the tape that fits each of the examples below and justify your answers, taking special care to mention any tapes that a less experienced student might easily mistake for the correct one.

1. A student walking through the laboratory at constant speed   A B C D E
   Justification?
2. A cart gradually slowing down on a level plane   A B C D E
   Justification?
3. A cart rolling freely down an inclined plane   A B C D E
   Justification?
4. Explain how one of the two remaining tapes might have been made, and briefly justify your hypothesis.

Sparks mark the position of the falling object on the ticker tape. The dot patterns can not be analysed readily by that third of US adolescents and adults who use only concrete reasoning.

sonal world with his own ego at the center ("The Sun is following me!"). He puts facts together to produce ad-hoc explanations, such as, "My dad mows the yard because he's a physicist."

The pre-operational child does not use causal reasoning. Some authors have used children's pre-causal explanations as the motif for humorous books. For Piaget, such explanations are clues as to how children think about the world in which they live.

The first two Piagetian stages are usually completed before a person is nine years old. The child's interaction with physical systems plays an essential role in his or her intellectual development during the first two stages. The role of physics in the development of reasoning in the elementary-school years was discussed in a special issue of PHYSICS TODAY.[4]

Concrete reasoning

To explain the qualitative differences in the reasoning patterns of older students' responses to the two puzzles described earlier we must look to Piaget's third and fourth stages of intellectual development, *concrete reasoning* and *formal reasoning*. Certain characteristics help identify reasoning patterns associated with these two stages.

Here are some of the characteristics of concrete reasoning patterns; illustrative examples are added in parentheses:

Class inclusion A person at this stage understands simple classifications and generalizations of familiar objects or events (can reason that all aluminum pieces can close an electric circuit, but not all objects that close a circuit are made of aluminum).

Conservation Such a person reasons that, if nothing is added or taken away, the amount or number remains the same even though the appearance differs (that when water is poured from a short wide container into a tall narrow container, the amount of water is not changed).

Serial ordering The person arranges a set of objects or data in serial order and may establish a one-to-one correspondence ("The heaviest block of copper stretches the spring the most.").

Reversibility A person using concrete reasoning mentally inverts a sequence of steps to return from the final to the initial conditions (reasoning that the removal of weight from a piston will enable the enclosed gas to expand back to its original volume).

Concrete reasoning enables a person to
▶ understand concepts and simple hypotheses that make a direct reference to familiar actions and objects, and can be explained in terms of simple associations ("A larger force must be applied to move a larger mass.");
▶ follow step-by-step instructions as in a recipe, provided each step is specified (carry out a wide variety of physics ex-

College Teaching and the Development of Reasoning

The islands puzzle

The puzzle below is a written task designed to display the variety of deductive-logic strategies used by adolescents (reference 2).

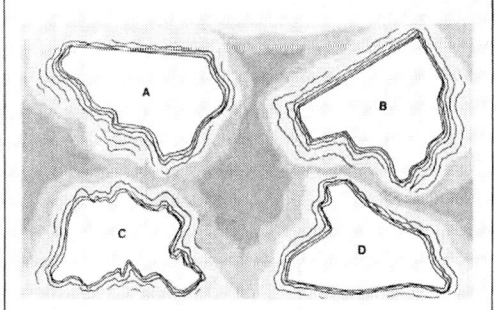

There are four islands in the ocean, Islands A, B, C and D. People have been travelling these islands by boat for many years, but recently an airline started in business. Carefully read the clues about possible plane trips at present. The trips may be direct or include stops and plane changes on an island. When a trip is possible, it can be made in either direction between the islands. You may make notes or marks on the map to help use the clues.

First clue: People can go by plane between Islands C and D.
Second clue: People can not go by plane between Islands A and B.
- Use these clues to answer Question 1. Do not read the next clue yet.
1. Can people go by plane between Islands B and D?
   Yes ___ No ___ Can't tell from the two clues ___ Please explain your answer.
Third clue (do not change your answer to Question 1 now!): People can go by plane between Islands B and D.
- Use all three clues to answer Questions 2 and 3.
2. Can people go by plane between Islands B and C?
   Yes ___ No ___ Can't tell from the three clues ___
   Please explain your answer.
3. Can people go by plane between Islands A and C?
   Yes ___ No ___ Can't tell from the three clues ___
   Please explain your answer.

periments in a "cookbook" laboratory), and
▶ relate his own viewpoint to that of another in a simple situation (be aware an automobile approaching at 55 mph appears to be travelling much faster to a driver moving in the opposite direction at 55 mph).

However, persons whose reasoning has not developed beyond the concrete stage demonstrate certain *limitations* in their reasoning ability. These are evidenced as the person:
▶ searches for and identifies some variables influencing a phenomenon, but does so unsystematically (investigates the effects of one variable without holding all the others constant);
▶ makes observations and draws inferences from them but without considering all possibilities (fails to see all of the major sources of error in a laboratory experiment);
▶ responds to difficult problems by applying a related but not necessarily correct algorithm (uses the formula $s = at^2/2$ to calculate displacement, even when the acceleration is not a constant), and
▶ processes information, but is not spontaneously aware of his own reasoning (does not check his conclusions against the given data or other experience).

The puzzle responses given by Fred and Deloris are examples of concrete reasoning.

Formal reasoning

The following are characteristics of formal reasoning patterns and examples from the history of physics to illustrate them:

Combinatorial reasoning A person systematically considers all possible relations of experimental or theoretical conditions, even though some may not be realized in Nature (for example, using the spectral response of the eye to develop the three-element theory of color vision),

Control of variables In establishing the truth or falsity of hypotheses, a person recognizes the necessity of taking into consideration all the known variables and designing a test that controls all variables but the one being investigated (for example, changing only the direction of the light to detect the possible existence of the ether),

Concrete reasoning about constructs A person applies multiple classification, conservation, serial ordering and other reasoning patterns to concepts and abstract properties (for example, applying conservation of energy to propose the existence of the neutrino),

Functional relationships A person recognizes and interprets dependencies between variables in situations described by observable or abstract variables, and states the relationships in mathematical form (for example, stating that the rate of change of velocity is proportional to the net force),

Probabilistic correlations A person recognizes the fact that natural phenomena themselves are subject to random fluctuations and that any explanatory model must involve probabilistic considerations, including the comparison of the number of confirming and disconfirming cases of hypothesized relations (for example, arguing from the small number of alpha particles scattered through large angles from gold foil to suggest a nuclear model for the atom).

Formal reasoning patterns, taken in concert, enable individuals to use hypothesis and deduction in their reasoning. They can accept an unproven hypothesis, deduce its consequences in the light of other known information and then verify empirically whether, in fact, those consequences occur. Furthermore, they can reflect upon their own reasoning to look for inconsistencies. They can check their results in numerical calculations against order-of-magnitude estimates. James and Myrna, in their responses to the puzzles, gave evidence of using formal reasoning.

In the table on page 28 we summarize some differences between reasoning at the concrete and formal levels. It is quite clear that a successful physicist makes use of formal reasoning in his area of professional expertise. In fact, formal reasoning is prerequisite for producing quality work in physics.

Many theoretical and experimental issues relating to Piaget's work are still being investigated. Piaget's original notion was that all persons use formal reasoning reliably by their late teens. Yet recent studies strongly suggest that, although almost everyone becomes able to use concrete reasoning, many people do not come to use formal reasoning reliably. These persons often appear to be reasoning at the formal level and/or comprehending formal subject matter when

Workshops and programs based on Piaget's concepts

Workshops that focus on physics teaching and the development of reasoning have been offered at professional meetings and on individual college campuses. The workshop materials for examing instructional aids in various subject areas are available from several sources:
▶ Physics Teaching and the Development of Reasoning Workshop Materials, AAPT Executive Office, Graduate Physics Building, S.U.N.Y., Stony Brook, N.Y. 11794;
▶ Biology Teaching and the Development of Reasoning Workshop Materials, Lawrence Hall of Science, Berkeley, Cal. 94720;
▶ Science Teaching and the Development of Reasoning Workshop Materials (includes physics, chemistry, biology, general science and earth sciences), Lawrence Hall of Science, Berkeley, Cal. 94720, and
▶ College Teaching and the Development of Reasoning Workshop Materials (includes anthropology, economics, English, history, mathematics, philosophy and physics materials), ADAPT, 213 Ferguson Hall, University of Nebraska–Lincoln, Lincoln, Neb 68588. Another such workshop is being sponsored by the American Association of Physics Teachers at the joint APS–AAPT meeting in Chicago this month.

College students are being encouraged to develop their reasoning in several programs, including:
▶ physical-science programs, such as those led by Arnold B. Arons, University of Washington (Amer. J. Phys. **44**, 834; 1976) and John W. Renner, University of Oklahoma (Amer. J. Phys. **44**, 218; 1976);
▶ the introductory physics laboratory course for engineering students developed by Robert Gerson, University of Missouri–Rolla, and
▶ two Piaget-based multidisciplinary programs for college freshmen, ADAPT at the University of Nebraska–Lincoln and DOORS at Illinois Central College, East Peoria.

By comparing the extensions of a coil spring at various points, these students are gaining insight into proportionality; such formal-reasoning patterns are attained through self-regulation.

they are actually only applying memorized formulas, words or phrases.

The development of formal reasoning represents an extremely worthwhile educational aim. Formal reasoning is fundamental to developing a meaningful understanding of mathematics, the sciences and many other subjects of modern life. The finding, by a wide variety of studies,[5] that more than one third of the adolescents and adults in the United States do not employ formal reasoning patterns effectively presents a real educational challenge. What can be done about the significant fraction of the population that appears to be stuck at the stage of concrete reasoning?

Self-regulation

As physicists, we can see the advantages to our profession of more widespread use of formal reasoning patterns. To see the role that physics would have to play in creating the necessary atmosphere for this, let us turn to another concept in Piaget's theory of intellectual development, that of self-regulation.

Self-regulation is the process whereby an individual's reasoning advances from one level to the next, an advance that is always in the direction toward more successful patterns of reasoning. Piaget considers this process of intellectual development as analogous to the differentiation and integration one sees in the biological development of an embryo, as well as analogous to the adaptation of evolving species.

A person develops formal reasoning only through the process of self-regulation. Concrete reasoning thus is a prerequisite for the development of formal reasoning.

The process of self-regulation is one in which a person actively searches for relationships and patterns to resolve contradictions and bring coherence to a new set of experiences. Implicit in this notion is the image of a relatively autonomous person, one who is neither under the constant guidance of a teacher nor strictly bound to a rigid set of precedents.

Self-regulation can be described as unfolding in alternating phases, beginning with *assimilation*. The individual's reasoning assimilates a problem situation and gives it a meaning determined by present reasoning patterns. This meaning may or may not, in fact, be appropriate. Inappropriateness produces what is called "disequilibrium." "cognitive conflict" or "contradiction," a state that, according to Piaget, is the prime mover in initiating the second phase—*accomodation*.

Accomodation entails

▶ an analysis of the situation to locate the source of difficulty and
▶ formation of new hypotheses and plans of attack.

Just how this is done varies from person to person and depends upon his analytical and problem-solving abilities. The results of these reflective and experimenting activities are new reasoning patterns that may include new understandings. In terms of assimilation and accommodation, self-correcting activities (accommodation) are constantly being tested (assimilation) until this alternation of phases produces successful behavior. The whole self-regulation process, directed at a stable rapport between patterns of reasoning and environment, is often called "equilibration" by Piaget.

Recall the self-regulation process that Count Rumford recounts in his essays on heat.[6] In Piaget's terms, Rumford experienced cognitive conflict by the extraordinary ability of apple pies to retain their heat, by the fact that heat had no effect upon the weight of objects and by the intense heat of the metallic chips separated from the cannons he bored. He could not assimilate these experiences with the caloric theory of heat, so he rejected that theory. He accommodated his reasoning to experience by developing the idea that heat was excited and communicated by motion.

The development of reasoning has two requirements: Exploratory experiences with the physical world, and discussion and reflection upon what has been done, what it means and how it fits, or does not fit, with previous patterns of thinking. This suggests that experiences gained through physics can play a key role in the development of reasoning and understanding.

Role of the physics community

Let us examine how physics could be used to foster self-regulation in a person. Two factors appear to be required:
▶ He must be faced with a physical situation that he can only partially understand in terms of old ideas and
▶ he must have sufficient time to grapple mentally with the new situation, possibly with appropriate hints, but without being told the answer—people must be allowed to put their ideas together for themselves.

The ideal situation would be one in which the problems experienced are felt to be solvable. The Piaget hypothesis is that a challenging but solvable problem will place persons into an initial state of disequilibrium. Then, through their own efforts at bringing together this challenge with their past experiences and what they learn from teachers or peers, they will gradually reorganize their thinking and solve the problem successfully. This success will establish a new and more stable equilibrium with increased understanding of the subject matter and increased problem-solving capability, that is, intellectual development.

One example of such a use of physics is an exhibit of a spring scale and an equal-arm balance mounted on the wall of an elevator in a public building.[7] The riders in the elevator noticed that the "weight" of the object on the scale varied while the balance remained stationary, a paradox that gave rise to some cognitive conflict. A small card beside the exhibit asked questions and offered hints to encourage the riders to accommodate to this experience.

Physics programs, done properly, can be effective means of promoting intellectual development. Such developmental-physics programs are not aimed at producing more physicists, but at enabling people to develop their potential for formal reasoning. This reasoning can serve them well in many aspects of our technological society.

If physics is an essential element in the growth of reasoning, why are persons so turned off by physics? It seems to us that the physics community has chosen to isolate itself from individuals using primarily concrete reasoning patterns. It has been suggested that *all* of the junior and senior high-school physics curricula that have been developed in the last 25 years have been intended for students who typically use formal reasoning.

True, modern secondary-school physics courses, such as PSSC Physics and the Project Physics course, have directed students toward laboratory experiments. Yet many of the experiments can only be understood within the hypothetical structure of the formal laws of physics. For example, the use of stroboscopic photographs to analyze the collisions of two objects appear to be at least as demanding as the Ticker-Tape Puzzle; yet we have seen that the solution to the Ticker-Tape Puzzle was inaccessible to students who used only concrete reasoning.

In short, our fixation on the formal aspects of physics instead of its concrete experiences has made physics unnecessarily difficult and dry. We have removed the sense of exploration and discovery from the study of physics for the majority of students. Several generations of public-school students have been alienated from physics.[8,9]

What can you do to make the study of physics less a slave to the formal structure of the discipline and more of a servant to the development of reasoning? You can
▶ become more familiar with the applications of Piaget's ideas to learning from physics;
▶ learn about the present attempts to offer Piaget-based programs for large numbers of students;
▶ encourage your school or college to initiate some programs that focus on the development of reasoning rather than the mastery of content;
▶ assist service clubs and other groups to present physics to the citizens by means of displays, exhibits and media, and
▶ develop your skills as a facilitator of self-regulation in others.[10]

The Box on page 27 lists some sources of workshop materials, as well as current college programs based on the Piaget concepts.

The human potential

As a result of our professional experiences, we of the physics community may possess a valuable insight: that carefully planned interactions of persons with the experimental systems and concepts of physics can contribute vitally to the full human potential. Perhaps our efforts to increase the appropriate people–physics interactions are as important to the future of mankind as our continuing efforts to increase our fundamental understanding of physical systems.

* * *

This material is based upon work done as a part of AESOP (Advancing Education through Science-Oriented Programs), supported by the US National Science Foundation under Grant No. SED74-18950. The opinions are those of the authors and do not necessarily reflect the views of the Foundation.

References

1. *Proceedings of the Workshop of Physics Teaching and the Development of Reasoning* (Anaheim, Calif. January 1975), American Association of Physics Teachers, Stony Brook, N.Y. (1975).
2. E. F. Karplus, R. Karplus, School Sci. and Math. **70**, 5 (1970).
3. B. Inhelder, J. Piaget, *The Growth of Logical Thinking from Childhood to Adolescence*, Basic Books, New York (1958).
4. PHYSICS TODAY, June 1972.
5. D. Griffiths, Amer. J. Phys. **14**, 81 (1976); G. Kolodiy, J. Coll. Sci. Teach. **5**, 20 (1975); A. E. Lawson, F. Nordland, A. DeVito, J. Res. Sci. Teach. **12**, 423 (1976); J. W. McKinnon, J. W. Renner, Amer. J. Phys. **39**, 1047 (1971); J. W. Renner, A. E. Lawson, Phys. Teach. **11**, 273 (1973); C. A. Tomlinson Keasey, Dev. Psychol. **6**, 364 (1972).
6. *The Collected Works of Count Rumford* (S. C. Brown, ed.), Harvard U. P., Cambridge, Mass. (1968).
7. L. Eason, A. J. Friedman, Phys. Teach. **13**, 491 (1975).
8. P. de H. Hurd, School Sci. and Math. **53**, 139 (1953).
9. M. B. Rowe, The Science Teacher **42**, 21 (1975).
10. A. B. Arons, Amer. J. Phys. **44**, 834 (1976).

Cultivating the capacity for formal reasoning: Objectives and procedures in an introductory physical science course*

A. B. Arons
Department of Physics, University of Washington, Seattle, Washington 98195
(Received 16 January 1976)

Experience in a physical science course for preservice elementary teachers, inservice elementary teachers, and other nonscience majors has led to the identification of certain specific factors and procedures that seem to assist the attainment of the formal operational level of intellectual development on the part of students who are initially at a concrete or transitional stage.

I. INTRODUCTION

Several years of observation of performance and development of students in an introductory physical course, the content and structure of which have been previously described,[1] have led us to sharpen our analysis and definition of the intellectual developmental objectives that are appropriate and desirable for the students concerned. These objectives and some of the procedures attendant on their implementation, are set forth in this paper.

The student population in the course has included preservice and inservice elementary teachers, preservice secondary teachers in nonscience areas, and nonscience majors discharging a general education requirement. We have found the initial state of intellectual development among these diverse groups to be essentially similar and to be entirely consistent with the statistical data being reported in recent years by numerous investigators.[2-8] Expressed in Piagetian terminology,[9] no more than 25% of the students have attained the level of formal operations; perhaps 25% are in transition between concrete and formal levels; and about 50% are essentially concrete operational.

It is a major goal of our program to lead as many students as possible (particularly among the pre- and inservice teachers) to attainment of formal operations as defined by the capacity to: control variables; do elementary syllogistic reasoning involving inclusion, exclusion, and serial ordering; discriminate between observations and inferences; recognize incompleteness of information in a line of reasoning; do inductive reasoning in the development of a scientific model and deductive reasoning in predicting consequences of the model; engage in hypothetico-deductive reasoning; do arithmetical reasoning, particularly that involving the consequences of division of one number by another.

Some of the objectives and procedures identified as contributing to progress toward the major goal are outlined in the following.

II. BASIC FRAMEWORK AND OBJECTIVES

The previously cited statistics on intellectual development indicate very strongly that the majority of students do not attain formal operations through being "told" about concepts, modes of thought, and lines of reasoning. The promising channel appears to reside in that being offered children in the new inquiry-oriented elementary curricula: direct personal experience with phenomena, evidence, inference, concept formation, and quantitative reasoning, as well as experience in verbalizing one's own growing insights and perceptions of relationship.

Sustained observation of student response and performance in repeated runs of the physical science course have led to identification of the following procedures and strategies as establishing a framework that impels students toward formal operational thought and draws them through iterations that, in Piagetian Terminology, lead to "equilibration" of the new intellectual level attained.

(1) *Exploratory activity and question asking prior to concept formation and model building.* Examples: exploration of the phenomenology of balancing prior to induction of the quantitative relationship; exploration of conditions necessary for lighting flashlight bulbs with 1.5-V cells prior to formation of concepts such as "circuit," "current," "conductor and nonconductor," and "resistance"; naked eye astronomical observations prior to formation of a picture accounting for phases of the moon or the geo- and heliocentric models of the solar system. Such exploration gives the students a much needed opportunity to use English in forming questions and describing observations prior to invoking technical terminology (which is misleading because it is not yet understood). It also provides opportunity for discrimination between observation and inference. It is necessary to watch the initial struggles toward clear expression and articulation to appreciate how little opportunity most students have had to form statements arising out of their own consciousness and experience and how much they have relied on the repetition of words, phrases, and statements drawn from others rather than from within themselves.

(2) *"Idea first and name afterwards."* Examples: Counting unit squares in an irregular surface and unit cubes in a three-dimensional space prior to introducing the names "area" and "volume" (most students consider "length × width" to be the *definition* of "area," do not recognize that the key aspect is the operation of counting, and have no idea what to do if the surface in question has an irregular rather than a rectangular shape); examining and interpreting the significance of the number mass/volume before giving it the name "density"; observing that effects, processes, or changes in an electrical system take place only when certain objects are connected end to end from one terminal of a battery to the other before giving the configuration the name "circuit"; developing evidence and examining phenomena from which one infers discreteness in the microscopic structure of matter before introducing the terms "atoms" and "molecules"; examining and interpreting the physical significance of the number obtained by dividing the change of position of an object by the time interval in which the change occurred before giving this number the

name "speed" or "velocity"; examining common thermal phenomena that lead to introduction of the concept of "heat" in addition to the concept of "temperature."

The maxim "idea first and name afterwards" underlies the concept of operational definition and its semantic overtones. The students we encounter have virtually no sense of the fact that words acquire meaning and communication becomes possible only through elements of shared experience. They almost invariably hold the unprobed assumption that knowledge and understanding reside directly in the technical terms they have learned. Competent articulation of operational definitions intelligible to another individual emerges only after repeated practice with each successive concept.

(3) *Translating words into symbols and symbols into words.* Examples: converting verbal problem statement into the corresponding arithmetical formulations; sketching position-time and velocity-time graphs of motions that have been described in words; interpreting verbally the significance of linearity of graphs (such as mass versus volume of a particular substance, circumference versus diameter of circles, net force versus acceleration imparted to a particular body) and recognizing the slopes as density, pi, and mass in the respective instances; interpreting in words the results of an arithmetical, algebraic, or geometrical analysis; interpreting in words graphs such as growth curves, position-time and velocity-time histories of a particle motion, cooling curves involving passage through a freezing point.

(4) *"How do we know . . . ? Why do we believe . . . ? What is the evidence for . . . ?"* Examples: How do we know the earth is round? Why do we believe that the earth and planets revolve around the sun? What is the evidence for discreteness rather than continuity in the structure of matter? What is meant by "like" electrical charges? How do we know when two charges are "alike"? Why do we believe there are only two varieties of electrical charge? How do we know that the phenomena taking place in a circuit connected to a battery or household outlet have any relation to phenomena that are observed in the frictional effects we call "electrostatic"? In what sense and on what basis do we view light as a wave phenomenon?

The great majority of our students (including the inservice teachers) have accepted these propositions on faith. They have almost never examined evidence or articulated in their own words any of the reasons that lead us to hold these views. They received them as end results from authority and pass them on to others in exactly the same manner. Eventually it does become necessary to take *some* end results of scientific inquiry on faith; we cannot develop extensive evidence in every single area we wish to study or interrelate. The students, however, have never discriminated between assertions such as "scientists know that . . ." and instances in which they have followed at least some of the evidence and understood how the particular result was validated and accepted. Before submerging them in further assertion of end results, it is essential to lead them to an understanding of the basis for some of our most fundamental and far reaching ideas concerning the physical world—ideas they have never realized they accepted without evidence and without understanding.

(5) *Inferences drawn from models.* Examples: How would stars, moon, and sun appear to pass through the sky at terrestrial locations different from our own (poles, equator, southern hemisphere, etc.)? What would things on earth be like if the ecliptic coincided with the celestial equator? If it passed through the poles? How do we visualize, in terms of the kinetic molecular model, the dissolving of a substance in water and the formation of a saturated solution? Given the concept of current in an electrical circuit, the concept of resistance (based on qualitative observation of the effects resulting from connecting more bulbs in series and inserting increasing lengths of michrome wire) and observation of the effect on bulbs in series when one bulb is short circuited: What can be predicted about the combined resistance of bulbs or lengths of wire in parallel? (Almost all students are astounded by the inference that the combined resistance in parallel must be less than that of the individual objects. Since there are more objects, they expect more resistance, an essentially concrete operational response, and they are often extremely loath to accept the opposite conclusion.) Is it possible to discriminate between the geo- and heliocentric models of the solar system on the basis of naked eye observations? (Many students have great difficulty understanding that it is impossible to discriminate between two models that equally well account for the available observations. They expect to be able to "prove" the one they "know" to be correct.)

It is essential that students have time to express the requisite lines of reasoning in their own words, drawing as much as possible on their own observations and experiences. Telling them the correct answers in lucid lectures, explanations, or text presentations is futile. This is what has been done before, and it has left no trace on the students' intellects.

(6) *"Backwards science; forwards science."* Examples: (a) Student: If the moon and sun are on opposite sides of the earth when we see a full moon, *why* is the moon not eclipsed each time by the shadow of the earth? Teacher: *Because* the moon, earth, and sun are not usually in a straight line. (b) Student: Why do two bulbs connected in series burn less brightly than one bulb alone? Teacher: *Because* of the resistance of the bulbs. (c) Student: Why does a charged rod attract an uncharged pithball? Text: because the pithball becomes polarized. (d) Student (referring to a cooling curve encompassing the freezing of a pure substance): *Why* is there a dip below the freezing temperature at the beginning of the flat portion? Text: Because of super cooling of the liquid before the solid begins to form.

Each one of these instances shows scientific reasoning being presented to students in a "backwards" way. A *because* answer to the *why* question carries for the student the clear implication that there existed an *a priori* reason for the phenomenon—a reason that the scientist had long ago discovered and that the student himself might also have known had he had the proper revelation. Answers of this kind strongly inhibit the progress of the student toward formal operations.

What is necessary in such instances is prompt reversal of the initial sequence. In example (a) the much more effective teacher response is: It is an observed *fact* that the full moon is not eclipsed every month; what can we infer from this observation about the character of the moon-earth-sun alignment? In (b): It is an observed *fact* that the two bulbs in series burn less brightly; what does this suggest concerning the effect of added material on the intensity of the "current" we visualize in the circuit? Can we test this notion by inserting michrome wire in series with a single bulb? (From this sequence emerges the concept to which we give the name "resistance.")

(7) *Interpretation of the results of multiplication and division in specific contexts.* Many students who are still essentially concrete operational do not interpret multiplication as a form of addition or counting in contexts where such an interpretation is appropriate. For example, they do not recognize the calculation of length × width for a rectangular surface as a short way of counting the unit squares; they dredge up "length × width" as a memorized operation somehow associated with the otherwise undefined technical term "area" [see item (2) above]. It is no use "telling" them or "explaining," however lucidly, that the operation length × width counts the unit squares; they have been told this before, and it did not register. The interpretation must be extracted from them in their own words by a sequence of questioning, and they must be led to give the explanation again on tests, as well as being led to give the parallel interpretation in the case of calculation of the volume of a parallelepiped.

Students who are somewhat further along toward formal operations may have little trouble with the interpretation of multiplication but frequently run into formidable obstacles in the interpretation of division. They have never interpreted division as calculating how much of the numerator is associated with one chunk of whatever is in the denominator. Example: "We have given the name density to the number obtained when we divide the mass (*M* grams) of an object by its volume (*V* cubic centimeters). How do you interpret the number *M/V*? What does it mean in simple terms?" Many students will bog down completely on this question or they will mutter something meaningless like "mass per volume." If one then says, "Let us take a different example. Suppose we find in the grocery store a box marked 75 cents and 14 ounces, what is the meaning of the number 75/14?," he finds that many students still have trouble, but the majority are able to say, however haltingly, that this is how much we pay for one ounce.

If this response is reinforced and one then says, "Now suppose we calculate the number 14/75. Does this have some basically similar interpretation or is it essentially meaningless?," he finds the majority of students in great trouble. There seem to be two difficulties superposed: (a) Although they have occasionally had to think about the cost of an ounce or a pound, they have almost never thought about how many ounces one gets for one cent or one dollar; (b) 75/14 involved dividing one number by a smaller number, and this is not very frightening while 14/75 is a frightening, unintelligible *fraction.*

After students have been led through interpreting 14/75 as the number of ounces obtained for one cent, one can usually go back to *M/V* and elicit the interpretation that this represents the number of grams in one cubic centimeter. One can then elicit the interpretation of *V/M* and the generalized interpretation of the result of a division.

Note the strategy that is involved. Although some of the students have responded to problems such as "calculate the cost of one ounce when 14 ounces cost 75 cents," virtually none of them have ever been asked to interpret the meaning of 75/14 and 14/75 in their own words; i.e., they have never reversed the line of thought, retracing it in the opposite direction. In the Piagetian lexicon, the word "operations" denotes reasoning processes that have the capacity of reversibility, and thus our evidence is that relatively few students have attained the operational level in the case of interpretation of the process of division; they do not reverse the line of thought.

Control of the operation is rarely attained with just the short sequence of examples cited above. Most students must carry through the same kind of reversible reasoning in several other contexts (e.g., what is the meaning of circumference divided by diameter in the case of a circle? If 16 g of oxygen combine with 12 g of carbon to form carbon monoxide, what is the meaning of 16/12? If a laboratory cart moves 180 cm in 2.3 sec, what is the meaning of 2.3/180?, etc.) Only after several such encounters, over a period of weeks, does the mode of thought become "equilibrated" and does "self-regulation" begin to take over.

N.B. if the teacher allows casual use of the word "per" in answers to the request for interpretation of the division, he falls into a trap. "Per" is a technical term, and few students know what it means. They inject it because they have a vague memory that it has always turned up for some reason or other in connection with division, but they do not explicitly associated it with terms such as "in," "for each," "corresponds to," "associated with," "combines with," etc. Similarly, very few know what the word "ratio" means. The students should always be asked to define "ratio" in their own words if they, the text, or the teacher invoke the term.

(8) *Arithmetical reasoning involving division.* Interpreting the consequences of division as illustrated in the preceding section is only the first step in a sequence; it is not sufficient by itself. The next fruitful step is made through questions such as "We have 800 g of material having a density of 2.3 g/cm³. What must be the volume occupied?" The first impulse of most students is to manipulate the density formula $\rho = M/V$. Investigation of what they are doing reveals that this is an essentially concrete operational response. They are not thinking either arithmetically or algebraically but are literally moving the concrete objects ρ and *V* around in a procedure they have been previously shown and have laboriously memorized. Obtaining a correct result to the initial question reveals no understanding or capacity for arithmetical reasoning. It should be pointed out that classical "proportional reasoning" suffers from a similar difficulty. Students have frequently memorized a "this-is-to-this as that-is-to-that" routine and manipulate quantities as concrete objects in a spatial arrangement. A correct result does not insure understanding of a line of reasoning and is frequently just a matter of chance.

The students must be led to articulate something like the following story: What does 2.3 g/cm³ mean? This is the number of grams in *one* cubic centimeter of the material. We can think of 2.3 g as a package. If we find how many such packages there are in 800, we obtain the total number of cubic centimeters because each package is associated with one cubic centimeter.

Similarly, when asked to find the diameter of a circle having a circumference of 28 cm, the students should be led to argue that they must find how many 3.14's there are in 28 cm since each "package" of 3.14 cm of circumference corresponds to 1 cm of diameter. Manipulation of the formula $C = \pi D$, however correctly, does not help lead them to formal operations because they are performing the manipulation in an essentially concrete rather than formal manner.

A way of helping equilibrate this level of thinking is to alter the preceding density problem to still another form:

"we have a block consisting of 1000 g of material with a density of 2.3 g/cm³. Suppose we add 800 g of the same material to the block. By how much have we *increased* the volume of the block?" Similarly one alters the circle problem by adding 28 cm of circumference to an initial 19 cm and asks for the *increase* in diameter. Students initially see these as problems entirely different from the originals and painstakingly calculate the final total volume of 1800 g of material and subtract the volume of 1000 g. When they grasp the point that 800/2.3 is the answer to both density problems, they have made a major additional stride toward equilibration of the lines of reasoning.

We have a strong subjective sense that a breakthrough on arithmetical reasoning of this variety is accompanied by a simultaneous breakthrough on other aspects of formal reasoning such as control of variables, making deductive predictions from a model, doing hypotheticodeductive reasoning, etc., but we have not had the resources to test this hypothesis objectively.

Our eventual test for attainment of the capacity for reasoning with division is to pose a question such as "How long will it take an object to travel 12.6 m if its velocity is 1.7 m/sec?," ask for an explanation of the arithmetical reasoning (without use of formulas) in the student's own words, and then ask the student to make up and solve a problem in some other context (density, circles, solubility, composition of compounds, etc.) in which the reasoning is essentially parallel. Some students begin to show the capacity to do this in the early stages of exposure, but we find that we have to spiral back to such reasoning about five times (in successive contexts) before we have reached as many as 85% of the students. A residual of 10 or 15% never do develop the capacity within the time and scope we have had available.

The reader should remember that the student population being referred to is not limited to undergraduates; it includes *inservice* elementary school teachers, and all the difficulties described and statistics cited apply to the latter as well as the former. It is clear that one reason our undergraduates have never developed these reasoning capacities must be that their teachers were unable to help; the teachers were unable to help because they did not have the capacities themselves. The teachers were graduates of our colleges and universities. Until we start producing teachers whom we have helped attain formal operations, we cannot hope to alter what is going on in the schools.

III. EFFECT ON STUDENTS

Resources have not been available for conducting a quantitative evaluation of the program with adequate controls. We can report one very rough datum (the one cited in Sect. II on development of the capacity for arithmetical reasoning), and we have accumulated qualitative observations of behavior. Some of the latter are described in the following.

In response to the demand of "idea first and name afterwards," students, within a few weeks after the beginning of the course, consciously and noticeably begin avoiding the use of undefined technical terms. They begin to describe observations and explain lines of reasoning with a minimum of jargon. Many volunteer descriptions of experiences in other courses (particularly the social sciences) where they have asked for clearer operational definition of terms. The inservice teachers visibly carry over this pattern both to their classrooms and to the workshops they conduct for their fellow teachers.[10]

To illustrate with a specific example: One inservice teacher reported the following incident with her second grade class. After demonstrating that both our breathing and a candle flame consume some of the air that is present and release a gaseous substance that turns lime water milky, she asked the class for an interpretation of the observations. Describing the incident to us, the teacher said, "One little girl said it so beautifully, she said it better than I could have. She said, 'I know what this means. It means that *we* take out of the air the same thing the candle takes out and we put back the same thing the candle puts back in.' " In an earlier period this teacher would have wanted the child to start using the undefined terms "oxygen" and "carbon dioxide" immediately. Now she valued and appreciated the beauty of the child's response.

The inservice teachers also noticeably carry over the basic model of teaching that is set before them. One teacher, after measuring the circumferences C and diameters D of a group of cylindrical objects, plotting C vs D and interpreting the slope of the graph, exploded with the comment frequently heard at this point, *"That* is what they meant by pi!" She then went on with the following, "I am going to call up that sixth grader who asked me about this and tell him . . . no, I will tell him to make these same measurements and interpret the graph." (Additional descriptions of teacher behavior are given in Ref. 10.)

Another type of response is exemplified by the student who was initially clearly concrete operational. It was necessary to lead her through every problem or line or inference with drawings or objects that she could manipulate. She exhibited every one of the difficulties with arithmetical reasoning described in parts (7) and (8) of Sec. II. She could not express herself clearly, could not discriminate between observation and inference, could not do simple syllogistic reasoning. As the weeks went by, her performance in each of these categories visibly improved as indicated by improving response on tests and examination. and in dialogs with the staff. At the 18th week there was a demonstration concerning the law of inertia and the concept of force. After observing the translational motion of a block of dry ice on a glass plate, attention was directed to the fact that the block kept on spinning indefinitely about its own axis if it had been given an initial spin. This student suddenly asked whether the vapor pouring off the block (which apparently no one else had noticed) also kept on spinning in the air after it left the block. She was duly reinforced for the quality and significance of the question, and attention was eventually turned to colliding carts in order to show that inanimate objects could impart changes in motion by interacting with each other. The first demonstration was the familiar one in which a moving cart collides with an identical stationary one. The first cart stops, and the second one moves off. The student looked carefully at the experiment, and, after observing a repetition asked, "If the first cart is made bigger, will it keep on moving instead of coming to a stop." These two questions marked the first instances of hypotheticodeductive thought this student had exhibited. The inception may not have been as sudden as it seemed, but there was no question about the qualitative intellectual change that had taken place over the 18 week period.

In summary, we feel we have made some progress toward

defining a framework and several procedures that stand up to analysis and assist in enhancing the capacity of students for formal reasoning. It is not our contention that this system is unique in the sense of being the only one capable of producing such effects nor do we feel that we have analyzed more than a minute fragment of possibilities. We hope that others will share the conviction that analysis of this kind might be fruitful to the teaching–learning process and that they will join the effort to enlarge the pool of available insights.

*Work supported in part by grants from The National Science Foundation.
[1] A. B. Arons, J. Coll. Sci. Teach. 1, 30 (1972).
[2] J. W. McKinnon and J. W. Renner, Am. J. Phys. 39, 1047 (1971).
[3] J. W. Renner and A. E. Lawson, Phys. Teach. 11, 273 (1973).
[4] A. E. Lawson and A. J. D. Blake, Advancing Education Through Science Oriented Programs (AESOP) Report, Lawrence Hall of Science, University of California, Berkeley, 1974 (unpublished).
[5] R. Karplus, E. Karplus, M. Formisano, and A.-C. Paulsen, AESOP Report ID-25, Lawrence Hall of Science, University of California, Berkeley, 1975 (unpublished).
[6] R. P. Bauman, paper delivered at AAPT Summer Meeting, Boulder, Colorado, June 1975; AAPT Announcer 5, 74 (1975).
[7] J. W. Renner and A. E. Lawson, J. Coll. Sci. Teach. 2, 89 (1975).
[8] G. Kolodiz, J. Coll Sci. Teach. 5, 20 (1975).
[9] J. Piaget and B. Inhelder, Growth of Logical Thinking (Basic, New York, 1958).
[10] L. C. McDermott, Am. J. Phys. 44, 434 (1976).

Self-Regulation in Reading a Story

by E. T. Carpenter

Any kind of situation in which one has to sort objects or ideas into various categories will involve several steps. First one must be acquainted with the objects and notice similarities and differences. Then similarities and differences need to be systematized and formulations of criteria for prospective classifications proposed. Once the criteria are formed and operational they are applied to the objects to be sorted. In this process the individual is actively engaging in assimilation and accomodation, so when the objects to be sorted do not readily fit what the sorter regards as conventional categories, some disequilibration is experienced and some search for a way to make the fit is made--providing the sorter is in some measure capable of at least concrete operations.

Sorting out ideas presented in the language of a story involves one in these same processes, and disequilibration may be expected to occur if there are contradictions implicit or explicit within it or if there are blatant misrepresentations of "facts" therein.

The following "story" bears interesting results when used as objects for such a classification exercise as the students' responses to it show. Although this exercise is not a reliable indicator of the line between the concrete operational and the formal operational student, it may serve to separate the students who are low concrete operational or preoperational providing they are given opportunity to work on the task over a period of more than one encounter and are thus encouraged to read it as carefully as they can.

Nice March Day*

On a nice March day our club organized a day's outing. Although it had been raining all night, the roads were quite wet and muddy in the morning; but this did not spoil our pleasure. We came through a woods consisting entirely of fir trees. Unfortunately, there were no leaves on the trees as it was still early in the season; how lovely this woods must be in summer time when the trees with their shade protect us against the sun. Then we saw in the distance a rabbit. I ran after it, but as it ran faster than I did, I could overtake it only slowly and finally caught it. I did not hurt it, but let it go again shortly.

Then we came past fields where the farmers were harvesting. At noon we arrived at the village where we intended to stay. About one year ago the village had suffered heavily from a fire; the tower of the church had burned down entirely; in memory of this event, there was a tablet at the place where the top of the tower had been. In a dairy we asked whether we could have milk and cheese, but as they didn't have any at that time they told us they would milk the cows in half an hour and that then we could have plenty of both. Of course, we were glad to wait and then enjoyed it very much. Most of the crowd now remained in the village, but together with a friend, I made a little jaunt up to a vantage point. We climbed up for half an hour, enjoyed the lovely view and then returned to the village on a path which was even steeper and also continually uphill.

With many games the afternoon passed quickly. We hardly noticed that the shadows grew shorter and shorter and we were surprised when we saw that the sun was setting. We sat down for a while on the shores of a lake. All of a sudden, a dense fog came up from the lake, but it did not spread over a large area; it just covered us and all the things close to us disappeared but all the objects in the distance remained distinctly visible. Tired but well satisfied, we reached home after complete darkness had fallen.

Directions: You may proceed in the following way:

(a) find "mistakes" or "errors" in the piece,
(b) explain why you take them as "mistakes" and, if possible, how you would "correct" them,
(c) try to characterize the "mistakes" by <u>kind</u> and group cases of similar kinds of mistakes together under one class heading.

---

*This three paragraph piece was used in a diagnostic instrument by J. McV. Hunt in 1935. See <u>American Journal of Psychology</u>, <u>47</u>, 458-463; article entitled; "Psychological loss in paretics and schizophrenics."

College Teaching and the Development of Reasoning 235

Before you read on to examine the way students completed this task please do the following:

A. List the "mistakes" or "errors" that you found in the story, explaining why they are "mistakes", and jot down for each "mistake" your prediction of how students might correct it:

Error found	Predicted correction
1.	1.
2.	2.
3.	3.
4.	4.
5.	5.
6.	6.
7.	7.
8.	8.
9.	9.
10.	10.
11.	11.
12.	12.
13.	13.

B. Can you suggest a way to classify the "mistakes" you mentioned above? How will you group them?

C. Now turn to the following pages and compare your responses to those of college students. Using your list and your predictions, evaluate the responses given by the two college students.

Absurdities: How do you deal with them? The Nice March Day story presents the student with the tasks of identifying difficulties in various parts of the story and then of classifying those difficulties with respect to kind; thus, he must formulate his rationale both for calling something an "error" and for grouping specific "errors" together--perhaps, giving criteria for his groupings.

However the student handles the task, it can be very illuminating of his ways of understanding written material. And if he is required to read large quantities of material, it may provide some insights into the sorts of misunderstandings or non-understandings that result. Note: It is not unusual to find freshmen college students completing the assignment:
a) on a sentence by sentence basis--fixing up the sense of one sentence at a time without paying attention to the possible contradictions resulting when two sentences are taken together; or
b) by criticizing the grammar or writing style--changing the placement of modifiers, the transition words between sentences, or the paragraphing and punctuation--skipping over entirely the logical problems in the meaning of the sentences of the story.

Preliminary results of a study of 380 University of Nebraska-Lincoln students' way of completing the task indicates that approximately 25% of them do (a) or (b) or simply do not even mention the sentences which contain the difficulties; and that percentage is not much lower than that of a group of Junior High School Students of 12 to 13 years of age.

Student Responses to the Nice March Day Task

Student A:

The transition from **although** to **because** is necessary in order to present a 'reason' statement rather than a 'pronounced' statement--'although' indicates that something happened even though something else happened; whereas 'because' expresses that something is or has occurred because of something else--it expresses a reason for the situation.

I must interject here that the reason for the additions of a few phrases is to extend on the story in order to make the transitions of thought from one paragraph to another fuller flowing and eradicate the awkwardness of the train of thought in the existing paragraphs. For example; the addition of "...We continued on with our plans and set out for the outdoors." indicates what was happening **before** so that the reader can understand how or why the next occurrence came about.

Many of the changes are self-explanatory--such as the fact that fir trees have needles and therefore there was shade. This makes the sentences describing the condition of the trees contraries, i.e., a) the trees cannot be fir trees if b) they are deciduous. They could not both be true (a fir and deciduous tree) but they _might_ be false together.

The next part of the story involving the chasing of the rabbit is highly improbable. Anyone running _slower_ than the rabbit would not be able to overtake it at all. This makes the propositions "...it ran faster than I did" and "I could overtake only slowly" contraries in their relationship together.

The next drastic correction I made was to reestablish a relationship between the church, the village, and the tower. In the original story it is stated that a tablet was placed on top of where the tower had been--this is impossible as the complete tower had burned and the tablet is not likely to be suspended in midair. Secondly, I doubt strongly that the villagers wanted the **memory** of the _fire_--more likely they were anxious to remember the church "...there was a tablet where the top of the tower had been" is contradictory to the statement "...the tower of the church had burned down entirely."

How many people can make cheese in half an hour or less? The statements regarding the milk and cheese are obviously contraries. "They would milk the cows in half an hour? and "then we could have plenty of both (milk and cheese)" just don't conform to reality or probability.

One of the more amusing sets of contradictories are the two phrases "...up to a vantage point" and "...even steeper and also continually uphill." The first phrase describes leaving the village and the latter the return trip. It is impossible to go up and return again also by going up.

The next set of phrases; "...shadows grew shorter and shorter" and "...the sun was setting" are also very improbable in relation to one another. These statements then are contraries as it is possible that they _might_ both be false together.

And finally the set of subcontraries are the phrases regarding the fog; "...it just covered us and all the things close to us disappeared" and "all the objects in the distance remained distinctly visible." Both _might_ be true if the fog was very low and only covered the ground, but because of the possibility, I feel they should be classified as subcontraries.

Other simple changes, i.e., rearranging some sentences and making more paragraphs simply help to better explain the story.

A's Rewrite:

On a nice day in March our club organized a day's outing. Because it had been raining all night, the roads were quite wet and muddy in the morning; but this did not spoil our pleasure. We continued on with our plans and set out for the outdoors.

We came to a woods consisting entirely of fir trees. Fortunately there was shade to protect us against the sun as we trekked through the tangle of trees.

Then in the distance we saw a rabbit. I ran after it, but as it ran faster than I did, I failed to overtake it and had to let it go.

Then we came past fields where the farmers were harvesting. How lovely the grains looked as they stood waving in the wind waiting to be reaped!

At noon we arrived at the village where we intended to stay awhile.

About a year ago the village had suffered heavily from a fire and the tower of the church had burned down entirely. In place of the tower a simple tablet had been laid to sustain the piety rendered by the tower until the village could afford to rebuild it.

Wandering through the village we came upon a dairy and inquired within about our obtaining some milk and cheese. They told us that at the time they had only cheese and that if we would return in half an hour they would milk the cows and give us some warm milk with the cheese. We decided not to wait as we were health nuts and didn't want to drink unpasteurized milk. (No telling what the cheese was like!)

Most of the gang remained in the village, but a friend and I made a little jaunt up to a vantage point. We climbed for about half an hour and then sat and enjoyed the lovely view of the surrounding countryside. Later we returned to the village on a rocky footpath and had to go slowly in order to avoid falling down the steep decline.

After rejoining our friends we played some games and the afternoon passed quickly. We hardly noticed that our shadows were growing longer and longer and we were surprised when we saw that the sun was setting.

We were sitting and regaining our breath along the shores of a lake when suddenly a dense fog came up from the lake, covering us and all the things close to us. Transfixed, we sat wondering what to do as the fog blocked our vision and the darkness was closing in.

Traveling carefully and slowly we gradually reached home after complete darkness had fallen.

Student B:

Although it had been raining all night, the roads were quite wet and muddy in the morning. This sentence is wrong because it sounds like you are saying - in spite of the fact A, the roads were A. You could say it like this - It had been raining all night, the roads were quite wet and muddy in the morning; although this did not spoil our pleasure.

Then we saw in the distance a rabbit. This sentence is wrong because there is no antecedent for the then to follow from. You could just say - We saw in the distance a rabbit.

I ran after it, but as it ran faster than I did, I could overtake it only slowly and finally caught it. This sentence is wrong because first of all the as is unnecessary because then it sounds like - I ran after it, but [equally] it ran faster than I did. The "only" isn't necessary in the - I could overtake it [only] slowly and finally caught it. You don't need the only because you already know that to overtake it slowly is the only way he could catch it since it ran faster than him the sentence could sound like this - I ran after it, but it ran faster than I did, I could overtake it slowly and finally catch it.

The sentence - About one year ago the village had suffered heavily from a fire; the tower of the church had burned down entirely; in memory of this event, there was a tablet at the place where the top of the tower had been is too long and spread out. You could shorten it by making two sentences out of it since the tablet brings in a different idea other than the fire. About one year ago the village had suffered heavily from a fire and the tower of the church had burned down entirely. You connect the two propositions by making them a conjunction and using the word "and". In memory of this event there was a tablet placed where the top of the tower had been: It is easier to simply say "placed" instead of saying "at the place".

In the sentence - In a dairy we asked whether we could have milk and cheese - the "and" should be replaced with an "or" making the sentence a disjunction because "whether" is used here as the same as "either - or". You should also leave out the "as" - "but as they..."--because it sounds like you are saying but [equally] they. The "then" is also unnecessary because "...in half an hour and that [then] we..." because you know it's an implication but since you don't use the "if" the "then" is unnecessary. The same thing goes for the next sentence. That passage should read like this - In a dairy we asked whether we could have milk or cheese, but they didn't have any at that time. They told us they would milk the cows in half an hour and that we could have plenty of both. Of course, we were glad to wait and we enjoyed it very much.

You make two sentences out of "they didn't have any at that time" and "they would milk the cows in half an hour" because they are separate ideas.

Most of the crowd now remained in the village but, together with a friend, I made a little jaunt up to a vantage point. This sentence is wrong because it isn't necessary to use both words - "together" and "with" both give the same general meaning. To make it correct you should omit one of them.

In the sentence - We climbed up for half an hour, enjoyed the lovely view and then returned to the village on a path which was even steeper and also continually uphill - it isn't necessary to say that the path was steeper or the continually uphill part.

The sentence - "We hardly noticed that the shadows grew shorter and shorter and we were surprised when we saw that the sun was setting," would sound better if you used a semi-colon after the shadows grew shorter and shorter and omitted the "and" connecting the two ideas.

We sat down for awhile on the shores of a lake. - It isn't necessary to say you sat for awhile because you naturally assume that if you know you sat down. It should sound like this - We sat down on the shores of a lake.

In the sentence - "All of a sudden, a dense fog came up from the lake, but it did not spread over a large area." it would sound clearer if you omitted the conjunction "but" and made "It did not spread..." a different sentence and omit the semi-colon after it and use a comma. A comma should also follow the word disappeared to separate the two ideas. All of a sudden, a dense fog came up from the lake. It did not spread over a large area, it just covered us and all the things close to us disappeared, but all the objects in the distance remained distinctly visible.

Note: You may wish to copy the <u>Nice March Day</u> task, as it appears on page 2, above, and give it to your students as an assignmmnt. If you would like to have our key for scoring students' responses on it, please write Dr. E.T.Carpenter, c/o ADAPT, 213 Ferguson Hall, University of Nebraska-Lincoln,Lincoln, Nebraska, 68588.

Can College Students Reason?*

Larry Copes

Independent Consultant in Educational Mathematics

<copes@edmath.org>

If X teaches Y, then X acts upon Y's environment in such a manner that Y develops in a desired way.

How Y develops in a given environment varies not only according to that environment but also according to the way Y perceives that environment.

Hence if X teaches Y, then X must consider not only how to act upon Y's environment but also Y's perception of his environment. Equivalently, if X is <u>not</u> sensitive to Y's perception of his environment, then X cannot be teaching Y.

Simplistic as this argument may sound, most of us who try to teach college mathematics have tended to ignore it and its implications. We rarely consider how various students perceive their learning environments--specifically, our classrooms. We also are mostly ignorant of recent research that dramatizes some important consequences of our omissions.

<u>Item</u>. Towler and Wheatley of Purdue University asked students in an introductory mathematics course whether or not changing the shape of a clay ball affected a) the amount of clay, b) the weight of the clay, or c) the amount of space occupied by the clay. Although most students realized that mass and weight of the clay were invariant, 39% of them believed that the volume changed when the ball was rolled into a sausage shape.[1]

Purdue University, of course, has no monopoly on such thinking; we all have experienced the student who just can't seem to catch on to our mathematics, no matter how hard he tried, the student who can do no more than memorize how to manipulate some formulas. Moreover, in this day of opening admissions and dropping enrollments, it is unlikely that the number

---

*Talk given at the spring, 1975 meeting of the Seaway Section, Mathematical Association of America; York University, Toronto.

of these students in our courses will decrease. Not all these students are lazy, or dumb. Some work very hard for us, meeting only frustration; some are quite successful in other courses. Is there anything we can do for them?

I believe we can find at least partial answers to such questions if we consider a psychological theory that makes good use of the concept of the learner's perception of his environmental stimuli. The framework I wish to oversimplify for you today is that developed by the Swiss investigator Jean Piaget.[2] Although Piaget began work in the 1920's, he was largely unknown in this country until the last decade or so. His work by now has influenced elementary and, to some degree, secondary school teaching, but still has not received the attention it deserves from most college educators.

Piaget describes the mental development of a human being in terms of an undefined concept that is roughly translated as "mental structure". An individual organizes environmental stimuli according to his mental structure and adapts this structure to assimilate such stimuli. Except for inherited reflexes, an infant's mental structure is very narrow; it can assimilate very few of the many stimuli encountered. But, given sufficient numbers of these stimuli, the structure accommodates itself for organizing a broadening range of them. A structure changes when it encounters stimuli that differ only slightly from those it can handle. If there is no incongruity, the stimuli will be assimilated without structural change; if there is too much incongruity, the stimuli will be ignored.

Although Piaget and his followers describe typical mental growth in terms of a refined system of stages and substages, the most important observation for our purposes is that persons encounter the stages in order. They do not backtrack, and, ideally, development does not involve skipping stages, which can lead to problems later in the growing period. (In an extreme case, a special educator might take a "slow" 8- or 9-year-old back to the crawling stage, and then teach him to walk again, and so forth, gradually rebuilding his mental structures to catch up with his physical development.)

With the hope that we can separate the wheat from the chaff, which is abundant in any psychological theory, we shall concentrate here on two of the major stages—those of "concrete operations" and "formal operations". Piaget uses the term "concrete operations" to refer to an extended period between the approximate ages of 7 and 11 in which a child has become able to set up one-to-one correspondences, to count, to recognize that the number of objects in a set is independent of its configuration, and to imagine himself in the position of others. He could perform none of these operations before reaching this stage, and his aptitude improves during this stage. On the other hand, he <u>cannot</u> yet operate <u>on these operations</u> by designing an experiment that requires holding all but one variable constant, or by formulating hypotheses, or by recognizing that volume is independent of shape or weight, or by responding to the form rather than the content of a logical argument. He will probably not take a fastidious interest in the rules of games. Ability to perform these operations on operations, or "formal operations", is acquired around the age of 11 or 12, according to Piaget.

> _Item_. At the University of Oklahoma, Renner and Lawson found that 58% of the 185 freshmen tested could not isolate variables sufficiently well to determine whether the period of a pendulum is affected by string length, weight of bob, both, or neither. The students were also asked to hypothesize whether a heavier or lighter object of identical volume would displace more water. Twenty-eight percent of the freshmen either predicted incorrectly or reasoned incorrectly in their prediction.[3]

So Oklahoma joins Purdue--and, of course, the rest of us. A growing body of research indicates that many college students, at least in North America, do not think at the formal operations stage. This means that a generous portion of students cannot be expected to "reason" in what we like to think of as a logical way (i.e., as formalized by the "laws of logic"). Since a favored assumption of most college mathematics teachers is that "reasonable" explanations promote understanding, the indications are that a large number of our students are incapable of learning from us if we teach in the ways to which we are accustomed.

Specifically, what can they not learn from us that we would like them to understand? Borrowing heavily from a recent paper[4] concerning the implications of Piaget's theory for teaching chemistry, I have stuck my neck out and prepared a list of concepts which I suspect most students who are not at the formal operations stage cannot really understand. (Figure 1.) If I am at all correct, it follows that they are not able to follow a formal argument, much less to come up with a proof of their own. They cannot grasp the concept of a function, because the concept of variable is not clear. And, in terms of attitude toward our field of study, they certainly cannot appreciate playing mathematics, seen as a rule-oriented game.

Concrete-operational students

can	but can't
make routine measurements and observations	measure "indirectly" quantities such as speed and acceleration, perhaps even area and volume
answer acceptably the question, "Are there more squares or rectangles in the diagram"? if they realize that all squares are rectangles	respond correctly to the choice, "If all squares are rectangles, then: 1. all rectangles are squares; 2. some rectangles are squares; 3. no rectangles are squares."
order a collection of sticks according to length	decide who is tallest if told that Bill is taller than Tammy and shorter than Sheila
count and perform elementary arithmetic operations	systematize counting procedures well enough to understand permutations and combinations
manipulate algebraic expressions, including fractions	given the equation $y=3x^2$ or $y=1/x$, decide what happens to y as x increases
generalize simply from given data: All quadratic equations (in x) represent parabolas	perform "once-removed" generalization Since quadratic equations in x represent parabolas, so do quadratic equations in y.

Figure 1.

Untested conjectures

Item. As long ago as 1944, a study presented college students with an argument for which they were to choose a correct conclusion. "Some ruthless men deserve a violent death; since one of the most ruthless of men was Heydrich, the Nazi hangman:
1. Heydrich, the Nazi hangman, deserved a violent death.
2. Heydrich may have deserved a violent death.
3. Heydrich did not deserve a violent death.
4. None of these conclusions logically follows."
More than 37% of the students chose number one.[5]

Item. Recent experimentation reported in the journal Science indicates not only that 50% of the freshman women at Penn State are unaware of the general principle that the surface of still water is invariantly horizontal, but also that they do not learn this principle by correcting their own errors.[6] My own informal experimentation verifies that a large number of college students, by no means limited to freshman women, do not understand this principle. (Figure 2.)

Sketch in the water:

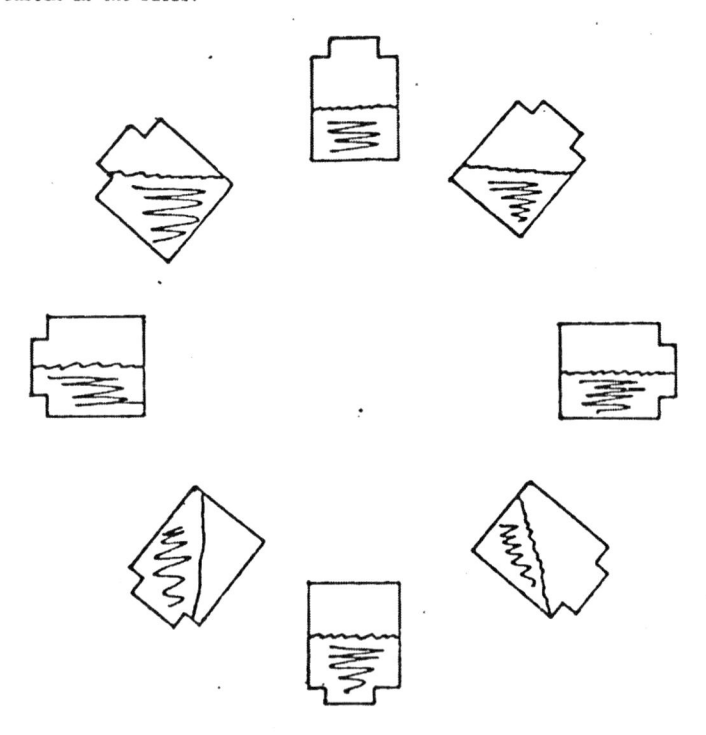

Figure 2.
Actual result of my own testing.

If it's not clear even how to teach these forms of abstract thinking, then, what should we do? Should we give up all hope of bringing about understanding and retention, and fall back on conditioning and drill? But then aren't we building our houses on sand? Or should we abandon altogether the notion of teaching mathematics to these students? But then, where do we find our new jobs? Or should we perhaps take our students back to a "crawl" stage, in some sense?

Although I don't pretend to have any final answers to these questions, I am growing increasingly in favor of the last alternative, of concentration on rebuilding mental structures—but only if we keep in mind a few caveats. For example, we should be aware that responses to "why" questions can be just as automatic as responses to "how" questions, as I believe some of the "new math" programs demonstrated. Thus we must be very careful in assessing progress. Also, we should probably at least consider Piaget's personal opinion that we should not unnaturally accelerate a person's development--in what he calls, of course, the "American Way"--although some limited experimentation indicates that it can be done.

Since I'm generally coming down on the side of optimism, though, I should probably go even farther out on our limb and speculate about techniques we can use for teaching mathematics to these college students. It seems clear by now that we must find ways to bridge the gap between concrete and formal operations--at least to the point of giving our students intuitive feelings for whatever mathematical concepts can be communicated this way. To do so would require at least paying a great deal more attention to concrete materials in the college classroom than we're accustomed to--and by "concrete materials" I mean paper and scissors and compass and measuring tape, not overhead projector and programmed text and teaching machine (although the extent to which these aids can provide relatively concrete operational experiences is a fascinating and unexplored question). The student we're discussing needs to "mess around" with basic mathematical concepts--independently of our telling him how to mess around--before he can begin to formalize them, or appreciate anyone's desire to formalize them.

While I'm at it, I should say that I suspect we only impede developmen
toward more abstract ways of thought if we continue to think of these students as dumb, or slow. To ask "What if . . ." kinds of questions, ofter o
requires an openness to new ideas that presupposes some degree of ease with
one's current view of the world.[7] Our labeling a student as "slow" cannot
help in building this self-confidence and thus will probably become a self-
fulfilling prophesy. Moreover, it is a prophesy that ignores the fact that
all of us are concrete-operational in some areas of thought.

So we need to provide learning environments that give a student concret
experiences yet don't insult his dignity. We need to find materials for thi
that are conducive to mental development. And we would like to find ways of
evaluating the success of such a program. I have gleaned some ideas about
these problems from student experiences in a few courses I have taught using
concrete materials in a college mathematics laboratory setting.[8] I'd like
to share a few of them with you before turning you loose to do your own
experimentation.

1. The Tower of Hanoi is an old puzzle, consisting of three spindles
and a stack of punctured disks, decreasing in size, which fit over the spind
The goal is to transfer the pile of disks from one spindle to another, movin
only one disk at a time and never putting a larger disk on top of a smaller
one.

Ideas for such concrete materials can come from many sources: articles
in mathematics education journals such as The Mathematics Teacher, NCTM year
books, catalogues of educational materials, browsing through toy stores, and
so on. In the case of the Tower, I believe I was originally inspired by
some Madison Project material.[9] I usually let students play with it for

while, devising strategies for transferring the disks if possible. Some never get beyond this point, although most do so in the course of a semester of periodic attempts. Then I ask them to vary the number of disks and to keep track of the minimum number of moves required to transfer the piles. Eventually many of them actually derive an expression for the function involved; some go on to explore deeper mathematical relationships exemplified by the Tower. Those who cannot generalize this way need more practice with concrete materials, so I suggest that they play with other puzzles and games that give similar experiences.

Incidentally, I have never encountered a student who was not intrigued by the Tower, no matter what his mathematical ability. One student last fall went on to derive a new method for moving disks, which, while not the most efficient, required little thought. She thus discovered what another student had once proudly proclaimed to me--that mathematics is the process of working very hard to find easier ways of doing things!

2. While studying polygons, one freshman was asked to cut some geometric figures out of construction paper--apparently the first time in her life she had applied scissors to paper! She enjoyed this, and went on to construct polygons out of popsickle sticks by weaving the sticks to make stable figures. (Interestingly, she was not satisifed that her early figures were stable until they had remained together for several days.) She also constructed polyhedra with the help of Superstructures, a modern plastic version of Tinkertoys. By the end of the course she was making fairly accurate predictions about two-dimensional patterns required for paper polyhedra, although she had a long way yet to go.

3. Many students are delighted with problems involving cutting and tracing graphs. They are usually attracted by the dual challenges of cutting each line segment of a given figure exactly once with a single continuous curve

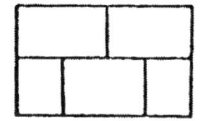

and of tracing various figures without repeating line segments or lifting t pencils. Some students derive conditions for traceability fairly quickly, and either continue to another project or expand into relationships demonstrating Euler's formula. On the other hand, one music major persisted with the tracing project for several weeks before finally coming across a relatic ship between order of vertices and traceability. The "discovery" came only after he had physically traced literally hundreds of graphs, mostly of his own making, and had constructed several charts. Even then the dawn was altc accidental--he was not yet comfortable with designing his experimentation s(as to eliminate variables methodically.

4. As I hinted before, we all seem to experience a need to work in the concrete-operational mode upon first approaching an area of investigation that is new to us. Of course, this is a primary justification for laboratories in the natural sciences and even in the social sciences, but it can be true for us as we intially confront an area of mathematics. We are like the person who first encounters Piet Hein's Soma puzzle. I have never seen anyone pick up the blocks for the first time and immediately form them into a cube. However, most of my acquaintances who have "messed around" with it for awhile eventually have come up with a solution--and, as time goes on, they have become quite conscious of combinations that will or won't be suc-

cessful, even without a logical analysis. Developing this intuitive feeling by "messing around" is the concrete operational work which, I suspect, must precede formal operational learning in any field.

It should be clear by now that the students we are discussing are not stupid or lazy. Perhaps they are not "reasoning", in our logical sense of the term, but we need to consider the possibility that this is due to gaps in the development of their mental structures rather than to inherent lack of growth potential. If we channel our impatience toward providing concrete, "hands-on" learning environments, I believe we may teach more effectively in the long run.

Therefore I encourage you to take Piaget's work seriously—if not for its specifics, at least for its metaphorical value—for it presents a very compelling model for describing the growth of our students. "Mess around" with the theory, be sensitive to the grain of students' mental structures, and experiment with some concrete teaching materials. And, please, let me hear from you.

References

1. J. O. Towler and G. Wheatley, Conservation concepts in college students: a replication and critique, Journal of Genetic Psychology 118: 265-70, 1971.

2. For background reading about Piaget's theory, see J. L. Phillips, The Origins of Intellect: Piaget's Theory (Freeman, 1969); H. Ginsburg and S. Opper, Piaget's Theory of Intellectual Development: an Introduction (Prentice-Hall, 1969); and R. W. Copeland, How Children Learn Mathematics: Teaching Implications of Piaget's Research (Macmillan, 1970).

3. J. W. Renner and A. E. Lawson, Promoting intellectual development through science teaching, Physics Teacher 11: 273-6, 1973.

4. D. Heron, Piaget for chemists, Journal of Chemical Education 52: 146-50 1975. See also D. W. Beistel, A Piagetian approach to general chemistry in the same issue.

5. J. J. B. Morgan and J. T. Morton, The distortion of syllogistic reasoning produced by convictions, Journal of Social Psychology 20: 39-59, 1944. Although the authors attribute such false reasoning to personal bias on the parts of the subjects, they admit that "even when a subject is presented with a syllogism in which the terms. . . have little or no personal significance, he has difficulty in selecting the correct conclusion. . . The only circumstance under which we can be relatively sure that the inferences of a person will be logical is when they lead to a conclusion which he has already accepted." (p. 39)

6. H. Thomas, W. Jamison, D. D. Hummel, Observation is insufficient for discovering that the surface of still water is invariantly horizontal, Science 181: 173-4, 1973.

7. For some fascinating ideas about the "What if not . . ."nature of mathematical exploration, see articles by M. Walter and S. I. Brown in Mathematics Teaching, Nos. 46 (Spring, 1969, pp. 38-45) and 51 (Summer, 1970, pp. 9-17).

8. A talk I gave last spring on some of these courses has been expanded into a paper, Multi-structured college courses in general mathematics and calculus, available from me. For an attempt to fit them into philosophic and psychological contexts, see my doctoral dissertation, Teaching Models for College Mathematics, available from University Microfilms, Ann Arbor, Michigan.

9. For example, Robert B. Davis, Explorations in Mathematics: A Text for Teachers (Addison-Wesley, 1967), pp. 257-63.

PROBLEMS OF EQUILIBRATION[1]

By Jean Piaget

I would like to start by thanking Dr. Annesley, Dean Eberman, and Dr. Macomber for their kind words of introduction. I would also like to express my thanks to Temple University and to the founders of the society which bears my name. It is the first time that I have ever spoken to a society with such a designation. I am very moved by it but I am also very anxious. I am not sure that I am up to it.

The title "Equilibration" refers to one factor that I think is essential in cognitive development. In order to understand the role of this factor we must relate it to the classical factors that have always been understood to be pertinent in cognitive development. There are three such classical factors: (1) the influences of the physical environment, the external experience of objects; (2) innateness, the hereditary program; and, (3) social transmission, the effects of social influences. It is clear that all three are important in cognitive development. I will begin by discussing them separately. But as we discuss them I think we will see that no one of the three is sufficient in itself. Each one of them implies a fundamental factor of equilibration, upon which I shall place special emphasis.

I will start by discussing the role of physical experience. It is clear that this is indispensable in cognitive development. There can be no development without contact with physical objects, i.e., contact with the physical environment. In terms of classical empiricism the role of acquired experience simply amounts to perceptions that we draw from objects and associations among perceptions. As I see it, there never can be pure association in the classical sense in which the empiricists mean it. The manner of linkage which always intervenes in the whirlpool of associations is in reality an assimilation in the biological sense of the term, an integration of external data into the structures of the subject.

Any action on the part of a subject gives rise to schemes of assimilation. That is, an object can be taken into certain schemes through the actions that are carried out on it; each of these schemes of assimilation goes hand-in-hand with an aspect of accommodation of the schemes to the situation. Thus when a subject takes cognizance of or relates to an object, there is a pair of processes going on. It is not just straight association. There is a bipolarity, where the subject is assimilating the object in his schemes and at the same time accommodating his schemes to the special characteristics of the object. And in this bipolarity and sharing of processes there is already a factor of equilibration between assimilation and accommodation.

Assimilation is a form of integration. It presupposes an instrument by which the data can be assimilated into the structures of the subject. An excellent example of assimilation as integration is the notion of horizontality of the level of water. Children see water in various forms every day. They see water in glasses from which they drink; they see water in bottles which they tip. Moreover they see water running in bathtubs and lakes and rivers. In all cases the water is horizontal. So the notion that water is horizontal should be a basic permanent notion. It even seems to assert itself in a more primitive manner as the child's own body is bound to positions where horizontality or verticality intervene, By the end of the first year the child is aware of the positions of his own body. He can tell whether he is standing up or whether he is lying down; he is aware of the sensori-tonic attitudes, You would expect this postural awareness to give him the understanding necessary to realize that water is always horizontal.

In some research we did many years ago, we asked the child to predict what would happen to the water inside a bottle if we tipped it. The child was unable to see the water inside the bottle because it was covered. He was asked to draw a picture of the water inside the bottle when it was tipped. The average age at which children could answer this correctly and draw a horizontal line was about nine years of age. I say average age because of course some children advance more rapidly than others. Moreover, the populations we studied were from an impoverished area of Geneva and it is possible that in more highly civilized regions the age is younger. It is possible that in Philadelphia, children are more precocious! However, in Geneva the average child is nine to ten years of age before he can predict where the water will be in the covered container when it is tipped. Before that he will always draw the line parallel to the bottom of the bottle as it is when the bottle is upright. Then there will be various intermediary stages between drawing a parallel and drawing a horizontal line. This seems to be quite strong evidence to the fact that seeing is not enough because children have been seeing this phenomenon all their lives. But, within the experiment we even gave the children a chance to see by taking the cover off the bottle. If the child had drawn the water parallel to the bottom of the bottle, when we uncovered and tipped the bottle and the child compared the bottle with his drawing, he would say, "Yes, that's just the way I drew it. Just like my drawing." He doesn't even seem to be able to see that the line is horizontal.

Why is the child unable to see that the line of the water is horizontal? The reason for this is that he does not possess the necessary instruments of assimilation. He hasn't yet developed the system of coordinates that will enable him to put the water into a frame of reference with points outside the bottle, such as the table top or the floor. As adults, we operate with a coordinate spatial system of verticality and horizontality at all times. The child doesn't have the framework which enables him to make the extrafigural comparison needed to go outside the framework of the bottle. He reasons only by an intrafigural frame of reference, until about the age of nine when these systems of coordinates are being built. He remains inside the framework of the bottle; his only points of reference are the base of the bottle which results in his drawing the water parallel to the base or to sometimes the corners of the bottle. He may draw a line from one corner to another which is slightly tipped but it is still not considered horizontal. His frame of reference remains the bottle itself.

This seems to me a very striking example of the complexity of the act of assimilation which always supposes instruments of integration. A well developed structure within the subject is needed in order to take in the data which is outside. Assimilation is clearly not a matter of passively registering what is going on around us. This leads us to the critical examination of the famous stimulus-response scheme, the classical model of behaviorism.

It is true, of course, that stimuli give rise to responses. However, this only raises much more basic, more preliminary questions. Why does a given stimulus give rise to a certain response? When is an organism sensitive to a particular stimulus? The very same organism may at one time not be sensitive to a particular stimulus, and not give any response to it, then later be sensitive to the stimulus and respond to it, and then later perhaps again not be sensitive to it. This may also vary from one organism to another. Some organisms may respond to certain stimuli and other organisms may not. So the fundamental question is: What makes an organism respond to a certain stimulus.

The organism is sensitive to a given stimulus only when it possesses a certain competence. I am borrowing this word from embryology in the sense in which Waddington has used it. He has referred to the influence of an inductor. Waddington has shown that an inductor which modifies the structure of the embryo does not act in the same way at all levels of development. If the inductor is present before the embryo has the competence to respond to it, the inductor will have no effect at all; thus, it will not modify the structure. The embryo must be at a point of being competent to respond to the inductor before the inductor can have its effect.

The phenomenon is the same in cognition. Stimulus-response is not a one-way road, a unilateral scheme. A subject is sensitive to a stimulus only when he possesses the scheme which will permit the response. In other words, the sensitivity to the stimulus is the capacity for response, and this capacity for response supposes a scheme of assimilation. We again have to create an equilibrium between assimilation, on the one hand, and accommodation to a given or an external stimulus, on the other hand. The stimulus-response scheme must be understood as reciprocal. The stimulus unleashes the response, and the possibility of the response is necessary for the sensitivity to the stimulus. The relationship can also be described as circular which again poses the problem of equilibrium, an equilibrium between external information serving as the stimulus and the subject's schemes or internal structure of his activities.

I would like to make two final remarks on the role of the physical environment. I will first discuss the development of the notion of conservation. As you know, if one transforms a ball of clay into a sausage shape, the young child will tell you that there is more clay in the sausage than in the ball because the sausage is longer. Secondly, even though no clay was added and no clay was taken away, the child believes that the sausage shape and ball will weigh differently. The child will also say that one would displace more water in a vessel than the other, indicating different volumes in the ball and sausage shape. These notions of conservation are acquired in a certain order: first, the conservation of the substance, that is the quantity of material; next, with quite a notable time-lag, the conservation of weight; finally, the conservation of volume, in the sense one can evaluate volume by the displacement of the level of water. What strikes me as very interesting is that the conservation of the amount of clay, the conservation of the substance, is the first concept of conservation that a child attains. But it is clear that conservation of substance, i.e., amount of clay, is not observable. The child can observe the size of the clay, perceive its volume and lift it to sense its weight, yet he believes they have changed. And yet somehow he believes that the amount of clay has remained the same even though it is not observable or clearly measurable.

It is, it seems to me, very important that conservation of sub stance can only be the product of reasoning. It is not a product of perception. The child has simply become aware that something must be conserved when things are transformed in order to make the process of rational thought at all possible. So the scheme of the conservation of the amount of clay imposes itself on the child for rational rather than for perceptual reasons.

Finally, I would like to distinguish between two kinds of experience in connection with the factor of external experience. Classical empiricists assume there is only physical experience. In physical experience information is drawn from the objects themselves. For example, you can have various objects and see that they differ in weight. But, there is a different kind of experience which plays a necessary role at the preoperational level. I will call this logico-mathematical experience. In logico-mathematical experience the information is drawn not from the object but from the subject's actions and from the subject's coordination of his own actions, i.e., the operations that the subject effects on the objects.

There is a very banal example of logico-mathematical experience that I have often quoted. One of my friends who is a great mathematician described to me an experience he had as a child. While counting some pebbles, he arranged them in a line, counted them from left to right and found that there were ten. Then he decided to count them from right to left and found there were still ten. He was surprised and delighted so he changed the shape again. He put them in a circle, counted around the circle and found there were still ten. With mounting enthusiasm, he counted around from the other direction and there were still ten. It was a great intellectual experience for him. He had discovered that the sum ten is independent of the order of counting. But unlike their weight, neither the sum nor the order is a property of the pebbles. The sum and the order come from the actions of the subject himself. It was he who introduced the order and it was he who did the counting. So logico-mathematical experience is experience where the information comes from the subject's own actions and from the coordinations among his actions. This coordination of actions naturally poses a problem of equilibrium much more than a problem of action from external experience.

I would like to say a final word on the role of experience. It is clear there is an undeniable role played by experience in cognitive development; however, the influence of experience has not resulted in a conception of knowledge as a simple copy of outside reality. In external experience, knowledge is always the product of the interaction between assimilation and accommodations, i.e., on equilibrium between the subject and the objects on which the knowledge rests.

The second factor I would like to discuss is that of the innateness or hereditary programming of development. It is, of course, obvious that the factor of innateness plays an equally fundamental role as does the maturation of the nervous system and is a condition of cognitive development. But it is only a condition opening up possibilities. The problem is how these possibilities are realized, i.e., how they are actualized. In sensorimotor development it is easier to see how hereditary transmissions playa central role. For instance, at the sensorimotor level, the coordination between grasping and vision seems to be clearly the result of the myelinization of certain new nervous paths in the pyramidal tract as physiologists have shown. This myelinization seems to be the result of hereditary programming. However, in the domain of higher, representative and especially operational cognitive structures, these structures are not innate. Logical transitivity, for example, imposes a necessity on the subject with an obviousness internal to the subject. Yet this necessity is not a proof of innateness.

We have conducted a very simple experiment to test the notion of transitivity. We asked children to first compare the length of two pencils. Children see that A is smaller than B. Then we hide A and show B and C; C is very obviously longer than B. We then ask the child, "Do you think that C is longer than the first one you saw, smaller than the first one you saw or about the same length?" The little children will say, "I can't tell. I didn't see them together." The child does not make the inference we would make from the information which allows for transitivity. It seems to impose itself on us with a feeling of necessity that C must be longer than A. But, small children do not have that same feeling of necessity. This feeling of necessity is tied to the operational structure I have been calling seriation or serial ordering.

As you know, if children are asked to put ten sticks in order of length from shortest to longest, their ability to do so develops through very varied stages in which they experience some laborious trial and error. Small children are likely to make pairs of short and long sticks but will fail to coordinate the pairs among themselves. They have recognized that some sticks are short and some are long, but not much more than that. Older children make trios, the repetition of a pattern of short, medium, and long, but do not coordinate the trios among themselves. Slightly older children are able to produce an incomplete empirical series, that is, with errors, gropings and corrections. Finally at about seven years of age, children have developed a method, a method which I call operational. They first look for the shortest of all the elements and place it on the table, then look for the smallest of those remaining and place it next to the shortest, and then look for the next shortest and place it. I refer to this method as operational because it implies a certain reversibility. It implies the comprehension of the fact that any element, say element E, is at once bigger than all those preceding it and smaller than those which remain. There is a coordination which permits a construction of the seriation without errors. By following this system, once you know that objects A, B, and C were the shortest on the table, it is not necessary to compare object D with objects A, B, and C. You know that it must be longer than them and it must be shorter than the others.

The notion of transitivity is, thus, tied to the operational structuration of the series. Transitivity feels necessary to us and imposes itself upon us because of the nature of the closed operational structure—it is a result of the closing of this structure. And this, of course, means equilibrium. The structure, until it is closed, is not in a state of equilibrium. Once it is closed, we again find equilibrium to be an important factor.

The notion of the influence of innate factors in development is gaining new acceptance these days. Two of its leading proponents are Chomsky, the linguist, and Lorenz, the ethnologist. Chomsky, of course, has done very great work in his development of the notion of transformational grammar, work which I admire greatly. He has hypothesized that from the beginning of these transformations, there is a fixed innate core which contains the most general forms of language, for example the relationship between subject and predicate. This innate core contains both the possibility of construction of language and a rational structure, which consequently would be innate.

It seems to me that this hypothesis is not necessary. As we all know, language develops during the second year of childhood, and not from birth. As we all also know it develops at the end of the period of sensorimotor development, with all the numerous stages of construction involved in this form of intelligence. It seems to me that sensorimotor intelligence, once achieved, contains all that is necessary to furnish Chomsky's innate fixed core without having need to appeal to a hereditary structure.

Konrad Lorenz, the great ethnologist, agrees with Kant: the important forms of our thinking, the important categories, are present in us before any experience, i.e., are innate. He goes as far as to say that the general ideas of the mind are pre-formed in the embryo before the individual has the need for them, just as the horses' hooves or fishes' fins are pre-formed in the embryo before they are needed by the adult. However, Lorenz, as a biologist, recognizes the limitations of such an explanation. Each animal species has its own heredity. Then, if one brings the ideas of intelligence or reason back to innate structures, that means that heredity can vary from one species to another following the hereditary patrimony of the species. Realizing this difficulty, Lorenz follows through very logically by concluding that these innate notions are not necessary as they might be if the hereditary program were constant across all species. Since hereditary programs vary from species to species and there is nothing necessary about them, these innate ideas must be only innate working hypotheses. Thus, this means that innate ideas have lost their aspect of necessity. This does not mean that essential categories are not *apriori* and cannot exist before any experience, but it does mean that they cannot be accounted for by their intrinsic necessity.

I would conclude in discussing the role of biology as a factor of development that what is important for us to take from biology is not the notion of hereditary programming since it is variable and it cannot lead to the kind of necessity that we feel. We should take the much more general notion of self-regulating mechanisms. Self-regulating mechanisms are important throughout every level of biological development. One finds regulation at the level of the genome, where self regulatory mechanisms are an essential condition of functioning. There are regulations in the course of embryological development, what Waddington calls homeorhesis. At the physiological level, homeostasis is a self-regulating mechanism; similarly, in the nervous system, the reflex arc is a homeostat. On the level of human conduct and even at the level of logical operational thinking, there are similar self regulatory mechanisms. It seems to me that this notion of self-regulation, which consequently is one of equilibration, is much more fundamental and much more general than the more narrow notion of variable hereditary programming. It is, then, self-regulation that is the important idea for us to take from biology.

I now come to the third classical factor of development: the social factor, the role of education and language in development. I will try to be very brief so that I can get on to equilibration. The role of education and language is clearly fundamental, but once again it is subordinated to assimilation. There can be no effect of social or linguistic experience unless the child is ready to assimilate and integrate this experience into his own structures. The special problem of the relationship between language and logic is one which I would like to discuss at some greater length. Many people are of the opinion that an individual's grasp of logic is dependent upon the syntax and the logical relationships imbedded in the language in which people are speaking to him. Logic develops out of the language. This is the position of the logical positivists.

In Geneva one of our colleagues, Hermine Sinclair, has done some work on the problem of the relationship between logic and language. Sinclair was a linguist before she came to Geneva to go into experimental psychology. In her research she first identified two groups of children. One group was non-conservers, in the sense that they thought that a change in shape would entail a change in the amount of substance. The other group was conservers, in that they knew that the change of shape did not alter the amount of the substance. Then, she looked at the language of these two groups of children in different situations. For example, the children were asked to compare short, long, fat, and thin pencils. She found that the children who were non-conservers did not use comparative terms in describing the pencils and did not contrast two dimensions. They would just say that one pencil is big and that one pencil is fat. The children who were conservers, however, used comparisons. They talked in sentences that contrasted variables, such as saying that one is fatter but shorter, the other thinner but longer,

Sinclair then trained the non-conservers to learn the verbal expressions of the other more advanced group. This language training was not easy, but it was possible. After the non-conservers had mastered the language expressions of the conservers she readministered the conservation experiment to see whether the training increased their ability to conserve.

Progress was only minimal; nine-tenths of the children made no progress toward conservation although they had mastered the more sophisticated language. One-tenth of the children made very slight progress. This would lead us to believe they would have made this progress normally in that period of time anyway. We have been pursuing other research in Geneva since Sinclair's study; it all supports the general conclusion that linguistic progress is not responsible for logical or operational progress. It is rather the other way around. The logical or operational level is likely to be responsible for a more sophisticated language level.

I am now discussing the role of equilibration, that is, the fourth factor in psychological and cognitive development. It seems to me there are two reasons for having to call in this fourth factor. The first is that since we already have three other factors, there must be some coordination between them. This coordination is a kind of equilibration. Secondly, in the construction of any operational or preoperational structure, a subject goes through much trial and error and many regulations which involve in a large part self-regulations. Self-regulations are the very nature of equilibration. These self-regulations come into play at all levels of cognition, including the very lowest level of perception.

I will begin with an example at the level of perception. We have studied a number of optical illusions, by asking subjects to make perceptual judgments of an optical illusion. For example, we have often used the Müller-Lyer illusion, an illusion of the diagonal of the lozenge, which is always underestimated. One can present the subject with a successive series of judgments to make between the standard and the variable. The variable varies between presentation but the standard is a constant. The subject has to judge whether the variable is shorter, longer or equal to the standard. I have always admired the patience of children under seven years of age who will sit through 20 or 30 or 40 presentations at a time.

In children under seven years of age we find no notable transformations. That is, at the end of thirty or forty trials, they make the same errors they did in the beginning. With adults, on the contrary, the repetition of the judgment results in a very clear diminishing of the illusion. Some are able to eliminate the effect of the illusion altogether. Among children from seven years (the beginning of cognitive operations) to adulthood, one can observe a progressive diminishing of errors. It is important to note that the subject does not know the results of his judgments. There was no external reinforcement, yet the perceptual mechanism seems to have its own regulations, such that after 20 or 30 or 40 trials, an adult subject can eliminate the effect of the illusion altogether.

At the representational level, in both preoperational and operational structures, we can distinguish three kinds of equilibrium. The first one is the relationship between assimilation and accommodation, of which I previously spoke. There is an equilibrium between the structures of the subject and the objects; its structures accommodate to the new object being presented and the object is assimilated into the structures. It is this first fundamental form of equilibration which was exemplified by the horizontality of water and the notion of conservation. I will not repeat these examples here.

The second kind of equilibrium is an equilibrium among the subsystems of the subject's schemes. In reality, the schemes of assimilation are coordinated into partial systems; referred to as subsystems in relation to the totality of the subject's knowledge. These subsystems can present conflicts themselves. This afternoon Dr. Inhelder will give examples of equilibrium of subsystems. But in general terms I will say that, for example, it is possible to have conflicts between a subsystem dealing with logico-mathematical operations (classifications, seriation, number construction, etc.) and another subsystem dealing with spatial operations (length, area, etc.). For example, when a child is judging the quantity of a number of sticks, there may be in one collection a small number of long sticks laid out. In another collection, a larger number of shorter sticks may be laid out. If he is basing his judgment on number, he would make one judgment of quantity. If he is basing his judgment on length, he would make a different judgment of quantity. These two systems can evolve at different speeds. Of course as they evolve there is a constant need for coordination of the two - an equilibration of subsystems.

The third kind of equilibrium in cognitive development appears to be fundamental. Little by little there has to be a constant equilibrium established between the parts of the subject's knowledge and the totality of his knowledge at any given moment. There is a constant differentiation of the totality of knowledge into the parts and an integration of the parts back into the whole. This equilibrium between differentiation and integration plays a fundamental biological role.

At the level of cognitive functions, there is a fundamental form of equilibrium because integration, as a function of differentiation, poses new problems. These new problems lead to the construction of new actions upon the previous actions, or new operations upon the previous operations. The construction of operations upon operations is probably the secret of development and of the transition from one stage to the next.

I would like to point out that the notion of operation itself involves self-regulatory mechanisms. They are, in the Ashby sense (in his cybernetic terms) the perfect regulations in that the outcome is anticipated before the act is actually carried out. The feedback, which at lower levels has incomplete reversibility, now becomes a feedback with perfect reversibility in the sense of inversion or reciprocity. This is an example of perfect compensation, otherwise said, attained equilibrium.

I would like to explain the reasons for the role of equilibrium. All operational subject structures, on the one hand, and all causal structures in the domain of physical experience, on the other hand, suppose a combination of production and conservation. There is always some production, that is, some kind of transformation taking place. Similarly there is always some conservation, something that remains unchanged throughout the transformation. These two are absolutely inseparable. Without any transformation we have only static identity. The world becomes rigid and unchanging in the sense that Parmenides (co 539 B.C.) conceived it. Without any conservation we have only constant transformation. There is total change; the world is always new and it becomes unintelligible. It becomes like the world of Hereclitis with its river in which one was never able to bathe twice. In reality, there are always both conservation and production.

Conservation demands compensations, and consequently equilibration. If something is changed, something else must change to compensate for it, in order to result in a conservation. Even in physics all the transformations that take place involve compensations in order to lead to a conservation. These compensations are organized in group structures in the mathematical sense of the term. Furthermore, there is no conservation without production, and production with conservation results in a constant demand for new construction.

Where I speak of equilibrium, it is not at all in the sense of a definitive state that cognitive functioning would be able to attain. Attained equilibrium is limited and restrained, and there is a tendency to go beyond it to a better equilibrium. I would speak of the law of optimalization, if this term did not have technical meanings too precise for its psychological use. So, simply stated, there is a continual search for a better equilibrium. In other words, equilibration is the search for a better and better equilibrium in the sense of an extended field, in the sense of an increase in the number of possible compositions, and in the sense of a growth in coherence.

I would now like to point out the fundamental difference between biological or cognitive equilibrium and physical equilibrium. In physics, equilibrium is a question of a balance of forces. Take, for example, a balance with two weights—one on each side. Between the two are the lever and the fulcrum which are only organs of transmission. They are passive mediators permitting the action from one side to the other.

In another example, the Le Châtelier-Braun experiment, a piston presses down on a container that is full of gas. The gas is compressed while the force of the piston increases the pressure. The force of the piston heats the gas making it agitate. This makes the gas hit back with pressure on the sides of the container and eventually back on to the piston. It compensates for the initial force that was pressing down on the piston and presses the piston back up again. Le Châtelier referred to this as the moderation of the original cause. Here again the container plays the role of the transmitter, a passive mediator which receives and sends back the shocks.

In biological or cognitive equilibrium, on the other hand, we have a system in which all parts are interdependent. It is a system which could be represented in the form of a cycle. A has its influence on B, which has its influence on C, which has its influence on D, which again influences A. It is a cycle of interactions among the different elements. It also has a special feature of being open to influences from the outside. Each of the elements can interact with external objects. For instance, the cycle can take in A^1 and B^1.

In the case of biological or cognitive equilibrium the links are not passive; they are the very sources of action. The totality presents a cohesive force which is specific and which is precisely the source of the assimilation of new elements of which we have been speaking since the beginning of this talk. The system forms a totality in order to assimilate the outside elements. This equilibrium between the integration and the differentiation of the parts in the whole has no equivalent in physics. It is only found in biological and cognitive equilibrium.

In closing I would just like to make two references on the matter of the cohesive force of the totality, the source of equilibrium in biological and cognitive structures. The first is from Paul Weiss, the great biologist, who in his work on cells pointed out that the structure of the totality of the cell is more stable than the activity of its elements. Inside the cell the elements are in constant activity but the total structure of the cell itself has a much more continuing stability.

My second reference will be in the cognitive domain. I would like to speak of the works of Presburger, cited by Tarski, which point out the existence of systems which as totalities are closed on themselves - and are completely coherent. All aspects are decidable, in the logical sense of the term, within the total system, while the subsystems are not so closed and every aspect is not entirely decidable. This seems to me a very fine example of the kind of equilibrium about which I am talking: the totality has its own cohesion and equilibrium by integrating and differentiating the parts at the same time.

So, I've come to the end of my talk. It has been very schematic. It has been only an offering of ideas, I'm afraid, and not the proofs that might have been necessary to convince some of you. This afternoon there will be proofs when Dr. Inhelder talks about the role of regulations in learning. Perhaps the order of our lecture should have been the reverse, but at any rate I have contented myself with giving you the theoretical thoughts. I thank you very much for bearing with me.

NOTE

1. Translated by Eleanor Duckworth.

ACKNOWLEDGMENT

Reprinted by permission of the Jean Piaget Society. Dr. Piaget made this presentation to the first symposium of the Society on May 26, 1971, at Temple University. It was published in printed form in 1972.

We have stressed this example of mathematics somewhat since there is no field where the "full development of the human personality" and the mastery of the tool of logic and reason which insure full intellectual independence are more capable of realization, while in the practice of traditional education they are constantly being hampered. There is nothing more difficult for the adult than to know how to appeal to the spontaneous and real activity of the child or adolescent. Only this activity, oriented and constantly stimulated by the teacher, but remaining free in its attempts, its tentative efforts and even its errors, can lead to intellectual independence. It is not by knowing the Pythagorian theorem that free exercise of personal reasoning power is assured; it is in having rediscovered its existence and its usage. The goal of intellectual education is not to know how to report or retain ready-made truths (a truth that is parroted is only a half-truth). It is in learning to master the truth by oneself at the risk of losing a lot of time and of going through all the roundabout ways that are inherent in real activity… That is, in every field where knowledge of facts has no value except in relation to the processes of discovery that enable it to be absorbed.

—Jean Piaget (1973)

APPENDIX B

PHYSICS TEACHING AND DEVELOPMENT OF REASONING MATERIALS © 1975 AMERICAN ASSOCIATION OF PHYSICS TEACHERS (AAPT)

The following pages are from the edited version of the original workshop that was offered at the Anaheim meeting of the AAPT in January, 1975. These materials were prepared under the direction of Professor Robert Karplus, University of California, Berkeley. These materials provided the basis for the contents of the first 11 chapters of this book. These materials were transformed into workshop materials that were used at more than 100 different college and university locations.

The complete version of the original materials are available to download in pdf files from the University of Nebraska Lincoln Digital Commons Web site: http://digitalcommons.unl.edu/adapt/.

We have selected pages from those original materials to avoid redundancy with the first 11 chapters of this book. We have chosen to include the transcripts of interviews with both Robert Karplus from workshop Module 2 and John Renner from workshop Module 9 because of the essential roles that Karplus and Renner played in the intellectual development movement in physics education at colleges and universities. In addition we have included the physics readings from that first workshop. We think that even non-physicists will find items of interest in those articles.

WORKSHOP ON PHYSICS TEACHING AND THE DEVELOPMENT OF REASONING

BY

Francis P. Collea, California State University, Fullerton, CA 92634
Robert G. Fuller, University of Nebraska, Lincoln, NE 68588
Robert Karplus, University of California, Berkeley, CA 94720
Lester G. Paldy, SUNY, Stony Brook, NY 11794
John W. Renner, University of Oklahoma, Norman, OK 73069

AMERICAN ASSOCIATION OF PHYSICS TEACHERS
Graduate Physics Building
SUNY, Stony Brook, N. Y. 11794

*Partially supported by the Office of Experimental Projects and Programs, National Science Foundation

© 1975 American Association of Physics Teachers

Preface

Are physics teachers in high schools, colleges, and universities knowledgeable concerning the reasoning patterns their students use? The personal experiences of many instructors and research carried out during the last few years indicate that a substantial fraction of physics students have difficulty applying functional relationships among variables, considering all necessary combinations of experimental and theoretical conditions in a problem, and examining their own reasoning critically to locate possible errors. The theory of intellectual development formulated by the Swiss psychologist and epistemologist Jean Piaget deals with these matters and can therefore be of help to physics teachers.

We have prepared these individualized workshop materials to present the two principal concepts of Piaget's theory, stages of development and self-regulation, with background and illustrations that will make clear their relevance for physics teaching. The complete workshop includes audio-visual materials, laboratory activities, and discussions among groups of participants and workshop leaders, as described more fully in the "Guide for Workshop Leaders" also available from AAPT.

The titles of the eleven workshop modules are as follows:

1. How Students Think
2. Concrete and Formal Thought
3. Proportional Reasoning of College Students (Videotape)
4. "Formal Thought" (Film)
5. Analysis of Physics Problems
6. Analysis of Instructional Materials
7. Self-Regulation
8. Learning Activities for Self-Regulation
9. Analysis of Physics Concepts
10. Teaching Goals and Strategies
11. Suggested Reading

You will begin your workshop experience by studying the Orientation Module prepared by your workshop leader to describe the procedures and schedule that will be followed in your workshop.

We are grateful for many thoughtful comments and suggestions to the more than one hundred participants in the workshop held at Anaheim, CA using the trial edition of these materials. We are also indebted to Arnold A. Strassenburg, Warren Wollman, and Anton E. Lawson for reviewing our drafts and providing extensive assistance in the preparation of these materials.

Module 1 How Students Think

Introduction

You have probably been curious at various times in your teaching career about the thinking strategies that students enrolled in physics appear to use to solve problems. It is difficult for most of us to understand that many students do not use reasoning patterns that seem to be obvious. Many students substitute numbers into a formula they remember, even though the formula may not be applicable to the problem at hand. This situation quite naturally leads us to wonder about the reasoning that students utilize when we would employ mental operations such as separating variables, excluding an irrelevant factor, or applying a mathematical relationship such as ratios.

Objectives

To assist you in distinguishing among various patterns of thought used to solve simple problems in physics and mathematics.

Procedure

This module includes three puzzles: the Volume Puzzle (page 1-2), the Ratio Puzzle (page 1-6), and the Islands Puzzle (page 1-10). Each puzzle is followed by several typical student responses to the puzzle. Please complete at least two of the puzzle activities by writing out your own solution to the puzzle and then comparing your ideas with those of the students. The puzzles may be used in any order. Then please answer the review questions before going on to the next module.

Copyright American Association of Physics Teachers 1975

Module 1 Instructional Materials

Volume Puzzle Activity

1. Please write your answers in the spaces below.

    VOLUME PUZZLE

    Here are drawings of two vertical tubes (cylinders) which are filled to the same mark with water: the cylinders are identical in size and shape.

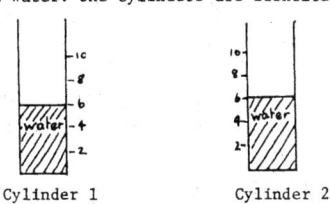

    Cylinder 1   Cylinder 2

    Here are two marbles, one made of steel and one made of glass. Both marbles have the same volume (that is, they are the same size). The steel marble is heavier.

    Glass   Steel

    The steel marble is heavier than the glass one, but both marbles will sink if placed in one of the cylinders. We are going to put one marble into each of the cylinders.

    After we have put the glass marble into cylinder 1, both cylinders and their contents look like this:

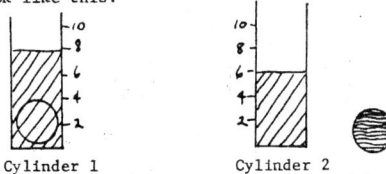

    Cylinder 1   Cylinder 2

    If we now put the steel marble into cylinder 2, what will happen to the water level in that cylinder? (Tell whether it will rise, fall, or stay the same; if it rises or falls, tell what the final water level will be in cylinder 2.)

    _____
    _____
    _____

    Explain why you predicted the result above.

    _____
    _____
    _____

2. This puzzle is accompanied by a videotape showing three girls working on the Volume Puzzle with the equipment described on the preceding page. The first girl (interviewed by Robert Karplus) is about fourteen years old*, the second (interviewed by John W. Renner) is seventeen, and the third (interviewed by Robert Karplus) is nineteen. Each girl's approach has a unique feature. Try to identify it while you are watching the videotape.

Please view the videotape now, and then describe the unique feature of each girl's thinking in the spaces below.

Fourteen-year-old:

Seventeen-year-old:

Nineteen-year-old:

3. The next pages present written student responses to the Volume Puzzle presented as a paper-and-pencil task. Study the responses and compare Students A with Students B.

Student A_1 (High School Junior)

    Prediction: "Rise to 8."
    Explanation: "Equal volume spheres displace the same volume of water."

Student A_2 (John Blake - Age 16)

    Prediction: "The water level in cylinder 2 will rise to the same height as in cylinder 1 after the glass marble is put in."
    Explanation: "Both marbles had the same volume, therefore the water level, after the marbles were put in, was the same in each cylinder. The weight in no way affected the degree to which the water rose."

Student A_3 (Barbara Downing - Age 21)

    Prediction: "Cylinder 2's water level will rise to the number 8.
    Explanation: "Since the 2 marbles have the same volume they will displace the same amount of water. Eureka! (weight has nothing to do with it)."

Student A_4 (Harold O'Keefe - Age 20)

    Prediction: "The level in cylinder 2 will also be 8; the same as in cylinder 1."
    Explanation: "If both marbles are heavy enough to sink and are the same size they will therefore displace the same amount of water thus raising the water level to the same numbers."

*Scene from PIAGET'S DEVELOPMENTAL THEORY: CONSERVATION. Compliments of Davidson Films, Inc., 3701 Buchanan Street, San Francisco, CA 94123

Student A₅ (College Junior)

Prediction: "The level of the water will be 8."
Explanation: "The reason that the water levels were both the same was because the objects both had the same volume and the cylinders which they were placed in were the same size with the same water level, therefore the objects displaced the same amount of water in both cylinders and their water level remained the same."

Student B₁ (High School Junior)

Prediction: "I think cylinder 2 would be higher to about the number 10 mark."
Explanation: "Because it put more pressure onto the water. This means it would push it upward. The steel ball seems to me like it would be heavier."

Student B₂ (High School Junior)

Prediction: "It will rise. The final water level in cylinder 2 will be 7."
Explanation: "The steel marble is heavier therefore the water will not rise as much."

Student B₃ (College Junior)

Prediction: "The water level in that cylinder will rise. I estimate the metal marble is twice as heavy so the water level will be at 10."
Explanation: "If you put an object that has the slightest weight into water, the level of the water will rise. The result would be the same as if you added water to the cylinder. Add something to something and you get more."

Student B₄ (College Junior)

Prediction: "The level of H_2O in cylinder 2 will rise to higher than 8 - probably 10."
Explanation: "Because the marble in cylinder 2 is heavier than the marble in cylinder 1. It's just like scales, the more weight the higher it goes up."

Student B₅ (David Kenting - Age 19)

Prediction: "The water in cylinder 2 will rise but not as much as in cylinder 1 because the glass marble has more volume."
Explanation: "Since the steel marble is heavier and smaller, it will sink faster but not have as much volume. Therefore the water level would rise, but not as much as the glass marble."

Student B₆ (Norma Kuhn - Age 20)

Prediction: "The steel marble will make it rise to a level of ten or more."
Explanation: "The reason for the increase in rise on the steel marble was because the steel marble is twice as heavy if not more than the glass marble."

Student B₇ (Deloris Johnson - Age 19)

    Prediction: "Cylinder level will rise because the marble is heavy. Final water level will be 10."
    Explanation: "Because the steel marble is heavier than the glass marble -- it took up more space than the glass marble."

Student B₈

    Prediction: "I think it will stay the same."
    Explanation: "I don't really know why. But it would seem the steel marble might have the weight to hold it down. The glass marble is lighter so it pushes the water up."

4. What similarities did you find among the responses of Students A? Please record your analysis here.

5. What similarities did you find among the responses of Students B? Please record your analysis here.

6. Please look at the responses again briefly and add any comments you may have about the differences between the two types.

Now proceed to another puzzle or to the Review Questions on page 1-14.

Module 2 Concrete and Formal Thought

Introduction

You have just completed several activities in which you examined student responses to various problems involving observation and reasoning. Observations of many children and young people attempting to perform similar tasks have led Jean Piaget and other psychologists to formulate theories concerning the mental processes an individual uses to deal with problem situations. In this module, we shall introduce you briefly to stages of reasoning, a feature of Piaget's theory we consider important for physics teachers. Modules 3 and 4 will give you more details and examples to illustrate what we say here. Modules 5 through 11 will help you to apply Piaget's ideas to physics teaching materials and teaching approaches.

Objectives

To assist you in describing and identifying student behavior that indicates concrete thought and behavior that indicates formal thought.

Procedure

Begin by reading the article, "Piaget's Theory in a Nutshell" included in the attached instructional materials. An audiotape with comments coordinated with the article is available; you may wish to listen to the tape during your first reading or during a review. To follow the article, we have provided two more activities for you in this module - - analyzing the student answers to the puzzles in Module 1, and participating in a group discussion - - each at a designated station arranged by your workshop leader. The order of these **two** activities is optional.

Piaget's Theory in a Nutshell is presented in revised form in
Chapter 2.
The audiotape presents a discussion between Dr. Karplus and Dr. Jane Bowyer, Professor of Science Education, Mills College.

Module 2 Audiotape "Piaget in a Nutshell"
A discussion by Robert Karplus and Jane Bowyer

Robert Karplus   Hello! This tape offers comments and examples of the use of concrete and formal reasoning patterns in physics. It accompanies Module 2 of the Workshop on Physics Teaching and the Development of Reasoning produced by the American Association of Physics Teachers. I'm Bob Karplus.

Jane Bowyer   And I'm Jane Bowyer. Have you read the article, "Piaget's Theory in a Nutshell" in Module 2? If so, you may find this tape instructive. If not, I'd suggest that you turn off the tape for now and read the article first, because it introduces the ideas on which this tape is based.

A transcript of the tape is included in your study guide beginning on page 2-10. If you'd like to follow the text, turn off the tape until you find the correct page and then turn it on again.

Robert Karplus   Piaget has described human intellectual development in terms of four stages during which individuals use certain patterns of reasoning.

Before continuing, I'd like to explain what I mean by a "pattern of reasoning." A pattern of reasoning is a mental process by which certain data, observations, or ideas are compared, organized, or transformed. For example, recognizing that a pendulum with mechanical energy of 20 joules and potential energy of 6 joules has kinetic energy of 14 joules, is a pattern of reasoning that involved comparing forms and amounts of energy. As another example, consider finding Mr. Ruthgren's telephone number between Rutherford and Ruthie; here one has to make use of the alphabetic order of letters and apply it successively to the first, second, third, fourth, and fifth letters in the names in the directory. A person who cannot conceptualize the alphabetic order of letters and apply it systematically is unlikely to find the listing.

Jane Bowyer   Piaget uses the term OPERATION rather than pattern of reasoning, and describes it in his article reprinted in Module 11. We have avoided the term OPERATION because of its other meanings in physics.

Let's now go back to the four stages. The first two, called sensory motor and pre-operational, are usually completed before a child is ten years of age. Only the last two are therefore of interest to us; they are called concrete operational and formal operational. Bob and I will give examples of some characteristic patterns of reasoning associated with these two stages.

General clues to identify concrete thought were listed on pages 2-2 and 2-3:

(C1) Does the individual make simple classifications and generalizations?

Robert Karplus — An example is consistently sorting a collection of objects into electrical conductors and electrical insulators after testing them in a circuit.

Jane Bowyer — (C2) Does the individual apply conservation logic?

Robert Karplus — When a rocket of mass M ejects exhaust of mass ΔM, the student concludes that the rocket has remaining mass $M-\Delta M$.

Jane Bowyer — (C3) Does the individual arrange a set of objects or data in serial order and establish one-to-one correspondence between the two sets?

Robert Karplus — Short organ pipes produce high pitched sound waves and long organ pipes produce low pitched sound waves.

Jane Bowyer — In these respects the individual can reason and solve problems beyond his/her ability in the preoperational stage. Items (C1), (C2), and (C3) are called concrete reasoning patterns, because they are applied to concrete objects and directly observable properties--electrical conductors, mass of a rocket, organ pipes, and audible pitch.

For comparison, we'll now describe a physics example that requires reasoning for which concrete patterns are not adequate. The example is an explanation of Archimedes's principle. Why is the buoyant force on body A when immersed in water equal to the weight of the displaced water?

Robert Karplus — First, imagine a hypothetical body B of exactly the same size and shape as A but composed of water. Since this water body is in equilibrium when immersed in water, the buoyant force it experiences is equal to its weight W_B. By the definition of body B, W_B is also the weight of the displaced water. Furthermore, the buoyant force on body B is the net force exerted by the rest of the water across body B's bounding surface. The buoyant force on body A is the net force exerted by the rest of the water across its bounding surface, which is identical with the bounding surface of B. Hence the buoyant force on A equals the buoyant force on B, and this in turn is equal to the weight of the displaced water.

Jane Bowyer — The reasoning involved here was not limited to concrete patterns because the hypothetical water body B and the "displaced water" were never perceptually distinct. Furthermore, the reasoning made use of certain propositions regarding the boundary surfaces and the equality of forces. The required reasoning comprised formal patterns.

Bob and I will now turn to formal reasoning patterns more broadly, with clues as listed on page 2-3:

(F1) Does the individual reason with propositions regardless of whether these are factual or hypothesized?

Robert Karplus — The student who correctly finds the thermodynamic efficiency of an ideal heat engine with black body radiation as working medium uses propositions such as the first law of thermodynamics, the equation of state of the radiation, and hypothesized processes making up the carnot cycle. Similar reasoning was used in our explanation of Archimedes's principle. It is also used when Newtonian mechanics, electrostatics, group theory, or other subjects are derived from definitions and postulates rather than being inferred from concrete examples and observations.

Jane Bowyer — (F2) Does the individual consider all conceivable combinations of experimental and theoretical conditions, even though some may not be realizable in nature?

Robert Karplus — To solve the Islands puzzle, for instance, the individual had to be aware of all possible ways Island C could be reached from Island A. When inferring the construction of an electric network from measurements at its terminals, the student has to consider all possible ways in which resistors, capacitors, and other circuit elements could be assembled.

Jane Bowyer — (F3) Does the individual recognize and interpret functional relationships in situations described by observable or abstract variables?

Robert Karplus — Students who use inverse proportion of weight and distance when equalizing a balance arm apply this formal reasoning pattern. When graphing and interpreting experimental data, they smooth out small irregularities in the measurements and describe the relationship by a simple analytic formula.

Jane Bowyer — (F4) Is the individual aware of and critical of his/her own reasoning?

Robert Karplus — The formal operational student checks an answer by comparing the results of a calculation with other similar calculations. He/she verifies that the solution of a motion problem with friction falls between the solutions to the same problem without friction and with very large friction (no slipping at all).

Jane Bowyer	On pages 2-3 and 2-4 there are additional examples of concrete and formal reasoning patterns. Unfortunately, we cannot give you a single, simple criterion for distinguishing between these two types of patterns.
Robert Karplus	You have to keep four additional points in mind, as described on page 2-4:
Jane Bowyer	First, a person may use primarily formal reasoning patterns in relation to ideas with which he is familiar, while using concrete reasoning patterns in other areas with which he is unfamiliar.
Robert Karplus	Second, the stage of formal thought is really open-ended, in that an individual may deepen his understandings, broaden the domains, and/or add new intellectual fields within which he can function formally with confidence.
Jane Bowyer	Third, one can enter the formal stage in any area only through self-regulation from the concrete stage, which must not be by-passed.
Robert Karplus	Fourth, by applying memorized formulas to familiar problems, a student may appear to use formal thought though the reasoning pattern is actually concrete.
Jane Bowyer	You may wonder whether you should test your students to identify their developmental stage. In view of what we have just said, and the fact that the stages are idealizations, such a testing effort is likely to give unclear results. I would recommend that you observe your students' work on their physics problems for a period of a week or two and try to identify the reasoning patterns they use.
Robert Karplus	This is the end of our comments. We hope you are finding the workshop interesting. Do discuss these ideas with your fellow participants--they may have a very different point of view from yours. Before turning off the tape player, please rewind the tape so it can be used by other participants. Thank you for listening. Goodbye!

Note: Modules 3 through 8 were revised to make Chapters 3 through 8

Module 9 Analysis of Physics Concepts

Introduction

Most physics teachers think about their courses in terms of topics covered, concepts explained, and principles applied. Our effort in this workshop has been to call your attention to another important dimension of physics teaching, your students' patterns of reasoning. By this time, you have probably concluded that most physics courses are addressed primarily to students who can use formal reasoning patterns with ease, and we would agree with that. Yet there are also the students who use formal reasoning patterns only with difficulty and in limited areas. To help you analyze course content and present it in a way that will be understandable to more of your students, we suggest that you classify physics concepts according to the reasoning patterns <u>necessary</u> to understand the meaning you wish to communicate. Concepts may then be called "concrete" or "formal," in analogy to the stages of reasoning. This module presents examples and explanations of "concrete" and "formal" concepts.

Objectives

To assist you in classifying physics concepts on the basis of the patterns of reasoning needed to understand them.

Procedure

We have arranged this module in the form of a learning cycle built around the distinction between concrete and formal concepts. Please find a partner with whom you can join in the activities. Then undertake the designated exploration, invention, and discovery activities described in the attached instructional materials. An audiotape to supplement the invention phase is available; we suggest you listen to it at a certain time as indicated in the text, but you may wish instead to proceed to some of the discovery activities before listening.

The audiotape transcript presents a discussion of self-regulation between John (Jack) Renner, Professor of Science Education, University of Oklahoma, and Robert (Bob) Fuller, Professor of Physics, University of Nebraska Lincoln.

College Teaching and the Development of Reasoning

Module 9 Audiotape "Self-Regulation and Physics Concepts"
A Conversation between Robert G. Fuller and John W. Renner

Robert Karplus: This is the audio tape accompanying Module 9 in the Workshop on Physics Teaching and the Development of Reasoning. The workshop was prepared under the auspices of the American Association of Physics Teachers with partial support from the National Science Foundation. The speakers are Bob Fuller, who is a little confused, and Jack Renner, who helps to explain.

Jack Renner: How are you doing?

Bob Fuller: Well, I'm a bit confused. These last two modules had something to do with the concept of self-regulation and I'm not sure I understand it. Think you could help me a little bit?

Jack Renner: Well, that is a confusing concept, and you know, it is so important for any teaching activities that are based on the intellectual development theory of Piaget that maybe I should take a few minutes to run over its meaning with you. Think of it like this. Whenever a student encounters an unfamiliar object, unfamiliar situation, or new event - in short, has a new experience - he interprets that new experience in terms of his existing patterns of reasoning, which form a system of understandings and operations called mental structures. Assimilation is Piaget's term. If the new experience is sufficiently complex and unfamiliar to the student, he will only understand it in terms of what he already knows and will not develop an appreciation of the entire meaning the teacher had intended. Development of a greater depth of understanding requires a change in the student's mental structures, a change Piaget calls accommodation. To change the structures, the student must have extensive exploratory experiences as was explained in Module 8. After an appropriate mental reorganization or accommodation, the intended impact of the new experience can be more fully felt. The process leading from assimilation to accommodation is self-regulation. After accommodation the student is in the position of reinterpreting his other knowledge in terms of the new mental structures.

Bob Fuller: Oh, I see. You start by assimilating into your present structures, then through self-regulation, you can accommodate to the new experiences. Sounds like some kind of new jargon to me. I wonder if you could give me some more specific example, maybe taken from physics.

Jack Renner: All right. The first physics course I ever had was in college. I remember the instructor very well, Dr. Tom Bedwell, who was a superior instructor, and he really drove home the concept of velocity. Velocity is the change of distance with respect to time. Thought I, "Big deal! That's speed. Just exactly

Renner (cont'd): what you read from a speedometer. Vectors are not important to the speedometer of my Model A." (That kind of dates me, doesn't it?) I promptly forgot all about the direction aspect of velocity.

Next, we encountered acceleration through an experience in the laboratory with a spark-gap device. That apparatus was, as I remember it, a free-fall apparatus and it delivered to me a nice tape that I could use to see that the carriage fell farther each successive unit of time. Therefore the carriage had to be traveling faster and the velocity had to increase during each interval of time. I could then appreciate the concept of acceleration, that is, a change of velocity with respect to time. I know my reasoning was, at best, early formal operational and that ratio of a ratio gave me some trouble; but in a short time I was saying centimeters per second per second just like everyone else. The holes in the tape made by the spark provided the concrete experience that led me to change my mental structures. Notice, Bob, that once again I did not pay any attention to the vector aspect of acceleration. Nor did the experience require this to be done! I had achieved self-regulation without it, I thought, and to a degree, I had.

Then the roof fell in. Uniform circular motion! Speed is constant and the object is accelerating. Impossible, said I. When the speedometer on my Model A reads constant, I am not accelerating. The patient instructor then reinforced the idea of velocity to a thoroughly confused physics student. I discovered that velocity and acceleration were completely different than I had thought them to be. My entire mental structure regarding velocity and acceleration had to be changed, I had to undergo a completely new self-regulation.

Now, when the instructor drew arrows over the V and A symbols, those arrows really meant something to me and led me to an entirely new set of understandings about Newtonian mechanics. I had finally changed my mental structures, the ultimate outcome of self-regulation (it was a lengthy and uncomfortable process, yet essential for my understanding).

Bob Fuller: Oh, yes, I think I've had similar experiences with self-regulation as a physics student myself. Now let me ask you a question that's really got me confused. I picked up this module that says something about analyzing physics concepts for formal and concrete concepts and now I find at the beginning all of this introduction to the idea of self-regulation. What has that got to do with it?

Jack Renner: That's a very good question. The basic answer to that question is that, in order to initiate self-regulation, you, the physics teacher, must do something with the physics subject matter. Think back to what I said earlier about how self-regulation starts. The student assimilates the outcome of a new experience to his present mental structures. If these mental structures are based on concrete reasoning

Renner (cont'd): patterns, and the student is presented with content that requires formal thought, he is in trouble. Without the aid of concrete experience and the opportunity for self-regulation, he will resort to rote memorization and learn a recipe. So you must begin with concrete concepts. Learners with concrete mental structures need exploration experiences that will lead them to comprehend concrete concepts. Data from such exploration plus the introduction of new concepts may then initiate self-regulation that will ultimately make the student think about the world in a formal way.

Bob Fuller: Oh, I see; so ability to be able to analyze physics concepts into concrete and formal categories might be very helpful for me as a physics teacher. What then is a concrete concept or a formal concept in physics?

Jack Renner: Well, Bob, a concrete concept is one about which the student can develop understanding through exploring concrete objects, concrete events, and/or concrete situations. Those explorations must produce concrete information that can be used to introduce the concept. In other words, for a concept to be concrete, the learner has to be able to develop understanding of it through actual experience. Consider the series circuit. A student can actually observe the fact that the elements in the series circuit are connected each one to the next, and that if you follow from one element to the next, you will come back to where you started. An aspect of the series circuit is that anything moving in the circuit, moves through or over every element. Furthermore, if you define an ammeter as a black box that measures what is moving in the circuit the student can insert the ammeter in the circuit at any one of several places and observe the same reading throughout. Thus a series circuit can actually be experienced. Many concrete discoveries can be made with the series circuit concept.

Temperature, Bob, is another concrete concept if it is related to hot and cold, which can be experienced, and can be measured with a thermometer. So, a concrete concept is one of which the student can develop an understanding through direct experience.

Bob Fuller: Oh, I get it, Jack, that seems fairly easy. Then just about anything I cover in the introductory physics course is probably a concrete concept.

Jack Renner: I wish that were true, but it isn't. Consider the idea of pressure. Now that's a common concept that we always have in physics courses. Pressure is normally defined as a ratio, force per unit area. To understand pressure, the student must understand force and area. While a single force can be experienced, generalizing the idea so force can be thought of as acting on one unit of area requires the student to use a formal reasoning pattern. Hence pressure viewed in

Renner (cont'd):	this way is a formal concept. Pressure viewed as the reading of a barometer, however, is a concrete concept, just as temperature defined as a thermometer reading was a concrete concept.
	Bob, the nuclear atom is another formal concept. For it to have meaning, the student must grasp the theoretical constructs of plus charge, minus charge, electron, proton, and neutron. None of those can be experienced; none is based upon experience.
Bob Fuller:	Oh, I see, Jack; so that really means that a lot of the concepts we use in the basic models we use in physics are formal concepts.
Jack Renner:	That's right. A formal concept is one that has meaning because of its position within a hypothetical deductive system. The concept of light polarization, for example, has meaning only in terms of the wave theory. Temperature viewed as mean molecular kinetic energy is a formal concept deriving its meaning from the kinetic molecular theory. Often teachers try to make formal concepts concrete by introducing a tangible model, such as styrofoam balls for atoms, ball bearings for molecules, water waves for light waves. Yet many students only learn about the model from such an experience. They do not construct the related system of postulates and deductions, and do not recognize the relationship of the theory to the concrete materials used to represent the idealized entities of the theory. Examples and careful explanations do help to clarify concepts, but models and examples do not of themselves turn formal concepts into concrete concepts.
Bob Fuller:	Now you've got me scared, Jack. What am I going to do with a course in which I have students who are still using concrete operational mental processes?
Jack Renner:	Well, students with concrete mental structures cannot properly assimilate formal concepts. Therefore, and this we believe to be the primary message of this module, these students can initiate self-regulation only if they have concrete experiences and the opportunity to begin with an understanding of concrete concepts in the topic to be mastered. After they reflect on the meaning of their experiences, self-regulation will lead them to build the formal mental structures with which they can then assimilate the necessary formal concepts.
Bob Fuller:	Oh, I see. Well, thank you very much, Jack. I am eager to go home and try these ideas out in my physics classroom.
Jack Renner:	Glad to help.
Robert Karplus:	This is the end of the Module 9 audio tape. Thank you very much for listening. Please rewind the tape back to the beginning so another workshop participant can use it. Goodbye.

Module 10 was revised to create Chapter 10 of this book.

Module 11 Suggested Reading

Introduction

This module contains reprints of several articles related to the ideas of stages of development and self-regulation and a bibliography of books and articles that you may wish to study after you complete the workshop.

Objectives

To provide you with examples of applications of the instructional techniques that you were introduced to in the workshop, and to make available a bibliography that you can use for further study.

Procedure -

If you would like further background information on Piaget's theory as related to physics instruction, read one or more of the three reprints selected from AJP and TPT that are included in the instructional materials for this module. If you would like additional information on Piaget's theory in general, read the article by Piaget reprinted here or consult the books and articles listed in the bibliography -- most are available in paperback and many can be obtained in any college or university bookstore.

INSTRUCTIONAL MATERIALS

This module contains the following materials:

1. Reading list of suggested books and articles.

2. Joe W. McKinnon and John W. Renner, "Are Colleges Concerned with Intellectual Development?" American Journal of Physics 39, 1047 (1971).

3. John W. Renner and Anton E. Lawson, "Piagetian Theory and Instruction in Physics," Physics Teacher 11, 165 (1973).

4. John W. Renner and Anton E. Lawson, "Promoting Intellectual Development Through Science Teaching," Physics Teacher 11, 273 (1973).

5. Anton E. Lawson and Warren T. Wolman, "Physics Problems and the Process of Self-Regulation" The Physics Teacher 13, 465 (1975).

Module 11 Instructional Materials

Books

1. Anderson, DeVito, Pyrli, Kellog, Kochendorfer and Weigand, <u>Developing Children's Thinking Through Science</u>, Prentice-Hall, N.J. 1970.

2. Ruth M. Beard, <u>An Outline of Piaget's Developmental Psychology for Students and Teachers</u>, Basic Books, Inc., N.Y. 1969.

3. David Elkind, <u>Children and Adolescence, Interpretive Essays on Jean Piaget</u>, Oxford Univ. Press.

4. Richard I. Evans, <u>Jean Piaget: The Man and His Ideas</u>, E.P. Dutton, Co. N.Y. 1973.

5. Hans G. Furth, <u>Piaget for Teachers</u>, Prentice-Hall, Inc., Englewood Cliffs, N.J. 1970.

6. Herbert Ginsburg and Sylvia Opper, <u>Piaget's Theory of Intellectual Development</u>, Prentice-Hall, Inc., Englewood Cliffs, N.J. 1969.

7. Richard M. Gorman, <u>Discovering Piaget</u>, Charles E. Merrill Publishing Co., Columbus, Ohio, 1972.

8. Bärbel Inhelder and Jean Piaget, <u>The Growth of Logical Thinking from Childhood to Adolescence</u>, Basic Books, N.Y. 1961 (There is a paperback classroom edition of this book)

9. John L. Phillips, Jr., <u>The Origins of Intellect: Piaget's Theory</u>, W. H. Freeman and Co., San Francisco, 1969.

10. Jean Piaget, <u>Genetic Epistemology</u>, W.W. Norton & Co., New York, 1970.

11. Jean Piaget, <u>The Psychology of Intelligence</u>, Littlefield, Adams, & Co., Paterson, N.J. 1968.

12. Jean Piaget, <u>Six Psychological Studies</u>, Vintage Books, Random House, N.Y. 1967.

13. Jean Piaget, <u>To Understand is To Invent</u>, Grossman Publishers, N.Y. 1973.

14. John W. Renner, Robert F. Bibens, and Gene G. Sheperd, <u>Teaching Science in the Secondary School</u>, Harper and Row, N.Y. 1974, Chapter 4.

15. M. F. Rosskopf, L. P. Steffe, and S. Taback, Eds., <u>Piagetian Cognitive-Development Research and Mathematical Education</u>. Reston, Va.: National Council of Teachers of Mathematics, 1971.

Selected Articles

1. Entire issue, Journal of Research in Science Teaching, Vol. 2, 1964, (Articles by Piaget, Karplus, Ausubel and Duckworth).

2. Arnold B. Arons, "Anatomy of an Introductory Course in Physical Science," Journal of College Science Teaching, April 1972.

3. Arnold B. Arons, "Toward Wider Public Understanding of Science," American Journal of Physics, 41, 769 (1973).

4. Arnold B. Arons and John Smith, "Definition of Intellectual Objectives in a Physical Science Course for Preservice Elementary Teachers," Science Education, 58, 3, pp. 391-400, 1974.

5. David Elkind, "Piaget and Science Education." Science and Children, Nov. 1972.

6. Elizabeth F. Karplus and Robert Karplus, "Intellectual Development Beyond Elementary School I: Deductive Logic," School Science and Mathematics, LXX, 5 (May, 1970) pp. 398-406.

7. Robert Karplus and Rita Peterson, "Intellectual Development Beyond Elementary School II: Ratio, a Survey," School Science and Mathematics, 70, 9 (December, 1970), pp. 813-820.

8. Edward G. Palmer, "Accelerating the Child's Cognitive Attainments Through the Inducement of Cognitive Conflict: An interpretation of the Piagetian Position." Journal of Research in Science Teaching, 3, 318-325 (1965).

9. Jean Piaget, "Intellectual Evolution from Adolescence to Adulthood," Human Development, 15, 1 (1972).

APPENDIX B CONTINUTED—READINGS FROM THE PHYSICS TEACHING AND DEVELOPMENT OF REASONING PUBLICATION

Are Colleges Concerned with Intellectual Development?

JOE W. McKINNON
Oklahoma City University
Oklahoma City, Oklahoma 73106
JOHN W. RENNER
University of Oklahoma
Norman, Oklahoma 73069
(Received 14 December 1970; revised 8 March 1971)

The assumption is often made by college professors that incoming freshman students think logically. Using tests designed by the Swiss psychologist Jean Piaget to evaluate logical thought processes, the authors found that 66 of 131 freshmen exhibited characteristics of the concrete operational thinker, while another 32 did not meet the criteria for formal operations. Professors further compound the problem by failing to recognize the kinds of experiences incoming freshmen students must have to move toward more logical thought. McKinnon, using a newly developed inquiry-oriented science course based upon Piagetian criteria, found a highly significant difference between those students who were exposed to the course and like students who were not. The authors concluded that secondary and elementary teachers do not take advantage of inquiry-oriented techniques so necessary to the development of logical thought because college professors do not provide examples of inquiry oriented teaching.

INTRODUCTION

Are colleges and universities making inadequate evaluations of student ability to think logically? Is the unrest today in many universities caused by student evaluation of problems based upon emotion rather than logic? Do student claims that curriculums are irrelevant, trivial, and inadequate in terms of the magnitude of the problems facing mankind today have substance, or are these students unable to evaluate logically the structure and necessity of those curricula? These questions, together with suspicions voiced by various professors of science about the inability of their freshman students to think logically about the simplest kind of problems, led the authors to question whether or not most college freshmen do think logically. This doubt about the ability of the entering freshman to think logically led to the following hypothesis: The majority of entering college freshmen do not come to college with adequate skills to argue logically about the importance of a given principle when the context in which it is used is slightly altered.

Since these students have been accepted by boards of admission that based their decisions upon high school transcripts and various established entrance examinations such as the American

J. W. McKinnon and J. W. Renner

TABLE I. A comparison of operational level of 131 students on Piagetian data.

	Male	Female	Total number	Per cent
Formal	25	8	33	25
Post-concrete	12	20	32	25
Concrete	16	50	66	50
Mean Piagetian score	12.82	9.45	Average 10.74	

College Test (ACT) and the Scholastic Aptitude Test (SAT), a different means of evaluation was sought. The evaluative system used is one based upon the ability of the student to think critically about problems, the answers to which would be found in his experiential background and could not be derived from memorized data.

WHEN DO STUDENTS BEGIN TO THINK LOGICALLY?

The scheme of evaluation of the ability to think logically which was used has been developed and verified by a Swiss psychologist, Jean Piaget, during many years' research with children. There is, however, no indication that his work has been extended to include entering college students, particularly American students. In addition, no work can be found with American children which verifies his conclusions that children begin to think logically between ages 11–15.

Piaget[1] found that children progress through various stages of mental manipulation and that these steps cannot be circumvented. Prior to thinking about abstract ideas, a student must undergo a period of physical manipulation of objects using the basic principles upon which the abstraction to be developed depends. This stage Piaget identifies as the *concrete stage* of thought. A student may handle concepts quite adequately, but until he has had many manipulative experiences he cannot recognize those concepts in the context of a broader generalization, of which the manipulative experiences and the concepts are simply a subset. Inhelder and Piaget[2] found that from 11–15 years of age most Swiss children should become *formal operational*, i.e., capable of abstract logical thought. The concern of this research was whether or not this was true for American college freshmen, i.e., had those students become formal operational?

A STUDY OF THE ABILITY OF COLLEGE FRESHMEN TO THINK LOGICALLY

McKinnon[2] studied responses to tasks given 131 members of the freshman class at an Oklahoma university in which students had to think logically about problems of volume conservation, reciprocal implication of two factors, the elimination of a contradiction, the separation of several variables, and the exclusion of irrelevant variables from those relevant to problem solutions. These tasks had initially been developed by Inhelder and Piaget[2] for determining the patterns of thought of children and the ages at which changes in those thought patterns occur.

Table I presents the test results for these 131 students using the foregoing tasks and the criteria specified by Inhelder and Piaget for demonstrating formal operational thought. Each student was graded from 0 through 4 on each of the tasks. Should a student score a total of 14 or more points on the five tasks, he was judged as definitely being at the formal operational stage. To achieve 14 points, he had to score at least 3 points on the

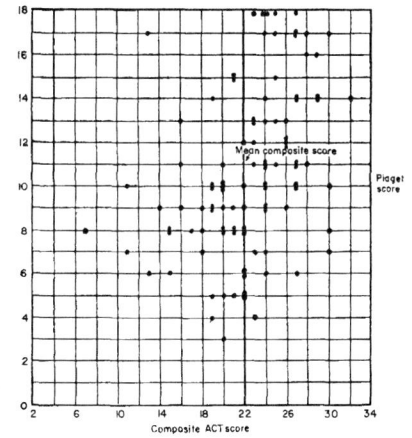

FIG. 1. A comparison of ACT score versus Piagetian score for 94 freshman students.

tasks for which 4 points were possible. If a student scored an average of 2 points or less on each of the five tasks, he was judged to be at the concrete stage of operations. Those students who scored more than 10 but less than 14 points were judged to be moving from the concrete stage to the formal stage of thought.

The findings, as shown in Table I, are that 50% of the entering college students tested were operating completely at Piaget's concrete level of thought and another 25% had not fully attained the established criteria for formal thought. The average score for all students was 10.74, with the males scoring significantly higher than females. An examination of the performance of the students on the various tasks used follows:

1. Of the college freshmen tested, 17% of them did not conserve quantity (the result of a change of form), while another 10% failed to recognize equivalence of volume. Thus, 27% of those students tested were at the lowest concrete operational state or less.
2. Reciprocal implication involved the student in the problem of reflecting a ball and the necessity to relate incident and reflected angles. This task was second only to the problem of density in the number of failures recorded—64% scored 2 or less.
3. The elimination of a contradiction involved the student in relating weight and volume of floating and sinking objects in a meaningful way. More than ⅓ of those tested did not relate weight and volume. Typically, they recognized weight only. Seldom was there a proportionality expressed; 67% of the students tested on this task were concrete operational.
4. The separation of variables task gave evidence that 50% of entering college freshmen could not recognize the action of a potential variable and find a way to prove the action of that variable.
5. The task of excluding irrelevant variables showed that 33% of the students tested could not eliminate variables of no consequence in a swinging pendulum, while another 18% could do no more than order the effects of weight.

In the research, a comparison was made of the score obtained by each student on the various Piagetian tasks given him and this score was correlated with his ACT composite score. (See Fig. 1.) A graph of these two scores shows that Pearson product–moment correlations were high for those students scoring at the average ACT composite of 22 or better, but correlations of -0.05 were found for students scoring less than that average. The university where this study was made ranks high in terms of the average ACT scores when compared with all other colleges and universities in Oklahoma[4] and is well above average for all regions of the United States.[5] Almost 75% of that university's entering freshmen, however, were either partially or completely concrete operational. What evidence exists, therefore, to demonstrate that logical thought can be promoted among all levels of students?

CAN INQUIRY-ORIENTED COURSES PROMOTE LOGICAL THOUGHT?

The University of Oklahoma Science Education Center has, for some time, been investigating the effects of inquiry-oriented teaching upon both teachers and pupils. Various new courses in science which utilize the inquiry approach have been evaluated. Porterfield[6] compared teachers of reading who had inquiry educational experiences in science with those who had not. He found that the former tended to use more questions requiring analysis and synthesis and other high-level cognitive thought patterns than did the latter group. Wilson[7] found much the same in a study of 30 classes of elementary children when fifteen of the teachers had been exposed to inquiry experiences in science and fifteen had not. Schmidt[8] found similar results by investigating the teaching in social studies done by teachers who had and had not been involved with inquiry in science. Friot[9] found in a study of seventh, eighth, and ninth grade science that courses placing emphasis upon the inquiry approach allowed students to be able to function at a much higher level of logical thought than those courses in which students did not have that inquiry experience.

Stafford used the development of conservation reasoning in children as an evaluative tool to determine whether or not inquiry-oriented science experiences move first graders toward the acquisition of concrete operational thought. The specific unit he used was *Material Objects*.[10] Stafford found: "... those first grade children who have experiences with the unit achieved the ability to

TABLE II. A comparison of the growth in logical thought processes of the experimental and control groups.

Group	Stage	Pre-test Females	Pre-test Males	Post-test Females	Post-test Males	Net gain Females	Net gain Males	Total
Experimental	Formal	4	11	14	16	10	5	15
	Post-concrete	14	6	17	8	3	2	5
	Concrete	24	10	11	3	−13	−7	−20
Control	Formal	4	14	7	17	3	3	6
	Post-concrete	6	6	11	7	5	1	6
	Concrete	26	6	18	2	−8	−4	−12

conserve much more rapidly than did those children who did not have these experiences."[11] *Material Objects* is an inquiry-centered unit and Stafford concluded: "... children so taught do show more rapid intellectual development than do those children not having such experiences."[11]

Finally, McKinnon,[12] in a study of the effect of an inquiry-centered science course on entry into the formal operational stage of concrete operational freshman college students, found a highly significant difference between those students enrolled in the course and a like group who had not been exposed to the course.

The data of Table I gave evidence of the ability of students to think logically. The data of Table II show the effect of the inquiry-centered course upon freshman students' ability to think logically. A net gain in favor of the experimental group resulted in 15 students moving into the formal stage of thought—compared with six for the control group. The post-concrete gain was, respectively, five and six, with the experimental group showing a net movement of 20 out of this category compared with 12 for the control group, a net gain of more than 50% for the group exposed to the influence of the new science course. The material of the science course did not include references to the tasks which were part of the test instruments; therefore, changes in ability to think logically were caused by added opportunities for inquiry. Another comparison in terms of the mean Piagetian scores for the two groups is shown in Table III.

After obtaining individual pre-test–post-test differences and summing them up for each group, an F ratio of 6.24 was obtained. This value is significant in favor of the test group at the 0.001 level of confidence; therefore, the hypothesis must be accepted that a properly designed course in science for freshman college students does enhance their logical thought patterns by increasing their ability to hypothesize, verify, restructure, synthesize, and predict.

The preceding research gives evidence that students do not think logically. However, research carried out on newly developed courses does give evidence that the logical thought processes can be enhanced. Therefore, who is at fault and what steps must be taken to alleviate the situation?

AN EVALUATION OF EDUCATIONAL RESPONSIBILITY USING THE INQUIRY APPROACH

If students do not think logically when they enter college, who has not discharged his responsibility? The immediate answer to the foregoing question is, the high school. That answer, however, needs to be examined.

Piaget states formal operations begin to emerge around 11 years of age. But Friot[9] found that 82% of eighth and ninth grade children (ages 13 and 14 years) were still concrete operational. Thus, children probably enter senior high school two to three years behind the age set by Piaget for

TABLE III. Pre-test and post-test Piagetian mean scores for both experimental and control groups.

Group	Experimental n	Experimental Piaget score	Control n	Control Piaget score
Pre-test	69	10.77	62	10.81
Post-test	69	12.32	62	11.14

entering into formal operation. While some of this age difference might be attributed to differences in the samples of Piaget and Friot, the entire 82% cannot be. The answer to the question of who is responsible for the lag in intellectual development seems to be the elementary school. But that answer, too, needs to be examined.

Begin that examination with another question. Who is teaching in the elementary and secondary schools? Teachers who have been educated in the existing colleges and universities. Those teachers have been subjected to four years of mainly *listening* experience. They have been lectured to, told to verify, given answers, and told how to teach. Lest you think the foregoing happens entirely in the colleges and/or departments of education, remind yourself that *all the content taken by a teacher* (which represents a substantially greater number of credit hours than do courses in education) *is taken in other colleges and/or departments*. Teachers are, in other words, not having the kinds of experiences with inquiry which Piaget says they must have in order to allow logical thought processes to develop. Future teachers are not having learning experiences in college which will permit them to learn the value of inquiry in educating a child. The foregoing rather dogmatic statement was substantiated by Gruber[13] when he found that only 25% of those attending NSF Institutes showed interest in inquiry-oriented science teaching, while Torrance[14] found that only 1.4% of elementary and 8.4% of secondary social studies teachers listed independent and critical thinking as important educational objectives. These statistics suggest that pre-college teachers place little value upon logical thought as an outcome of 12 years of schooling. Considering the paucity of research on implementation of logical thought as an educational objective, these educators' values will not change. The responsibility, then, for the small percentage of high school students attaining formal operations rests in part at the door of the institutions of higher education. They have assumed that their role is to tell. Future teachers, therefore, assume that telling is teaching and when they get their first class, they tell, tell, tell! All the while, very little, if any, intellectual development is going on. If, then, a college student develops logical thought, such development is more by accident than design.

One of the criteria Piaget cites for intellectual development is that of social transmission. Just possibly more intellectual development goes on in dorms, fraternities, sororities, and student hangouts than in the classroom because social transmission occurs in these places and little occurs in classes. To test our assertions, walk down the hall of any building on any campus and stop outside any classroom door and listen to who is talking. In most instances only information is being transmitted by the instructor.

Stafford and Renner[11] hypothesized that "... specialized educational experiences in inquiry-centered science teaching encourage a teacher to become sensitive to children, functionally aware of the purposes of education, and equipped to lead children to learn how to learn in all subject areas." The importance of this hypothesis is in the phrase "... all subject areas.", for inquiry methodology is not only the province of science, but all the other disciplines as well. Unfortunately, few other teaching areas have recognized the importance of the inquiry approach.

With the exception of a few new courses in the social science areas, most educators have chosen to ignore the lead taken by science and mathematics in devising new courses from kindergarten through the 12th grade. In many cases, the colleges have failed to use inquiry even when teaching the new curricula. This point was well illustrated by Gruber. Therefore, the blame must, in the last analysis, be placed, at least partially, upon the shoulders of those who teach at the college level and who insist upon ignoring the rapidly accumulating evidence in favor of the inquiry approach.

Renner and Stafford also pointed to the necessity of the teacher becoming "... functionally aware of the purposes of education ..." which in far too many cases they are not now. Unless teachers are aware of the primary purpose of education being the development of the learner's intellectual ability, they will not pursue teaching by giving the student opportunities for exploration using all his senses. Rather, they will continue to teach students what the teacher wants them to know and not what the students want to learn.

Finally, the total accumulation of research to date leads to the following hypotheses: (1) The secondary educational experience does not now promote logical thinking in most students. (2) An abundance of inquiry-oriented courses taught by teachers who are products of college and university professors who practice and profess inquiry must come into being in the secondary schools before an alternative to the first hypothesis can be accepted. Those experiences will have to be developed by many colleges.

Those hypotheses have profound educational implications since a serious problem has been shown to exist and the means for its alleviation have also been shown to be available to the profession. If colleges and universities do not try to solve the problem by assuming the responsibility for the intellectual development of their students, but continue to look at their primary purpose as the transmission of information about the several disciplines, the elementary and secondary schools will continue to fail in their mission of truly educating students. The needed changes, however, can come only through acceptance of inquiry by *all* of those who teach the teachers.

[1] J. Piaget, J. Res. Sci. Teach., 2, 176 (1964).
[2] J. Piaget and B. Inhelder, *Growth of Logical Thinking* (Basic Books, New York, 1958), p. 337.
[3] J. W. McKinnon, dissertation, University of Oklahoma, 1970.
[4] J. J. Coffelt and D. S. Hobbs, *In and Out of College* (State Regents for Higher Education, Oklahoma City, Ok., 1965.
[5] *American College Testing Program: College Student Profiles* (ACT Publications, Iowa City, Iowa, 1966).
[6] D. Porterfield, Ph.D. dissertation, University of Oklahoma, 1969.
[7] J. L. Wilson, Ph.D. dissertation, University of Oklahoma, 1967.
[8] F. B. Schmidt, Ph.D. dissertation, University of Oklahoma, 1969.
[9] F. E. Friot, Ph.D. dissertation, University of Oklahoma, 1970.
[10] *Science Curriculum Improvement Study*, University of California at Berkeley. (Rand-McNally, Chicago, Ill., 1970.)
[11] J. W. Renner and D. G. Stafford, Sci. Teacher 37, 55 (April 1970).
[12] J. W. McKinnon, Ref. 3, p. 37.
[13] H. E. Gruber, J. Res. Sci. Teach. 1, 124 (1963).
[14] E. P. Torrance, Ph.D. dissertation, University of Minnesota, 1960.

APPENDIX B CONTINUED

Piagetian Theory and Instruction in Physics

John W. Renner and Anton E. Lawson

Jean Piaget and his associates have been gathering data and formulating important theoretical observations about the intellectual development of children since 1927. Although it has taken American psychologists and educators a relatively long time to become acquainted with his work, it is becoming apparent that we can gain much by a careful evaluation of his efforts and their educational implications.

Numerous texts[1] have become available in recent years attempting to explain Piaget's theory and its educational significance. The primary purpose of this paper is similarly to explain his ideas, and further to expand a scheme of instruction and classroom procedures that arise as a consequence of that theory.[2] When possible these ideas will be put forth using examples in physics context in an effort to elucidate difficult ideas.

Mental Structures

A central idea in Piaget's work and fundamental in understanding his theory is the concept of mental structure. It would be satisfying to be able to indicate the physiological and chemical nature of these structures, but at this point in the study of human mental functioning that is not possible.[3] Instead their existence in the brain is hypothesized from observable behavior; determination of their exact nature awaits further research. These hypothesized mental structures function to organize the environment so that the organism can function effectively. In this sense the construction of these structures carries adaptive value for the individual. An analogous situation is found in the genetic adaptation of evolving species. Basically, then, mental structures represent a more or less tightly organized mental system to guide behavior.

During development of the human infant to adulthood, these structures must be built within the brain. A complete developmental sequence of the structures is not genetically given to the child, they must be learned. According to Piaget, the building and rebuilding of these mental structures is what underlies the process of intellectual development. These structures control how and what we think and guide behavior. In other words, structures actually represent our knowledge.

Since science educators are deeply concerned with intellectual development and the building of mental structures about everything from the metric system to the theory of relativity, two questions need to be asked: (1) How are structures built? (2) Once the structure is built is it static or can it be altered?

These two questions are not mutually exclusive, and we will answer the second one first. Structures can be altered, and that may be a more than

Professor Renner holds B.A. and M.A. degrees from the University of South Dakota and a Ph.D. from the State University of Iowa. He has taught at various levels, worked on a national curriculum project (S.C.I.S.) and with professional groups. He has authored or co-authored six books and over 70 journal articles. (Dept. of Physics, University of Oklahoma, Norman, Oklahoma 73069.)

Anton E. Lawson (M.A., University of Oregon) is a Graduate Assistant of Science Education. He has taught in elementary and junior high schools in California, and is currently investigating selected aspects of Piagetian theory and their educational implications. (Dept. of Physics, University of Oklahoma, Norman, Oklahoma 73069.)

adequate definition of education—the building and rebuilding of structures. The answer to the first question should then give us good insights into how learning takes place and how instruction should be planned.

The Building of Mental Structures — A Problem

An important point must be made before examining the process by which mental structures are formed according to Piaget. Structures do not come from simply making a mental record of the world by keeping eyes and ears open. Unfortunately, it would appear that many teachers subscribe to this view. Work done by Van Senden with congenitally blind persons provides an interesting example of this point.[4] These persons, who had gained sight after surgery, could not identify objects without handling them. They were unable to distinguish a key from a book, when both lay on a table. Also they were unable to report seeing any difference between a square and a circle. The important idea to note is this: Whether the task is to simply distinguish objects in the environment or complex relationships such as $F = ma$, acceleration, or velocity, the ability to develop the understandings requires much more than a simple photographing of the environment.

According to Piaget a person is unable to perceive things until his mind has a structure which enables its perception. Without the development of a mental structure things which seem obvious to an adult, such as the difference between a key and a book, a square and a circle, are simply not perceived by beginners. But this leads us to a fundamental problem. If learning is the building or rebuilding of mental structures, and if structures are needed in order to perceive and learn and are not derived from simply copying the external world, then where do they come from?

Plato's answer to this question was simple. The structures were innate and developed through the passage of time and the growth of the brain. Of course at the other end of the spectrum is the belief that these structures derived directly from the environment. This is the classical empiricist's view; but we have already seen that this view is untenable.

Piaget rejects the Platonic view, except to admit that certain very primary structures must be present at birth. Piaget's view is that the development of structures derives from a dynamic interaction of the organism and the environment which he calls equilibration.

The Building of Mental Structures — Equilibration

From birth, basic structures enable the child to begin interacting with his surroundings. As long as that interaction is successful the basic structures continue to guide behavior. However, owing to the child's inborn drive to interact with his environment he meets contradictions, i.e., things which do not fit his present mental structures. These contradictions produce a state of disequilibrium. In other words, his present mental structures are disrupted and must be replaced. Through continued investigation and guidance from others, the child alters or accommodates his disrupted mental structure. Once this is accomplished he is then able to assimilate the new situation. The new structure that is developed is then tried. If the structure guides behavior so that the child's efforts are rewarded (reinforced) the structure is also reinforced. In this manner the child builds new mental structures and adapts to new situations.

The above-described process underlies all development according to theory. The entire process of development of mental structures is viewed as a process of *equilibration* or self-regulation. This process results in the development of progressively more complex and useful mental structures.

The Building of Mental Structures — Contributing Factors

The role of three main factors, *experience, social transmission,* and *maturation* can be isolated in the process of equilibration. It is apparent that experience is a necessary part of learning. With no contact with the environment, no contradictions of present structures arise and no possibility for further exploration into the situation that produced the contradiction is possible.

There are basically two kinds of experience—physical, and logical–mathematical. This distinction is important because the different experiences lead to different kinds of mental structures.

Physical experience is exactly what the phrase connotes—actual physical action on the objects in the world. This physical experience leads to the development of structures about objects. At some point, however, the learner begins to see more in his interaction with the world than just objects. He sees that his actions with objects produce some kind of order themselves. An example of this is when a learner discovers that ten objects, when counted left to right provide the same result as when counted right to left. In other words, the action itself has properties. The learner now can make the generalization that the sum of any set of objects is independent of their order. Now the student has a mental structure that he can utilize in many situations and that is a logical–mathematical structure. The structures then enable the learner to operate logically within his environment. The basic behavioral patterns directed by the mental structure are called operations. In the early structure-building stages the opportunity for the learner to interact with concrete material is mandatory.

Piaget has not projected to what academic level the necessity for interaction with material exists; he says, "...coordination of actions before the stage of operations needs to be supported by concrete material."[5] A literal interpretation of that statement would be that, regardless of age, the student must have materials to perform actions with until he can begin to utilize logical–mathematical operations. Our research with kindergarten and elementary school children,[6] junior high school students,[7] and college freshmen,[8] all studying science, supports our interpretation of the foregoing quotation.

The factor of experience, then, helps students to build operational-structures which can ultimately lead them to think abstractly about the world around them. In other words, it is experience with the materials of the discipline that produces the person who can understand abstract content and *not* studying abstract content which produces students who can interact with the materials and invent abstract generalizations. This says to science teachers that the laboratory *must precede* the introduction of an abstract generalization

296   R. G. FULLER ET AL.

Fig. 1. *Jean Piaget. Photograph by the Science Curriculum Improvement Study.*

Piaget's second factor, *social transmission*, also provides a basis for structure building. The very young child — and some not so young — operate from a very egocentric frame of reference. He cannot see things objectively because he always looks at them as related to himself. Such a thinker cannot objectively view and/or evaluate anything. In order to shake the learner from an egocentric view of anything, he must experience the viewpoints and thoughts of others. He must, in other words, interact with other people. If he does not, he has no reason to alter the mental structures which he gained from an egocentric frame of reference. Social interaction can lead to conflict, debate, shared data, and the clear delineation and expression of ideas. All of these require that the student carefully examine his present beliefs which will, according to the Piagetian model, develop and change structures. In order to have all of this happen, however, students must be encouraged to talk with each other and their teachers. Data from an experiment must be shared, discussed, retaken, and rediscussed. Students, "... should converse, share experience, and argue."[9] The factor of social interaction is valuable in building and rebuilding structures, but it is insufficient because the learner can receive valuable information via language or via education directed by an adult only if he is in a state where he can understand this information. That is, to receive this information he must have a set of experiences that enables him to assimilate this information.

Maturation, the third factor, must also be considered. Evidence indicates that these structures require time to develop. Old structures cannot be accommodated to new experiences all at once. The process of development is slow, as any teacher can attest.

Perhaps this personal example will help clarify how these three factors interact in the process of equilibration to change structures. Our first contact with $V = IR$ was a rather traumatic experience. We vaguely understood that it involved the conservation of energy, but concentrated upon memorizing what the symbols meant and how to juggle the formula. In short, an advanced state of disequilibrium was our lot! When meter readings were substituted for the very abstract terms of potential difference and current, the symbols began to have meaning, and after a good deal of thinking equilibrium was achieved. Then a series circuit with one source and more than one resistor and parallel circuit was introduced. The notion that in a series circuit the total potential difference, V_t, of the source equaled the sum of all voltage drops, V_i, $i = 1,2,3,...n$, around the circuit brought on another disequilibration. Once again meter readings (objects) were salvation; we began to really understand that

$$V_t = \sum_{i=1}^{n} V_i, i = 1,2,3,...n,$$

really was a conservation of energy statement. Now $V = IR$ was a concept which was available for use and once again equilibrium was achieved. Parallel circuits presented no problem and Kirchhoff's laws were nearly obvious.

This example demonstrates that the science laboratory clearly has a place in promoting equilibration and disequilibration. Data from an experiment can be very threatening, because they too often produce disequilibrium. But to the sensitive, concerned science teacher, disequilibrium is an opportunity; he can now introduce the student to the major conceptualizations of the discipline which will produce equilibrium. This sequence of events suggests that perhaps the principal role of the teacher is to promote disequilibrium and equilibrium, because through the process of equilibration structures are built and rebuilt. Equilibration proceeds through experience with the materials worked with and the social interaction of those around us.

The Learning Cycle

An instructional technique incorporating much of Piagetian theory has been developed and refined by the Science Curriculum Improvement Study, University of California,

Berkeley. Their procedure is basically a three-phase process: (1) exploration, (2) invention, and (3) discovery.

Exploration involves the students in concrete experience with materials. As a consequence of these initial explorations, which sometimes may be highly structured by the teacher or on other occasions relatively free, the learner encounters new information which does not fit his existing structures. This produces disequilibrium. At the appropriate time, determined by the teacher, he suggests a way of ordering the experiences. In essence, the teacher invents a new structure which often involves a new concept. This phase, termed *invention*, is analogous to Piaget's structure building and promotes a new state of understanding or equilibrium. The question now is: Can the new situation be applied in other situations? During phase three, *discovery*, further application of the inventions are discovered by the students. Discovery experiences serve to reinforce, refine, and enlarge the content of the invention.[10]

Again an example from physics may help to clarify these points. Experience in the laboratory with voltage and resistance, seeing the effect these have on current, and recording all these data is exploration. These exploratory experiences, if provided at the appropriate time, will promote disequilibrium and lead students to question relationships. Since it would take a brilliant student to invent the notion that $V = IR$, the formal statement of that relationship is left up to the teacher. The teacher, having explained the relationship, has in effect provided a way of ordering the student's experience. This is invention. Now the student is in a position to make discovery with this new concept. He can apply it to various types of circuits, magnitudes of voltage, current, and resistance, practically any type of situation he can design. That is the true notion of discovery. Exploration, invention, and discovery are the three phases of the learning cycle and represent a process which will lead the learner to move from physical action to abstract mental operations. Science in general — and in our opinion physics in particular — has a unique opportunity to lead students to build structures. Are we utilizing it? There is much evidence to suggest we are not.[11]

Levels of Thinking

Piaget's theory has gone further than describing how mental structures are formed. He has outlined the basic structures that dictate behavior from birth to adulthood. The structures fall roughly into four categories. Each category or stage incorporates and adds to the structure of the previous stages. If Piaget is correct, it becomes imperative for educators to understand these stages of development. They provide a possible key for adapting instruction to the learner's capabilities. They further suggest types of activities which could promote intellectual development.

The child at birth is in a state Piaget calls *sensory–motor*. During this period, which lasts until about 18 months, the child acquires such practical knowledge as the fact that objects are permanent. The name of the second stage describes the characteristics of the child — *preoperational*, the stage of intellectual development before mental operations appear. In this stage, which persists until around seven years of age, the child does not, for example, reverse his thinking; he exhibits extreme egocentricism, centers his attention upon a particular aspect of a given object, event, or situation, reasons transductively, and does not demonstrate conservation[12] reasoning. In other words, the child's thinking is very rigid.

At about seven years of age the thinking stages of children begin to "thaw out" — they show less rigidity. The stage the child has entered is called *concrete operational*. Those structures which permit the reversal of thinking *et al.*, which are denied a pre-operational thinker, begin to show themselves as the child moves more and more deeply into the concrete operational stage. The child can now perform what Piaget calls mental experiments — he can assimilate data from a concrete experience and arrange and rearrange them in his head. In other words, the concrete operational child has a much greater mobility of thought than when he was younger.

The name of this stage of development — concrete operational — is representative of the type of thinking of this type of learner. As Piaget explains this stage: "The operations involved...are called 'concrete' because they related directly to objects and not yet to verbally stated hypotheses."[13] In other words, the mental operations performed at this stage are "object bound" — operations are tied to objects. This point must be firmly entrenched in the minds of teachers, because when working with students who are moving through this stage they must focus their teaching on the object — the actuality — and not on the abstract. Density, for example, is an abstraction — lenses are concrete.

As the child begins to emerge from the concrete operational stage of thought, according to the Piagetian model, he enters the last stage called *formal operational*. According to Piaget, this occurs between 11 and 15 years of age. A person who has entered that stage of formal thought "...is an individual who thinks beyond the present and forms theories about everything, delighting especially in considerations of that which is not."[14] Formal operational thought is capable of reasoning with propositions only and has no need for objects. It should be pointed out, however, that for this type of thought to occur it must be developed through the use of objects. For that reason this type of thought can be described as propositional logic. An analysis of formal operations reveals that they "...consist, essentially of 'implication'... and 'contradiction' established between propositions which themselves express classifications, seriatations, etc."[15] The formal thinker can form hypotheses and test them. To do this, he must isolate and control variables and exclude irrelevant ones. This type of thought can truly be described as abstract.

The maximum educational gain that comes from the study of science is derived from the isolation and investigation of a problem. Quite obviously this involves the formulation and stating of hypotheses and using a form of thinking which can be described as, if..., then..., therefore. That is, of course, propositional logic. In other words, science teaching should promote formal thought. But it cannot do so if concrete operational thinkers are asked to interact with science on a formal operational level and their teacher teaches them as though they think formally. Concrete operational learners must interact with science at that level, they *cannot* do otherwise. Only then will they build the struc-

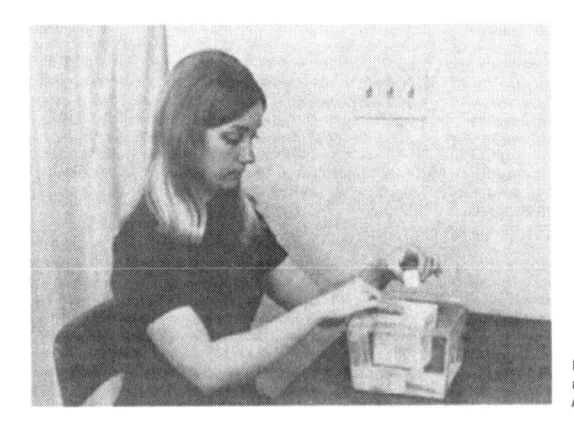

Fig. 2. *Eliminating the contradiction in the sinking-floating problem is useful to identify formal thinking.*

tures that promote their intellectual development toward formal thought.

Where are today's science students in the development of formal thought? If the programs of study available for high school physics are examined, for example, the fact that they require the use of abstract thinking is immediately apparent. The same can be said for most of the new curriculum developments in science. As Kohlberg and Gilligan recently said: "Clearly the new curricula assumed formal operational thought rather than attempting to develop it."[16] Is such a statement justified? Can science taught at the pre-collegiate and college levels promote formal thought? What can teachers do, if anything, as they select and arrange curricula and interact with students to promote formal thought? A later article in this journal will address itself to those questions.

[The second part of this article will appear in the May issue of *The Physics Teacher*.]

References

1. Examples of those texts are: Herbert Ginsburg and Sylvia Opper, *Piaget's Theory of Intellectual Development* (Prentice-Hall, Englewood Cliffs, N.J., 1969); Richard Gorman, *Discovering Piaget: A Guide for Teachers* (Merrill, Columbus, 1972). John L. Phillips, Jr., *The Origins of Intellect: Piaget's Theory* (San Francisco, Freeman, 1969). John G. Flavell, *The Developmental Psychology of Jean Piaget* (Van Nostrand, Princeton, N.J., 1963).
2. This scheme of instruction also incorporates theoretical observations detailed in Chester A. Lawson, *Brain Mechanisms and Human Learning* (Houghton Mifflin, Boston, 1967).
3. For hypothesized neural mechanisms see Lawson, Ref. 2, pp. 9–16.
4. D.O. Hebb, *The Organization of Behavior*, (Wiley, New York, 1949), pp. 31–36.
5. Jean Piaget, J. Res. Sci. Teach. 2, No. 3, 180 (1964).
6. Don G. Stafford and John W. Renner, "SCIS Helps the First Grader to the Logic in Problem Solving," School Sci. Math. 70, 159 (Feb. 1970).
7. Faith Elizabeth Friot, *The Relationship Between an Inquiry Teaching Approach And Intellectual Development*, unpublished doctoral dissertation, University of Oklahoma (1970).
8. Joe W. McKinnon and John W. Renner, Amer. J. Phys. 39, 1047 (1971).
9. Ginsburg and Opper, Ref. 1, p. 228.
10. Chester A. Lawson, *So Little Done: So Much To Do* (Regents University of California, Berkeley, Calif. 1966) Monograph, p. 7.
11. Robert J. Whitaker, *Teaching Practices In Introductory Physics Courses In Selected Oklahoma Colleges*, unpublished doctoral dissertation, University of Oklahoma (1972).
12. Ginsburg and Opper, Ref. 1, p. 164.
13. Jean Piaget and Barbel Inhelder, *The Psychology of the Child* Basic Books, New York, 1969), p. 100.
14. Jean Piaget, *Psychology of Intelligence* (Littlefield, Adams & Co., Totowa, N.J., 1966), p. 148.
15. See Ref 14, p. 149.
16. Lawrence Kohlberg and Carol Gilligan, *Daedalus* 100, No. 4, 1051 (Fall 1971).

APPENDIX B CONTINUED

Promoting Intellectual Development Through Science Teaching

John W. Renner and Anton E. Lawson

The previous article in this series, ["Piagetian Theory and Instruction in Physics," Phys. Teach. 11, 165 (1973)] discussed the process of intellectual development and the intellectual level concepts of Jean Piaget and briefly commented upon the relation of those ideas to teaching and learning physics. The purpose of this article is to comment upon the thought patterns of secondary school and first-year college students and to suggest types of experiences students need to have to enable them to move toward acquiring formal thought.

We start with the assumption that all students deserve the opportunity to develop the capacity to think with the "If..., then..., therefore..." form — in other words, to develop formal thought. Three questions immediately arise:

(1) What type(s) of thought do secondary school and first year college students use?

(2) How can the student's level-of-thought be assessed?

(3) What can educational institutions do to change the type(s) of thinking students do?

Levels of Thought, Students, and Content

If you reflect back to the first article we prepared on the topic of learning, you will recall that we pointed out that learners begin to leave the pre-operational stage at around seven years of age. At this point, they enter the concrete operational stage of thought and, according to Piaget, move more and more deeply into that stage until somewhere between 11 and 15 years of age. That is the time when they begin to move into the last stage of intellectual development — formal operational thought.

Now the transition from concrete to formal thought is of the utmost importance to teachers who work with students in grades 10-12 in the secondary schools and in their first years of college. *If* students have achieved the ability to think formally, the teacher can proceed to lead them to deal in the great abstractions of science because they can think with form, "if..., then..., therefore...," or propositional logic. These teachers need not be as concerned with providing students direct experience with the materials of the discipline as those teaching concrete operational thinkers. But if students are concrete operational, they cannot think with propositional logic and *all* they learn will come from interacting with the materials of the discipline. These statements carry with them serious implications for science teaching; indeed for all types of teaching which deal with abstractions. Therefore, the validity of these statements must be carefully evaluated. At this particular time such an evaluation has not been carried out to any satisfactory extent. However, to any teacher who has had the experience of having his students simply not comprehend what to him seemed eminently clear, Piaget's hypothesis becomes extremely compelling.

Professor Renner holds B.A. and M.A. degrees from the University of South Dakota and a Ph.D. from the State University of Iowa. He has taught at various levels, worked on a national curriculum project (S.C.I.S.) and with professional groups. He has authored or co-authored six books and over 70 journal articles. (Science Education, University of Oklahoma, Norman, Oklahoma 73069.)

Anton E. Lawson (M.A., University of Oregon) is a Graduate Assistant of Science Education. He has taught in elementary and junior high schools in California, and is currently investigating selected aspects of Piagetian theory and their educational implications. (Science Education, University of Oklahoma, Norman, Oklahoma 73069.)

Basically one can grasp why Piaget asserts that "if..., then..., therefore..." thinking is required to understand abstract concepts if you understand the nature of the abstract concepts themselves. The abstractions in physics, as well as in biology and chemistry, are in actuality models created by scientists to explain observable data. These models do not arise directly from the observations; rather, they simply represent attempts to construct an explanation or model which implies what is observed. The scientist creates the model (we do not know how) and reasons *if* his model is true, *then* consequences should be found. If the predicted consequences are indeed found, he has *therefore* supported his model. The process is hypothetico-deductive or in the if..., then..., therefore... form. For a student to fully grasp the meaning of the abstract models he, too, must be able to think in the if..., then..., therefore... form. The inertia principle, for example, has to be deduced and verified from its implied consequences. Strictly speaking, it does not give rise to observable empirical evidence.

Consider Newton's second law, $F = ma$. That law is always stated (and properly so) in terms of the mass of a body. Now mass is not a concrete concept — it is an abstraction. All matter that students have *experienced* exists in a gravitational field. Therefore what students have experienced is not mass but weight. This point is of little consequence to a formal operational thinker; mass is an abstract concept he can comprehend and do mental experiments with. To succeed in understanding $F = ma$ (particularly when identifying its units) however, the learner must be able to do mental experiments with abstract concepts. Now look at acceleration — a rate of change of a rate of change. A rate of change is a concrete concept; miles/hour, cents/pound, and pounds/foot are all situations with which a learner can have concrete experiences. But when you change that rate of change so that you are referring to miles/hour/second, providing experience which will lead a student to that is nearly impossible. (To make acceleration even more abstract, it is usually written, for example, as ft/sec^2.) About the best that can be done is to let the student experience the fact that as an object slows down, the time intervals required to travel equal distances get progressively longer. Now consider the experience students have had with forces. Those experiences have no doubt been pushes and pulls and have probably been measured in pounds. Now a student takes an abstract quantity (mass) which he has not experienced and multiplies it by a second very abstract quantity (acceleration) and produces a third quantity called force. But here the force is not measured in pounds but in kilogram-meters/second[2] and is called a newton. *There is nothing concrete about that entire process. It is a complete abstraction.* Now if a student is a formal thinker, he can probably handle that abstraction — *he can't if he is concrete operational*. Do not misread *can?* to mean "doesn't want to"; it means exactly what it says, *can?*.

Couple Newton's second law with the calorie, transverse waves, the particle theory of light, the gauss and maxwell, and the second law of thermodynamics and you have a pretty good sampling of a first-year physics course. You also have a fair list of abstractions. Those are abstract topics for which formal operations are a necessity. How does a teacher determine whether or not his class can handle such abstract topics?

Assessing Student Level of Thought

What we have done in the area of determining student success with tasks which reflect formal operational thought has been greatly influenced by four sources:

1. Bärbel Inhelder and Jean Piaget, *The Growth of Logical Thinking From Childhood to Adolescence* (Basic Books, New York, 1958), Chaps. 1-7.

2. *The Developmental Theory of Piaget: Conservation* (John Davidson Film Producers, San Francisco, 1969).

3. Elizabeth F. Karplus and Robert Karplus, "Intellectual Development Beyond the Elementary School: I. Deductive Logic," [School Sci. Math. **LXX**, 398 (May 1970)].

4. Robert Karplus and Rita W. Peterson, "Intellectual Development Beyond Elementary School II: Ratio A Survey," [School Sci. Math. **LXX**, 813 (Dec. 1970)].

The foregoing sources contain many more tasks than will be described here, and you are urged to try them. Here are two tasks which we have used quite extensively.

(1) *The Conservation of Volume* (Source 2, above). This task requires two cylinders of exactly the same size but having different weight (we have used one made of brass and the other of aluminum); those properties of the cylinders are pointed out to the student. He is next presented with two identical tubes partially filled with water and allowed to adjust the water levels until he is convinced that each tube contains exactly the same amount. The student is then asked if when the cylinders are put in the tubes, the heavy cylinder will push the water up more, if the lighter cylinder will push the level up more, or if the cylinders will push the levels up the same. The examiner requires the student to explain his answer, and often it is the explanations and not the initial responses that are most revealing of thought patterns. If the student completes the task successfully, he has provided evidence of beginning formal operational thought.

(2) *The Exclusion of Irrelevant variables*[1] (Source 1, above). The student is presented with a pendulum whose length can be easily changed and three different sized weights which can be used for the pendulum bob. He is told to do as many experiments as he needs to, using many different lengths of string and all the various-sized weights until he can explain what he needs to do to make the pendulum go fast or slow. Again, note that the examiner bases his evaluation on the student's explanations. The variables of string length, angle, and push are also pointed out to the student. If the examinee recognizes that length is the only relevant variable, he is about to enter into the formal operational thought period. If he not only excludes the irrelevant variables but hypothesizes a solution to the problem and demonstrates his solution, he has entered the formal period. If the student can state a general rule about pendula in such a way that it can be tested, he is probably capable of working with propositional logic. Although the concept of an oscillating pendulum and its period is not an abstract concept itself (its discovery and construction related directly to a concrete physical experiment), solution of the pendulum problem does indicate the use of propositional

logic and that is a prerequisite to the understanding of abstractions.[3]

Student Performance on the Tasks

Physics is normally taught in the high schools to students in grades eleven and twelve. We administered these tasks, therefore, to 99 eleventh graders and 97 twelfth graders from Oklahoma public schools. The schools were randomly selected, and students in each selected school were also randomly selected. Table I shows what we found.

Table I. *Performance of formal operational tasks by a random sample of high school students.*

Population	Conservation of volume	Exclusion
11th Grade (N=99)		
Females (N=54)	19	14
Males (N=45)	26	23
12th Grade (N=97)		
Females (N=47)	18	16
Males (N=50)	34	20

The data in Table I suggest that out of the population from which physics students are drawn, not many are formal operational. You are urged to administer these tasks to your students. If you are interested in doing some group evaluations of your students, study sources three and four listed earlier. Source three deals with determining student ability to reason abstractly by presenting a problem and then providing one clue at a time. The clues and the original statement of the problem must then be analyzed and used to draw conclusions. Source four assesses student ability to apply the concept of ratio. When using ratios, the student is utilizing proportional thinking which is an essential component of formal thought. Please do not make the assumption that by the time students get to physics in high school only those who think formally enroll. Our high school data from those enrolling in high school physics, though not extensive enough to make a definite statement, suggest that such is not the case. Data will be presented later which show that many concrete operational thinkers are found at the first year college level.

Kohlberg and Gilligan[4] report that in a study of the ability of 265 persons to perform successfully on the pendulum task (exclusion), these results were obtained:

age 10-15 – 45%;   age 21-30 – 65%;
age 16-20 – 53%;   age 45-50 – 57%.

If you assume that performance on the pendulum task is an indication that formal operational thought is present, the foregoing data suggest what our data do – a large percentage of the adolescent population is not formal operational. Unfortunately, our age ranges and those of Kohlberg and Gilligan do not coincide exactly, and so no more definite statement can be made from those two groups of data.

The conservation of volume and the pendulum tasks were taken by college freshmen. The results shown in Table II were obtained.

Table II. *Performance of college freshmen for formal operational tasks.*

Number of college freshmen	Conservation of volume	Exclusion
185	133	77

The data shown in Table II clearly reflect that the majority of college freshmen have not moved deeply into the formal operational stage of thought – 77 of 185 experiencing success on the exclusion task is not too impressive. We do not mean to infer that performance on the pendulum task is an absolute measure of the achievement of formal operational thought. We *do* mean to infer that performance on these tasks is a strong indication of student ability to use propositional logic. We tested our inference that these two tasks do help isolate formal thinkers – those that use thought patterns which are "the stock in trade of the logician, the scientist, or the abstract thinker."[5] In searching for a test population we ruled out all quantitative fields because the tasks are quantitative in nature. We were reminded that the "if..., then..., therefore" construct is also the stock in trade of the lawyer. In order to survive in the study of law, students have to think mainly on the abstract level. We asked several groups of second and third year law students to react to the two tasks we just described. Table III reflects our results. A total of 66 students reacted to the tasks and 50 of them demonstrated formal operational thought. We feel, therefore, that these two tasks have a good probability of identifying formal thought.

Table III. *Performance of second and third year law students on two formal operational tasks.*

	Concrete Operational	Formal Operational
Conservation of volume (N=22)	3	19
Exclusion of irrelevant variables (N=44)	13	31

What Educational Institutions Can Do to Foster Formal Thought

Our research has shown us that the level of thought of junior high school students[6] and college freshmen[7] can be changed by providing them inquiry-centered experiences in science. We believe that the principal reason our research has shown an increase in the thought levels of students is because *we accepted that most of them participating in the experiments were concrete operational.* That put squarely upon us the responsibility for providing concrete experiences with the objects and ideas of the discipline. These students were involved in actually creating some knowledge of their very own. We know that this was the first time some of them had been given that opportunity. We believe that actual involvement with the materials and ideas of science and being allowed to find out something for themselves accounts for the movement toward and into formal thought which we found.

Science teachers in general and physics teachers in particular have a vehicle at their command that makes active student involvement convenient. That vehicle is the laboratory. Both of our research studies had the laboratory at its nerve center. In the case of the college study that laboratory did not too frequently involve hardware and chemicals, but it was a place where data were gathered, ideas were honed, hypotheses were made and tested, and verifications were carried out. That is the true laboratory.

In teaching the majority of physics courses (both college and high school) the laboratory can be used to lead students, through inquiry,[8] to develop understandings of the concepts to be learned. The teacher, then, has three responsibilities to discharge before ever meeting a class:

(1) Isolate those concepts which, when learned, will provide students with an accurate and adequate understanding of the discipline. The teacher must use his understanding of the structure of the discipline in order to select the concepts, and his goal is to provide the learner with *his own* understanding of the discipline's structure. Textbooks are of little help here.

(2) Find those laboratory investigations which when cast in an inquiry framework will, upon completion, allow the student to develop an understanding of the concept being considered. Textbooks are of no help here.

(3) Make sure the investigations are cast into an inquiry framework and be sure the necessary materials are available.

Now classes start.[9] The teacher becomes an asker of questions, a provider of materials, a laboratory participant, and a class chairman and secretary. Perhaps most importantly, he is a discussion leader. He gathers the class together (chairman) and solicits the data they have gathered (secretary). He then leads a discussion on what the data mean (discussion leader). He also makes the necessary conceptual inventions at the proper time, decides when discovery can take place, and when the present concept needs to be related to the next one by exploration. He must also decide when exploration of a completely new concept must begin. This teacher is not a teller, he is a director of learning. Traditional teaching methods embrace the notions that (a) teaching is telling, (b) memorization is learning, and (c) being able to repeat something on an examination is evidence of understanding — those points are the antithesis of inquiry.

The development of formal thought must become the focus of attention of every teacher in the country. The Educational Policies Commission said, in 1961, that the *central* purpose of the school must be to teach students to think and they operationally defined thinking.[10] Such good advice! We would add that the central role of the school must be to teach children to think with form not objects — in other words, to move students into the stage of formal operational thought. Science has the structure to enhance greatly the achievement of this objective. We must not blow our chances to make a maximum contribution to education in general and education in science in particular. Let's establish an environment in our classrooms that encourages and promotes formal thought!

References

1. For a nearly complete picture of one research with formal operations, see John W. Renner and Don G. Stafford, *Teaching Science in the Secondary School* (Harper and Row, New York, 1972), Appendix A, and Joe W. McKinnon and John W. Renner, Amer. J. Phys. 39, 1047 (1971).
2. Renner and Stafford, Ref. 1, p. 294.
3. Barbel Inhelder and Jean Piaget, *The Growth of Logical Thinking From Childhood to Adolescence*, (Basic Books, New York, 1958), Chaps. 1-7, p. 309.
4. Lawrence Kohlberg and Carol Gilligan, Daedalus 100, 1051 (Fall 1971).
5. Jerome S. Bruner, *The Process of Education*, (Vintage Books, New York, 1960), p. 37.
6. Faith Elizabeth Friot, "The Relationship Between an Inquiry-Teaching Approach and Intellectual Development," unpublished doctoral dissertation (University of Oklahoma, Norman, Okla., 1970).
7. Joe W. McKinnon and John W. Renner, Amer. J. Phys. 39, 1047 (1971).
8. Refer to John W. Renner and Anton E. Lawson, Phys. Teach. 11, 165 (1973), under the section "Learning Cycle" for an explanation of this term and its phases of exploration, invention, and discovery.
9. John W. Renner and Don G. Stafford, *Teaching Science in the Secondary School* (Harper and Row, New York, 1972). This book contains suggestions which will be helpful in classroom implementation of inquiry.
10. Educational Policies Commission, *The Central Purpose of American Education* (NEA, Washington, D.C., 1961).

Physics Problems and the Process of Self-Regulation

Anton E. Lawson and Warren T. Wollman

In two previous articles[1,2] Jean Piaget's theory of intellectual development and its general implications for physics teaching were discussed. The purpose of this article is to examine more closely one aspect of that theory and discuss its implications for designing and using homework problems. We will briefly describe the process of self-regulation (the process Piaget hypothesizes governs all intellectual growth) and suggest a way in which homework problems can be used to provide students an opportunity for self-regulation. Further, we will discuss deficiencies of typical homework problems and provide a number of example problems which we believe can initiate self-regulation. Through the process of self-regulation initiated by thought-provoking problems, we believe students will not only be able to develop understandings of the concepts involved but will also progress from relatively concrete (or limited) to more abstract (or generalizable) modes of thinking.

The process of self-regulation

The process by which Piaget hypothesizes that patterns of reasoning are refined, extended, or combined with other patterns of reasoning is called self-regulation. Initially, basic reasoning patterns serve to guide an individual's actions within his surroundings. As long as those actions promote satisfactory interaction, the basic patterns continue to guide behavior. However, owing to the individual's extended interaction with his environment he meets contradictions, that is, situations for which his initial patterns of reasoning do not serve as effective guides to behavior. These contradictions produce a state of disequilibrium. In other words, his patterns of reasoning are found wanting and must somehow be changed. If the disequilibrium is not too great, he will spontaneously begin to alter his patterns of reasoning in an attempt to assimilate the new situation. The process by which an individual actively seeks to reestablish equilibrium is termed self-regulation. The altered reasoning patterns which develop are then tried. If the patterns guide behavior successfully so that the person's efforts obtain positive feedback the patterns are reinforced. Continued positive feedback then produces an increasingly stable set of reasoning patterns. In this manner the person gradually builds new reasoning patterns and adapts to new situations.

Homework problems can initiate self-regulation

The gradual process of reestablishing equilibrium through self-regulation affords the possibility of initiating interactions between students and subject matter with the use of homework problems provided the following two factors are present: Problems must be chosen so that the student can partially but not completely understand

Anton E. Lawson (M.A. University of Oregon, Ph.D. University of Oklahoma) is a science educator at the Lawrence Hall of Science. He is now investigating the transition period between the concrete and formal reasoning stages as described by Piaget. Dr. Lawson is also developing curricular material in the health sciences and is co-authoring a book (with Chester A. Lawson). (Lawrence Hall of Science, University of California, Berkeley, California 94720.)

Warren Wollman (Ph.D. from University of California, Berkeley, Theoretical Physics) studied psychology under Piaget in Geneva. He has taught at various levels and is currently studying intellectual development and its relation to the school environment. (Lawrence Hall of Science, University of California, Berkeley, California 94720.)

Typical homework problems seldom require a student to examine his own thinking.

---

them in terms of old ideas (i.e., a moderate state of disequilibrium must result from the problem); and sufficient time must be allowed for the student to grapple with the new situation, possibly with appropriate "hints" to direct his thinking, but allowing him to put the ideas together himself.

An important facet then in selecting problems which encourage self-regulation is to obtain a careful match between what the student knows and the kind of problem he is asked to work through. The ideal situation would seem to be one in which the problems are challenging but are felt to be solvable. The hypothesis is that a challenging but solvable problem will place a student into an initial state of disequilibrium. However, through his own efforts at bringing together what he has done in the laboratory, read in the textbook, heard in lectures, learned from other past experiences, and obtained from teacher or peer discussions he will gradually organize his thinking about this information and successfully solve the problem. This success will then establish a new and more stable equilibrium. The new state of equilibrium will be one with increased understanding of the subject matter and increased problem-solving capability. Before giving examples of the kind of problem we believe can initiate self-regulation a few comments will be made regarding deficiencies of standard homework problems.

What's wrong with typical homework problems?

Typical homework problems seldom require a student to examine his own thinking, make comparisons, and raise questions which, in fact, are crucial to scientific inquiry. These problems usually require students to apply an equation or sometimes two or three equations to obtain a solution. Students quickly come to realize that the name of this game is "Can you discover the correct equation?" This is a game of recognition—a sort of high order matching process involving little thought. Although this process can be an important one, we believe that little if any self-regulation takes place in this way. Typical homework problems do not require the student to think about:

1. *The data of the problem.* Usually there is just the right amount, no more nor less, whereas in real situations there is either a dearth or superfluity of information and the problem is to discover what is relevant.
2. *The approach to the problem.* Usually this is determined by the chapter heading. If, for example, a mechanics problem can be solved either by Lagrange's equations, Newton's laws, or energy conservation, the choice is dictated by irrelevant considerations, e.g., the problem comes from the chapter on Lagrange's equations. It is important for students to learn that many approaches may seem reasonable and the problem is to decide whether one is particularly appropriate.
3. *The tacit assumptions of a problem-solving strategy,* for example deciding between use of Boyle's law or the Van der Waals equation. This decision is usually made for the student, not by the student.
4. *The physical arguments involved in the problem as opposed to the mathematical ones.* Too often problems are only exercises in using mathematical tools (a necessary exercise) without ever demanding that the student try either to arrive at or qualitatively justify the mathematical result by physical (phenomenological) arguments utilizing both principles and order of magnitude calculations. Indeed, the physical or intuitive argument often precedes the mathematical in real research.
5. *The statement of a problem.* Problems are tailored to fit the text when, in fact, the real problem is doing the tailoring by conceptualizing a real situation in terms of a model. This involves all of the above points.

How to encourage self-regulation

A few points should be kept in mind when designing, discussing, using, and scoring problems to encourage self-regulation:

1. Open-ended problems (problems with no single solution) are often excellent tools to encourage thinking.
2. Problems which present an apparent paradox produce disequilibrium and can initiate self-regulation. Paradox problems by their nature are generally short and incisive. Leighton in his foreword to the exercise workbook written to accompany *The Feynman Lectures in Physics*[5] discussed the kinds of problems which appeared most suitable to him. He suggested that problems of a kind that are numerically or analytically simple, yet incisive and illuminating in content were particularly useful.
3. To encourage self-regulation it is often helpful to ask students to record and hand in all the various ideas they tried and found unsuccessful as well as the ones which were successful in arriving at the problem

"Real" problems should, and indeed must, involve a certain amount of trial and error.

solution. Discussions of these steps in an atmosphere in which these ideas are recognized not only as worthwhile but as necessary, clue students into the fact that "real" problems *should* and indeed *must* involve a certain amount of trial and error, albeit informed trial and error.

4. Have the students search for necessary data so they examine their conceptualization of the problem. Either give superfluous data or omit necessary data. To account for the latter, students should have to make plausible assumptions or introduce suitable symbols for quantities that are needed to solve the problem.

5. Require students to draw a diagram of the physical situation. To do this students have to think deeply about the spatial relationships of the interacting objects, and may find discrepancies as they compare their preconceptions with the diagram.

6. Provide for a "problem clinic" or tutorial service where students can get help with problems while they are solving them, and before they have to be turned in. Interaction with other persons can be very helpful and is often even necessary if students are to conceptualize, then critically analyze their own thinking.

7. For problems designed to engage a student over a period of, say, two weeks, the teacher should consult with the student several times in order to:
   A. Discuss with him his initial approach. If this approach is reasonable but known in advance to be inappropriate, the teacher should *not* intervene at this point, but rather let the student discover for himself why the approach will not work.
   B. Discuss with the student alternative approaches both when the initial approach is appropriate and when it is reasonable but not appropriate. In either case, let the student first discover which approach will work. *Then* discuss alternatives, *even* if the first approach worked. It may be that he will accept inappropriate alternatives as reasonable. He may then discover on his own why they are not.
   C. Discuss both semi-quantitative (order of magnitude) and qualitative arguments anticipating the outcome of more rigorous approaches. Limiting cases should be used as a check when solutions to simpler problems are already known.
   D. Discuss alternatives to an inappropriate and *time-consuming* approach. This is to *avoid* having the student spend too much time discovering the inadequacies of an approach. Overall, the student should get from the teacher a feeling for the general considerations appropriate to choosing and comparing strategies, i.e., a feeling for the process of inquiry.

8. Although solutions (numerical or algebraic) should be provided for all problems (not just the "odd-numbered" ones), students must understand that a premature glance at a solution will surely affect their conception of the problem and distort the problem solving procedure. Knowledge of the solution can provide stimulating feedback *after* the student has completed and carried through a formulation of a solution.

Examples of problems that can promote self-regulation

Problem 1 Since the net force on the spring scale shown in Fig. 1 is zero how can the scale register a non-zero reading? What does the scale register? Why isn't it 20 since it is pulled by 10 lbs at each end?

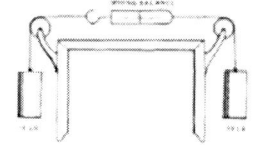

Comment: This example, which is especially useful when associated with a demonstration, illustrates how a little knowledge can go a wrong way. At first, concepts are only vaguely grasped and thus over-extended. Here we obviously have two forces whose sum is equal to zero and yet the scale does not read zero. Or, we might think that each force contributes 10 lbs of tension to the scale to give 20 lbs. These two approaches use unrestricted (over-extended) concepts which must be coordinated, via self-regulation, with other concepts, e.g., free-body diagrams and action-reaction, in order to resolve the discrepancy.

Fig. 1. Spring balance and suspended weights

Problem 2 A capacitor and resistor are connected in a circuit as shown in Fig. 2. The values are $C = 250$ μμf, $R = 10\,000\,\Omega$, and $E = 400$ V. Initially the switch is closed and then it is opened suddenly. Use two methods to calculate the energy dissipated in the resistor after the switch is opened. Do both methods give the same result? Should they give the same result? If so, why? If not, why not?

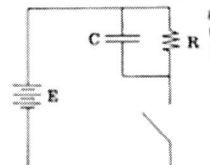

Comment: This problem calls for two quantitative analyses of the same situation. If the student is able to think of two methods of solution and obtain the same answer using both methods no disequilibration will result. However, if two different answers are obtained the student should check his own work. The discrepancy could be resolved quickly if the source of the difference was an error in calculation. If, however, the difference was due to difficulty in conceptualization, then the check will promote self-regulation.

Fig. 2. Circuit diagram showing the capacitor, resistor, switch, and battery.

Problem 3 The gas temperature at one level of the upper atmosphere is about $1000°$K. The temperature at the surface of a burning match is about the same. Yet a person would be very cold in the upper atmosphere. How can that be?

Comment: This problem presents a paradox because $1000°$K is a very high temperature and yet it is "cold up there." Resolution through self-regulation leads to a more scientific and less everyday notion of the relation between temperature and "cold" or "hot."

Problem 4 A glass is exactly full of water at $0°$C and has a cube of ice floating in it. When the ice melts (still at $0°$C) the water will not overflow, because the ice displaced a volume of water equal to the volume of the water into which the ice melted. OK. Let us look at some fine points. In what *direction* (slight overflow or the opposite) would each of the following affect the result? Give only the *direction*.
(a) The ice cube contained some grains of sand.
(b) The ice cube contained some air bubbles.
(c) The water (and the glass) were not at $0°$ to start with, but were at room temperature.
(d) The "water" is not water at all, but is a Martini which is close to $0°$ but, due to its alcoholic content, has density less than that of water.

Comment: This problem originally appeared in an article by Richard Crane.[4] It, as well as other problems in that article (for example, problems 8, 17, 18, 26-29), are excellent examples of problems which will promote self-regulation. Problems 34, 41, 42, and 48 which appeared in a second article by Crane[5] also are thought provoking and should encourage self-regulation.

Problem 5 If internal energy is partly molecular motion, what is the difference between a hot, stationary golf ball sitting on a tee and a cold golf ball rapidly moving off the tee.

Comment: Of course, the molecular motion part of internal energy refers to *random* motion. Thus, self-regulation refines or sharpens a global or relatively diffuse concept. It is typical of students that they only assimilate parts of a concept at first. By provoking them to discover or recover all the parts, the concept becomes more sharply defined.

Problem 6 When a cylinder, open at one end, is placed over a burning candle which is sitting in a container of water the candle flame goes out and water rises into the cylinder. Why does the flame go out and why does the water rise? Note: Not all observations are mentioned in the description. What other observations do you think you would make if the phenomenon was observed? Obtain the necessary materials and try the experiment yourself. Try the experiment varying the number of candles used, the amount of water in the container, the size and shape of the cylinder, the speed with which you place the cylinder over the candle, and anything else you can think of.

Comment: This problem is one which often yields a quick but erroneous solution. Most students will hypothesize that the candle goes out because it burned up all the oxygen in the cylinder and the water then came in to replace the oxygen. Selected items of information or questions could be supplied at this point to provoke students to abandon this idea and continue their search. For example: What is produced when a flame consumes oxygen? Two burning candles make more water rise than one. Small bubbles were observed escaping from the bottom of the cylinder. Why might this have occurred? These observations contradict the initial explanation and should provoke disequilibrium. Once other explanations are offered they can be analyzed to determine their suitability. They may lead

Problem 7 Everyone "knows" that to win a tug of war, a team has to pull harder than the other team. What everyone doesn't know is that, in fact, each team always pulls equally hard, even the winning team. Under these circumstances, how can one team ever win (short of the other team just letting go)?

Comment: Obviously one normally thinks that good teams pull harder than poor teams and this is why they win. This problem makes one apply the free-body diagram method and the action-reaction idea to resolve a problem already believed solved by common sense but now made to appear strange. This nonroutine use of physics concepts makes it more likely they will *not* be overlooked in the future.

Problem 8 Polishing surfaces reduces friction between them unless you polish them extremely well, then friction will increase. How can that be true?

Comment: One never expects polishing to increase friction. Resolution of this paradox leads to better understanding of the relation of macroscopic effects to microscopic phenomena, e.g., friction, to microscopic and molecular interaction.

Problem 9 (a) See Fig. 3a. The focal lengths of two identical, thin, convex lenses are the same and measured to be 20 cm each ($F_1 = 20$ cm, $F_2 = 20$ cm). The two lenses are placed next to each other as shown in Fig. 3b and taped together at their edges only. The focal length of this combination, F_c, is 10 cm. Write an equation that gives the focal length of a lens combination that consists of two lenses having identical focal lengths.

(b) One of the 20 cm focal length lenses is replaced by one having a focal length (F_3) of 5 cm. The focal length of the resulting combination is measured to be 4 cm. Write an equation that can be used to calculate the focal length of a lens combination that consists of two lenses of unequal focal lengths.

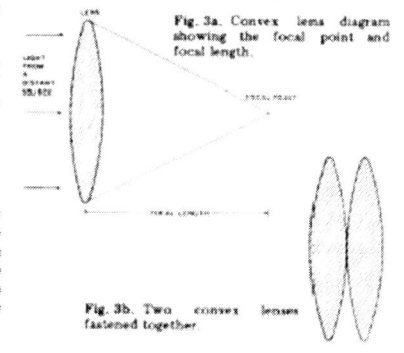

(c) Now check your two equations. Are they the same? Do you think they should be the same. If so, why? If not, why not? If you believe they should be the same but you have two different equations rethink the problem and try to reduce the two situations to one equation.

Comment: Students will generally solve parts (a) and (b) with little difficulty. However, they will seldom write an equation general enough to account for both situations. The suggestion in part (c) that the equations should be the same and the student's intuitive feeling that a general equation could be found, coupled with the original incompatible equations should produce disequilibrium and provoke the student to rethink the problem.

Fig. 3a. Convex lens diagram showing the focal point and focal length.

Fig. 3b. Two convex lenses fastened together.

Problem 10 A student measures his weight by climbing onto the large platform of a big spring scale. He takes a step to one side and notices that just as he started to do this, the scale registered less than his weight. Before he could puzzle this through, he noticed that just as he completed the step, the scale now registered more than his weight. If there is nothing wrong with the scale, then what was going on?

Comment: "Weight is weight is weight," a famous poet might have said. So how can a scale read less than one's weight? Worse, how can it also read more? Still worse, if it isn't the scale that must be fixed, then how am I, the student, to fix my ideas?

Problem 11 A brick is supported by a string A from the ceiling, and another string B is attached to the bottom of the brick. If you give a sudden jerk to B it will break, but if you pull on B steadily, A will break. Since the force is the same both ways, how could this occur?

Comment: To be most effective this problem should be demonstrated. Anything actually seen makes a much greater and longer lasting impression than anything simply heard or read about. This comment of course applies to other problems as well. Since the student is used to thinking in a temporal terms, he will think that force is force and so equal forces have equal effects. So how can the string break in one instance and not in the other? Again, common sense is in conflict with observation and this use of physics to set the world straight is likely to be retained.

Acknowledgment

The authors wish to express sincere appreciation to Professor Robert Karplus and Professor Lester Paldy for their helpful suggestions in the formulation and presentation of the ideas put forth in this manuscript. Credit is due also to Professor John Renner for the ideas used in problems 6 and 9 and to Robert Karplus for problem 2. Ideas for some of the other problems came from D. Halliday and R. Resnick, *Physics* (Wiley, New York, 1966). In all cases the problems were edited and modified.

AESOP (Advancement of Education in Science Oriented Programs) is supported by a grant from the National Science Foundation.

References

1. John W. Renner and Anton E. Lawson, "Piagetian Theory and Instruction in Physics," Phys. Teach. 11, 165 (1973).
2. John W. Renner and Anton E. Lawson, "Promoting Intellectual Development Through Science Teaching," Phys. Teach. 11, 273 (1973).
3. Robert B. Leighton, *The Feynman Lectures on Physics-Exercises* (Addison-Wesley, Palo Alto, 1964).
4. H. Richard Crane, "Problems for Introductory Physics," Phys. Teach. 7, 371 (1969).
5. H. Richard Crane, "Problems for Introductory Physics," Phys. Teach. 8, 182 (1970).

APPENDIX C

PETALS AROUND A ROSE

In an attempt to simulate the intellectual and emotional experience of a student using only concrete reasoning patterns in a class that requires formal reasoning, we have chosen a dice game called the Petals Around A Rose. Our purpose in introducing this activity to you is to encourage you to have a learning experience that may serve as background for Piaget's second key concept, Self-regulation. To this end, as you complete this exercise please note your reasoning processes.

The dice game Petals Around A Rose is very simple but seems quite baffling to some college teachers. It has only two basic directions.

1. The name of the game tells you what the rule is.
2. No one is EVER TOLD what the rule is. Everyone must discover the rule for one's self.

In a workshop setting to begin the game, someone who knows the rule will roll several dice (we will start with six) and will tell you how many petals around a rose are showing for that roll. This procedure will be repeated as often as necessary for workshop participants to discover what the rule is which determines the number of petals showing on a roll. The same rule will work for any number of dice.

Each of the pages here reduces the number of dice being used until on the last page there is only one die.

310   R. G. FULLER ET AL.

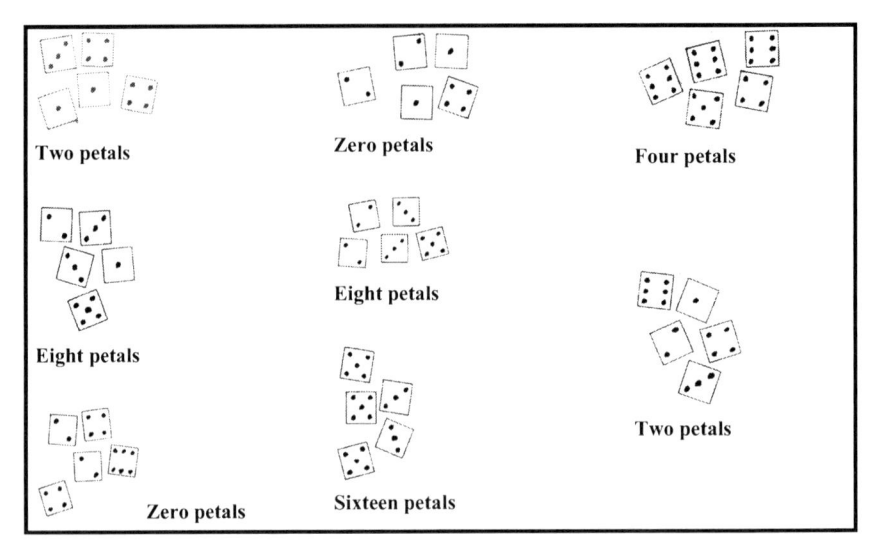

Figure C.1.   Petals Around a Rose—Five Dice Configurations.

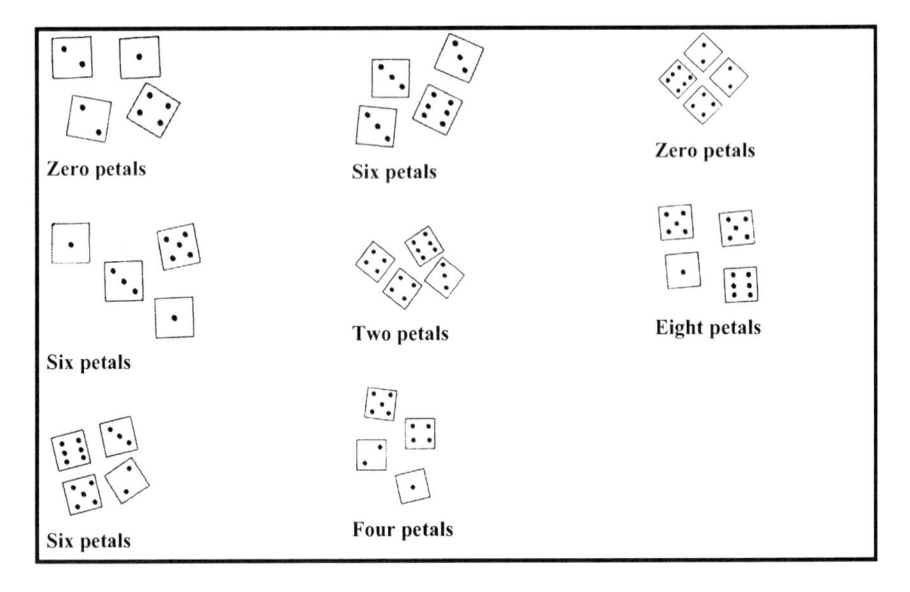

Figure C.2.   Petals Around a Rose—Four Dice Configurations.

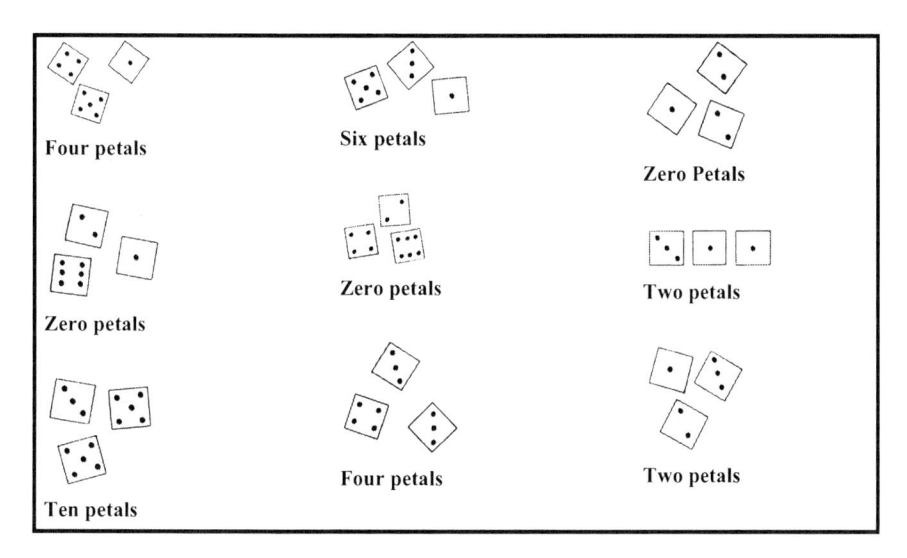

College Teaching and the Development of Reasoning 311

Four petals
Six petals
Zero Petals
Zero petals
Zero petals
Two petals
Ten petals
Four petals
Two petals

Figure C.3. Petals Around a Rose—Three Dice Configurations.

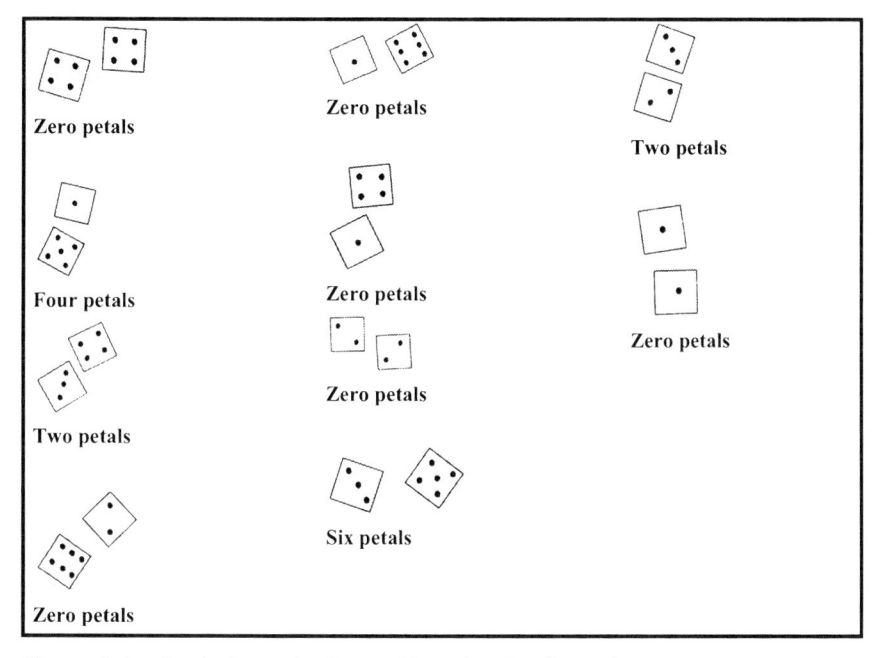

Zero petals
Zero petals
Two petals
Four petals
Zero petals
Zero petals
Two petals
Zero petals
Zero petals
Six petals
Zero petals

Figure C.4. Petals Around a Rose—Two Dice Configurations.

312   R. G. FULLER ET AL.

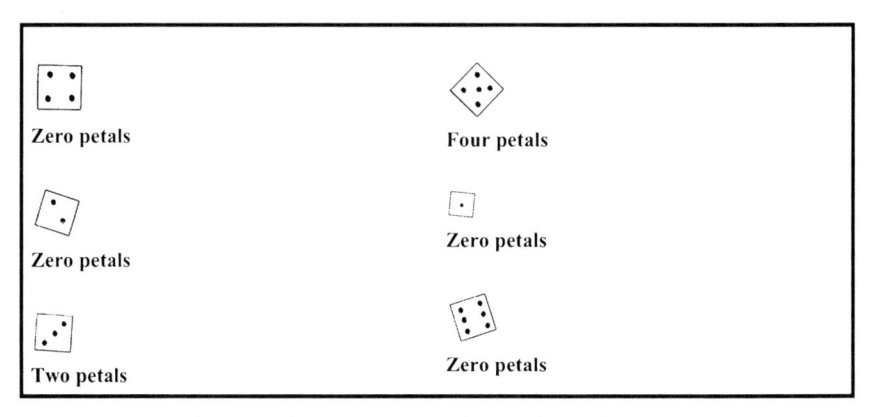

Figure C.5.   Petals Around a Rose—One Die Configuration.

The pedagogical point to be stressed in conclusion is that this type of discovery teaching appears to be strongly motivating and rewarding. Yet, the teaching seems also to be reasonably efficient even when compared with a more verbal expository approach. The pupils come to the point where they know they will discover something, and they know what their discovery will mean. Hence, perhaps they did not invent the new concepts, but they did make discoveries.

—Robert Karplus (1962)

APPENDIX D

College Cognitive Development Programs and Their Acronyms

Program	Acronym	Funding	College or University
Accent on Developing Abstract Processes of Thought	ADAPT	Exxon Ed. Fund. $100,000	Univ. of Nebraska, Lincoln
Development Of Operational Reasoning Skills	DOORS	FIPSE, $100,000	Illinois Central College
Consortium for Offering and Managing Programs for the Advancement of Skills	COMPAS	FIPSE, $100,000	Umbrella Program for seven community college programs
?	PATH	FIPSE	William Rainey Harper CC, IL
Reasoning and Intellectual Skills Enhancement	RISE	FIPSE	Prairie State CC, IL
Steps To Abstract Reasoning	STAR	internal	Metropolitan State College, Denver
Student Talent Enhanced through Practical Positive Experiences	STEPPE	FIPSE	Joliet Jr. College, IL
Freshmen Abstract Reasoning	FAR	NSF, $50,000	College of Charleston, SC
Stress On Analytical Reasoning	SOAR	Kenan Fund.	Xavier Univ. of LA
Development Of Reasoning In Science	DORIS	NSF	Cal. State Univ. Fullerton
Lessons In Formal Thinking	LIFT	FIPSE	CC of Allegheny Co., PA
Student Training in Advanced Reasoning Skills	STARS	FIPSE	Seminole CC, FL

Table continues on next page.

Table continued

Program	Acronym	Funding	College or University
Concrete Reasoning and Exploration Applied to Thinking and Experience	CREATE	FIPSE	Surry CC, NC
The 4th R	(none)	FIPSE	Piedmont Tech. College, SC
The Cognitive Program	(none)	internal	Essex County College, NJ

Quotation Sources and Locations

Source of Quotation	Chapter	Location Page No.
Rita Peterson (2002). In R. G. Fuller (Ed.), *A Love of Discovery Science Education—The Second Career of Robert Karplus* (p. 11). New York: Kluwer Academic/Plenum.	3	50
Rita Peterson (2002). In R. G. Fuller (Ed.), *A Love of Discovery Science Education—The Second Career of Robert Karplus* (p. 12). New York: Kluwer Academic/Plenum.	5	68
Fuller, R. G., & Dykstra, D. I, (2009). *Informal coment by Fuller and Dystra.*	7	106
Eleanor Duckworth (1996). In *The Having of Wonderful Ideas and Other Essays on Teaching and Learning* (2nd ed., p. 14). New York: Teachers College Press, Columbia University.	8	114
Robert Karplus (1977). In Science Teaching and the Development of Reasoning. *Journal of Research in Science Teaching, 14*(2), 169-175.	9	134
Jean Piaget (1965). In *Science of Education and the Psychology of the Child* (English translation published in 1970)	10	146
William G. Perry, Jr. (1985). *Different Worlds in the Same Classroom:? Students' Evolution in Their Vision of Knowledge? and Their Expectations of Teachers*, Reprinted from On Teaching and Learning, Volume 1. Derek Bok Center for Teaching and Learning, Harvard University	11	152
William G. Perry, Jr. (1978). Sharing in the Costs of Growth. In C. A. Parker (Ed.), *Encouraging Development in College Student* (p. 270). Minneapolis: University of Minnesota Press.	14	218
Jean Piaget (1973). In *To Understand Is To Invent, The Future of Education* (pp. 105-106). New York: Grossman.	App. A	266
Robert Karplus (with J. Myron Atkins) (1962). In Discovery or Invention? *The Science Teacher, 29*(5), 47.	App. C	312
Jean Piaget (1973). *To Understand Is To Invent* (pp. 123-125). New York: Grossman.	App. E	318

APPENDIX E

ADAPT Anthropology

by Dr. Martin Q. Peterson

This anthropology class taught the scientific method of observing human social behavior. We adopted Piaget's Aphorism; "To Understand Is to Invent." The students used class time to understand how to conduct their own research. We starting with research design and ending with accepting or rejecting working hypotheses. We developed strong hypotheses as the method of research.

The students generated their own testable hypotheses about categories of campus social behavior. This placed the instructor as a fellow learner and hooked the students' interest. We observed only in public spaces and maintained individuals' privacy. We limited investigations to simple provable and measurable predictions of behavior.

An early example: Discover rules of non-verbal behavior that will elicit a smile from a stranger approaching on a sidewalk.

The instructor followed Sir Karl Pearson's original proof of chi-square as a class approach. The instructor used neither the term "statistics" nor "chi-square." The instructor did not start with the chi-square formula.

Instead, we started with five pennies, shaken and dropped on a desk, and made bets on which categories one would be seen least and most often. These results disconfirmed most of students' predictions. We now had both a Piagetian task, "In Order to Learn, First Disconfirm," and the basic components of chi-square, "Observed, Expected, and Predicted."

Because students used data in ADAPT math and physics, they began to explore relationships between observed and expected. The instructor helped the students discover Pearson's insights. This process of understanding required refocusing of many, many questions, and large numbers of false starts and dead ends.

These students and this instructor would have failed without the parallel investigation processes in ADAPT math and physics. Anthropology, math, and physics problem solving required the same intellectual and computational skills.

The process from basic methodology through chi-square took about 5 weeks, leaving 10 weeks to do many projects investigating rules of social behavior.

Once the students understood how to accept or reject a hypothesis using a chi-square analysis, they carried out simple behavioral studies. Students asked a question, framed a working hypothesis and the null hypothesis, generated the expected data, and collected data on paper. Students did initial calculations with hand-held calculators.

Many students found the process challenging. One of the students told the instructor during class, "I can't to do that!" The instructor asked if he could shout his refusal to the class. He shouted. Another student said, "Aw, sit down. We'll help you." The student said, "OK" and joined her team.

The instructor found the process equally challenging. From time to time, he fantasized shouting at the students, "Enough. Just open a book. Find the formula. Use it. Stop asking questions. The book will answer your questions."

The instructor had severe doubts that first year college students could figure out anything Sir Karl Pearson discovered. He doubted his own ability. Without the support of his team, his ADAPT colleagues, he feared one day he would say to the students, "Please listen. Take notes. I'll show you the formula. Please don't tell Professor Fuller."

The students' progress humbled this instructor. Students began coming into class with research notes showing that they had started with a question, made and rejected a dozen hypotheses, each one flowing from the one before, ending with a hypothesis they could not reject. Their final test involved using the social behavior rules to see if they worked.

As the instructor looked at one student's field notes, he saw the counts of the various categories, the chi-square number, the degrees of freedom and the conclusion that most hypothesis did not meet a .05 significance level. He saw no calculations. "Did you forget to enter the calculations?" he asked. The student shook his head, "No, that takes too long. I just do the calculations in my head. I memorized the "point zero five" number at three, four and five (degrees of freedom), and if my answer is larger, I dump that hypothesis and start on the next one."

The students understood chi-square as a simple heuristic to sharpen focus, allowing generation and testing of hypotheses on the fly. Because they had taken the time to internalize, instead of memorize, they considered it a rule-of-thumb, not a statistic.

Piaget captured the process perfectly: "To Understand Is To Invent."

In an Ed Psyc course evaluation, graduate students learned that they had to use a calculator to do what the first year ADAPT students did in their heads.

What did this instructor learn?

One: Did the instructor's internalizations change learning and teaching approaches?

Yes. In all subsequent courses, students developed their own knowledge and skills, rather than retention and regurgitation. Students and the instructor spent class time tackling project problems, with students offering most of the solutions. The instructor became a resource instead of an encyclopedia.

Two: Did the instructor's frustration diminish?

Yes. After the ADAPT program, the instructor experienced frustration only during the walking encyclopedia mode. Dealing with the concrete project problems frees one from frustration. Individual projects allow constant renewal and fun.

Three: Did discovery replace content?

No. In each project, a literature review informed the problem statement. The students used both the Science and Social Science Citation Index to find recent literature. Using content to solve problems focuses on understanding, not memory.

Four: Did the instructor use the method with other activities, and with what result?

Yes. This instructor took advantage of an early retirement, opening up a national consulting firm. The consulting involves helping clients make presentations in high stress environments. The ADAPT approach helps clients internalize their knowledge. The client presents from experience, rather than memorized set pieces. Clients have paid this instructor to have fun for the last 25 years.

On the whole, whether it is a question of education of the mind and of intellectual functions, or of education of the ethical conscience, if the "right to education" implies that it envisions "full development of the human personality and ... the strengthening of respect for human rights and fundamental freedoms," it is important to understand that such an ideal cannot be attainted by any of the common methods. Neither the independence of the person, which is assumed by this development, nor the reciprocity that is evoked by this respect for the rights and freedoms of others can be developed in an atmosphere of authority and intellectual and moral constraints. On the contrary, they both imperiously demand a return, by their very make-up, to the "lived" experience, and to freedom of investigation, outside of which any acquisition of human values is only an illusion.

—Jean Piaget (1973)

APPENDIX F: LEARNING BY DESIGN

Constructing Experiential Learning Programs

Daniela Weinberg and Gerald M. Weinberg

How can we assure that our students really learn? If we want to improve the learning process, we'll have to decide what we mean by "learn." Recall a time when you learned something new-a new skill, a new technique, a new word, a new hobby, a new way of interacting with people- and consider the following three questions: First, why did you bother? You knew that learning would change you, and that change meant stress. Why would anyone volunteer for additional stress? Second, how did you feel during the learning process? Was it difficult or easy? Was it a delight or a bore? Third, what was the outcome? Did your behavior change? Did it stay changed or did it fade? Would you consider it a successful learning experience?

A TYPICAL LEARNING EXPERIENCE

A typical learning experience we observed was Dani's learning how to use a word processor. Let's consider Dani's answers to the three questions. Why bother? Jerry and his secretary, Judy, made a quick transition from the typewriter to the new machine. Dani observed the process and felt curious about this new addition to the family, as well as increasingly excluded by the new language around the office. Not to be conquered by a glorified typewriter, she asked for instruction. How did you feel? Dani's first reactions to the new technology were mostly negative. The keyboard was not laid out exactly like a typewriter's, nor did it have the same "feel." There was no carriage return, the familiar typing sound was absent, and the small video screen had a nasty habit of displaying cryptic error messages such as: 62, FILE NOT FOUND, 00, 00 And with all her intelligence, Dani could not seem to memorize the simplest formatting commands but had to look up everything in the manual, over and over. No question about it, this was a stressful situation that made her feel lost, dumb, and angry! What was the outcome? With time and practice, Dani's irritation gradually gave way to excitement, which she noticed when she found herself actually looking forward to the next session at the machine. She knew she had mastered it when she realized that she no longer referred to the manual, or even to her little sheaf of penciled notes.

Piaget's Model of the Learning Process

How can we explain this process of learning? And, once explained, can we generalize the model to apply to other kinds of learning? Jean Piaget, the Swiss philosopher and psychologist, proposed that learning was a process of constructing-not receiving-new knowledge. The learner could not simply sit back passively, and obtain learning through the manipulations of another person-a "teacher." The learner was neither an "empty vessel" to be filled with knowledge or a "blank slate" on which knowledge could be inscribed, but a system that learned through its own interaction with its environment. What we like best about Piaget's model is the way it makes the learner an active participant in the learning process. The process begins when the learner is provoked-the learner examines his or her existing cognitive models because of some pressure from the outside environment. It might be provoked by necessity, as when a businesswoman struggles to learn Japanese to retain a major overseas client. It might be simple curiosity or, as in Dani's case, a feeling of being left out of the group. Whatever the case, learning doesn't just happen. Learning is the result of decision and action by the learner. And not learning can also be a conscious decision and action-to ignore the provocation and proceed as if nothing had happened (until provoked again, perhaps this time too significantly to be ignored.). Once the decision is made, the learner plunges into an unfamiliar sea filled with unknown flora and fauna. At first, nothing fits or even makes sense in the learner's vision of the world. The world seems filled with cryptic messages. Piaget called this stage disequilibration. The learner is literally off balance in the new environment. What to do? From the disequilibrated state, we may try to restore equilibrium by changing the environment. When Dani said "this is nothing more than a glorified typewriter," she was bending the environment so she could retain her own model of the world. Piaget called this process assimilation, which was one pole on a continuum of choices we can make to restore equilibrium. At the other pole, we can throw out our old model and embrace the new one totally. Piaget called this choice accommodation. Jerry was closer to the accommodation pole because he could no longer type competently on the typewriter without ruining 50 sheets of paper. Generally, neither pole by itself provides a satisfactory outcome. Instead, we move between these poles in a dynamic equilibrium that Piaget called self-regulation. We partially surrender our earlier models of the world, and at the same time we twist the world into their static shape. In the process, we build for ourselves a new model of reality that somehow reconciles the old and the new. Although Dani no longer calls the word processor a typewriter, she still needs a printout and a red pencil before she can "really" edit her work. When we complete the self-regulation process, we have constructed new knowledge. And then the process begins anew-moving from a state of comfort, into a provocation, through a state of discomfort, and finally into a new region of comfort.

The *Learning Cycle*

As trainers and educators, we can use the Piaget model to design teaching strategies that allow this process to develop. We must first put our students into a provocative environment. We must encourage them to experiment-to play with the materials in that environment. We must challenge some of their preexisting notions of the world-to provoke disequilibirum, but without utterly frightening them away. We must support and guide them through the self-regulation process. And finally, we must provide opportunities for them to consolidate and feel comfortable about their newly-constructed knowledge. The teaching design we use to accomplish all this is called the learning cycle. The original *Learning Cycle* was developed by Robert Karplus of the University of California at Berkeley to assist students in the development of logical thought. Robert Fuller worked with Karplus at Berkeley and brought the learning cycle idea back to the University of Nebraska, where it was modified for college instruction by the ADAPT faculty. In our own work, we have adapted the *Learning Cycle* for adult learners. In all its variations, the *Learning Cycle* has three phases, called exploration, invention, and application.

The Exploration Phase

In the exploration phase, students-usually working in small groups-are invited to explore a new environment on their own, with minimal intervention on the part of the instructor. The exploration phase is the learner's personal encounter with the new material. Working with these materials, the students attempt to complete an apparently simple task. They soon find, however, that there is some fly in the ointment. Resolving the difficulty requires even more interaction with the materials, as well as active discussion with peers. Eventually, the students complete the task and possess a set of data about the new environment. Here's an example of an exploration taken from one of our workshops for systems analysts. We want the students to learn a new way of designing questions, one that will be effective at extracting information from users in the fuzzy early stages of the system development process. We give them a work order for a new system, with instructions to prepare a list of questions for the user. The user is played by one of the instructors, who carefully answers their questions without volunteering anything not covered by their questions. The students are aware of some difficulties as they interview the user, but other difficulties become apparent only after they are given a complete list of all the information they might have obtained if their questions had been better framed. The instructor's principal role in the exploration phase is designing a task that will force the students to call their existing models into question. Sometimes these tasks work too well, so the instructor may have to encourage a student who feels unable to proceed, but this is rare. Sometimes the instructor plays a role, as in our fuzzy-question simulation. Mostly, however, the instructor simply observes the explorations, gathering data to be used in the next phase, invention.

Invention

The invention phase brings the entire group together, with the instructor playing a leading role. The group tries to make sense of the data generated during the exploration phase. They are now working in an analytical mode, trying to generalize from their data by inventing new concepts or tools. The instructor may provide the standard technical terms for these "inventions," or present a model in current use, or even deliver a mini-lecture to illuminate or integrate the students' inventions. For instance, in our fuzzy question simulation, the instructor might guide the discussion by listing students' examples of information that their questions failed to elicit. Alongside each piece of information, the students write questions that might have succeeded. The instructor then asks the students to identify systematic differences between the successful and unsuccessful questions. Out of 10 principles that the instructor had in mind, the students might develop 7 on their own, get 2 more with tiny hints from the instructor, and need a bit of a push to catch the last. The instructor might then finish the invention by relating all ten principles to a model based on information theory. Regardless of the instructor's contribution, the knowledge that emerges has been constructed by the students themselves, rather than provided by the instructor. The instructor may have provided conventional names, or accelerated the convergence of invention, but has in no sense filled the empty student vessels with knowledge. That is done by the student's own active involvement.

Application

The application phase completes the learning cycle by creating the opportunity for the students to interact with the world once again-this time using their newly acquired models. As in the exploration phase, the instructor merely provides a structure and observes the students working in their small groups. In our fuzzy-question learning cycle, the application involves a work order for another system, more or less repeating the structure of the exploration phase. In many cases, the application phase for one learning cycle becomes transformed into the exploration phase of the next. The fuzzy-question learning cycle is actually a series of case studies. In each case, the students progress a bit further by applying their learnings from the previous case-then run into trouble on the next type of difficulty. Such a series of linked learning cycles makes learning more efficient, but, more important, integrates different conceptual models.

Experience With the *Learning Cycle*

We have used the learning cycle approach in a great variety of educational settings, ranging from undergraduate college courses to intensive residential workshops for technical leaders in industry. Whenever principles are to be learned, rather than simple procedures, the *Learning Cycle* is appropriate and effective. Virtually any subject can be learned using the *Learning Cycle* approach. Our experience, and the experience of our colleagues, has included anthropology, computer science, management, English, systems analysis, philosophy, logic, economics, communication skills, and leadership training. We have used the *Learning Cycle* effectively in groups ranging from 5 to 150. *Learning Cycles* may be designed for a variety of available resources, including what the students carry around in their heads. A *Learning Cycle* may be built into a 1-hour class meeting or planned to run for a full 16-week semester or a 6-day workshop. It may be integrated with readings, films, field trips, laboratory experiments, guest experts, and even lectures. In this book, we'll provide a broad sample of experiential learning situations we have used with great success throughout the past half-century. Using these as models, our readers should be well started on the way to designing their own experiential learning situations- adaptations of these, or brand new ones.

Learning Versus Teaching

Piaget's model highlights the difference between learning and teaching. In other educational approaches, the "teacher" acts on the "student," hoping to transfer knowledge from one to the other. As one wag described the lecture method, "It's a way of getting material from the teacher's notes into the student's notes-without passing through the brain of either one." Not all lectures for all students may share this characteristic, but it's certainly a frequently observed phenomenon-one that's simply not possible with the learning cycle. In the learning cycle approach, the material must pass through the student's brain because the student acts on and interacts with the material to be learned-transforming the material rather than mechanically copying it. In the learning cycle, the student has responsibility for her or his own learning, which is virtually a requirement for success with adult learners. And through this responsibility, all students, whatever their age, develop a greater sense of ownership of the products of the learning process. Not only is understanding of the material much deeper, but retention is far better than in other approaches. Experiments show that most of what is taught is rapidly forgotten, but what is learned stays learned-until it's unlearned in some new disequilibrating environment. And that is our job, not as teachers, but as leaders of learning-to create environments in which everyone is empowered to contribute to their own learning.

INDEX

accommodation, 110-111, 113, 166-167, 181, 184, 253, 255, 261, 321
ADAPT, xiv, 3, 10, 14, 32, 82-84, 86, 87, 88, 89, 90-97, 99, 102-104, 136, 142, 145, 147, 149, 203-211, 214, 313, 315-317, 321
Algae Puzzle, 51, 53
APPLICATION, 117-128, 131-133, 136-138, 158, 161-164, 166, 321, 323
Aronsxiii, xv, 149, 153, 166, 167, 221, 228
assimilation, 110-112, 166-167, 193, 253-255, 257, 260-262, 264, 321

balance beam (equal arm balance), 45, 50, 68

Campbell, 51, 53-54, 59-61, 65, 205, 207
Chemical Mixtures, 43
COMPAS, 205, 210, 217
concrete operational reasoning, 19, 21-25, 28-30, 33-34, 35, 37, 45, 47-48, 51-52, 69-74, 108, 143-144

demonstrations, 119, 132, 139, 158-159, 166, 177, 181

disequlibration, 110-111, 118, 120, 123, 125, 128, 132, 143, 150, 157, 161, 184, 189, 320
DOORS, 52, 62, 205, 207-211, 313
Duckworth, 114, 150-151, 220, 264
Dykstra106, 156-157, 167, 179, 189-190, 200-201

Equilibration, viii, 21, 110, 119, 122, 124, 142-143, 149, 183-184, 186-188, 199, 202, 219-220, 253, 260-263, 320
Elkind, 149-150
EXPLORATION, 117-121, 123-128, 131-134, 136-141, 148, 157, 161-164, 166, 321-323

Flexibility of Rods, 39-40, 45
folk theory (of teaching), 178, 186-188, 190, 196, 199, 200, 202
formal operational reasoning, xiv, 19, 21-29, 33-34, 35-37, 39, 43, 45, 48, 51-52, 63, 66, 69-70, 74-75, 108, 119, 122, 139, 143-144, 154, 204
Frog Puzzle, 23, 27, 30-31, 33, 51-52, 55-56, 66

325

Fuller, xiii-xv, 65, 102, 106, 112, 149, 170, 172-173, 177, 180, 205, 222, 281-284, 316, 321
Furth, 150, 219, 220

Glasersfeld, 188, 196, 202

INVENTION, 117-128, 130-133, 136-138, 322
Islands Puzzle, 3-4, 6, 18, 28

Kalman, 167, 180, 200, 202
Karplus, xiii-xv, 25, 35-50, 68, 113, 115, 134, 136, 145, 149, 151, 153-154, 167, 190, 219, 221-222, 267-268, 276-279, 281, 287, 312, 314, 321

Lawson, xiii-iv, xvi, 65-66, 149, 154-155, 180-181, 222, 294, 299, 303
Learning Cycle, 115-128, 131-133, 136-138, 142, 144, 148, 163-164, 166, 207-208, 212-213, 321, 323-324
lecture, 117, 120-121, 156, 158-160, 163, 170, 215

Mealworm Puzzle, 2, 7-9, 18, 23, 27-28, 51-52, 58-59
memorization, 165
Mr.Short/Mr. Tall Puzzle, 2, 10-11, 13, 18, 23, 29, 36

Open-ended questions, 137, 140

Perry, xv-vi, 106, 152, 218, 314

Petals Around A Rose, 107-111, 184, 309-312
Piaget, xiv-xv, 19-22, 24-27, 35, 39, 43, 45, 49, 51, 64, 66, 68, 105, 110-112, 115, 125, 133-136, 142, 146, 147, 148-151, 153-154, 162, 166, 168, 181, 183-184, 186-188, 190-202, 208, 212, 217, 219-220, 221, 222-227, 232, 242, 244, 251-252, 253, 265-266, 269, 272, 275-276, 281, 285-287, 289-300, 302-303, 314, 315, 317-318, 320-321, 324
Piagetian model, 207-208, 211
Piagetian theory, 26, 166

Questioning Skills and Strategies, 137-139

self-regulation, 21, 25, 75, 107-108, 110-113, 116-126, 128, 130-133, 135-136, 139, 142-144, 148-149, 161, 183-184, 259-260, 309, 321
Stevens, 169, 174, 180, 182, 205
Student Population Puzzle, 27, 30, 32-33, 66

transitional reasoning, 27-28
Treasure Hunt Puzzle, 14-15, 18, 29

Vygotsky, 162, 181, 183, 190-202

Wait-time, 137, 145

Zollman, 170